Islamic Post-Traditionalism in Indonesia

The **ISEAS–Yusof Ishak Institute** (formerly Institute of Southeast Asian Studies) was established as an autonomous organization in 1968. It is a regional centre dedicated to the study of socio-political, security and economic trends and developments in Southeast Asia and its wider geostrategic and economic environment. The Institute's research programmes are the Regional Economic Studies (RES, including ASEAN and APEC), Regional Strategic and Political Studies (RSPS), and Regional Social and Cultural Studies (RSCS).

ISEAS Publishing, an established academic press, has issued more than 2,000 books and journals. It is the largest scholarly publisher of research about Southeast Asia from within the region. ISEAS Publishing works with many other academic and trade publishers and distributors to disseminate important research and analyses from and about Southeast Asia to the rest of the world.

Islamic Post-Traditionalism in Indonesia

RUMADI

With a Foreword by
ABDURRAHMAN WAHID
Translated by
REBECCA LUNNON

YUSOF ISHAK INSTITUTE

First published in Singapore in 2015 by ISEAS Publishing
ISEAS–Yusof Ishak Institute
30 Heng Mui Keng Terrace
Singapore 119614

E-mail: publish@iseas.edu.sg
Website: <http://bookshop.iseas.edu.sg>

All rights reserved. No part of this publication may be reproduced, stored in a retrieval system, or transmitted in any form or by any means, electronic, mechanical, photocopying, recording or otherwise, without the prior permission of the Institute of Southeast Asian Studies.

© 2015 ISEAS–Yusof Ishak Institute

Originally published as *Post Traditionalisme Islam: Wacana Intelektualisme dalam Komunitas NU* (in Indonesian)

© Fahmina Institute, Indonesia, 2008

The ISEAS–Yusof Ishak Institute gratefully acknowledges both the generous contribution of the Asian Law Centre at the University of Melbourne in funding the translation of this book, and the work of Tim Lindsey, Director of the Centre for Indonesian Law, Islam and Society at Melbourne Law School in initiating and managing the translation project.

The responsibility for facts and opinions in this publication rests exclusively with the authors and their interpretations do not necessarily reflect the views or the policy of the publishers or their supporters.

ISEAS Library Cataloguing-in-Publication Data

Rumadi, 1970–
   Islamic Post-traditionalism in Indonesia.
   1. N.U. (Organization)—History.
   2. Ulama—Indonesia—Intellectual life.
   3. Islam and politics—Indonesia.
   I. Title.
BP10 N83R93   2015

ISBN 978-981-4260-42-0 (soft cover)
ISBN 978-981-4620-66-6 (e-book, PDF)

Typeset by Superskill Graphics Pte Ltd
Printed in Singapore by Markono Print Media Pte Ltd

CONTENTS

Foreword vii

Preface xi

1. Introduction 1

2. NU Intellectualism: Foundations 15

3. NU and the Islamic Post-Traditionalist Discourse 95

4. Islamic Post-Traditionalism and the Future of NU Intellectualism 169

5. Conclusion 283

Bibliography 291

Index 301

About the Author 309

FOREWORD

POST-TRADITIONALISM IN NU?
By Abdurrahman Wahid

In this book, the predicate "post-traditionalist" is applied to anyone who desires change within Nahdlatul Ulama (NU). This of course is inherently problematic and must be resolved immediately. However, there is one aspect in the history of NU's foundation that Dr Rumadi does not cover, namely the dialogue between Islam and nationalism, which has been around since before NU was established.

In all his enthusiasm, Rumadi has the tendency to take anything that appears as a "deviation" from old traditionalism, and consider it part of the student revival that is needed today. This attitude, of viewing post-traditionalism as the essence of NU "revival", is frankly quite dangerous because it can be easily misused.

In fact, there is also a "revival" of older parties to strengthen this old traditionalism, including within NU, in reaction to the attitude that rejects tradition. This does not complement or serve post-traditionalism, but rather opposes it. The most obvious example of this is the emergence of figures such as KH Ma'ruf Amin and KH Sahal Mahfudz. They do not lead NU to "oppose" traditionalism; instead, they uphold traditionalism but in "deviation" to other parties who hold to the old traditionalism. How do we explain the attitude of the Indonesian Council of Ulama (MUI), which is so quick to deem others deviant? Is it not so that this leads to the religious formalism that NU has fought against from the very beginning? Rumadi does not explain this issue. This could well encourage others to consider all NU members as post-traditional.

Thus, it is clear that within NU there is also a denial of the creative dialogue between Islam on the one hand and nationalism on the other. So where then do we place people like Bung Karno, let alone our friends in dialogue such as KH M. Hasjim As'yari and NU *kyai* in general who are not usually considered? And what of the Mecca chapter of Syarikat Islam that was established in 1913 and went on to inspire a number of efforts to enforce religious traditionalism, but also freed religion from stagnation? What do we label it? And how should we consider the actions of H.O.S. Tjokroaminoto and his son-in-law Soekarno, along with KH M. Hasjim As'yari from Tebu Ireng *pesantren* in Jombang, his cousin KH A. Wahab Chasbullah, his nephew Ahmad Joyosugito (founder of the Ahmadiyah movement in Indonesia), his son KH A. Wahid Hasjim and his cousin KH A. Kahar Mudzakir (who later became a member of Muhammadiyah's national leadership)?

We must be careful here in judging those who, at the end of the day, have become the "NU Ulama". Indeed, it is not easy to follow the developments of an organization like NU over the decades. The creative dialogue between NU and the spirit of nationalism is by no means easy to explain. Before NU had been established, the Majelis Taswirul Akfar (Council for the Awakening of Thought) was formed, and before it the Nahdatu Al-Tudjar (Awakening of the Merchants) and the Nahdlatu al-Wathon (Revival of the Motherland). This was followed by the NU Congress in 1935 in Banjarmasin. All of this deeply influenced NU, and we do not now know whether it should be labelled as post-traditionalism or not.

In the Congress in Banjarmasin, NU decided it was not a religious obligation to establish an "Islamic State". That in itself was startling, and still we do not know what label to give this. In Banjarmasin five figures rejected the decision, holding tight to their convictions that an Islamic State had to be established. They later changed their tune in 1950, accepting the Republic of Indonesia that they had initially rejected. In fact, they became the "Pancasila Heroes" and essentially regarded the President of the Republic of Indonesia as the legal ruler of state (*waliyul amri al-dlaruri*) with effective authority for a set period of time (*bi al syaukah*). For how long? Forever, until doomsday. The phrase "for a set period of time" was used because the requirements for the President of the Republic of Indonesia were not the same as the requirements for the ruler of state. These results from the National Conference in Medan in 1957 are rarely used in considerations of NU's stance and attitudes.

Foreword

It is clear from the discussion above that examining the term post-traditionalism requires a willingness to use all the materials available. However, this book is of great value as it reveals the enormous process currently taking place within NU. Whatever it may be called, it is of immense interest to studies of the changes occurring within the Muslim community in Indonesia. No matter the labels used, this book details with interest how the traditional ulama are reacting to challenges from within and from outside of their community. This is the most important thing to be obtained from this book.

The process through which NU was born was a result of historical developments, and not the cause of the changes that subsequently took place. This is the great value of the book you hold in your hands.

Jakarta, 7 February 2008

PREFACE

No words suffice but praise to God the Almighty for it was with His help that I was able to complete this dissertation through much hard work. Although the completion of this dissertation took much sweat, time, and money, I am aware that there are many gaps that were unable to be explored. This was a consequence of limitations I faced in being able to examine everything related to the research topic. However, this is not an excuse for any academic errors in this research. I take full responsibility for all the shortcomings in this book.

This work does not represent the end of my academic career, but rather the beginning of a long and more challenging academic journey. Consequently, I accept criticism from readers in order to become a more responsible intellectual.

Although I worked hard to finish this research, I feel indebted, both directly and indirectly, to many; those who helped, who gave motivation, who were discussion partners, who continually asked if my dissertation was finished, and to those who helped collect data in the field.

First of all, to my parents. They both worked hard, expending much energy and time to guide me while I obtained my degrees, from undergraduate through to doctoral. In all their simplicity and with all their restrictions, they have always been a light in my life that has never flickered nor died. To my father, who is now in the presence of God (7/1/2005), I hope you are peaceful by His side. Your sacrifice was not in vain.

To my beloved wife, Emmamatul Qudsiyah who wished that I would finish this dissertation quickly in amongst the busyness of making a living. My two children, Affan F. Azka and Najma Fuaida, who have forgone their right to my love and attention, you always give me inspiration.

To my supervisors, Prof. Dr Azyumardi Azra and Dr Bahtiar Effendy, who encouraged me to finish this dissertation, and who were both teachers and discussion friends. Thank you for your advice and input in perfecting this dissertation.

To the management and academic staff at the Bengkulu State Islamic College (STAIN Bengkulu) who permitted me to study while I was still teaching there. Your assistance and flexibility helped me greatly in my studies. Similarly to the staff of the Syarif Hidayatullah State Islamic University in Jakarta (UIN Syarif Hidayatullah Jakarta), especially in the Faculty of Islamic Syariah and Law, who willingly allowed me to forgo my duties as I finished my dissertation.

To my friends who became discussion partners and critiqued my dissertation. Yenni Wahid, Ahmad Suaedy, Abd. Moqsith Ghazali (The Wahid Institute), Ulil Abshar-Abdalla, Khamami Zada, the late Maskur Maskub, M. Imdadun Rahmat, and Fawaid amongst others (Lakpesdam NU's *Taswirul Afkar Journal*), Farid Wajdi (Yogyakarta/Leiden), Jadul Maula (LKIS), and others at P3M, Desantara, JIMM, ISIS, eLSAD (no longer active), Averoes (Malang), LAPAR (Makassar), and the Liberal Islam Network (JIL). I cannot forget Mr Masykuri Abdillah and others at Jakarta UIN's Center for Development of Human Resources (PPSDM) who were happy to give me room to do as I needed and obtain self-actualization. These friends have all helped me greatly in completing this dissertation, although perhaps they are not aware of this.

Hopefully the kind favours of all are rewarded accordingly. I hope that this work is beneficial to all.

Kampung Semanggi, 16 July 2005

RD

1

INTRODUCTION

Contemporary developments in religious (Islamic) thought within the Nahdlatul Ulama (NU) community reveal an interesting phenomenon, especially amongst the young cadres. They have progressive religious ideas in responding to modernity that stem from the traditional knowledge base they possess, but that are also shaped by the new knowledge they have gained from modernity. They are not only concerned with modernity, which they critique and view very carefully, but also with revitalizing tradition. This revitalization of tradition is not about glorifying and sacralizing tradition, but deeply critiquing it, both in terms of action and thought. In fact, even the pillars of the *ahl al-sunnah wa al-jamâ'ah* doctrine (belief in the Qur'an, the Prophet's Sunna, and the Muslim community) do not escape criticism. The NU youth's thoughts and ideas are generally more responsive in facing the challenges of modernity when compared to their seniors.

Nevertheless, studying the development of thought within the NU community is no easy task. Although NU is known as a traditional organization, tracking the dynamics of its intellectualism involves many complex elements and variables. This is because although the roots of NU's intellectual tradition are relatively similar, their expression by different

NU thinkers is quite varied. This diversity demands that care be taken so as not to arrive at erroneous conclusions. This is even more important when taking a haphazard approach, such as applying the categories of traditionalism versus modernism. These categories are by now well and truly outdated when it comes to looking at where NU is at currently. In short, the spectrum of NU intellectualism has no single face.

This difficulty is also related to the reality that NU intellectualism is a field often neglected by academic studies. Those researching NU, both foreign and native, have the same tendency to examine NU purely from the aspect of politics and power. Meanwhile, the socio-intellectual aspects of NU remain largely unexplored.[1] This is evident in the number of books and works on NU, from the early years right up to the latest developments, that focus largely on the political rather than the socio-intellectual. Although it is clear that NU developments cannot be separated from national politics in general, this does not mean all NU activities are geared towards politics and power.[2] Very few, if any, serious studies of NU concentrate on tracing the intellectual roots of the NU ulama (religious scholars) and the Islamic discourse that has been developed.

This is of course quite concerning and not at all beneficial for NU. Why? Because it gives the impression that NU, both organizationally and culturally, is a community so preoccupied with political issues throughout its entire history that it has neglected the intellectuality which is in fact the very soul of the movement. This assumption is clearly at odds with the reality that NU — where ulama form the backbone of the organization — has embraced the mission of becoming the bridge between the wealth of classic Islamic intellectualism and the reality of modernity. On a macro level, it also gives the impression that Islamic intellectualism in Indonesia is very poor.

HISTORY OF NU INTELLECTUALISM

The emergence of a new passion within NU intellectualism has a long history and has been influenced by many things. The success of the modernists in developing educational institutes helped motivate NU *kiai* (religious scholars) to reform their education by adopting a system of secular education, while still keeping the old *pesantren* (traditional Islamic boarding school) system. For instance, Tebuireng *pesantren*, established by KH Hasyim Asy'ari (1874–1947), adopted a school system, especially in studies of the Qur'an, from as early as 1916. The following decade, there were at least two pioneers who introduced educational reformation to this *pesantren*, namely Kiai Muhammad Ilyas (1911–70) and Kiai Wahid Hasyim (1914–53). The former was the nephew of Kiai Hasyim Asy'ari's wife, who completed his studies at HIS (Hollandsch Indlansch School) and led the Madrasah Salafiyah (the Salafi School) in Tebuireng *pesantren*. The latter was the son of KH Hasyim Asy'ari, who after returning from Mecca in 1935, introduced Dutch lessons to the madrasah (formal Islamic school).

Since the 1950s, a number of *santri* (Islamic students studying at *pesantren*) and sons and daughters of *kiai* have gone on to study at tertiary institutes, both in Indonesia and overseas. At the same time, in 1951, the Minister for Religious Affairs KH Wahid Hasyim established the state Islamic college known as Perguruan Tinggi Agama Islam Negeri (PTAIN), which later became the State Islamic Institute (IAIN) in 1960. Subsequent developments have seen no fewer than fourteen IAIN campuses across the archipelago; and in 1997, faculties that had been part of the IAIN network became part of the State Islamic College (STAIN), which now has thirty-three campuses.[3] Besides this, there are many private Islamic Tertiary Institutions (PTAI) that also help spread developments in Islamic education throughout Indonesia. Their existence plays an important role for the continued mobility of *santri* after they have graduated from *pesantren*. This fast-paced modernization of education means that NU youth are increasingly more educated, attending tertiary institutions, and living in academic environments.

The emergence of a number of religious non-governmental organizations (NGOs) has also greatly influenced the NU youth. NGOs do not only invigorate religious life, but also play a role in creating a progressive religious discourse. Since the 1970s, young NU cadres became active in NGOs working towards the development of village communities. These activities gave NU youth the opportunity to openly participate in the intellectual discourse and have a direct impact on social reality.

Several NGOs influenced the development of NU intellectualism, including P3M (Perhimpunan Pengembangan Pesantren dan Masyarakat/ The Indonesian Society for Pesantren and Community Development), which was established in 1983, and Lakpesdam NU (Lembaga Kajian dan Pengembangan Sumber Daya Manusia NU/NU's Institute for Human Resource Studies and Development), which was established in 1985, shortly after NU announced a return to the Khittah of 1926 (a socio-religious rather than political orientation) in 1984. In the 1990s a number of NGOs emerged, motivated by the NU youth. They included LKiS (Lembaga Kajian Islam dan Sosial/The Institute for Islamic and Social Studies) in Yogyakarta, the Desantara Institute in Jakarta, Ilham in Semarang, eLSAD in Surabaya, Avveroes in Malang, INCReS in Bandung, Bildung in Cirebon, LAPAR in Makassar, and Syarikat in Yogyakarta.

The emergence of this new passion in NU intellectualism cannot be separated from NU's decision to leave the bustling life of practical politics and return to the NU Khittah of 1926. This important decision forced the NU elite and community to step away from the busyness of practical political affairs. Much of their time instead was channelled into responding to issues of education, poverty, injustice, and realignment to the NU framework of thought. The election of Achmad Shiddiq as chairman of the 'Âm Syuriah (central legislative body of NU) and KH Abdurrahman Wahid as head of the Tanfidhiyah PBNU (NU executive body) in Situbondo in 1984 further facilitated critical and progressive religious thought in NU circles.

KH Abdurrahman Wahid's leadership from 1984 brought two important changes. The first one was a repositioning of politics with the decision to return to the Khittah of 1926, which represented a transition from formal politics on the New Order's platform to informal politics without a platform. This repositioning allowed NU to create its own political platform and gave it a bargaining position with the New Order government, though it also made the New Order government continually suspicious of NU. In addition, the reorientation allowed NU to struggle for the development of society, rather than being oriented towards securing political positions. Secondly, Abdurrahman Wahid provided room for the growth of new thought, related to theology, fiqh (Islamic jurisprudence), *tasawuf* (mysticism), and the doctrine of *ahl al-sunnah wa al-jamâ'ah* (belief in the Qur'an, the Prophet's Sunna, and the Muslim community). This theological repositioning was crucial because, in accordance with the Khittah of 1926, NU was returning to being a religious organization (*jam'iyyah diniyah*) concerned with social issues (*ijtima'iyyah*). In this context, NU placed theological belief as the basis of community development through promotion of universal issues such as human rights, democracy, civil society, and gender equality.[4]

Abdurrahman Wahid's leadership stimulated change in NU's religious discourse. Without hesitation, he published articles in several journals, magazines, newspapers, and other media forms on a variety of issues, including criticism of the NU and *pesantren* traditions. Abdurrahman

Wahid's criticism and appreciation of new thought motivated the NU youth to think critically in a way that broke away from the establishment. On this basis, it can be reasoned that under Abdurrahman Wahid's leadership, NU's religious thought appeared more dynamic compared to that of other religious organizations.

Today, the progressive thought of the NU youth has continued to develop, both through NGOs and tertiary institutions. Recently, their thoughts have become increasingly crystallized and marked by their own unique characteristics, which they refer to as Islamic post-traditionalism. However, this transformation within Islamic intellectualism is not well known amongst the public. How intellectual dynamics within the NU community moved from the traditional–conservative to the outbreak of Islamic post-traditionalist thought, the factors that influenced this change, the issues and Islamic discourses that have developed, and the implications and future of this post-traditionalist movement within the context of NU intellectualism, are all topics that need to be elaborated further in an academic manner.

NEGLECT OF SOCIO-INTELLECTUAL STUDIES

Academic elaboration is also important in response to the general conception of NU, which has been stereotyped as a traditional community that is old-fashioned, anti-modernity, and static, amongst other things, but which is in fact leading developments in very progressive new thought in Indonesia.

This misconception is a result of at least three factors. First, although recently I have been paying much greater attention to NU developments by reading academic studies of NU for my honours, Masters, and PhD, from both within Indonesia and overseas, the majority of these studies look at developments in NU's political behaviour instead of its intellectual dynamics.

Secondly, the development of progressive thought in NU is quite startling. This is understandable given that NU, which has always been seen as the guardian of Islamic orthodoxy, the most loyal heir to tradition, and a group which is nearly without intellectual dynamics, has suddenly produced a generation of NU youth who have developed NU's intellectual character as if to separate it from its traditional foundations.

Thirdly, studies of socio-intellectual dynamics in Indonesia are generally neglected. As a result, research on NU intellectualism would make an important contribution to the study of socio-intellectual developments in Indonesia.

To date, there are very few academic studies of NU compared with studies of modern organizations such as Muhammadiyah and Persatuan Islam (Persis, Islamic Union). This is of course very worrying. In-depth research into NU only really took off at the end of the 1980s and the beginning of the 1990s. It was then that NU's changing role in the second half of the 1980s caught the interest of (Western) scholars.

This led to the publication of a foreign-language book, albeit an edited collection, which specifically discussed NU, titled *Nahdlatul Ulama: Traditional Islam and Modernity in Indonesia*. It was edited by Greg Barton and Greg Fealy and published by Monash University, Australia, in 1996. The book was later translated into Indonesian and published by LKiS, Yogkakarta, with the title *Tradisionalisme Radikal: Persinggungan Nahdlatul Ulama-Negara/Radical Traditionalism: NU-State Interaction* (1997). Three years after this initial publication, a second foreign-language book was written in French by Andree Feillard and later published by LKiS under the title *NU vis a vis Negara: Pencarian Bentuk, Isi dan Makna/NU vis a vis the State: A Search for Form, Content and Meaning* (1999).

Native Indonesian scholars produced more works on NU, including Choirul Anam (1985), *Pertumbuhan dan Perkembangan Nahdlatul Ulama/ Growth and Development of Nahdlatul Ulama*; Kacung Marijan (1992), *Quo Vadis NU: Setelah Kembali ke Khittah 1926/Quo Vadis NU: After the Return to the 1926 Kittah*; Mahrus Irsyam (1984), *Ulama dan Partai Politik, Upaya Mengatasi Krisis/Ulama and Political Parties, An Attempt to Overcome the Crisis*; Bahtiar Effendy (1988), "The Nine Stars and Politics: A Study of Nahdlatul Ulama's Acceptance of Asas Tunggal and Its Withdrawal from Politics", MA thesis at Ohio University; Einar Martahan Sitompul (1989), *NU dan Pancasila: Sejarah dan Peranan NU dalam Penerimaan Pancasila sebagai Satu-Satunya Asas/NU and Pancasila: The History and Role of NU in Accepting Pancasila as the Sole Basis*; A. Gaffar Karim (1995), *Metamorfosis NU dan Politisasi Islam di Indonesia/NU Metamorphosis and Politicisation of Islam in Indonesia*; Ellyasa KH Dharwis, editor (1994), *Gus Dur, NU dan Masyarakat Sipil/Gus Dur, NU and Civil Society*; Ali Haidar (1994), *Nahdlatul Ulama dan Islam: Pendekatan Fiqih dalam Politik/Nahdlatul Ulama and Islam: A Fiqh Approach in Politics*.

Almost all of these books favour a political approach. More recently, Djohan Effendi (2000) wrote a dissertation that took an intellectual development approach more than a political one, entitled "Progressive Traditionalists: The Emergence of a New Discourse in Indonesia's Nahdlatul Ulama during the Abdurrahman Wahid Era", at Deakin University, Australia.

In 2002, two dissertations that discussed contemporary NU developments were written. The first was Laode Ida (2002), "Gerakan Sosial Kelompok Nahdlatul Ulama (NU) Progresif/Nahdlatul Ulama's Social Movement", written for her doctoral degree at the University of Indonesia, and the second was Robin L. Bush (2002), "Islam and Civil Society in Indonesia: The Case of the Nahdlatul Ulama", written for her doctoral degree from the University of Washington. Both dissertations discuss the NU social movement, but with emphasis on different aspects. While Laode Ida emphasized the social movement brought about by the progressive NU community that is spread through a variety of institutions, Robin focused more on the dynamics of the civil society movement within NU circles, and as a result the variable of politics is quite dominant in her analysis. One thing that is very clear is that both dissertations failed to delve into the religious discourse developed by the NU youth, whose references are taken largely from Arabic books. This appreciation is important at the very least to cross-check the sources used. In addition, Robin sees all activities of the NU youth within the context of civil society, although civil society is a political concept and not a religious one. Such a focus means that both dissertations were unable to pay much attention to the dynamics of religious discourse within the NU community. Although Robin mentioned several themes of thought that were developing, it was only very briefly, as the dissertation was in fact a study of politics.

An examination of these previous studies shows that the new current of thought in the NU community, which reflects themes of Islamic post-traditionalism, has not been studied in any depth except in a handful of short articles. On this basis, research that places emphasis on NU's socio-intellectual history, especially in relation to the growth of progressive youth groups, is an area that remains untouched by many academics.

TRADITION, THE TRADITIONAL, TRADITIONALISM, AND POST-TRADITIONALISM

In the Indonesian dictionary, tradition has two meanings: hereditary customs that are still followed by the community; and the assessment or assumption that the ways that exist are the best or most correct.[5] As such, tradition is a generic term used to refer to everything that has been brought from the past and exists in the present.

In Islam, Sayyed Hossein Nasr explains that tradition refers to God's revelation and its expression throughout history. Nasr states that tradition encompasses three aspects: first, *al-dîn* (the religion) in the widest understanding possible, which incorporates all religious aspects; secondly, *al-sunnah* (the Prophet's example), which was formed and developed based on sacred models until it became a tradition; and thirdly, *silsilah* (genealogy), or the chain that connects all periods, episodes, or steps in life. In short, tradition is interpreted as being the sacred truth, eternal, perennial wisdom in its application in any one place and time.[6]

The term tradition is also often translated as referring to the Hadith,[7] the Sunna, and customs. However, these three terms are unable to completely encapsulate the meaning of tradition in this discussion. This is not to say that tradition is unrelated to these three terms. The Sunna, for instance, is often referred to as a tradition which is alive, and NU, as an organization that holds firmly to this tradition, calls itself a follower of *ahl al-sunnah wa al-jamâ'ah*.[8]

Muhammed 'Abid al-Jabiri examined different forms of traditions and pointed out the relevance of explaining the term. He argued that tradition has several forms, including: (1) meaningful traditions (*al-turâs al-ma'nawî*), in the form of cultural traditions or traditions of thought or thinking; (2) material traditions (*al-turâs al-mâdî*), such as monuments or objects from the past; (3) cultural traditions, or everything that we possess from our past; (4) universal humanitarian traditions, or everything present amongst us that comes from the pasts of others.[9]

The term "traditional" is an attitude, a way of thinking and acting that holds to hereditary norms and customs.[10] The word is usually used to refer to a person or group of people who still hold firm to tradition. In the context of Indonesian Islam, traditional Islam has the following features. First, it is very much connected to traditional Islamic thought, which can be traced back to the thought of ulama who were experts in fiqh (Islamic jurisprudence), the Hadith, *tasawuf* (mysticism), *tafsir* (exegesis) and *tauhid* (the oneness of God), and who lived between the seventh and thirteenth centuries.[11] Adherents of traditional Islam are happier to follow the opinions of the great ulama from the past than to draw their own conclusions based on the Qur'an and the Hadith. Secondly, a large number of them live in villages, and *pesantren* form the basis for their education. Initially, they tended to be an exclusive group that neglected worldly issues because of their involvement in the world of Sufism and mysticism (*tasawuf*); they also resisted modernization and the way of thinking of urban *santri*, defended their possessions, and bowed down to their *kiai* almost without limit. Thirdly, the more ideological characteristic of those who adhere to traditional Islam is that they are attached to a particular understanding of *ahl al-sunnah wa al-jamâ'ah*. This understanding does not just differentiate between the Sunnis and non-Sunnis, but also between the traditionalists and the modernists.[12]

Meanwhile, traditionalism is an understanding or teaching based on tradition.[13] Traditionalism therefore represents teachings that are structured in such a way so as to become the living practices within a community. When related to Islam, Islamic traditionalism refers to a specific Islamic understanding or doctrine, both in the form of religious thought and practices that are inherited from one generation to the next.

Post-traditionalism etymologically means passing or going beyond traditionalism. As a term, post-traditionalism is considered uncommon; besides not being in the dictionary, no academics use the term to study Islamic thought. Nevertheless, Anthony Giddens, a sociologist from Cambridge University, used the term post-traditional society to refer to modernity. Consequently, modernity is post-traditional.[14] However, post-traditionalism here is not used in the way Giddens used it, although several aspects are relevant.

The word "post" in this sense can indeed be understood as passing by, going beyond, or even discarding and leaving behind tradition. However, the soul of the post-traditionalist movement and revitalization of tradition does not mean leaving tradition behind. Thus, post-traditionalism contains a sense of both continuity and change[15] — continuity in the sense of using tradition as a basis for transformation (change).

In the context of NU, the term post-traditionalism is used to refer to the NU youth to symbolize their break with tradition. This break does not mean discarding or leaving tradition behind, but using it as the basis of their movement for transformation. It is at this point that the group can be differentiated from other communities. NU youth are characteristically determined to hold to and use tradition as a social model to develop thought and push for change. Nevertheless, this does not mean that they accept tradition blindly, without criticism. Rather, they do not hesitate to criticize their own traditions and those of others. Criticism of their own traditions does not equate to a hatred and dismissal of said traditions, but instead a revitalization to make tradition more useful. Consequently, their movement and thinking remains within the bounds of tradition.

THE MODERN, MODERNISM, AND NEO-MODERNISM

The term "modern" has several meanings, including a period of time (the modern era from 1500 CE to the present) or the adaptation of the latest methods, ideas, and technology. The term originates from the Latin *modernus*, which is derived from the word *modo* meaning "recently" and "current". Modern civilization is marked by two main features: rationalization (rational thinking) and technicalization (a more technical way of acting).

Modernism is interpreted as a modern view or method, and particularly the tendency to regulate tradition and religious belief so that it is harmonious with modern thought. The Webster dictionary defines modernism as the movement of adapting religion to modern thought, especially to reduce the presence of supernatural elements that are considered traditional.[16] Thus, Islamic modernism can be understood as a movement that emerged during the modern period of Islamic history in which Islamic doctrine was adapted to modern thought and institutions.[17]

Harun Nasution (1919–98), a professor of Islamic thought and philosophy at Syarif Hidayatullah UIN in Jakarta, tends to avoid using the term *modernism*, preferring instead the term *pembaruan*, meaning renewal or reform. The term *modernism*, he believes, has a negative connotation in addition to its positive ones. The negative connotation that Harun Nasution refers to is the Western connotation inherent in the term, which might give the impression that Islamic modernism is a continuation of the modernism that emerged in the West.[18]

In Arabic, modernism is often translated as *tajdîd*, which has the same meaning of renewal or reform. The term (renewal or reform) refers to the purification movement that began before the nineteenth century. Meanwhile, modernism is used to refer to reformation movements since the nineteenth century that were aimed at adapting Islamic doctrine to modern thought. In Indonesia, Islamic modernism began with the renewal of religious thought (theology), institutions, social and educational aspects, and politics.[19]

Neo-modernism then is Fazlur Rahman's typology of thought, created to depict developments in — and the nature of — Islamic intellectualism.

Rahman divided movements in Islamic thought into four categories. First, there was the revivalist movement at the end of the eighteenth century, which was marked by the emergence of the Wahabi movement in Saudi Arabia, the Sanusi movement in North Africa, and the Fulani movement in West Africa. These movements did not make contact with the West. Secondly, there was the classic modernism movement which emerged in the mid-nineteenth century and beginning of the twentieth century, and was highly influenced by Western ideas. This movement expanded what could be subject to *ijtihad* (independent interpretation and reasoning) to encompass matters such as the relationship between divinity and rationality. It also allowed for social reform, including reform in the education sector and concerning the status of women, as well as political reform and democratic forms of governance. Thirdly, there was the neo-revivalist movement, which was based on the classical modernist idea that Islam encompasses all aspects of life, both collective and individual. However, in its attempt to differentiate itself from the West, the movement did not accept the method and spirit of classical modernism, but was also unable to develop its own methodology to express its position. Fourthly, there was the neo-modernist movement that attempted to find a way to achieve progressive synthesis between modernist rationality and *ijtihad* of classical traditions. According to Fazlur Rahman, although there is indeed a spirit of classical modernism, the movement has at least two fundamental weaknesses. First, it does not thoroughly analyse the method which is semi-implicit in addressing the specific issues and the implications of its fundamental principles. Secondly, it is unavoidable that neo-modernism should actually become an agent of westernization. Neo-modernism is thus viewed by Fazlur Rahman as developing a fitting and logical methodology that differentiates itself from classical modernism.[20] According to Fazlur Rahman, although neo-modernism attempts to integrate modernism and traditionalism, in fact it cannot escape the hegemony of modernism, which places traditionalism as a historical ornament and not the spirit of social transformation.

OVERVIEW

This book consists of five chapters. This first chapter consists of an introduction that presents the background and significance of the book, a number of key issues that will be discussed, an elaboration of related studies, and the book's position amongst socio-intellectual studies in Indonesia.

The second chapter discusses the foundations to the formation of NU intellectualism. This section first presents the initial formation of the tradition of intellectualism in the archipelago, and then moves on to the tradition of *ahl al-sunnah wa al-jamâ'ah* as the foundation to the formation of NU intellectualism that encompasses the three scientific traditions of fiqh, *tasawuf*, and theology. In addition, NU's socio-intellectual model and NU's response to a number of socio-religious developments are examined.

The third chapter specifically looks at the development of Islamic post-traditionalism within the NU community. It discusses the discourse of post-traditionalist thought within Islamic thought; the emergence of a new current of progressive thought within NU; factors that influence this; and the dimension of Islamic post-traditionalist thought in the NU community.

The fourth chapter contains the real essence of this book, analysing the discourse of post-traditionalist thought in NU and looking at future projections. This chapter more specifically discusses the struggle between liberal and conservative thought in NU; the position of post-traditionalist thought in the development of intellectualism in Indonesia; the religious discourse that is being developed; the implications and future for post-traditionalism; and the direction and tendencies of the future of post-traditionalist thought.

The fifth chapter is a final summation of the key issues discussed.

Notes

1. This tendency is evident in all studies of Islam, including Islam in Indonesia. Many scholars of Islam are more interested in studying the religion from the perspective of politics and power than from the perspective of culture, intellectualism, or doctrine. This gives the less-than-helpful impression that the history of Islam is identical to the history of kings, the rise and fall of dynasties, power struggles amongst political elites, and so on. Meanwhile, the very rich socio-intellectual dynamics of the Muslim community are often left out of historiographies.
2. This includes for instance Mahrus Irsyam, *Ulama dan Politik: Upaya mengatasi Krisis* (Jakarta: Yayasan Perkhidmatan, 1984); Choirul Anam, *Pertumbuhan dan Perkembangan Nahdlatul Ulama* (Sala: Jatayu, 1985); Kacung Marijan, *Quo Vadis NU setelah Kembali ke Khittah 1926* (Surabaya: Erlangga, 1992); Martin van Bruinessen, *NU: Tradisi Relasi-Relasi Kuasa dan Pencarian Wacana Baru*

(Yogyakarta: LKiS, 1994); Ellyasa KH Dharwis, ed., *Gus Dur, NU dan Masyarakat Sipil* (Yogyakarta: LKiS, 1994); Ali Haidar, *Nahdlatul Ulama dan Islam: Pendekatan Fiqih dalam Politik* (Jakarta: Gramedia, 1994); A. Gaffar Karim, *Metamorfosis: NU dan Politisasi Islam di Indonesia* (Yogyakarta: LKiS, 1995); Greg Fealy and Greg Barton, eds., *Tradisionalisme Radikal: Persinggungan Nahdlatul Ulama Negara* (Yogyakarta: LKiS, 1997); Andree Feillard, *NU vis a vis Negara: Pencarian Bentuk, Isi dan Makna* (Yogyakarta: LKiS, 1999); and Marzuki Wahid et al., eds., *Geger di "Republik" NU, Perebutan Wacana, Tafsir Sejarah, dan Perebutan Makna* (Jakarta: KOMPAS-Lakpesdam, 1999).
3. Recently, five IAIN and one STAIN merged to form the State Islamic University (UIN), namely Syarif Hidayatullah IAIN in Jakarta, Sunan Kalijaga IAIN in Yogyakarta, Sunan Gunung Djati IAIN in Bandung, Alauddin IAIN in Makassar, Sultan Syarif Kasim IAIN in Pekanbaru Riau, and Malang STAIN.
4. Syafiq Hasyim and Robin L. Bush, "NU and Discourses: Islam, Gender and Traditional Islamic Society" (unpublished paper presented at the Conference on Islam, Civil Society and Development in Southeast Asia, University of Melbourne, 11–12 July 1998).
5. Compilation Team for the Comprehensive Dictionary of Indonesian Language, *Kamus Besar Bahasa Indonesia* (Jakarta: Balai Pustaka, 1988), p. 589. An almost identical meaning can be found in Edward N. Teall, A.M., *Webster's New American Dictionary*, vol. 4 (New York: INC., 1965), p. 1059, which explains that tradition has three meanings: (1) the handing down of knowledge, beliefs, and customs from one generation to another; (2) a belief or custom so taught; (3) anything handed down from the past and strongly rooted as to be as inviolable of law.
6. Sayyed Hossein Nasr, *Traditional Islam in the Modern World* (London: Kegan Paul International, 1990), p. 13.
7. In John L. Esposito, ed., *The Oxford Encyclopedia of the Modern Islamic World*, vol. 5 (Oxford: Oxford University Press, 1995), p. 230, tradition is equated with the Hadith.
8. For more see Azyumardi Azra, "Islam Tradisional dan Modernitas di Indonesia", book review in *Studia Islamika* 4, no. 4 (1997): 217–40.
9. Muhammad Abed al-Jabiri, *Post-Tradisionalisme Islam*, translated by Ahmad Baso (Yogyakarta: LKiS, 2000), pp. 24–25. See also Muhammad Abed al-Jabiri, *Nahnu wa al-Turâs, Qirâ'ât Mu'âshirah fî Turâsinâ al-Falsafî*, 5th ed. (Casablanca: al-Markaz al-Tsaqafi al-Arabi, 1986), pp. 11–19.
10. Compilation Team for the Comprehensive Dictionary of Indonesian Language, *Kamus Besar*, p. 959.
11. Zamakhsyari Dhofier, *Tradisi Pesantren: Studi tentang Pandangan Hidup Kyai* (Jakarta: LP3ES, 1982), p. 1.
12. For further information see Fachry Ali and Bahtiar Effendy, *Merambah Jalan*

Baru Islam, Rekonstruksi Pemikiran Islam Indonesia Masa Orde Baru (Bandung: Mizan, 1990), pp. 48–52.
13. Compilation Team for the Comprehensive Dictionary of Indonesian Language, Kamus Besar, p. 959.
14. See Anthony Giddens, Masyarakat Post-Tradisional, translated by Ali Noer Zaman (Yogyakarta: Ircisod, 2003).
15. In the NU tradition there is a famous principle which says al-muhâfadhah 'alâ al-qadîm al-shâlih wa al-akhdzu bi al-jadîd al-ashlah (preserve old [traditions] that are good, and adopt new [traditions] that are even better). Simply speaking, continuity is preserved in al-muhâfadhah 'alâ al-qadîm al-shâlih, while change comes from al-akhdzu bi al-jadîd al-ashlah.
16. Edward N. Teall, A.M., Webster's New American Dictionary, vol. 3, p. 626.
17. Nia Kurnia and Amelia Fauzia, "Gerakan Modernisme", in Ensiklopedi Tematis Dunia Islam, vol. 5, edited by Taufik Abdullah et al. (Jakarta: Ichtiar Baru van Hoeve, 2003), p. 349.
18. See Harun Nasution, Pembaharuan dalam Islam, Sejarah Pemikiran dan Gerakan (Jakarta: Bulan Bintang, 1992).
19. Nia Kurnia and Amelia Fauzia, "Gerakan Modernisme", p. 350.
20. For more on this see Fazlur Rahman, Neomodernisme Islam, Metode dan Alternatif, 2nd ed., edited by Taufik Adnan Amal (Bandung: Mizan, 1989), pp. 17–21. See also Greg Barton, Gagasan Islam Liberal di Indonesia, Pemikiran Neo-Modernisme Nurcholish Madjid, Djohan Effendi, Ahmad Wahib dan Abdurrahman Wahid (Jakarta: Paramadina, 1999).

2

NU INTELLECTUALISM: FOUNDATIONS

FORMATION OF ISLAMIC INTELLECTUALISM IN THE ARCHIPELAGO

Before discussing the foundations of NU intellectualism, it is necessary to examine the initial process behind the formation of the tradition of intellectualism in the Indonesian archipelago more generally. It is necessary to show that the formation of NU intellectualism was not something that happened out of the blue. Rather, the process involved connections with and continuity of the development of thought that was occurring across the Islamic world, especially in Mecca and Medina, which represented the centre of Islamic development. However, it is important to note that in addition to continuity, there was also a dynamic change of past traditions. NU's connection with the tradition of intellectualism in the past was what prevented NU from severing ties with the classical intellectual tradition, and as such, NU is often known as a traditional organization.[1]

The question is, how was NU connected to the intellectual heritage of the ulama (Islamic scholars) of the archipelago? This question is quite important because the tradition of NU intellectualism that has developed tends to reveal a greater connection to Middle Eastern intellectual heritage than to intellectualism within the archipelago. This is apparent in the wealth of classical books or *kitab* taught in *pesantren* (traditional Islamic boarding schools), which for the most part are written by Middle Eastern ulama. On this basis, tracking the tradition of intellectualism in the archipelago is intended to form the foundation on which to view the relationship between NU and Indonesian intellectualism. In order to do so, patterns in Indonesian Islam will first be discussed.

Understanding Islam in Indonesia is possible through an examination of how Islam came to Indonesia. There are several theories as to the origin of Islam in Indonesia. The key questions answered by these theories are: when, from where, by whom, and how was Islam brought to Indonesia? In Azyumardi Azra's study,[2] there are at least three theories as to how Islam came to Indonesia. The first theory is that Islam entered Indonesia in the seventh century CE or the first century H (of the Islamic calendar), directly from Saudi Arabia (Handramaut) to the coast of Aceh. This theory was also confirmed in a 1962 seminar in Medan on the coming of Islam to Indonesia. Those who defend this theory include Naquib al-Attas and "indigenous" historians such as HAMKA, A. Hasjmi, and M. Yunus Jamil. This "Arab theory" is also upheld by foreign scholars such as Crawfurd, who noted that the interaction between people of the archipelago and Muslims from the east coast of India was an important factor in the spread of Islam to the archipelago. Similarly, Keijzer argues that Islam in the archipelago came from Egypt because of the shared belief in the Syafi'i school of thought. Niemann and De Holander also adhere to this theory, albeit with minor revisions, where they view Islam as coming not from Egypt but from Handramaut.[3]

The general view of Western scholars who support the "Arab theory" differs from that of "indigenous" scholars who argue that Islam came directly from Saudi Arabia (not from India), and not in the twelfth or thirteenth century CE, but in the seventh century CE, as evidenced by the presence of Arab merchants in Indonesian ports. For instance, Abdul Rahman Haji Abdullah[4] states that in the seventh century CE, camphor business relations had already been established between the indigenous inhabitants of the archipelago and Arab merchants. This theory is often promoted by Islamic historians and originates from their desire to prove that Islam in the archipelago is authentic, and not a peripheral or syncretized Islam as many Western scholars proclaim.

Nevertheless, the Arab theory fails to answer questions about how religious conversion took place and how Islamization occurred. This is understandable in light of the fact that merchants and traders were not purely out to spread Islam, and as such, religious conversion and the process of Islamization were not yet taking place. Yet these two elements are necessary for the spread of religion.

Secondly, there is a theory proposed by Dutch historians such as Pijnappel and G.W.J. Drewes. They propose that Islam in the archipelago came from the Indian subcontinent; not from Persia or Saudi Arabia, but from Gujarat and Malabar. They argue that there were Arabic people from the Syafi'i school of thought who migrated to and settled in India, and later took Islam to the Indonesian archipelago. This theory was developed by Snouck Hurgronje, who proved that Islam had a strong foothold in several port cities of the Indian subcontinent and that Deccan Muslims were the first to go to the Malay-Indonesian world to spread Islam. They were then followed by Arab lords and nobles (*sayyid* and *syarîf*) who completed the spread of Islam to the archipelago by becoming "priests" and even "priest-princes" or sultans. This process occurred in the twelfth century, as the period most likely to have facilitated the spread of Islam to the archipelago.

The third theory was developed by Fatimi and states that Islam came from Bengal (Bangladesh), based on the fact that the majority of prominent figures in the coastal regions were Bengali people or their descendants. Islam first emerged in the Malay Peninsula on the eastern coast, not from the west (Malacca), via Kanton, Phanrang (Vietnam), Leran, and Trengganu. Fatimi argued that Islam on the Peninsula was, in terms of doctrine, the same as the Islam in Phanrang, while inscriptions found in Trengganu resembled those in Leran. Drewes, an expert on Indonesian history, criticizes this theory, particularly in relation to the inscriptions, which he regards as "wild conjecture". Moreover, the dominant school of thought in Bengal is the Hanafi and not Syafi'i school of thought.[5]

As for who brought Islam to the archipelago, many Western historians hold to the theory that it was spread by Muslim merchants while they were trading in the region and through marriage to local women. This differs from A.H. Johns's idea expressed in his book *Sufisme as a Category in Indonesia Literature and History,* as quoted by Azyumardi Azra,[6] that it is difficult to believe that Muslim traders also functioned as propagators of Islam. If they were indeed active in spreading Islam, why did it not appear before the twelfth century CE when Muslim merchants were present in the archipelago as early as the seventh century CE? In other words, although the indigenous inhabitants had already met and interacted with Muslim traders since the seventh century CE, there is no evidence of a significant number of them having converted to Islam or of any substantial Islamization in the archipelago.

From here A.H. Johns proposes the theory that there were Sufi nomads who, thanks to their charismatic authority and magical powers, were able to spread Islam to the archipelago and successfully convert masses of indigenous inhabitants to Islam from the thirteenth century CE onwards. Their success was a result of the Sufis' ability to present Islam as an attractive option, particularly through the emphasis on adjusting it to local culture rather than changing local practices and cultures. Thus Islam in the region, especially in Java, has been described as syncretic Islam[7] by many scholars, including Harry J. Benda,[8] Clifford Geertz,[9] W.F. Wertheim,[10] Robert Jay,[11] and Howard M. Federspiel.[12]

The question then becomes: why were the Sufi wanderers only active in the thirteenth century? A.H. Johns, as cited in Azyumardi Azra, showed that Sufi *tarekat* (orders) were not a dominant feature in the Muslim world until the fall of Baghdad in 656 H/1258 CE. Only then did Sufi orders gradually become a stable and disciplined institution, able to develop affiliations with trade and craft groups that helped to shape urban society.

Adhering to A.H. Johns's theory of Sufi domination in the spread of Islam to the archipelago, consciously or not, means that Indonesian Islam was shaped to be more Sufistic or mystic. This in turn influenced the growth of Sufistic life and nature, in comparison to a philosophical intellectual nature, in Indonesia, which in turn also produced Sufi figures like Nûr al-Dîn al-Raniri, Hamzah Fansuri, Abd al-Rauf al-Sinkili, Muhammad Yusuf al-Maqassari, and the Walisongo (Nine Saints) in Java. As a result, it is no surprise that throughout history the discourse of Indonesian Islamic intellectualism has been coloured by a Sufistic-syncretic discourse. This is further compounded by the fact that when Islam arrived in Indonesia it was during a period of anticlimax, when the gate of *ijtihad* had already been closed, although it was not known who had closed it.

Indonesian Muslims therefore no longer had the opportunity or ability to develop Islam, either in terms of the politics of social administration or in terms of science or scholarship. As compensation, they immersed themselves in a life of Islamic mysticism that was assumed to be an ascetic life that paid little attention to worldly issues. This situation continued until it eventually led to stagnation of Islamic thought.

This less than ideal state of affairs influenced the nature of Islam that was spread and subsequent developments. In other words, because Islam was spread systematically in Indonesia in an era of decline, it led to an ascetic lifestyle. As a result, Islam's adaptive and accommodative approach towards traditional values was an indirect result of the Sufistic nature of the Islam that took root in Indonesia.

As explained above, the Islam that entered Indonesia was nuanced with Sufism. The success of the Sufis in spreading Islam throughout Indonesia is supported by a number of facts. First, the Sufis succeeded in presenting Islam in a very attractive manner. They were tolerant of the local practices and thought that some people labelled as *bid'ah* (heresy) or *khurafat* (superstition). Secondly, and in relation to this, the local communities had no reservations and felt that Islam suited the background and culture of their local traditions.[13]

Quite separately from the service the Sufis performed in bringing Islam to Indonesia, later developments saw a sharp disagreement between those ulama following a *tasawuf* (mystical) orientation (esoteric) and those following a fiqh (Islamic jurisprudence) orientation (exoteric), both of whom were very strongly represented. In studies of Islam in the archipelago, these two currents are represented by Hamzah Fansuri (died around 1600 CE) and Syams al-Dîn al-Sumatrani (d. 1040 H/1630 CE) who represented the Sufis with their belief in *wujûdiyah* (existentialism) on the one hand, and Nûr al-Dîn al-Raniri (d. 1068 H/1658 CE) who represented the fiqh current on the other, although al-Raniri did not know the first thing about *tasawuf*.[14]

The conflict between these two groups sometimes reached worrying heights, with one side claiming that the members of the other were kafir (infidels). Such claims are apparent in Nûr al-Dîn al-Raniri's writing in *Hujjah al-Shiddîq li Daf' al-Zindiq*, which reads as follows:

> Thus there are two *qawm* (groups) in *wujûdiyah* (existentialism): one is the *muwahhid(ah)*, and the second is the *mulhid(ah)*.... The *muwahhid(ah)* group incorporates all the *ahl al-shufî* or Sufis (*Haqq Ta'ala*, God's truth, seems to have descended upon this *qawm*!), and the *mulhid(ah)* group incorporates all the *zindiq* (heretics) — *na'ûdzubillâh minhâ* (may God's curse be upon them)! The reason this group is part of the *wujûdiyah* group is because their language, words and *i'tiqad* (intentions) focus on God's existence.[15]

The above quote does not explicitly state that Hamzah Fansuri and Syams al-Dîn al-Sumatrani belong to the *mulhidah* group, but other statements in *Tibyân al-Ma'rifat al-Adyân* voice this accusation even more harshly. A number of labels are applied to Hamzah Fansuri, Syams al-Dîn al-Sumatrani, and their followers, not just describing them as deviants, infidels, or heretics, but also equating them with other currents of thought that were considered deviant, such as the Jahmiyyah, Tanasukhiyyah, Watsaniyyah, Barahimah, Hindus, Samaniyyah, Hululiyyah, and Falasifah (philosophers). These currents of thought were considered to contradict the *ahl al-sunnah wa al-jamâ'ah* doctrine that al-Raniri saw as the true understanding.[16]

In *Raniri and the Wujudiyyah of the 17th Century Acheh*, as quoted by Abdul Rahman Haji Abdullah, S.M.N. al-Attas explains that in al-Raniri's eyes Hamzah Fansuri's opinions can be summarized as follows:

1. Hamzah Fansuri's opinion on God, nature, humans, and social interaction is the same as those held by philosophers, the Zoroasters, metempsychosists, incarnationists, the Brahmin, and so on.
2. Hamzah Fansuri's beliefs are "pantheistic" in the sense that God's presence is immanent in nature.
3. God is a simple being.
4. As with the Qadariyah and the Mu'tazilah, he believes that the Qur'an is a creation.
5. Hamzah Fansuri also believes that nature is *qadim* (eternal, without beginning or end).[17]

S.M.N. al-'Attas argues that al-Raniri's accusation of Hamzah Fansuri was not solely due to differences in Sufi understanding and practices, but also because of the political rivalry between the two. This rivalry grew because al-Raniri and Hamzah Fansuri's beliefs were the same, as both Ibn al-'Arabi and 'Abd al-Karim al-Jilli believed.[18] Their political rivalry can be understood through an examination of their historical background. After Sultan Iskandar Muda died, his son-in-law Iskandar Stani was appointed to replace him. As a "foreigner", Iskandar Stani did not receive as much support from the Acehnese people. The situation became more complex due to a dispute with his wife, Safiat al-Dîn, who liked to read Hamzah Fansuri's works. The conflict led Iskandar Stani to leave the palace and live in the yard of the Bayt al-Rahman Mosque.

Al-Raniri emerged in the midst of this situation and collaborated with Iskandar Stani, who appointed him Syeikh al-Islâm (The Sheikh of Islam) because of his enmity towards Hamzah Fansuri. With this new appointment, Iskandar Stani found new strength to restore his position, which he was aware had become increasingly weak as a result of the influence of the *wujûdiyyah* (the existentialists). By incorporating al-Raniri into the political arena, as a man who persistently opposed Hamzah Fansuri, political stability was restored and Iskandar Stani consolidated his power.[19] From this perspective, it is not wrong to suggest that behind the Hamzah Fansuri and al-Raniri polemic there were private motives that were political in nature. Al-Raniri's domination over the *wujûdiyyah* did not last long, because in 1644 CE, seven years after the events described above, al-Raniri returned to India, after Safiat al-Dîn successfully took over the reign of Aceh from 1641 to 1675 CE. During this time the *wujûdiyyah* rose again.

Besides these private and political motives, history clearly shows that there were two mutually opposed religious currents. On the one hand was the fiqh current with its own logic, while on the other was the *tasawuf* current, also with its own logic that was at times difficult to understand from a fiqh point of view. On this basis, a new current emerged that attempted to bring together the two extremes. The tendency for excessive mysticism was gradually balanced with a *syari'ah* (Islamic law) orientation.[20] This shift in orientation, according to Martin,[21] was a result of the renewal or purification that began in the seventeenth century with the Padri movement (inspired by Wahabism), the youth and modernist movements such as al-Irsyad and Muhammadiyah, and puritan movements such as Persatuan Islam (Persis, the Islamic Union). The end of the nineteenth century also saw the emergence of the Naqsyabandiyah Sufi order that placed more emphasis on *syari'ah* than had previous orders.

It was these processes that revived enthusiasm in the Qur'an and the Hadith, as Muhammadiyah was calling for, across the archipelago. This is reflected for instance in the translations of orthodox Sufi texts into the Malay language. This in turn brought the fiqh-oriented ulama and the mystics closer together, which then gave rise to neo-Sufism.[22]

Azyumardi Azra mentions several important figures who were considered crucial to this "rapprochement" process, namely al-Raniri, Abd al-Rauf Singkel (1615–93 CE), Muhammad Yusuf al-Maqassari (1627–99 CE), Abd al-Shamad al-Palimbani (1704–85 CE),[23] Arsyad al-Banjari (1710–1812 CE), and Dawud bin Abdullah al-Fatani (1847 CE).[24]

In later developments, this rapprochement between fiqh-oriented and *tasawuf*-oriented ulama was to become a general religious tendency in the archipelago. This is not a new thing in Islamic tradition. Well before this, al-Qusyairi and al-Ghazâlî (d. 1111 CE) had taught on this subject, which was greatly appreciated within the Sunni tradition.

NU AND ISLAMIC TRADITIONALISM IN INDONESIA

In Indonesia, the terms "Islamic tradition" and "traditionalism" are often polarized with the terms "modern" and "modernism". The first group is assumed to be left behind, uneducated, closed, old-fashioned, static, rural, ascetic and conservative; while the latter is seen as having progressive thought, being dynamic, urban, educated, and open. Deliar Noer, in his work that is fast becoming a classic,[25] could be held most responsible for the above distinction. In adopting Charles Adam's typology on modernism in Egypt and Azis Ahmad's on modernism in India and Pakistan, Deliar made a division between modern Islam as represented by Muhammadiyah (established in 1912 in Yogyakarta), Persatuan Islam (1920 in Bandung), Jamiat Khair (1905 in Jakarta), and al-Irsyad (1913 in Jakarta); and the traditionalists as represented by NU (1926 in Surabaya), Mathla'ul Anwar (1916 in Menes Banten), Persatuan Umat Islam (1917 in Majalengka), Persatuan Tarbiyah Islamiyah (1926 in Minangkabau), al-Jami'ah al-Wasliyah (1930 in North Sumatra), Nahdlatul Wathan (1934 in Lombok), and Dewan Dakwah wal Irsyad (1938 in South Sulawesi).[26] Separating the Islamic movement into such a binary opposition has recently received much criticism from a number of circles as it is felt to have become increasingly irrelevant.[27]

There are, however, several characteristics attributed to the traditional groups. First, their Islamic thought is strongly connected with the ulama who lived in the seventh to thirteenth centuries, in terms of *tasawuf*, the Hadith, fiqh, *tafsir*, and theology.[28] Secondly, the main adherents of Islamic traditionalism are *kiai* (Islamic teachers) and local figures who have their basis in *pesantren* education. Thus, *pesantren* are simplistically viewed as an agent of traditionalism that preserves the teachings and doctrine of ulama from the past. Nevertheless, as Snouck Hurgronje acknowledges, this does not mean that traditional Islam has not undergone development. Rather, traditional Islam that may seem to be static and chained to the thinking of medieval ulama has in fact undergone fundamental changes, though observing such changes is difficult and complex. Change has not only affected the social life of this group, as suspected by Fachry Ali and Bahtiar Effendy,[29] but has also influenced aspects of teachings and other fundamental thoughts. This research attempts to further explore these fundamental changes in greater depth.

Thirdly, the majority of traditionalists live in rural areas; or if they do indeed live in cities, their social origins can be traced back to rural areas. This is a result of the new mobility of the traditionalist youth who have better access to education and make their way to the cities. Fourthly, a more ideological feature is their connection to the *ahl al-sunnah wa al-jamâ'ah* doctrine, which is understood in a very specific way. On one level, the organized strengthening of the traditionalists is a result of their efforts to protect this understanding and ideology from the threat posed by the modernists, who campaign for Islam not to be chained down by tradition. As such, the Sunni understanding does not just emphasize differences with non-Sunnis such as the Shi'ites and the Kharijites, but also differentiates between the traditionalists and modernists.

NU, as a religious organization (*jam'iyyah diniyyah*), exists within this particular psychological atmosphere. As is well known, NU bases its religious understanding on three traditions: (1) in terms of fiqh, it follows one of the four *madzhab* or schools of thought (Hanafi, Maliki, Syafi'i, and Hanbali); (2) in terms of theology, it follows the teachings of Abu Hasan al-Asy'âri and Abu Mansur al-Matûridi; (3) in terms of *tasawuf* or mysticism, it follows the teachings of Imam Ghazâlî and Abu Qâsim al-Junaid al-Baghdâdî.[30]

The first NU generation created this doctrinal trilogy in an attempt to restrict the flow of modernization that stemmed from the Wahabi movement in Saudi Arabia. This is very much related to the birth of NU; however, the birth of NU will not be discussed in any depth here as it is not directly related to the topic of the book. Other researchers such as Martin van Bruinessen,[31] Andree Feillard,[32] M. Ali Haidar,[33] and Choirul Anam[34] have sufficiently examined the birth of NU. This research shows that there were at least two things that gave the traditional ulama momentum to consolidate the ranks and form Nahdlatul Oelama (The Awakening of the Ulama).

The first was the reaction of the modernist Islamic movement, which called for renewal through criticism of the religious practices of certain groups. The arrival of this movement in Indonesia cannot be separated from the increasing number of Indonesian Muslims who made the hajj or pilgrimage to Mecca after the opening of the Suez Canal (1869), several of whom also took religious studies there. Besides the many Muslims studying in Saudi Arabia, ulama from other areas, mostly from the Arab world, also travelled to Indonesia to teach in palaces and religious schools.[35] Prior to this, Saudi Arabia had witnessed the birth and burgeoning of a movement initially pioneered by Muhammad bin 'Abd al-Wahhâb (1703–87 CE) which became known as the Wahabi movement, as well as the pan-Islamism of Jamâl al-Dîn al-Afghâni (1839–97 CE), which was then continued by Muhammad Abduh (1849–1905 CE) and Rasyid Ridla (1865–1935 CE). These last three figures inspired the birth of Muhammadiyah (1912) in Yogyakarta, although vague elements of Wahabism are apparent. Meanwhile, the Wahabi movement inspired the birth of Persatuan Islam (1923) in Bandung, which promoted the purification of the Islamic faith.

From a religious point of view, the figures of these organizations voiced the same issues — namely, the attempt to return to pure Islamic teachings by purifying those teachings that were felt to be inauthentic or mixed with local traditions. The traditional ulama who were based in *pesantren* were of course accused by the movement. In short, the struggle between the two entities led the puritans to take every measure possible to eradicate all local elements from religious life, even from highly instrumental issues such as the *qunut, ushalli,* and *tahlilan* prayers. This was already taking place as early as the beginning of the twentieth century. In the 1910s for instance, there was a trader from Minangkabau in Surabaya known by the name of Faqih Hasjim[36] who provoked a harsh response from the traditionalists.

The most ruthless criticism of traditional practices concerned the relationship between the dead and those still living. An understanding had developed within traditional Islam that those who had died could still communicate with those who were still alive. In fact, it was believed that even when dead, a saint could bless the living. The puritans criticized this understanding, arguing that it tarnished the purity of *tauhid* (the oneness of God). They firmly rejected the belief in seeking help from the spirits of those who had died and other forms of spiritual help, including worshipping those considered to be *wali* or saints. Religious traditions such as *tahlilan* (prayers for the dead), *slametan* (thanksgiving offerings), and *ziarah kubur* (grave visits) were despised by the reformers.[37]

Besides theological issues, other matters were cause for criticism by the reformers, including the issue of heretical fiqh. Traditional fiqh demands a dogmatic belief in the four orthodox schools of thought or *madzhab*, especially the Syafi'i *madzhab*. The puritans rejected this dogmatic belief and called for a return to the Qur'an and Hadith and a resort to *ijtihad* (independent interpretation) in order to resolve new problems as they emerged. They also rejected the concepts of traditional mysticism and faith which, they argued, were influenced by Jewish philosophy and Christian and Persian thinking during its formative period.

Over quite a long period of time, despite disagreements over understandings, religious life remained relatively undisturbed, as any attempt at spreading disagreement was limited to word of mouth. G.F. Pijper likened socio-religious life until the beginning of the tenth century to a body of water whose surface remained calm and was only disturbed by a wave every now and again. However, this all changed about twenty years later, and the body of water became a flowing river that proved unable to contain the water within its banks.[38] The peak of tension occurred in 1922 when the Islamic Congress (Kongres al-Islam) was held in Cirebon. A heated debate ensued over the religious issues which had to date been at the crux of the dispute between the two groups. The congress nearly failed because of the atmosphere in which both parties declared one another to be kafir (infidels), or idolatrous because of their somewhat trivial difference in beliefs.[39] During the congress, the *pesantren* network was attacked by the reformers because they maintained their dogmatic beliefs and refused to undertake *ijtihad* or interpretation, since they felt that the requirements for it were not fulfilled. The two hostile parties were represented by Muhammadiyah and al-Irsyad on the one side, and the *pesantren* ulama were represented by Kiai Abdul Wahab Hasbullah[40] and Kiai Asnawi in the name of Tashwir al-Afkâr on the other.[41] The hostility continued until the Islamic Congress of 1924 in Surabaya and the 1926 Congress in Bandung.

Outside of these congresses, conflict broke out in other forums. One such example occurred in the Ampel Mosque in Surabaya between Ahmad Surkati from al-Irsyad and ulama from various *pesantren*. Initially, Surkati had written a piece analysing three issues, namely: (1) *ijtihâd* (interpretation) and *taqlid* (dogmatism); (2) Sunna (following the Prophet's example) and *bid'ah* (heresy); (3) grave visits and *wasîlah* (mediation) through the prophets and saints. The discussion of these issues was in rebuttal to the religious practices of the *pesantren* community. However, because it was deemed that the debate that was to ensue in the Ampel Mosque would have a negative impact, it was called off and Surkati was given the opportunity to present a written explanation of his actions.

The above illustration reveals how the religious practices of the traditional community were accused of being heretical or an impure form of Islam. An interesting phenomenon is revealed if we further examine NU's important documents. There are at least two key documents in which NU makes the same claim about "pure Islam" and "heresy". The concept of pure Islam was expressed by KH Achmad Siddiq in his monograph *Khittah Nahdliyah*, when he writes: "NU understands that the essence of *ahlussunnah wal jamâ'ah* (as understood by NU) is a pure Islamic teaching as taught and practised by the Prophet and his companions".[42] Meanwhile, the concept of heresy appears in a historical document, paragraph 3b, in which one of NU's objectives is to differentiate between which books are Sunni books and which are heretical. The two concepts are interesting, because either directly or indirectly, the formation of NU was related to the increasingly frequent attacks against it from the puritans. However, NU itself took the same stance on pure Islam and heresy, which formed the basis of its movement, although its understanding of the two concepts was different. This reached the point of one group claiming to represent pure Islam while accusing the other of heresy, with both blaming, if not denying, one another.

The theory that NU was born in response to modern Islam is not satisfactory, as it fails to answer the question of why NU was only established on 31 January 1926, while the puritan movement had emerged well before, at least since the foundation of Muhammadiyah in 1912. Nevertheless, tension with the modernists did play an indirect role in crystallizing solidarity within the *pesantren* community. As a result, it is perhaps better seen as an indirect cause of the birth of NU.

The second element that led to the formation of NU was the response to developments in Islamic politics on a global scale. This was related to the events at the beginning of 1924, when Musthafa Kemal Attaturk abolished the *khilâfah* or caliphate system. In response to the international political situation, a meeting was held in Surabaya on 4 August 1924, attended by Muhammadiyah, al-Irsyad, Tashwirul Afkâr, Ta'mîr al-Masâjid, and several other groups. Meanwhile, in the Arabian Peninsula itself there was a power struggle between 'Abd al-'Azîs Ibn Sa'ûd and Syarif Husein. Prior to this there had been two political meetings planned to discuss the issue of the caliphate: one in Cairo by Syaikh al-Azhar and one in Hijaz, Northwest Saudi Arabia, by Syarif Husein. However, because Syarif Husein lost in a war to Ibn Sa'ûd, his planned meeting failed, while the Cairo meeting lacked support because of poor preparation. A meeting to discuss the issue was eventually facilitated by Ibnu Sa'ûd in Hijaz. This newly planned meeting stirred Indonesian Islamic leaders into busy preparation. A series of meetings was organized to prepare for the meeting in Hijaz. The Khilâfah Committee Meeting was intense, and after the 1924 Congress, others were held in August 1925, February 1926, September 1926, and December 1926.[43]

Ibn Sa'ûd's victory and the planned meeting in Hijaz polarized Islam in Indonesia, especially in Java. Within the *pesantren* community it was felt that Ibn Sa'ûd's victory was a threat because he was known to be a fanatical Wahabi. They expressed their worries through Kiai Wahab Chasbullah in the Khilâfah Committee Meeting, while others expressed the desire to honour the initial agenda and go to Hijaz. The *pesantren* community wanted an agenda that included the preservation of the *ahl al-sunnah wa al-jamâ'ah* tradition, improvement in administration of the hajj, and in particular preservation of the traditions of Sufi orders and the practice of *wirid* (optional prayers said after the obligatory prayers), reciting of praise for Muhammad, and teaching books from the four schools of thought to be taken to Hijaz so that such practices could continue to be permitted. However, this agenda received no response from the non-*pesantren* community, and in fact the delegation sent to Hijaz did not include anyone from the *pesantren* community.[44] In light of this, ulama from the *pesantren* agreed to form their own alliance under the name Komite Merembuk Hijaz (the Hijaz Consultation Committee).[45] This committee later changed its name to Nahdlatul Ulama in a meeting in Surabaya on 31 January 1926. During this meeting it was decided that the organization would send a delegation to Mecca to meet King Ibn Sa'ûd and present its aspirations.[46] As already mentioned briefly, a number of issues were raised to King Ibn Sa'ûd, namely: (1) The request to King Ibn Sa'ûd to continue to allow freedom to follow the four schools of thought or *madzhab*: Hanafi, Maliki, Syafi'i, and Hanbali; (2) The request to allow people to continue to frequent historical sites because they had been irrevocably dedicated to mosques; (3) The request that all matters pertaining to the hajj be made publicly known across the world every year before the hajj season; (4) The request that all laws valid in Hijaz be written as legislation so that no violations would be made only because the law had not been put in writing; (5) NU asked for a written response confirming that the delegation had met King Ibn Su'ûd and delivered its suggestions.[47]

It is clear from the above discussion that the direct cause of the formation of NU was pressure from international Islamic politics, although internal dynamics, in the form of tension with the reformers, cannot be totally ignored as a force that helped unify the Islamic traditionalists.[48] This is further reinforced by the fact that before 1926, when the *pesantren* community started to be attacked by the reformers, Kiai Wahab Chasbullah had already consulted with Kiai Hasyim Asy'ari to form an organization to fight for the interests of the *pesantren*. This suggestion was made in 1924, but at the time Kiai Hasyim Asy'ari did not see any urgency. Two years later, after the Wahabi-oriented Raja Ibn Sa'ûd took control of Mecca, the need to form such an organization became more urgent and Kiai Hasyim Asy'ari gave his blessings to its establishment.[49]

The above discussion gives a strong enough impression that the birth of NU was to defend the freedom to follow one of the four *madzhab*, or schools of thought, which had become an element in the NU understanding of *ahl al-sunnah wa al-jamâ'ah* (in addition to theology and mysticism), and which was a part of NU's unique religious understanding. The trilogy of religious understanding that is often seen as the definition of *ahl al-sunnah wa al-jamâ'ah* à la NU can be found in the *Statuten Perkoempoelan Nahdlatoel Oelama* (Charter of the Association of Nahdlatul Ulama), formulated in 1926. Article 2 reads:

> The intention of this association is to hold firm to one of the *madzhab* of the four *imam*, namely Imam Muhammad bin Idris asj-Sjafi'i, Imam Malik bin Anas, Imam Abu Hanifah An-Ne'man, or Imam Ahmad bin Hambal, and to do anything for the good of Islam.[50]

Following on from here, Article 3 states:

> In order to achieve the intention of this association the following efforts will be made:
> a. Forming a nexus between the *ulama* who follow one of the *madzhab* mentioned in article 2.
> b. Examining books before they are taught, in order to establish if they are *ahl al-sunnah wa al-jamâ'ah* or heretical.
> c. Spreading Islam based on the *madzhab* mentioned in article 2 in whichever way is best.
> d. Attempting to increase the number of Islamic schools.
> e. Paying attention to matters pertaining to mosques and schools, as well as matters pertaining to orphans and the poor.
> f. Establishing bodies to promote agriculture, commerce and businesses that are not forbidden by Islamic law.[51]

This charter, which originates from the NU *Qanûn Asâsi* or fundamental charter and was formulated by Kiai Hasyim Asy'ari (1871–1947), does not completely depict what is meant by *ahl al-sunnah wa al-jamâ'ah* except that it firmly follows the four *madzhab*. The aspects related to theology and mysticism are not touched on in the least. Hasyim Asy'ari's formulation was more recently formulated by KH Bisri Musthafa in *Risalah Ahl al-Sunnah wa al-Jamâ'ah* (Kudus: Menara Kudus, 1967).[52] In this monograph, besides raising the fact that fiqh must follow one of the four schools of thought, he also emphasizes the theological doctrine that follows the ideas of Abu Hasan al-Asy'âri (d. 324 H/396 M) and Abu Manshur al-Matûridî (d. 333 H). Meanwhile, the doctrine on mysticism follows one of two imam, namely Abu Qasim al-Junaid al-Baghdâdî (d. 297 H/910 CE) and Abu Hamid Muhammad al-Ghazâlî (d. 505 H/1111 CE).

FORMATION OF NU INTELLECTUALISM

The roots of NU intellectualism can be traced back to the seventeenth and eighteenth centuries.[53] Azyumardi Azra's research reveals that during this era Islam in the archipelago was already showing some impressive intellectual dynamics, although in comparison to intellectual dynamics in other parts of the world it was quite left behind.[54] These dynamics were apparent in the involvement of ulama in — to borrow Azyumardi Azra's phrase — the network of ulama based in Mecca and Medina. The first representative ulama from Java were figures such as Nûr al-Dîn al-Raniri (d. 1068 H/1658 CE), Abd al-Rauf al-Sinkili (1024–1105 H/1615–93 CE), Muhammad Yusuf al-Maqassari (1030–1111 H/1629–99 CE), and Muhammad Arsyad al-Banjari (1710–1812 CE).[55]

This intellectual network was maintained up until the nineteenth and twentieth centuries, when — to borrow from Zamakhsyari Dhofier — the intellectual genealogy of the NU ulama was very apparent. Thus, over quite a long period of time before the first NU ulama established an intellectual network with Mecca and Medina, the Javanese ulama were already applying Middle Eastern traditions and developing a religious discourse that encompassed aspects of theology, fiqh and *tasawuf* which in turn became the Islamic standard for ulama in the archipelago.

In the second half of the nineteenth century, religious discourse in the archipelago was marked by the increasingly established nature of this network. However, during this era there were significant changes in the position that ulama from the archipelago held in Mecca and Medina. If during the previous centuries the "*Jawi*"[56] ulama were more like students of the Mecca and Medina ulama, by the nineteenth century ulama from the archipelago had attained an international standard and became the "teachers" in the geographical centre of Islam. These teachers in turn would establish the Southeast Asia Connection (a networked branch in Southeast Asia). The most prominent figures were Nawawi al-Bantani (1230–1314 H/1813–79 CE), Ahmad Khatib al-Sambasi (d. 1875 CE), Abd al-Karim al-Bantani, Ahmad Rifa'i Kalisalak (1200–86 H/1786–1870 CE), Ismail al-Khalidi al-Minangkabawi, Daud Ibnu Abdullah al-Fatani, Junaid al-Batawi, Ahmad Khatib al-Minangkabawi (1276–1334 H/1816–1916 CE), Syaikh Ahmad Nahrawi al-Banyumasi (d. 1346 H/1928 CE), Muhammad Mahfudz al-Tirmasi (1285–1338 H/1842–1929 CE), Hasan Musthafa al-Garuti (1268–1348 H/1852–1930 CE), Sayyed Muhsin al-Falimbani, Muhammad Yasin al-Padani (1335–1410 H/1917–90 CE), Abd al-Karim al-Banjari, Ahmad Damanhuri al-Bantani, and so on.[57]

The NU ulama initially involved in the intellectual network were involved with these figures. While Hasyim Asyari (d. 1945) was the central figure of NU intellectualism, several other ulama can be described as forming the core of the NU intellectual network, namely Mahfudz al-Tirmasi, Nawawi al-Bantani, Ahmad Khatib al-Minangkabawi, and Kiai Khalil Bangkalan. Members of the first NU generation[58] of the same time or a little after Hasyim Asy'ari, such as Bisri Syansuri (1886–1990) and Wahab Hasbullah (1888–1971), were also an integral part of the network.

In addition to the domestic network, the NU ulama, as with the ulama before them, also made Mecca and Medina the centre of their intellectual orientation. All NU ulama of this initial period had studied in Mecca.[59] For instance, Hasyim Asyari, the driving force behind NU, lived in Mecca for eight years at the age of twenty, and studied under Ahmad Khatib Minangkabawi, Mahfudz al-Tirmasi, and Nawawi al-Bantani.

These men were ulama with international reputations and were to have a large influence on the discourse of Islamic intellectualism in the archipelago. Nawawi al-Bantani, who was praised by Snouck Hurgronje as the most pious and humble man of his time in Indonesia, was an ulama who wrote many books across a wide range of disciplines that were studied in *pesantren*.[60] It is fitting to describe Nawawi al-Bantani as the axis in the formation of NU intellectualism.

However, in terms of influence, as Zamakhsyari Dhofier explains, the most influential teacher for the NU ulama, particularly for Hasyim Asyari, was Syaikh Mahfudz al-Tirmasi.[61] Mahfudz's intellectual authority can be equated to that of Nawawi al-Bantani, although the two had a teacher-student relationship. Mahfudz's writings cover several areas of study, including fiqh, the principles of fiqh (*ushûl al-fiqih*), *tauhid* (the oneness of God), and *tasawuf*. His most popular work is on the Hadith, both on research methodology and on the history and works of the great ulama.[62]

As with Hasyim Asy'ari, ulama like Wahab Hasbullah made use of similar channels for intellectual transmission. After wandering from his parents' house in Tambak Beras in Jombang, to Langitan Tuban, Mojosari Nganjuk, Tawangsari Surabaya, Kademangan Bangkalan (where Kiai Khalil lived) and finally to Tebu Ireng in Jombang, Wahab travelled to Saudi Arabia. There he studied with ulama who had previously nurtured Hasyim Asy'ari, including Mahfudz al-Tirmasi, Kiai Muhtaram, Ahmad Khatib al-Minangkabawi, Kiai Bakir, Kiai Asyari, and Syaikh Abdul Hamid.[63] Other wandering *santri* or students were to do likewise, including Bisri Syansuri, Wahid Hasyim, Kiai Munawir,[64] Kiai Ma'shum,[65] As'ad Syamsul Arifin, and Ahmad Shiddiq.[66]

Affirmation of the intellectual tradition within the community of NU ulama cannot be separated from this network. With the principle *al-muhâfadhah 'alâ al-qadîm al-shâlih wa al-akhdzu bi al-jadîd al-ashlah* (maintaining [the wealth] of the past that is good, and adopting that which is new and better), the wealth of NU intellectualism grew from the period of the Prophet Muhammad (Peace Be Upon Him), the Classical Period, and the Middle Ages through to the modern era.[67] This wealth represents an extraordinary cultural-intellectual capital through which NU can converse with modernity.

However, this section concentrates more on the initial formation of the tradition of Islamic intellectualism in the archipelago, and as such it is necessary to discuss several key aspects in Islam. They include the elements in Islam that encompass theology, fiqh, and *tasawuf*, as well as the dialectic between the three that led to the emergence of what has been called Malay reason.

AHL AL-SUNNAH WA AL-JAMÂ'AH AS NU'S RELIGIOUS ORIENTATION

Ahl al-sunnah wa al-jamâ'ah (often referred to as "Sunni") is the ideology that is both the orientation and soul of the NU religious movement. It is not just the basis of NU thought, but has also become an identifying factor to differentiate between those from NU and everyone else. The belief in the truth of the *ahl al-sunnah wa al-jamâ'ah* ideology is so strong because of the belief that those who adhere to this ideology will be saved on the Day of Judgement, as all sects in the Islamic community will enter hell except for one group, the community or *al-Jamâ'ah (mâ anâ 'alaihi wa ashhâbî)*.[68] This belief is indeed debatable, especially concerning what and whom the ideology refers to. In this context, the NU community adopts the *ahl al-sunnah wa al-jamâ'ah* identity and challenges other groups who are identified as deviant groups.

Nevertheless, the *ahl al-sunnah wa al-jamâ'ah* doctrine has strong roots in the discourse of Islamic theological thought. As a result, self-identification as a follower of the ideology is part of the effort to continue implementing the Islamic tradition. It is through this that the NU community displays its self-authenticity as a part of the true or valid Islam. The sheer strength of this identity and ideology has transformed *ahl al-sunnah wa al-jamâ'ah* into a tradition of thought and the basis of NU's intellectualism.

In this sense, there are at least three intellectual bases for NU's *ahl al-sunnah wa al-jamâ'ah* ideology: theology, fiqh, and *tasawuf*. In order to obtain a more detailed picture of this trilogy of NU religious understanding, a general overview of the three is presented below.

1. Theology

Theology or faith is a fundamental element in Islam which discusses God and all of His attributes and behaviour. The theological discourse in the archipelago in the initial period was fundamentally a continuation of the theological discourse that had developed quite rapidly in the initial and middle period of Islam's spread through the Arabian Peninsula. It is thus not surprising that the theological thought that developed in the archipelago was more of a defence of theology from the past which had fragmented into several schools of thought. That is, theological thought did not depict so much the Islamic intellectual struggle in the archipelago, but was more an attempt to preserve the schools of thought. This is understandable because the Islam that entered Indonesia was already fragmented into various schools of thought, in the fields of theology, *tasawuf*, and fiqh.[69] Moreover, this fragmentation had led to competition, if not conflict, between the schools of thought.

For an initial description, it is necessary to briefly examine the theological schools of thought that formed the standard of theological thought in the archipelago. Theological discourse in Islam discussed three main issues, namely: (1) *iman* (belief) and *kufur* (unbelief); (2) the position of *akal* (reason/logic) and *wahyu* (divine revelation); and (3) human actions.

Belief and unbelief was the first theological problem to emerge in Islam. Debate over the two concepts emerged at the time of the political battle between the forces of Ali bin Abi Talib (d. 661 CE) and those of Mu'awiyah bin Abu Sufyan (d. 680 CE), known as the Battle of Siffîn. An interesting event occurred during the battle, which is seen by historians of theology as the starting point for the rise of different theological groups in Islam. The incident occurred when Mu'awiyah's forces were under pressure and nearly defeated, and 'Amr ibn al-'Âs, a follower of Mu'awiyah who was known to be sly, asked for peace and raised a copy of the Qur'an on a spear. Part of Ali's forces then pushed for the offer of peace to be accepted, though a small minority strongly objected. After sufficient discussion, Ali decided to accept the offer through a process of arbitration. The diplomats representing each side were Abu Musa al-Asy'âri from Ali's forces and 'Amr ibn al-'Âs from Mu'awiyah's forces. History tells that an agreement was reached between the two to have the two warring leaders, Ali and Mu'awiyah, step down. However, after Abu Musa announced Ali's resignation, 'Amr ibn al-'Âs announced Mu'awiyah as the caliph.[70]

This incident was to have a significant impact on the development of Islam, both politically and theologically. In terms of politics, the incident is seen as the starting point of political disintegration within the Muslim community. On the other hand, the incident brought hidden wisdom to the world of theology because from that point onwards, speculative theological thought started to develop.

Several groups were involved in debate over theology, although they were initially involved because of political issues. The discourse that emerged after this first civil war or *fitnat al-kubrâ* was about the issue of belief and unbelief involving the Kharijites[71] and the Murji'ites.[72] They debated about whether the status of a person who had committed a terrible sin was kafir (an infidel) or not. According to the Kharijites, those guilty of terrible sins were infidels and became *murtad* or apostates, and as such had to be killed. In later developments, infidels were not only those who committed great sins but also those who did not agree with the Kharijite interpretation, and people who did not see non-Kharijites as infidels. At the most extreme level, those Kharijites who did not live in the same region (which was called the realm of Islam, *dâr al-Islâm*) were considered infidels (for living in the realm of war or *dâr al-harb*) and thus had to be fought against.

Consequently, those involved in the process of arbitration described above, namely Ali bin Abi Talib, Mu'awiyah bin Abu Sufyan, and the two delegates, 'Amr bin 'As and Abu Musa al-Asy'ari, were infidels because they had committed a great sin, and because they did not make a decision based on God's law, *wa man lam yahkum bi mâ anzala Allâh fa ulâika hum al-kâfirûn* (QS. 5: 44). They took from this Qur'anic verse the slogan *lâ hukma illâ lillâh* (no rulership except by God alone). In a similar manner, those who participated in the Battle of Jamal between Ali and Aisyah were also considered infidels.

Meanwhile, for the Murji'ites, sinners remained Muslims and judgement fell to God on the day of reckoning. They held this belief because even those who sinned continued to acknowledge that "There is no God but God, and Muhammad is His prophet". Humans cannot determine whether an individual has sinned or not because that is the right of God. The neutral attitude of the Murji'ites meant that it was easy for any ruler to accept them. This is evident in their change in attitude when Mu'awiyah came to power, and a large majority sided with Mu'awiyah, although they had been neutral during the reign of Ali bin Abi Talib. Their siding with Mu'awiyah made the government promote the spread of their teachings, which in the following phase would crystallize under the Jabarites (predeterminists/predestinarians).

After this debate over the status of sinners, the following theme concerned human actions. Generally speaking, debate on this issue was represented by two groups, the Qadarites and the Jabarites, although recently other variations have emerged. The Qadarites believed that humans had independence and freedom in choosing their path in life. They argued that humans had the power and energy to determine their own actions. This was known as the belief in free will and free action. This is based on the understanding of the justice of God, which argues that because humans act on their own behalf, then it is only fair for God to demand that they take responsibility for those actions.

The Jabarites beg to differ. They believe humans have no independence in determining their will and actions. Humans, they argue, are tied to God's absolute will, and as such have no freedom to determine their own will.[73]

Another theological theme concerned logical reason and divine revelation. This theological discourse revolved around four aspects, namely: knowing God; obligations in knowing God; knowing what is right and what is wrong; and obligations in doing good and avoiding evil. For al-Asy'âri,[74] logical reason (without divine revelation) could only provide the answer to one of these issues, namely, knowing God. That is, without divine revelation, humans could use their logic and would be capable of knowing that there was a God. However, for anything more, the human mind was powerless. Reasoning could not lead to the knowledge that there were obligations to knowing God, to knowing right from wrong, or the obligation to do good deeds and avoid evil. These last three could only be known through divine revelation. Thus, murdering or stealing cannot be deemed wrong if there is no divine revelation saying that they are wrong.

However, al-Maturidî[75] saw things differently. He argued that reason could reveal the first three aspects, but not the last. Divine revelation was only necessary to know the obligation to do good deeds and avoid evil. Thus, according to al-Maturidî, a deed could be called wrong if it was substantially wrong, and it could be called good if it was overwhelmingly good. Al-Maturidî's conviction was very similar to that of the Mu'tazilites, who reckoned that logical reasoning could reveal all four aspects. These opinions on reason and divine revelation also influenced theories on human action, where al-Asy'âri's stance was closer to the Jabarites, while al-Maturidî was closer to the Qadarites.[76]

Another theme concerned the attributes of God. It was debated by two large groups, the Asy'ârites and the Mu'tazilites. The main issue of debate was whether God had attributes or not. In answer, the Mu'tazilites argued that God had no attributes. This did not mean that God did not know, did not rule, or did not live, and so on. God did know, did rule, and did live, but these aspects were not attributes of God. Rather, God knew of things through His Essence, ruled through His Essence, and so on.

The Asy'ârites argued the opposite, saying that God had the characteristics of being eternal and everlasting, although they refuted anthropomorphism[77] in the sense that God had physical attributes like humans. God knew of things through His attribute of knowledge, God willed things through His attribute of intention, and so on. These attributes were not identical to His Essence, but were not separate from His Essence either, *lâ hiya huwa wa lâ hiya gairuhu*.[78] This last argument was an effort to avoid the creation of many eternal or beginningless entities *(ta'addud al-qudamâ)*, which the Mu'tazilites accused the Asy'ârites of doing.

Over time, al-Asy'âri's religious scholarship developed and expanded under Abu Bakar al-Baqillâni (d. 403 H/1013 CE), although al-Baqillâni did not accept all of al-Asy'âri's teachings. For instance, they had different views on God's attributes, which for al-Baqillâni were things (*hâl*) in accordance with the views of Abu Hâsyim of the Mu'tazilites. Another difference was over human actions, where al-Asy'âri argued that all human actions were created by God, but al-Baqillâni believed that humans contributed towards their actions. God only created movement within humans, while the form and characteristics of those movements were produced by humans.[79]

Besides al-Baqillâni, al-Asy'âri's teachings were sustained by 'Abd al-Mâlik al-Juwaini (d. 478 H), though again his opinions differed slightly from those of al-Asy'âri. For instance, while al-Asy'âri did not accept *ta'wîl* (explanation or interpretation), al-Juwaini accepted *ta'wîl* of the anthropomorphic verses, such as interpreting "God's hand" to mean God's rule, "God's eyes" to mean God's vision, "God's face" to mean God's being or existence, and the presence of God on the throne of His kingdom to mean God who is Powerful and Most High.

On human action, al-Juwaini believed that the energy within humans had an effect, where that effect was the result of a domino or butterfly effect. That is, the form of an action depended on the energy within a human being, and the form of that energy depended on other factors, and the form of those other factors depended on yet others, and so on, right back to the cause of all factors, namely, God.

The most influential of all of al-Asy'âri's followers was al-Ghazâlî (1058–1111 CE). Unlike al-Baqillâni and al-Juwaini who held slightly different views to al-Asy'âri, al-Ghazâlî was closer to al-Asy'âri, though again there were some differences. Under al-Ghazâlî's influence, al-Asy'âri's theological teachings spread across the Islamic world, especially amongst adherents of the *ahl al-sunnah wa al-jamâ'ah* ideology, as well as to Indonesia.

These theological understandings entered the archipelago not as an intellectual discourse that allowed people to think about them critically, but more as a religious doctrine that required people to accept them without question. It is thus understandable that when Islam first entered the archipelago, these theological issues were not a source of debate or dynamic discourse.

This in turn is understandable because abstract theology did not directly influence religious practices, and as such was viewed more as a doctrine to be believed in than as something to be discussed. This reality is different with fiqh which is more *'amalî* or practical, which directly impacted on daily religious practices, was structured and in some ways more secular, so that people did not have theological issues preventing them from questioning fiqh, although there was still some theologizing of fiqh.[80] If in theology, boundaries are often set with words such as "kafir" (infidel) and "Muslim", "believer" or "unbeliever", in fiqh the terms are softer, such as "may" and "may not". As such, theological thought did not develop dynamically because of the reluctance to question theological aspects, even though within theology there are a variety of different thoughts. This is caused by the fact that theology is very theocentric, so that questioning anything in theology is considered to be a questioning of God. This is different in fiqh, and although there are also elements of its transcendence, it presents a face more open to criticism in accordance with its worldly disposition.

Separately from this, another issue to be emphasized here is that when these theological understandings entered the archipelago, the inhabitants were not without faith; rather, they adhered to a number of local beliefs that had been passed down through the generations until they formed a particular world view. The meeting of (Arab) Islamic theology and these local beliefs or theologies gave rise, on the one hand, to tension to maintain the purity of said theologies, but, on the other, to compromises that led to syncretism.[81]

The syncretism between Islam and local traditions occurred largely in the spread of Islam throughout Java by the Sufis known as the Walisongo (Nine Saints). In inculcating Islam's doctrine of *tauhid* (the oneness of God), they were famous for their tolerance towards local religious practices that were the tradition within communities. Their tolerance of local traditions, especially ancient mysticism that originated from Hinduism and Buddhism, had two effects: on the one hand, Islam was easily accepted by locals because it was seen as similar to the traditions to which they already held; but on the other hand, Islam (especially Javanese Islam) was often accused by observers (especially foreigners) of being impure, and of being mixed with local traditions to the extent that one could not differentiate between what was Islam and what was customary tradition. Such accusations have been made by the likes of Harry J. Benda,[82] Clifford Geertz,[83] W.F. Wertheim,[84] Robert Jay,[85] and others.

There are at least two arguments in support of this assumption. First, geographically Indonesia is far from the centre of Islam: Mecca and Medina. As a result, it is difficult to believe that the purity of Islam could be maintained over such a distance; especially since, given the regions Islam had to pass through on its way to Indonesia, it is likely that they mixed Islam with the local traditions of each region. In other words, it is possible that on its way east (to Indonesia, Malaysia, and so on), Islam had already been mixed with and influenced by local values. Secondly, the historical reality is that Islam arrived in Indonesia not directly from Muslims of the Arabian Peninsula, but from traders from Persia and India.

These arguments seem valid at a glance, although there are fundamental aspects that can be questioned, including the parameters used to measure the purity or impurity of Islam, and the validity of the assumption that pure Islam can only be found in the Middle East (Saudi Arabia) while Islam in other areas is no longer pure. In fact, the above arguments have received criticism from a number of academics. Nikki R. Keddie (1987) disputes the idea in her research, which compares Southeast Asian Islam — in this case the Islam of Minangkabau — with Middle Eastern Islam. On one level, her study can be seen as the antithesis of the foreign researchers mentioned above, such as Van Leur who argues that Islam in the archipelago is only a thin veneer over the top of local culture and, as such, is easily influenced by local culture. In fact, he continues, Islam in the archipelago brought no reformation whatsoever, either socially, economically or politically.[86] The arrival of Islam did not bring much change to society in the archipelago in terms of faith or world view, except to add to and enrich traditional cultural elements. As such, according to Abdul Rahman Haji Abdullah, what emerged was not a significant change to traditional belief, but a change that went side by side with continuity.[87]

This is difficult to accept because Islam in the archipelago has had a significant effect on the dynamics of social life. Azyumardi Azra[88] summarizes a rebuttal to the above arguments using the opinions of Najib al-Attas, Husein al-Attas, and Nikki Keddie. Najib al-Attas argues that Islam changed the sociocultural lifestyle and spiritual traditions of the Malay-Indonesian society. The arrival of Islam also influenced the enlightenment in Southeast Asia through its support of intellectualism. Meanwhile, Husein al-Attas suggests that the intellectual opinions of scholars like Van Leur have built an argument on the basis of an erroneous historical reading, to the extent of creating a shallow historical perception of Islam in Southeast Asia. Keddie also refutes the argument by quoting Edwin E. Leob (1972), who researched the Minangkabau society that believed in witches, supernatural forces, and other superstitions considered to be a deviation from Islam. If these beliefs and practices are viewed as evidence that Islam is only a thin veneer, an already deviant form of Islam, the same conclusion must then be valid for Islam in North Africa and the Near East. Muslims there must also be seen as nominal and less authentic because these same beliefs are also widely practiced there. Keddie further contends that praying, as the most obvious form of worship of the pillars of Islam, is implemented more routinely by Muslims in Minangkabau than by Muslims in Iran in the pre-revolution era. A similar finding is apparent in their respective enthusiasm to make the hajj.

This discussion is intended to emphasize that the encounter between Arab Islamic theology and the local theologies of the archipelago opened up the possibility for discourse, which then saw Islam upheld as a historical religion that was thought about and practised by its adherents. Islam as a historical religion acknowledges that Islam has been sent to earth and has existed alongside other historical realities. On this basis, the claim that Islam in the archipelago is not (or less) authentic loses its relevance. Kiddie's argument as described above is well grounded. *Tauhid* (the oneness of God) as the essence of Islamic doctrine does not prevent interpretation from a variety of perspectives in accordance with the traditional conscience of local communities. The emergence of the various theological groups such as the Jabarites, the Qadarites, and the Mu'tazilites is proof that *tauhid* as the essence of Islamic doctrine allows for its interpretation from a variety of perspectives without any having the right to claim that any one view is most authentic. All the theological currents or sects within Islam are aimed at purifying (*tanzih*) and upholding the unity of God, although their individual opinions are not infrequently at odds with each other.

I now turn to an examination of the struggle of theological thought as it occurred in the archipelago as a continuation of the religious thought discussed above. Theological discourse in the history of Islam in the archipelago only became evident during the reign of the Samudra Pasai kingdom (1042–1444), particularly during the governance of Sultan Malik al-Shalih (1261–89) and Sultan Malik al-Dhahir (1326–50). At the time, the large-scale process of Islamization was under way, and Pasai could be described as the centre of Islam and the centre to which people came to seek reference in regards to religious matters. This situation continued until Pasai started to weaken politically after the rise of the Malacca kingdom. Even then, Pasai remained the reference for religious issues in Malacca.

The theological issues that emerged during the reign of the Pasai Kingdom — under Sultan Mahmud Syah — concerned *qadla'* and *qadar* (predestination). The *Sejarah Melayu*, as cited by Abdul Rahman Haji

Abdullah, states that ulama from Iran and Khorasan sent a letter to Pasai stating:

> Peace be upon my older brother Seri Sultan Azmu al-Mukarram Zillullah fi al-'Alam. As you have sent the wealthy Tun Muhammad and Minister Sura Dipa to meet me and ask about the issue: "*man qala: innallaha khaliqun wa raziqun fi al-azali faqad kafara*" that is, that anyone who says that God bestows blessings upon men [without them having to work], is an infidel. "*Wa man qala: innallaha lam yakun khaliqun wa raziqan fi al-azali faqad kafara*", that is, that anyone who says that God does not bestow blessings upon men [and it is through work that man is rewarded], is an infidel. With this you desire that I give you an answer.[89]

This is evidence that at the time there was a debate over the issue of predestination or divine will and decree between the Jabarites and Qadarites. As described above, the Jabarites believed that the fate of humans had been preordained by God and that humans did not have the ability to change God's will. Conversely, the Qadarite understanding, to which the Mu'tazilites also adhered, supported the freedom of human effort that meant humans had to take responsibility for their own actions.

Although the *Sejarah Melayu* does not detail how Pasai reacted to the letter, one thing is certain: Pasai had authority and prestige as the centre of Islam in the archipelago. As a Sunni kingdom, it is highly likely that the answer to their issue would be closer to the understanding held by the Jabarites than the Qadarites, even though as a theological sect the Sunnis wanted to remain between the two extremes that these groups represented.

In addition to the above issue, Malacca also asked Pasai to interpret the book *al-Dûr al-Mandzum* which was written by the Sufi Maulana Abu Ishak al-Shirazi and discussed faith, especially the issues of God's essence, attributes, and actions. The book was difficult to understand, so Sultan Mansur Syah (1456–77) ordered that it be sent to Pasai to be interpreted by the ulama there. Again, this indicated that although Pasai was politically weak, other kingdoms continued to respect its religious authority.[90]

In later developments, the centre of Islamic intellectualism in the archipelago began to shift from Pasai and Malacca to Aceh. After the fall of Malacca to the Portuguese in 1511, Aceh began to control and represent the centre for religious orientation in the archipelago. In relation to theological matters, in the seventeenth century when Aceh was at the height of its glory, the Asy'ârite and Maturidî theologies emerged. One of the figures responsible was Bukhari al-Jauhari, who wrote the book *Tâj al-Salâtîn* in 1603. Although this book cannot be described as a comparative religious study (*ushûl al-dîn*) in its true meaning, it was not only the first book to discuss the self and God in the Asy'ârite understanding in accordance with the teachings of Imam al-Ghazâlî (d. 1111 CE), but was also a Malaysian book with an identifiable author.

Two other figures that must be mentioned are Nûr al-Dîn al-Raniri (d. 1658 CE) and Abd al-Rauf Sinkel (d. 1693 CE). Nûr al-Dîn al-Raniri was more interested in discussing the Maturidî understanding that followed the Hanafi school of thought than the Asy'ârite belief that followed the Syafi'i school of thought. This is evident in his translation of Sa'ad al-Dîn al-Taftazani's *Syarh al-Aqâid al-Nasafiyah*, which he titled *Durrat al-Farâid bi Syarhi al-Aqâid*. This work of al-Taftazani was based on the opinions of Umar ibn Muhammad al-Nasafi (1143). Al-Nasafi and al-Taftazani were two ulama who followed the Hanafi school of thought in the field of fiqh, but according to W.M. Watt they were actually Asy'ârites who taught in areas that were dominated by the Maturidî understanding so that they tended to cover Maturidî theology.[91]

The influence of the Maturidî theology can also be seen in Nûr al-Dîn al-Raniri's work titled *Hidâyat al-Imâm*. The book discusses issues of God's essence, attributes and actions, the veracity of the Prophet, and the pillars of Islam. When discussing God's essence and attributes, he mentions the classification of attributes into *ma'âni* (part of the essence of God) and *ma'nawiyah* (not essential aspects of God's being), which is unique to the Maturidî theology.

Meanwhile, Abd Rauf Singkle's review of scholastic theology (*ilmu kalam*) can be found in his mystical book *Umdat al-Muhtajîn*. The book reveals him to be the first ulama in the archipelago to discuss the twenty obligatory attributes of God, the impossible attributes, and the possible attributes. He divided the twenty obligatory attributes into four categories: the *nafsiyah, salbiyah, ma'âni*, and *ma'nawiyah*. He also touched on the obligatory and impossible attributes of the Prophet, though very briefly because the book was intended as a mystical book.[92] From the very beginning, the Maturidî and the Asy'âri schools of thought were therefore popular in Aceh.

Thus, in Aceh two streams developed: one of scholastic theology that was supported by the ruling elite, and the other being the traditional belief still practised by society. As in other areas in the archipelago, despite the emergence of several scholastic streams of theology, local beliefs were not just wiped out. Local religious practices continued to thrive amongst communities, both those originating from indigenous traditions and from Buddhist/Hindu culture.

Entering the eighteenth century, the most prominent figure was Muhammad Zain Faqih Jalâl al-Dîn al-'Asyi. As described by A. Hasymi, al-'Asyi was the most well-known ulama of the Aceh Sultanate under Sultan 'Alâ' al-Dîn Mahmud Syah (1174–95 H/1760–81 CE).[93] His most important contribution was in 1757 CE, when he translated the book *Umm al-Barâhin* by Abu Abdullah Muhammad bin Yusuf al-Sanusi (d. 895 H/1490 CE) that discussed the twenty attributes of God. The translation was titled *Bidâyat al-Hidâyah*, which together with another book, *Kasyf al-Kirâm*, was prepared in Mecca in 1170 H/1757 CE and 1171 H/1758 CE and completed in Aceh. After its publication, several books on scholastic theology emerged based on *Umm al-Barâhin*, including *Zuhrat al-Murîd fî Bayân Kalimat al-Tawhîd* by Abd al-Samad al-Falimbani in 1764 in Mecca. At the time, there was a famous ulama in Mecca by the name of Syeikh Nawawi al-Bantani who also published an explanation of the *Umm al-Barâhin* titled *Zari'at al-Yaqîn*.[94]

During this period, Islam in Java experienced an interesting dynamic related to theology, although the theological dynamic itself cannot be entirely separated from fiqh and *tasawuf*. Syekh Ahmad al-Mutamakkin (d. 1740 CE) deserves a mention here.[95] He was quite a legend in Kajen, Pati, in Central Java. The fiqh ulama who were represented by Ketib Anom Kudus once accused him of spreading deviant understandings. In fact, they submitted a petition to the King of Kartasura, Sunan Amangkurat IV (1719–26), to punish Mutamakkin by burning him alive. The petition failed after Paku Buwono II (1726–49), Amangkurat IV's replacement, refused the proposal. The story was told in *Serat Cebolek* which was written by Raden Ngabehi Yasadipura I (1729–1803), a poet of the Mataram Sultanate under the reign of Paku Buwono II and Paku Buwono III (1749–88).[96]

At the end of the eighteenth century and beginning of the nineteenth century in Java there was another often controversial figure, KH Ahmad Rifa'i (1786–1876), who was born in 1786 in Kendal, Central Java but settled in Kalisalak, Batang. Ahmad Rifa'i studied in Mecca for eight years (1833–41) under Syaikh Abdurrahman, Syaikh Abu Ubaidah, Syaikh Abdul Azis, Syaikh Usman, and Syaikh Abdul Malik. After returning home from Mecca, he became known as a man who would not compromise with the Dutch colonial government. As a result, he moved from Kendal to Batang, where he built a religious community based on *pesantren* values.

Ahmad Rifa'i's work is known as the *Tarajumah*,[97] and as such his *santri* or students are often called *tarajumah santri*. He has written no fewer than fifty-three books, which span across the fields of theology, fiqh, and *tasawuf*.[98] Some of his works include: (1) *Syarîh al-Imân*, written in 1255 H/1840 CE in prose. This book discusses belief, an issue whose discussion often revolves around unbelievers and their fate, and the prohibition against Muslims from approaching them; (2) *Ri'ayat al-Himmah*, written in 1266 H/1851 CE. This work covers issues of theology, fiqh and *tasawuf* oriented towards the Syafi'i school of thought and the *ahl al-sunnah wa al-jamâ'ah* ideology. It holds a unique position as it is regarded as a primary source in comparison to Ahmad Rifa'i's other books; (3) *Kitâb Bayân*, written in 1256 H in verse. This book talks about the requirements for potential teachers, but it contains anti-ulama elements which sided with the Dutch colonizers; (4) *Tasyrihat al-Muhtâj*, written in 1266 H, which discusses fiqh concerning economic transactions (*mu'âmalah*), from trade (*bai'*) to lost property; (5) *Nadham Tasfiyah*, which is concerned with the meaning of *al-fâtihah* (the first verse of the Qur'an) and its connection with the validity of prayer; (6) *Abyân al-Hawâij*, written in 1264 H/1847 CE, which discusses theology, fiqh, and *tasawuf*; (7) *Asnal Miqsâd*, written in 1260 H/1844 CE, also on theology, fiqh and *tasawuf*; and (8) *Tabyîn al-Islah*, written in 1264 H/1847 CE, presenting a discussion of the issues pertaining to marriage.[99]

In the field of theology, Ahmad Rifa'i always identified himself as a follower of *ahl al-sunnah wa al-jamâ'ah*. He talked mostly about faith or belief. He believed that the element needed for an individual's belief to be legal and valid was confirmation within that individual's heart, which was then complemented by an attitude of resignation and obedience to religious rules. Thus, people could not be said to be believers if they only believed in their heart but did not observe religion. Observance was proof of belief; and as such, immorality decreased one's faith, to the point of making one a non-believer.[100]

Ahmad Rifa'i also believed that there was only one essential pillar in Islam (*suwiji blaka*), which was to read the *syahadat* or confession of faith. Meanwhile, the other pillars of Islam became obligatory after an individual embraced Islam. The other four pillars were considered to be a necessary perfection, but lack of observance of them could not terminate an individual's status as a Muslim.[101]

In the nineteenth century, there were several books on scholastic theology that discussed the belief in the "twenty attributes", including Sayyid Usman bin Yahya al-Betawi's book *Ini Kitab Sifat Dua Puluh* in

1886; *Sirâj al-Hudâ* by Zain al-Dîn ibn Muhammad Badawi al-Sambawi, written in 1885 or 1886; *'Aqîdat al-Najjîn* by Zain al-'Abidîn Muhammad al-Fatani in 1890; and *al-Dûr al-Tamîm* and *Sifat Dua Puluh* by Syaikh Dawud ibn Abdullah al-Fatani. In Kalantan, there was the book *Bi Kifâyat al-Awwâm* by Abd al-Samad Ibn Muhammad Sâlih (1840–91 CE), more commonly known as Tuan Tabal; and in Kedah, *Miftâh al-Jannah* was written by a descendant of Arsyad al-Banjari called Muhammad Taib ibn Mas'ûd al-Banjari, who also discussed the twenty attributes. In addition, on Penyengat Island in Riau, the book *Umm al-Barâhin* was taught by Raja Ali ibn Raja Ahmad alongside other books, including *Minhaj al-'Âbidîn* by al-Ghazâlî and *Jawhar al-Tauhîd* by Ibrahim al-Laqani.[102]

This was followed by a phase where theology in the archipelago went through very little significant intellectual development, because there was no longer any productive attempt at discussing different theological understandings. Instead, efforts were made to conserve and defend theological orthodoxy. The purification movement that spread throughout several regions in the archipelago, especially that of Muhammadiyah and its Wahabi ideology, is evidence of this conservation. It is thus not surprising that during the twentieth century and the centuries before, no monumental works were produced.

Martin van Bruinessen's research into books on scholastic theology taught in several educational institutes shows that developments in this field in the archipelago were purely in the form of exposure to al-Asy'âri thoughts concerning the twenty attributes, the possible and impossible attributes of God, and the attributes of the Prophet.[103]

It is clear from the above discussion that the tradition of scholastic theology that developed in the archipelago was a product of thought that developed elsewhere, and was just accepted, followed, and not questioned. The result is that such thought, most regrettably, became orthodox, standardized, and monolithic. As a result, the immense wealth of scholastic thought within Islam never reached or became part of the debate in the life of Muslims. The quite rational scholastic thought of the Mu'tazilites and the Syi'ites was lost in the process of history which was dominated by one particular line of scholastic theology, the Asy'âri line, with all its pros and cons.

This domination of the Asy'ârite theological understanding was spread via a process I call the "ideologization" of theology, through judgements concerning who was a believer and who was an unbeliever. That is, this understanding was socialized through its claim of being the truth, as if to deny the presence of any plurality within the theological understanding itself. Although in fiqh, people were willing to use a variety of legal opinions from ulama, in theology people were not prepared (or were at least reluctant) to do so. It was thought that playing with theological issues would plunge people into the abyss of non-belief. The world of fiqh, therefore, is more tolerant of pluralism than is the world of theology. In fiqh, sharp differences are still tolerated, but if those differences enter the realm of theology, they result in an immediate judgement as to what is Muslim and what is not.

2. Fiqh

Fiqh is a measurable element of the NU *ahl al-sunnah wa al-jamâ'ah* ideology that it is often used in daily life to differentiate the NU cultural community from other religious groups. This difference may be in the ritual practices of everyday worship, the method of applying law, or the way the legal schools of thought are viewed. It is not going too far to say that the nature of NU thought is the nature of fiqh thought. Thus, all actions, both those related to organizational policies and those related to interpretation of social interactions, always use a fiqh framework,[104] including NU political decisions which are always based on fiqh theorems and logic.[105] This indicates that fiqh has a more important position in NU culture than does theology and mysticism. While theology and mysticism are considered complete products that must only be believed in and practised, this is not so with fiqh, which is always alive and used in response to a variety of social phenomena. Because of its measurable characteristic, fiqh is almost always used as the parameter to measure an individual's piety. In other words, it is through the observance of fiqh principles that an individual is immediately judged to be religiously observant.

The important position that fiqh holds in the life of the Muslim community has a long and dynamic history. As a result, before discussing the fiqh that developed within NU, it is first necessary to discuss the fiqh dynamics that developed in the archipelago. Examining this allows us to see how much continuity was maintained and how much change occurred in the fiqh tradition that developed within NU, compared to the fiqh tradition of the archipelago. It might even be the case that NU fiqh has few ties at all with the fiqh tradition of the archipelago, but is more an adoption of the fiqh that developed in the Middle East. Within this framework, this section begins with a brief look at the fiqh dynamics from the seventeenth century to the beginning of the twentieth century.

The fiqh that developed in Indonesia was largely based on the Syafi'i discourse,[106] from Imam al-Syafi'i's school of thought. This is understandable because, first of all, the process of Islamization of Indonesia in the twelfth and thirteenth centuries occurred at a time when developments in Islamic law were in crisis as the door to *ijtihad* had already closed, although many people contested this later. The experts no longer had the courage to think as freely and as creatively as they could; instead, they found themselves busy with activities to support their own schools of thought. Secondly, the activists who launched the process of Islamization in Indonesia, as historians allege, were of the Syafi'i school of thought; although later developments saw some Indonesian Muslims basing their religious behaviour on other frameworks of thought besides Imam Syafi'i's fiqh, particularly at the beginning of the twentieth century when the reformation movement gained momentum.

The following will examine the fiqh discourse in Indonesia from the seventeenth century because, as Martin acknowledges, information on Indonesian Islam before this time is minimal.[107] In addition, more emphasis is placed on the intellectual dynamics on a cultural level, not on the level of legal politics such as the institutionalization of justice in the kingdoms of the archipelago and the laws enforced. Not only are studies of politics too frequent, they also tend to neglect developments in thought, even though the dynamics of thought at the cultural level cannot be separated from political dynamics.

In connection to this, Aceh will be taken as the starting point, as it represents the area in the archipelago which not only has a long history of Islam, but is also home to extraordinary intellectual dynamics. In this sense, it is not misleading to describe Aceh as the centre of Islamic intellectualism in its time. In the seventeenth century, there were many Islamic ulama from a variety of schools of thought living in Aceh. This was related to the enthusiasm of Sultan Iskandar Muda Mahkota Alam Syah (1016–46 H/1607–36 CE) and the sultans who came after him in promoting the arrival of ulama for the sake of Islamic propagation or *dakwah*.

A key figure of the seventeenth century was Nûr al-Dîn al-Raniri (d. 1068 H/1658 CE). Born in Indonesia, he settled in Aceh on 31 March 1637 and represented the relationship between Indonesia and India.

Al-Raniri was indeed better known as an expert in *tasawuf* than as an expert in fiqh. This is understandable, given that the twenty-nine works al-Raniri produced[108] were largely on issues of mysticism and faith, especially those concerning the debate over the followers of *wujûdiyah* (pantheism, *wihdat al-wujûd*) led by Hamzah Fansuri and Syams al-Dîn al-Sumatrani (d. 1040 H/ 1630 CE).[109] In addition, al-Raniri was a member of three Sufi orders: the Qadiriyah, Rifa'iyah, and al-Audarusiyah orders.[110]

Although al-Raniri did not write much on fiqh, this does not mean he did not know much about it. On the contrary, he had a significantly deep understanding of fiqh which influenced his mysticism, making it unique to the mystic teachings that had gone before him. The polemic over the followers of *wujûdiyah* can be understood from this perspective, where he tried to reveal and emphasize elements of harmonization between *syari'ah* and mysticism.[111] One of al-Raniri's works in fiqh was *Shirâth al-Mustaqîm*.[112] The book was written in 1634 CE and finished in 1644 CE, as the first book on fiqh in the archipelago.[113] Al-Raniri specifically discussed issues of worship, such as cleansing, praying, fasting, zakat (alms), the hajj, and sacrifice. Although at first glance the book provides a simple explanation of the fundamental fiqh principles, its significance for Malay–Indonesian Muslims cannot be overlooked, especially when excessive and speculative mysticism was rampant. As a result, in his chapter on praying, al-Raniri wrote that the prayers of a person who believed in the atheistic *wujûdiyah* ideology, as held by Hamzah Fansuri and Syams al-Din al-Sumatrani, were not valid.

Al-Raniri's fiqh provocation towards the *wujûdiyah* belief is also evident when he discusses the conditions for halal slaughter and hunting of meat. He argued that the meat slaughtered by the Zoroasters, the pagans, or the followers of the atheistic *wujûdiyah* belief must not be eaten (haram). Here al-Raniri equates followers of *wujûdiyah* with apostates or other idolaters in terms of the way they slaughter or hunt their meat. This opinion was an attack against the followers of *wujûdiyah* in Aceh, who al-Raniri believed were heretical and heterodox.

Al-Raniri did not only provoke followers of *wujûdiyah*, but also Christians. This is apparent when he explains *istinja'* (cleansing after urinating or defecating). Al-Raniri wrote that it was forbidden to cleanse with animal bones or skin that had not been cured. In replacement, an individual should cleanse with pages from the Torah or the Bible, which he argued had already deviated, or from forbidden books such as Sri Rama and Inde-Rapura, which do not contain God's name. On the basis of this provocation, Steenbrink judged al-Raniri as a hard and callous man.[114]

Although the *Shirâth al-Mustaqîm* is controversial, al-Raniri based it on standard Syafi'i texts such as *Minhaj al-Thâlibîn* by al-Nawawi, *Fath al-Wahhâb bi Syarh Minhaj al-Thullâb* by Zakariya al-Anshari, *Hidâyat al-Muhtâj Syarh al-Mukhtashar* by Ibnu Hajar, *al-Anwâr* by al-Ardabili, and *Nihâyah al-Muhtâj (Ilâ Syarh al-Minhaj* by al-Nawawi) by Syams al-Dîn al-Ramli.[115] In light of the sources al-Raniri used, Azyumardi Azra suggests that he was more than just an enthusiastic Islamic sheik who used his political and religious influence to oppose the followers of the *wujûdiyah* ideology to the point of having them sentenced to death. Rather, he was an educated scholar full of arguments, who investigated the nitty-gritty of mystical doctrine in order to find the true and correct path. In addition to his fiqh text *Shirâth al-Mustaqîm*, another of al-Raniri's books known as *Jawâhir al-Ulûm fî Kasyf al-Ma'lûm* was written in 1642 CE and analysed fiqh in accordance with principles found in mystical thought.

Al-Raniri wrote the book *Kaifiyat al-Shalât* on the ways to worship. On the practice of optional prayers, he also wrote *Tanbih al-'Awâm fî Tahqîq al-Kalâmi fî al-Nawâfil*. Another figure that deserves to be mentioned from this century is Abd al-Rauf al-Sinkili (1024–1105 H/1615–93 CE).[116] Al-Sinkili was one of the archipelago's quite productive interpreters. He wrote about twenty-two books — both in Arabic and Malay — which discussed a variety of religious aspects such as interpretation, scholastic theology, *tasawuf*, and fiqh. Al-Sinkili's main work in the field of fiqh was *Mir'at al-Thullâb fî Tasyi al-Ma'rifah al-Ahkâm al-Syar'iyah li al-Mâlik al-Wahhâb*.

Al-Sinkili wrote this book on command from the Sultan of Aceh, Sayyidat al-Dîn,[117] and finished it in 1074 H/1633 CE. It was largely this order that made al-Sinkili stutter when he was asked about the legal basis for a woman to rule. This kind of question is actually an old problem that has been settled, but not resolved satisfactorily. Al-Sinkili himself seemed to be unable to answer it adequately. In *Mir'at al-Thullâb* he did not directly discuss the issue; however, his opinion on women as rulers can be inferred from his discussion on the requirements for judges (rulers in a wider understanding of the term). In relation to this, al-Sinkili intentionally did not give a Malay translation of the term *dzakar* (male/men).

Azyumardi Azra suggests that al-Sinkili had already compromised his intellectual integrity, not only by accepting an order from a woman, but also because he did not resolve the issue. Nevertheless, this also gives an indication of his personal toleration.[118]

Differing from al-Raniri who concentrated his discussion of fiqh on the issue of worship, al-Sinkili tried to explore several aspects of fiqh, such as *munakahat* (rules of marriage), *mu'amalat* (financial transactions), and *farâidl* (inheritance). The issues concerning financial transactions that he discussed included, amongst other things, regulations concerning trade, interest, *khiyâr* (the right to choose), *syarikah* (contract or partnership), *qirâdl* (mutual loan), *sulh* (termination), *hiwalah* (transfer of debt), *wakalah* (contract of agency), and *iqrâr* (pledge or acceptance of an agreement).[119]

The nature of al-Sinkili's interpretation as reflected in the *Mir'at al-Thullâb* shows a fiqh with a high mystical tendency, to the extent that his teachings belong to the category of neo-Sufism. He wanted to reconcile science and spirituality. From here, it is apparent that al-Sinkili wanted to unite the exoteric and esoteric aspects of Islam. It was this characteristic that led him to become a tolerant reformer, with A.H. Johns, as cited by Abdurrahman, viewing al-Sinkili as the peacemaker between the *wujûdiyah* and al-Raniri.[120] As a sheik from the Syaththariyah Sufi order, al-Sinkili did not agree with the *wujûdiyah* ideology, yet he did not confront it directly as did al-Raniri.[121]

There were of course other figures in the seventeenth century whose intellectual exploration took them far, including Syekh Yusuf al-Maqassari (1615–99 CE). His life journey was coloured by quite an intense intellectual struggle, beginning in South Sulawesi but following him through Banten, Saudi Arabia, Sri Lanka, and South Africa.[122] Al-Maqassari was also a symbol of the expansion of the spectrum of Islam in the archipelago, which had initially been Aceh-centric.

According to available information, al-Maqassari was not an expert on fiqh, but on *tasawuf*. This is understandable, because not only did al-Maqassari not produce a representative work on fiqh, but he geared his life towards *tasawuf*, more precisely neo-Sufism. Al-Maqassari's neo-Sufism was a direct rejection of the *wujûdiyah* and *al-hulûl* beliefs.[123] Moving into the eighteenth century, a figure who must be discussed is Syaikh Muhammad Arsyad al-Banjari (1710–1812). Arsyad's relatively well-known work on fiqh is *Sabîl al-Muhtadîn li Tafaqquh fî Amr al-Dîn*, which generally speaking represents an explanation of al-Raniri's *Shirâth al-Mustaqîm*. As an explanatory book, the methodology used and the material discussed do not differ significantly from the book being explained. Only the discussion is developed further, as Dutch historian Karel Steenbrink states, through the use of a variety of rather theoretical and at times speculative cases. In fact, in certain circumstances the issues discussed were not based on the real conditions within Banjar society itself.[124] It seems Arsyad was inspired by the fiqh tradition in the Middle East which was often called *fiqih iftirâdli* or "hypothetical fiqh", although not all fiqh was like this, created through assumptions that were often quite impossible. Nevertheless, this kind of hypothetical fiqh can also be seen as an effort on behalf of the fiqh experts to anticipate the variety of possibilities that could occur.

From information presented in the introduction and conclusion of the book, it is apparent that it was written between 1193 H/1779 CE and 1195 H/1781 CE, when the Sultanate of Banjar was led by Tahmidullah bin Sultan Tamjidullah. The references Arsyad used were standard Syafi'i fiqh books such as *Syarh Minhaj* by Zakariya al-Anshari, *Tuhfah* by Ibnu Hajar al-Haitami, and *Nihâyah Jamâl* by al-Ramli. In addition to the ideas on fiqh he expressed in *Sabîl al-Muhtadîn*, there are several interesting incidents involving Arsyad. One event, as Steenbrink describes, involved changing the direction to Mecca. In 1186 H/1773 CE, Arsyad returned from Mecca via Batavia. There he took the opportunity to change the direction to Mecca in a number of mosques based on his expertise in astrology. In the *mihrab* (the niche in a mosque from which the imam leads the prayer, facing towards Mecca) of the Jembatan Lima Mosque in Jakarta, is a written reminder in Arabic that the direction to Mecca of the mosque had been moved 25 degrees to the right by Arsyad.[125]

Later in 1892, there was much furore in Banjarmasin because an astrologist proved that the direction to Mecca of the Great Mosque of Banjarmasin was not accurate. Strangely enough, the Mufti of Banjarmasin did not have the courage to change the direction to Mecca of the mosque because it had been set by Arsyad al-Banjari. This incident highlights how much authority Arsyad had in astrology that no one was willing to oppose him even though he had already passed away.

Another interesting incident was over a strange marriage. When he was still in Mecca, Arsyad received news that his daughter Syarifah, who was in Banjar, had matured into a young adult. One day he married her by force (*ijbar*) and without her knowledge to his fellow classmate in Mecca, 'Abd al-Wahab Bugis. But when Arsyad returned to Banjar, he discovered that the sultan (her legal representative) had already married her off to a man named Usman.

According to the Syafi'i school of thought in Islam, both marriages were legal and valid when they occurred. Faced with an unprecedented case,

Arsyad resolved it in an interesting manner, by examining the time of her marriage through his expertise in astrology. The result of his investigation found that the marriage in Mecca occurred several moments before the marriage in Banjar, and on the basis of these findings Syarifah's marriage to Usman was considered null.

Arsyad al-Banjari's expertise in the field of fiqh does not mean that he deviates from mysticism. In another book, *Kanz al-Ma'rifah*, he discusses everything about mysticism. Thus, in addition to being an expert in science (*'ilm al-dhâhir*), he was also an expert in spirituality (*'ilm al-bâthin*), fiqh, and *tasawuf*.[126] In addition, Muhammad Arsyad took several important steps towards reinforcing Islamization in South Kalimantan by reforming the administration of justice by the Sultanate of Banjar. Besides making fiqh doctrine a reference in criminal justice, he established an Islamic court — with the Sultan's support — to prosecute purely civil matters. He also introduced an institute for the muftis which was responsible for issuing social and religious fatwa (decrees).[127]

Another figure worthy of attention in the eighteenth century is Syaikh Abd al-Malik bin Abdullah Trengganu, who lived in Aceh during the reign of Zaenal Abidin I (1138–46 H/1725–33 CE). He had a number of works in the field of fiqh, including:

1. *Risâlat al-Naql*, which discusses the legal number of people needed to establish a Friday congregation or gathering.
2. *Risâlat Kaifiyat al-Niyat*, which examined the issue of *niat* or intention and several aspects related to mysticism. This book was an excerpt from the work by his teacher Syaikh Ibrahim al-Kurani, entitled *A'mâl al-Fikri wa al-Râwiyat*, and the work by Syaikh Ibnu Atha'ullah entitled *Miftah Ûlâ*.
3. *Kifayah*, a combination between a theological study and mysticism.[128]

In addition to Arsyad al-Banjari, another figure, Jalâl al-Dîn al-Tursani, deserves a mention. He wrote the book *Safînat al-Hukkâm* at the request of Sultan Alaiddin Johan Syah (1147–74 H/1735–60 CE). Jalaluddin al-Tursani was a senior ulama with extensive knowledge of law, politics, and economy. He was a *qadli* (magistrate) and senior mufti during the reign of Sultan Alaiddin.

Differing from other fiqh books, *Safînat al-Hukkâm* was a detailed exploration of justice in Islam, or more precisely, the "procedural law" of religious justice that judges had to adhere to. In accordance with the issues it discussed, the book was written as a guide for judges, officials of the kingdom, and the king. The aspects discussed included the laws of trade, marriage, homicide and bodily harm, and inheritance.[129]

Jamâl al-Dîn al-Tursani, the son of Jalâl al-Dîn, was also a well-known ulama who wrote *Hidâyat al-'Awâm*, a book on fiqh which begins with a theological discussion of the twenty attributes of God. Although thin, this book discusses several matters that were not discussed in works that preceded it. For instance, while many books discussed the pillars of faith and the pillars of Islam, Jamâl put forward the following:

> Know this, my students! When a descendent of Adam reaches puberty, he should, as required by religion, know the fifteen pillars that reveal an understanding of God the Most High (*ma'rifatullah ta'ala*). That is, the five pillars of Islam, the six pillars of faith, and the four pillars of the confession of faith (*syahadat*).[130]

Another interesting thing about this book is the belief that the crow of a rooster could be used as a sign for the time to pray. Jamâl also stated that the correct requirement for the Friday sermon was that it be in Arabic. On the issue of trade, to avoid usury, Jamâl decreed:

> The way to avoid usury for those who trade gold for gold, silver for silver, wheat for wheat, rice for rice and so on; is to willingly give every right to their friends or relatives or to give a loan of that right because of God the Most High, which makes the transaction *halal* in the eyes of God for both parties.[131]

On polygamy, Jamâl also decreed that only free men were allowed to marry as many as four times, while slaves were only allowed to marry two times. On transferral of guardianship (*wali ab'ad*), Jamâl believed that if a righteous person could be found and the judge had no concerns about vilification, then a female could put herself in the hands of that person and marry a man. If no pious person could be found, or the judge feared vilification, then the female need not resign herself.

Another figure is Syaikh Muhammad Zain bin Faqih Jalâl al-Dîn. In the fiqh of the Syafi'i school of thought, he only compiled the books *Kasyf al-Kirâm fî Bayân al-Nihâyat fî Takbirat al-Ihrâm*, *Farâidl al-Qur'ân*, and *Tahsîn al-Falâh fî Bayân al-Ahkâm al-Thalâq wa al-Nikâh*. Syaikh Abd al-Muthalib Aceh then compiled these books with those of others and published them under the title *Jam'u al-Jawâmi' al-Mushannifât*.

As mentioned briefly in the previous section, at the beginning of the nineteenth century there was a figure rarely given attention in the context of the development of fiqh in the archipelago — namely Ahmad Rifa'i Kalisalak, from Batang. The works he had published discussed fiqh. Although seemingly on the periphery, he is worthy of mention as part of the fiqh dynamics in the archipelago, and in fact several of his opinions triggered significant controversy in Central Java.

In the field of fiqh, Ahmad Rifa'i was a firm follower of the Syafi'i school of thought. This is evident, amongst other things, from his penchant for quoting popular fiqh texts amongst the Syafi'i's, such as *Minhaj al-Âbidîn* by al-Ghazali, *Hasyiyah al-Bajuri* by Ibrahim al-Bajuri, and *I'ânat al-Thâlibîn* by al-Bakr bin Muhammad Syatha' al-Dimyâti. Nevertheless, several of his ideas triggered controversy, including those on the implementation of the Friday congregation. He argued, as with Imam Syafi'i's belief, that the Friday gathering must be attended by at least forty people. However, Ahmad Rifa'i took this further, arguing that that meant not only forty people in terms of quantity, but also in quality. In other words, those forty people must be experts in Friday prayers (*ahl al-jum'at*). If even one person failed to fully understand the conditions and pillars, then the entire Friday prayer in that mosque was null.

His thoughts on marriage were also controversial. The problem lay in the assumption that Ahmad Rifa'i did not legalize marriages involving village heads (*penghulu*) because the parties involved in the marriage, such as the legal representative and witnesses, were considered not to have fulfilled the necessary conditions. According to Ahmad Rifa'i, the legal representative of a marriage must fulfil seven conditions, one of which was to be a *mursyid*, or a person who had never performed an ungodly act. Meanwhile, the witnesses of a marriage needed to fulfil sixteen conditions, two of which were that they must have dignity and self-respect, and also must not have performed ungodly acts. Both witnesses and legal representatives must be fair and just. Here, the terms "fair/just" and "ungodly acts" were used in the context of the colonial era. The *penghulu*, according to Ahmad Rifa'i, were not just or fair because they worked with the colonial power.[132] This issue disturbed ulama and local officials in Pekalongan. Eventually, in September 1859, Ahmad Rifa'i was invited to the Pekalongan Town Hall to be challenged to an open debate with religious officials and indigenous residents of the city. During the debate, Ahmad Rifa'i's defeat was pronounced — a defeat that ended in his eviction to Ambon.[133]

From the nineteenth century, one important figure was Syaikh Nawawi al-Bantani.[134] Born in Banten (Serang) in 1813, he died in 1879 as an ulama who was very productive in writing on a variety of subjects, including fiqh, exegesis, history, *tauhid*, morality, the Hadith, and the Arabic language. His most famous fiqh work is *'Uqûd al-Lujain*, which is a compulsory text for female *santri* in several *pesantren*.[135] Nawawi also wrote commentaries on the book *Fath al-Qarîb* by Ibnu Qâsim al-Ghazi, and *Qurrat al-'Ain* by Zain al-Dîn al-Malibari in the book *Nihâyat al-Zain*. He wrote two books on harmony: *Sulâm al-Munajat* which was a commentary of *Safînat al-shalât* by Abdullah bin Umar al-Hadharami, and *Kasyifat al-Sajâ* atas *Safînat al-Najah* by Salim bin Abdullah bin Samir, an Arabic ulama who lived in Jakarta around 1850.[136] Most of Nawawi's books were written in Arabic and were reviews of commentaries of other fiqh texts. It was this that led Martin to conclude that Nawawi was the most famous commentator of all commentators. This is also evidence of Nawawi's tie to fiqh texts produced before his time, which reinforces the main characteristic of the era as one of decline of Islamic law as explained above.

Another figure from this period is Abd al-Hamid Hakim, an ulama from Minangkabau whose books were not only studied in Indonesia, but also in Malaysia and South Thailand. His books on fiqh include *al-Mu'în al-Mubîn*, which was printed in four volumes, while on *ushûl al-fiqh* (Islamic jurisprudential principles) he wrote *Mabâdi' Awwaliyah, al-Sullâm*, and *al-Bayân*.[137] At the end of the nineteenth century and beginning of the twentieth century, Kiai Mahfudz Abdullah from Termas (d. 1919) left his mark. He wrote an explanation of *al-Muqaddimat al-Hadlramiyah* by Abdullah ibn Abd al-Karim Bafadhal. According to Martin, it was never printed, although senior *kiai* have copies of it.[138]

Finally, two Indonesian ulama who wrote simple modern texts on fiqh that are used in madrasahs must be mentioned. The first is Abd al-Rahman al-Sagaf, a man of Arab descent who lived in Surabaya and wrote four small volumes to a book titled *al-Durûs al-Fiqhiyah*. The other is Mahmud Yunus, who wrote several volumes of *Fiqh al-Wâdlih* that were compiled quite differently to traditional fiqh in reflection of his different perspective on education.

This leads into a discussion of the twentieth century. There was a tendency for reformation of fiqh in several different ways in the second half of the twentieth century that were influenced by academic nuances.

The emergence of the State Islamic College (PTAI), which later became the State Islamic Institute (IAIN), was to play a significant role in the development of fiqh thought in Indonesia. Here, the most popular figure was Hasbi ash-Shiddieqi, who was often called the Indonesian fiqh locomotive — although before him, Hazairin had come up with the same ideas.

In reality, Hasbi was not just an expert on law. An examination of his work (6 exegeses, 8 Hadith, 36 works on fiqh, 5 works on *tauhid*/scholastic theology, 17 general works, and more than 49 papers) reveals that he was an expert across a variety of fields. Nevertheless, the majority of his attention was given to fiqh. Most of the senior positions he held were in the field of law, and his honorary doctorate in *Syari'at* from Unisba Bandung in 1975 further strengthened his position as a reliable legal expert.

His most monumental breakthrough was on Indonesian fiqh. The fundamental idea to his thought was that the fiqh applied in Indonesia should adopt Indonesian characteristics and Indonesian insight. This kind of thinking was clearly different from the reformers who had gone before him and who were still Arabic in orientation.

While traditionalist ulama adhered entirely to one school of thought when discussing law, and as such rejected *talfiq* (choosing the best from each), Hasbi bravely accepted *talfiq*, and effectively selected what was most suited to the Indonesian condition. While other reforming ulama, both individually and collectively, discussed material for legal provisions concerning one issue such as transplantation of organs, Hasbi not only discussed material for laws such as blood transfusions, or the management of bequeathed property, but also concentrated on the methodology of finding legal bases, an aspect that did not receive much serious attention from experts before his time.

This is in line with his conviction that those who can be rightfully called interpreters or philosophers in Islamic law are experts of *ushûl al-fiqh* (Islamic jurisprudential principles), and not experts of fiqh. However, unlike Hazairin who wrote his concept of a national inheritance law in a book that was easy to study, Hasbi's idea that fiqh should adopt Indonesian characteristics is scattered across texts. His idea about an Indonesian-oriented fiqh was actually based on the concept of *maslahat* (issuing Islamic law for the benefit of humankind), as reflected in his scientific oration titled "Syari'at Islam Menjawab Tantangan Zaman", given during the first anniversary of Sunan Kalijaga IAIN in 1961:

> The aim of studying Islamic law in Islamic universities these days is so that Islamic *fiqh/syari'ah* can accommodate for the benefit of society and can be the principal founder of the development of law in our beloved country. Our intention is to compile a *fiqh* that reflects our very own characteristics.

This illustration is too simple to fully portray Hasbi's thoughts. However, it gives at least an indication of the substance of his ideas concerning Islamic legal reformation in Indonesia.

In addition to Hasbi's culturally nuanced ideas, reformation of Islamic law in Indonesia in this century was also influenced by state politics. This was a result of the desire of Indonesian Islamic legal figures to nationalize Islamic law, which they felt was being increasingly sidelined. The struggle continued, leading to the formation of Law No. 1/1974 on Marriage, Law No. 7/1989 on Religious Justice, the establishment of the Indonesian Mu'amalat Bank (BMI), and the birth of the Islamic Legal Compilation (KHI), amongst other things.[139]

It is thus apparent that right from the start, the dynamics of Islamic intellectualism in Indonesia displayed characteristics of being a continuation of the dynamics of Islamic intellectualism that developed in other parts of the Islamic world. This is particularly evident in the field of fiqh, much of which is a continuation of the fiqh that developed in the geographical centre of Islam. It is now time to enter into a discussion of what kind of fiqh developed within NU.

THE DEVELOPMENT OF NU FIQH

Fiqh is NU's heartbeat. It is positioned as a very important science because through fiqh one can know what is allowed and what is not allowed in Islam. In fact, it could be said that NU intellectualism is highly fiqh-oriented. The tradition of fiqh thought within NU was institutionalized through the Bahts al-Masâil forum. The forum actually existed before NU was established. At the time, there was a tradition of discussion in the *pesantren* circle which involved the *kiai* and *santri*, the results of which were published in the LINO (Lailatul Ijtima' Nahdlatul Oelama) bulletin. The bulletin, besides publishing the results of the Bahts al-Masâil, also became an arena for interactive discussion amongst the ulama.[140] After NU was established, the tradition was maintained in order to gather, discuss, and resolve legal issues (*waqi'iyyah*) that arose in the community.

The forum was present at all organizational levels within NU, from the central board down to the branches, although not in a structured institutional form. For years, the Bahts al-Masâil was a forum to discuss religious issues without any particular institution managing it. The NU central board accommodated the issues and questions that arose, and then formed a commission, the Bahts al-Masâil commission, which would arrange hearings during national conferences, congresses, or at other opportunities. However, the 28th Congress in Yogyakarta in 1989 recommended that the NU central board form the Bahts al-Masâil Diniyah Body as a permanent institute to specifically discuss the religious issues that arose in society. The recommendation was eventually reinforced with the NU Central Board Decree No. 30/A.I.05/5/1990 on the formation of the Bahts al-Masâil Diniyah Body.

In relation to this, Article 2 of the NU Charter of 1926 states that the objective of NU is to hold firmly to one of the four schools of thought, namely the Hanafi, Maliki, Syafi'i, or Hanbali schools, and doing anything necessary to benefit Islam. The Charter suggests that right from the beginning, NU fiqh was designed to exist within the scope of all four schools of thought, although in practice there was a visible tendency towards the Syafi'i school of thought. This is apparent in the fiqh decisions made in the NU Bahts al-Masâil,[141] almost all of which referred to fiqh texts from the Syafi'i school.

KH Hasyim Asy'ari, a founder and highly respected figure within NU, believed that following one of the four Sunni schools was very important. As is apparent in the *Muqaddimat al-Qanûn al-Asâsî al-Nahdlat al-'Ulamâ* (Introduction to Nahdlatul Ulama's Statutes), KH Hasyim Asy'ari supported the position of fiqh law while denying the arguments that opposed the fiqh schools of thought.[142] He stated that following one of the four fiqh schools (Hanafi, Maliki, Syafi'i, or Hanbali) would bring prosperity (*maslahah*) and immeasurable goodness, because Islamic doctrine (*syari'ah*) could not be understood except through *naql* (revelation) and the formulation of law using specific methods (*istinbâth*). Transmission would not be pure and correct unless each generation obtained Islamic teachings directly from the generation before them.[143]

Ulama from the past were considered to be the door to understanding Islamic doctrine. Hasyim Asy'ari wrote more explicitly:

> Oh pious *ulama* and leaders of the *ahlu assunnah wa al-jamaah* community who follow the four *madzhab* [schools of thought]! You have received

knowledge from those before you, and those before you received it from those before them through an unbroken *sanad* [chain], and you have also been cautious in deciding from whom you take your religion. So you of today are the source of that knowledge, and you are the door to it, and anyone who wants to enter the house without using the door will be called a thief.[144]

This perspective strongly influenced the development of NU fiqh, which is evident for instance in the way NU ulama formulate and apply law (*istinbâth al-ahkâm*). The meaning of *istinbâth al-ahkâm* within NU does not refer to the activity of formulating or applying laws directly from the Qur'an and Hadith, although it is acknowledged that the two are the primary sources in Islamic law. In this context, *istinbâth al-ahkâm* refers to the formation of law through a method of dynamically applying or adjusting (Syafi'i) fiqh principles in order to set valid legal provisions.[145] In this sense, it is fitting that NU's legal provisions do not refer directly to the primary legal sources using a specific method of *ushûl al-fiqh* (Islamic jurisprudential principles), but refer instead to fiqh texts defined as *kutub al-mu'tabarah*. Meanwhile, the *ushûl al-fiqh* method and *qawâid al-fiqhiyah* (fiqh standards) are only used to reinforce the legal decisions arrived at.

Istinbâth, or the formation of law directly from primary sources, tends to produce absolute interpretations, and is considered difficult for NU ulama because of the limitations they are aware of, particularly concerning the additional knowledge that interpreters have to master. Meanwhile, interpretation within the limits of the schools of thought (*ijtihâd fi al-madzhab*) is not only more practical, but can be performed by all NU ulama able to understand the *'ibarah* (explanations) given in fiqh texts. As a result, the term *istinbâth* is not so popular amongst NU ulama, and it may well be the case that the use of the Bahts al-Masâil discussion forum was an attempt at avoiding the use of *ijtihad* and *istinbâth*.

As such, the concept of the four schools of thought in NU is based on the thoughts and utterances (*qawl*) of the imam of these schools. NU has followed this concept for a long time, although theoretically speaking, since the National Conference of Ulama in 1992 in Lampung, there was a shift which saw the introduction of the term *ijtihad manhaji* (method of interpretation). Theoretically, this can be seen as a progressive step of the NU Bahts al-Masâil towards the formulation of a new fiqh paradigm, although in practice the effort remains half-hearted. Within the National Conference, the procedures and steps in formulating laws were devised as follows:

1. In the case where the solution can be provided by an *'ibarat kitab* (explanation of a text) where there is only one *qawl* (teaching), then that *qawl* should be used as explained in the text.
2. In the case where the solution can be provided by an *'ibarat kitab* where there is more than one *qawl*, then one *qawl* should be chosen collectively (*taqrir jama'i*).[146]
3. In the case where there is no *qawl* that provides a solution, then a collective interpretation of fiqh texts (*ilhaq al-masâil bi nadhairihâ*)[147] is undertaken by experts.
4. In the case where there is no *qawl* and it is not possible to undertake a collective interpretation of fiqh texts, then a collective legal ruling (*istinbâth jamâ'i*) is undertaken using methodical (*manhaji*) procedures of interpretation from the schools of thought by experts.[148]

In addition, the National Conference also determined the procedures for determining *qawl* as follows:

1. If there are several *qawl* for one issue, then an attempt must be made to choose one opinion.
2. Choosing one opinion is done through the following procedure:
   a. Taking the opinion that is most beneficial and/or strongest.
   b. To implement the stipulations of the first NU Congress as best as possible, which state that difference of opinion should be resolved by choosing:
      1) The opinion agreed to by the two sheiks (al-Nawawi and al-Rafi'i).
      2) The opinion held only by al-Nawawi.
      3) The opinion held only by al-Rafi'i.
      4) The opinion supported by the majority of ulama.
      5) The opinion of the most intelligent/respected ulama.
      6) The opinion of the most pious (*wara'*) ulama.[149]

In relation to this last procedure, in practice the Bahts al-Masâil does not pay much attention to the process of selecting the stronger opinion of two or more opinions.[150] Rather, in practice the Bahts al-Masâil indicates that there is a methodological problem within NU. KH MA Sahal Mahfudh, the chairman of the NU Central Board, acknowledged this when he stated that the Bahts al-Masâil within NU was not satisfactory, either academically/scientifically or as a practical effort through which to address the challenges of the era. One reason for this was NU's ties to only one school of thought (Syafi'i), despite NU's charter enabling other schools of thought to be adhered to. Another was due to the textual way of thinking, which tends to reject reality that does not accord with the classical texts, without proposing a solution.[151]

As such, the Bahts al-Masâil requires serious improvement, so that it will be able to practise what it introduces as *taqlid fi al-manhaj* (following methodology) through *ijtihâd jamâ'î* (collective interpretation), and not just implement the cases only based on formulated references. Furthermore, an explanation of the thinking and methods used in determining laws is needed, as it has received almost no attention of late from NU ulama who have been too busy dealing with the *qawl* (utterances/thoughts) found in fiqh texts. As a result, the legal decisions of the Bahts al-Masâil are based only on *qawl* from ulama. The method used is not known, although at the processing level of the forum, methods are discussed very briefly.

This practice cannot be separated from the concept of fiqh within NU, which is seen as a scientific study of *syari'ah* law (not *i'tiqâdiyah* or faith) related to human actions taken and concluded (*muktasab*) from detailed theorems (*tafshilî*). These fiqh laws are established by expert interpreters based on the foundations from which they were formed, namely the Qur'an, the Hadith, *ijmâ'* (consensus), and *qiyâs* (analogy).[152] It is on this basis that NU ulama assume that the laws taken from the fiqh texts have undergone a methodical process.

Standard books (*al-kutub al-mu'tabarah*) used by NU ulama as references, both in the Bahts al-Masâil forum or in classes at *pesantren*, include: *I'ânat al-Thâlibîn, Raudlat al-Thâlibîn, Anwâr al-Tanzîl, Bughyat al-Mustarsyidîn, Hâsyiyat al-Syarwânî 'ala al-Tuhfah, Hâsyiyat al-Bujairimî 'ala Fath al-Wahhâb, Hâsyiyat al-Bâjurî 'ala Fath al-Qarîb, Tasyîh al-Mustafidîn, Hâsyiyat al-'Iwadl 'ala al-Iqnâ', Hâsyiyat al-Kurdî 'alâ al-Bâfadlal, Radd al-Mukhtâr, Fath al-Mu'în, Asna al-Mathâlib*, and *Tanwîr al-Qulûb*. These texts are standard Syafi'i texts that have greatly influenced the development of fiqh in NU. Recently, the Bahts al-Masâil has also referred to books on exegesis and the Hadith that are well known in all schools of thought, such as those by al-Thabari, Ibnu Katsir, al-Qurthubî, Shahîh Bukhârî, Shahîh Muslim, and also books by modern writers that have no clear affiliation to a specific school, such as 'Abd al-Qâdir Audah, Yûsûf Mûsâ, Sayyid Sâbiq, al-Jurjâni and Husain Makhlûf.[153]

The results of Martin van Bruinessen's research into the genealogy of Syafi'i fiqh texts must be mentioned. Martin successfully traced the roots of the Syafi'i school of thought in many of the texts mentioned above, most of which are used in *pesantren* in Indonesia, especially in Java. The genealogy begins with the book *Muharrar* by Abu Qâsim al-Rafi'i (d. 623 H/ 1226 CE) and passes through *Minhâj al-Thâlibîn* by Muhyi al-Dîn Abu Zakariyya Yahyâ bin Syârif al-Nawâwi (d. 676 H/1227–28 CE). These two books then influenced five others: (1) *Kanz al-Râgibîn* by al-Mahalli (d. 864 H/ 1460 M); (2) *Minhaj al-Thullâb* by al-Anshâri (d. 926 H); (3) *Tuhfat al-Muhtâj* by Ibnu Hajar (d. 973 H/1565–66 CE); (4) *Mughnî al-Muhtâj* by al-Syarbînî (d. 977 H/1569–70 CE); and (5) *Nihâyat al-Muhtâj* by al-Ramli (d. 1004 H/ 1596 CE). These five texts were annotated and explained in turn by al-Qalyûbî dan Umaira, al-Anshari, al-Syirwânî, al-Subramâlisî (d. 1087 H/ 1676 CE), and al-Maghrabî. *Fath al-Wahhâb* by al-Anshârî, which was an explanation of *Manhaj al-Thullâb*, was further annotated and explained by al-Bujayrimî (d. 1221 H/1806 CE) and Jamal (d. 1204 H/1789–90 CE). Several books were translated into Javanese, Sundanese, Madurese, and Indonesian.[154]

Up to this point, it is clearly evident that NU ulama highly respected the opinions of the leaders or imam of the schools of thought, especially the Syafi'i school of thought. This choice saw NU often positioned as a supporter of *taqlid* (imitation) rather than *ijtihad* (independent interpretation), and as such, NU ulama were often cynically criticized as resembling a herd of buffalo in tow who "do not know where they will be taken and do not know anything at all, they just follow the flow".[155] NU ulama responded to this accusation by differentiating between *taqlid* according to laymen and *taqlid* according to Islamic legal experts (*fuqahâ*). While the first (according to laymen) involved following and imitation without understanding the arguments, the second (by *fuqahâ*) involved knowing the intricacies of the arguments used.

In relation to this, Hasyim Asy'ari recommended that Muslims (NU ulama and community) not follow fatwa or decrees issued by people who did not possess the necessary qualifications to interpret texts. Thus, *taqlid* became natural and proper for Muslims to do, except for those able to interpret. Anyone unable to interpret must therefore follow one of the four schools of thought.[156] Thus, for Hasyim Asy'ari and NU ulama in general, *taqlid* was recognized as a method for finding legal resolutions. It was this kind of practice that NU ulama engaged in to resolve legal issues through the Bahts al-Masâil forum almost throughout the entirety of its history.

3. Tasawuf/Tarekat

To say that Sufism has a special place in NU is not at all surprising. Besides acknowledging that the Sufis played an important role in the spread of Islam throughout Indonesia, NU is also known as a community that highly regards the Sufi tradition, especially as it exists in Sufi *tarekat* (orders). It is this characteristic that often differentiates NU from other Islamic groups like Muhammadiyah which view Sufism and mystic orders as a desecration of Islam.

The existence of *tasawuf* (mysticism) in Islamic society, which then led to the formation of *tarekat* (Sufi orders), has been a controversial matter throughout Islamic history, not just in Indonesia but throughout other parts of the Islamic world. Throughout history, mysticism has been an esoteric religious practice that tends to be more individualistic in appreciating and internalizing Islamic spiritualism. As it developed, these individual practices and experiences were followed, practised and institutionalized on a mass scale by society in the form of *tarekat*. Thus, the formation of *tarekat* was the final step in the development of *tasawuf*.[157]

Etymologically, *tarekat* means "path/road" or "method" through which to arrive at a destination/objective. The term itself has several interpretations, including: (1) a specific path travelled by a Sufi (*sâlik*) in his quest to move closer to God by climbing up the tiers of spirituality;[158] (2) A method of practice that leads or guides a student in a planned manner by controlling the way of his mind, thoughts, feelings, and actions in order for him to continue to exist in a series of tiers (*maqâmât*) so that he can experience the real essence of truth.[159]

Tarekat literally means "path", referring to a system of meditation and ritual worship (*muhâsabah, mu'âtiyah, murâtabah*) which is associated with a line of Sufi teachers and organizations that grew around the unique Sufi method. *Tarekat*, or Sufi orders, therefore represent an effort to systematize *tasawuf* teachings and methods. The members of a specific *tarekat* obtain spiritual progression through a series of degrees based on their level of spirituality. The first level is that of general member (*mansub*), which becomes student (*muqaddam*), assistant sheik (*khalîfah*), and finally teacher (*mursyid*).[160]

Within *tarekat* the genealogy used to determine the validity of a *tarekat* system is very important. Genealogy refers to the line of teachers or the sequence of names of teachers who taught the basics about the *tarekat*, and who are connected from generation to generation through an *isnad* system that can be traced back to the Prophet Muhammad. It is through this system that assessments about the validity (*mu'tabarah*) and doubt (*gairu mu'tabarah*) of a *tarekat* stem are made.

Generally speaking, the *tarekat* system that developed in NU is neo-Sufi, that is, it adheres to *tasawuf* that integrates the two orientations of *syari'ah* (*ahl al-syarî'ah*) and essence (*ahl al-haqîqah*).[161] Neo-Sufism is primarily marked by a rejection of the ecstatic and metaphysical side of Sufism and a preference for strict experience within the provisions of *syari'ah*.[162] These characteristics are related to the success of Junaid al-Baghdâdî (d. 859 CE) and al-Ghazâlî (d. 1111 CE), who worked hard to pacify and bring back together the two opposing tendencies. For al-Ghazâlî, the two (*syari'ah* and *haqîqah*) represent two sides of the same coin, and cannot be separated from one another.

This new tradition of moderate Sufism, which gained momentum in the third and fourth centuries of the Islamic calendar, has been examined by writers such as al-Sarraj al-Thûsî (d. 377 H/987 CE) in his work *al-Lumâ'* and al-Kalabadzi in his *al-Ta'arruf li al-Madzhab ahl al-Tashawwuf*. This was continued by al-Qusyairî (d. 465 H/1073 CE) in his book *Risâlat al-Qusyairiyah*, published in 438 H. The movement was perfected by al-Ghazâlî in his famous book, *Ihyâ' 'Ulûm al-Dîn*.[163] The figures of al-Ghazâlî and Junaid al-Baghdâdî have special significance amongst Sufi followers, because of their success in halting heterodox Sufism that ignored *syari'ah*. Due to this service, Junaid al-Baghdâdî was awarded the titles Sayyid al-Thâifah (leader of a sect or congregation) and Thâwus al-Fuqarâ (the peacock of the Sufis/poor), while al-Ghazâlî received the title Hujjat al-Islâm (defender of Islam).

Al-Ghazâlî held so strongly to *syari'ah*, that he made adopting such an attitude the first step an individual must take before being able to walk in God's path to become a *sâlik*/Sufi. If a *sâlik* violates the provisions of *syarî'ah*, although he may be able to walk on water with all the knowledge he possesses, in essence he is Satan.[164] As a result, al-Ghazâlî strongly opposed the Sufi practices that underestimated religious rites, arguing that religious rituals had to be performed and could not be exchanged by anyone to achieve perfection. In addition, he believed it was not sufficient to perform religious rituals in a purely physical manner in order to fulfil fiqh formalities, but that they must be performed with complete understanding of the meaning and significance inherent in such rituals. Thus, in *Ihyâ' 'Ulûm al-Dîn*, al-Ghazâlî gave an esoteric understanding of the exoteric provisions of fiqh. When explaining purification (*thahârah*) for instance, al-Ghazâlî stated that people using their logic would surely know of and understand the requirement to physically cleanse themselves, but what is actually meant by the requirement is spiritual cleansing.[165] The method of Sufism that al-Ghazâlî promoted was accepted by many because of its ability to synthesize the formalism of fiqh and the substantialism of heterodox mysticism or *tasawuf*.[166]

Given such a paradigm, it has been difficult for NU Sufism to accommodate figures such as Abu Yazid al-Bustami (875 CE) and his concept of *ittihâd* (the sense of a Sufi being one with God), Husain Ibn Mansur al-Hallaj (928 CE) with his idea of *al-hulûl* (the understanding that God descends to unite with the bodies of chosen humans), Ibn al-'Arâbi's *wihdat al-wujûd* (pantheism), and Syaikh Siti Jenar who was famous for his expression *Anâ al-haqq* (I am the creative Truth). Rather, they have been considered a danger to the Islamic faith, and thus their teachings have been avoided, to the extent that both Junaid al-Baghdâdî and al-Ghazâlî are seen as a radical critique of these figures.[167]

Generally speaking, the strand of *tasawuf* which is considered Sunni is one that sees reason as a tool to help understand the texts, even though reason must yield to the texts. When reason is used, it is purely as a means to strengthen the power of the texts. As a result, strands of *tasawuf* that are considered extreme are not seen as being Sunni. NU accepts Sufism that remains within the bounds of Sunni Islam. It is as if NU wants to place itself as the guardian of the purity and sanctity of *tasawuf* from deviant practices.

An understanding of NU Sufism can also be obtained from KH Hasyim Asy'ari's thought. Hasyim Asy'ari displayed *tasawuf* behaviour and thoughts that differed from the majority of NU people, even though he remained, generally speaking, a follower of al-Ghazâlî. Hasyim Asy'ari's ideas on Sufism were published in his books *Al-Durâr al-Muntatirah fî al-Masâil al-Tis'a 'Asyarah* (Scattered Pearls of Nineteen Problems) and *al-Tibyân fî al-Nahyi al-Muqâtha'at al-Arhâm wa al-Aqârib wa al-Akhawân* (Explanation of the Prohibition against Severing Relations with Relatives and Friends), written in 1360 H. In both books, Hasyim Asy'ari harshly criticizes deviations of Sufi teachings.[168]

One issue that received KH Hasyim Asy'ari's serious attention was the prohibition against idolizing a Sufi teacher (*mursyid*), because he argued that deviations of Sufi teachings were a result of deviations of the Sufis themselves because they glorified their elders and teachers too much. KH Hasyim Asy'ari thus called for moderate attitudes and behaviour towards Sufi teachers, and refused to be called a Sufi teacher. In fact, Hasyim Asy'ari forbade his students or *santri* from following the Sufi brotherhood. Moreover, he also forbade his descendants from celebrating the anniversary of his death (*hawl*), a tradition that was practised by a number of *pesantren* and considered *bid'ah* (heretical) by the modernists.[169]

According to Hasyim Asy'ari, there are four regulations that must be adhered to should an individual decide to join a *tarekat* or order, including: (1) avoiding authorities who do not uphold principles of justice; (2) respecting those who try with all sincerity to attain happiness in the world and hereafter; (3) helping the poor; and (4) praying together in a congregation.[170] These four points suggest that Sufism in Hasyim Asy'ari's eyes was not purely about honing individual piety through rituals, *wirid* and *dzikir*, but about enforcing justice and fighting to help the oppressed (the poor).

The Sufism proposed by Hasyim Asy'ari was in many ways a continuation or repetition of al-Ghazâlî's Sufi principles; that is, a model of Sufism appropriate to (orthodox) Islamic doctrine. Al-Ghazâlî's Sufism was different from other Sufi models which were often considered deviant (heterodox), such as those developed by Ibn al-'Arâbi and al-Hallaj. In the archipelago, these teachings were developed by Hamzah Fansuri, Abd al-Rauf al-Sinkili, and Syams al-Sumatrani in the thirteenth century. Al-Ghazâlî tamed these heterodox *tasawuf* practices by reverting back to the pure Sufi practices.

NU continued to develop this kind of *tasawuf* that had been stripped of heterodoxy. Differing from the modernist Islamic groups who rejected *tarekat* practices because they felt they were *bid'ah* (heretical) and could encourage idolatry, within NU the Sufi practices were accommodated within a brotherhood that was recognized in the NU organizational structure. This brotherhood was given the name Jam'iyyah Ahl al-Tarîqah al-Mu'tabarah al-Nahdliyyah.[171] It was established in 1957 by the *kiai* of Javanese *tarekat* who wanted to differentiate themselves from sects that were more syncretic and emphasize that their faith and practices alone were *mu'tabar* (valid). Martin van Bruinessen states that validity here referred to their compatibility with the belief in the *ahl al-sunnah wa al-jamâ'ah* doctrine and their genealogy that could be traced right back to the Prophet Muhammad.[172]

The organization was formed to control the number of *tasawuf* sects that existed and were practised by the NU community so that none became deviant. The *tarekat* or Sufi orders that were recognized as *mu'tabar* and developed within NU included the Qadiriyah wa Naqsyabandiyah, Syathâriyah, Shiddiqiyah, Syadziliyah, and the Wahidiyah orders.[173]

However, the Qadiriyah wa Naqsyabandiyah order was the most popular of them all. Qadiriyah wa Naqsyabandiyah was initially two separate *tarekat*, each with their own spiritual traditions and techniques from the fourteenth century. However, the Qadiriyah wa Naqsyabandiyah order then established itself as a *tarekat* by combining the two groups' spiritual techniques. These included the form of meditation without sound that was part of the Naqsyabandiyah *tarekat* and *dzikir* that involves reading in a certain rhythm and in a loud voice the sentence *Lâ ilâha illa Allâh* (There is no God but God). Those who joined this Sufi order did so by pledging one single oath (*bai'at*) rather than pledging two oaths separately to a *mursyid* (teacher) from each of the Naqsyabandiyah and Qadiriyah orders.[174]

SOCIAL-INTELLECTUAL CAPITAL AND THE EMERGENCE OF A NEW TRADITION IN NU INTELLECTUALISM

Social capital is the socio-cultural foundation of a community which encompasses values, norms, relations, world view, ties of solidarity, and so on. The mention of social capital usually refers to institutions, relations, and norms which influence the quality and quantity of social interaction within society. In a wider understanding of the term, social capital encompasses the positive and negative aspects of a number of groups within society, their behaviour, and the resources they possess.

Social capital is apparent in different forms, including: first, information channels within society that act as a means for spreading ideas; secondly, norms of reciprocity, whose sustainability depends on social networks to bring together various individuals; third, collective action by social networks; and fourth, broader identity and solidarity that emerges as a result of social networks.[175]

Before further discussing socio-intellectual capital, it is necessary to first give a general illustration of NU and the nature of its people. There are several aspects that deserve attention. First of all, as an organization with deep roots in village communities since its establishment, NU has always been aware of the importance of economically empowering the people. The *Statuten Perkoempoelan Nahdlatul Oelama* (Article 3a) lists a number of efforts to be made by NU, including "establishing bodies to promote agriculture, commerce and businesses that are not forbidden by Islamic law". This awareness in turn led to the birth of the *mabâdi' khaira ummah* (the principles of a good community) concept, triggered in the 13th NU Congress of 1935 that was known as the "economic movement" of the *nahdliyyîn* (NU members). *Mabâdi' khaira ummah* saw principles such as honesty, trust, and helping one another as the foundation of business ethics.

Programmes for economic development were indeed implemented, such as Syirkah Mu'âwanah, the corporation KH Machfoezh Siddiq established for the economic interests of its members. The most ambitious programme was KH Abdurrahman Wahid's plan in the beginning of the 1990s to establish 2,000 branches of the People's Credit Bank (BPR) over twenty years. Although the programme eventually fell apart due to the collapse of Bank Summa which was a business partner of NU's Central Board at the time,[176] the plan alone signified an awareness of the need for large-scale economic development.

This reality cannot be separated from the organizational characteristics of NU itself, which represent a second feature. Structurally speaking, NU as a congregation adopted a modern organizational system by establishing a neat structure from the Central Board right down to the branches at village level, implementing division of work areas, compiling a charter and so on. Although the superstructure was arranged and orderly, NU dynamics were relatively unorderly, undisciplined, and less than professional. Many of the organizational regulations had to submit to the charisma of select NU individuals. Another factor was the independence of the *pesantren* upon which NU movements were based, which made it difficult for the NU board to intervene. As a result, it is understandable that a lot of instructions, appeals, and the like were not followed at the lower levels because the *pesantren kiai* refused to accept them. This is no secret within NU circles. Although NU's formal structure adheres to the principle of centralism, in practice the organization remains decentralized.

This explanation does not thoroughly depict the processes and social capital that exist within NU, especially those related to the ideas and wealth of its traditions. The wealth of tradition that has been institutionalized through the *pesantren* in particular is the most influential socio-cultural capital in NU life. As a result, it is the focus of this section.

As mentioned above, NU is known as a traditional society (traditional Islam) that is often confronted by Islamic modernism. On the one hand, traditionalism is a barrier to the development of NU, yet on the other it provides both socio-cultural capital and strength for NU. Any attempt to change the face of NU must therefore take into account the reality of NU society. This incorporates several aspects. First, the NU community largely lives in villages, although recently there has been some vertical mobility in the elite circles of the villages, especially amongst the young educated NU members. They no longer live in villages, but have started to become agents of change in cities. Nevertheless, the majority of NU members live in villages with their own unique characteristics. One such characteristic is that villages tend to be less dynamic, resistant to change, and more defensive towards modernity, although this does not mean that there is no change at all in village communities.

Secondly, NU has an extraordinary intellectual wealth and foundation that will always be handed down from generation to generation through the *pesantren* network. *Pesantren*, although often criticized for their culture and way of teaching, have played a substantial role in conserving Islamic scholarship. This wealth has made NU highly appreciative towards old thought, although certain groups claim that such thought is heretical and superstitious. Through its long and complicated intellectual genealogy, affirmation of the intellectual tradition among NU ulama cannot be separated from the network formed by NU's pioneering scholars, especially KH Hasyim Asy'ari.[177] Through the principle *al-muhâfadhah 'alâ al-qadîm al-shâlih wa al-akhdzu bi al-jadîd al-ashlah* (maintaining the wealth of the past that is good, and adopting that which is new and better), NU's wealth of intellectualism stretches from the time of the Prophet Muhammad, through the Classical Period and the Middle Ages, to the modern era. This wealth is an extraordinary cultural-intellectual capital for NU in its dialogue with modernity.

Unfortunately however, for quite some time NU's intellectual wealth has not undergone any significant development. As a result, NU with all its tradition and education is little more than a kind of kitchen in which to preserve Islamic scholarship. There has been no serious effort to revitalize, let alone to transform this wealth of knowledge.[178] This is understandable, given that most NU ulama have uniform religious knowledge in the fields of theology, *tasawuf*, or fiqh. The source of their knowledge, both in the sense of intellectual genealogy and the texts that they refer to, is much the same, and as such there has been no diversification of knowledge. Given the situation, it is understandable that observers are less interested in NU these days. Consequently, up to the beginning of the 1990s it has been difficult to find quality works on NU. When people do look at NU, it is at most a glance at the political rumblings that appear on the surface, while the dynamics of NU thought are hardly paid any attention to. In short, until the second half of the 1980s, NU had no appeal. This was acknowledged by observers such as Mitsuo Nakamura, who seems to have been biased not only from his experience in researching Muhammadiyah in Kotagede, but also because of an intellectual bias that saw NU purely as an organization of ulama who were left behind and backwards in Javanese villages, who lacked intellectual sophistication, who were politically opportunistic and were culturally syncretic.[179]

Thirdly, NU possesses a well-established educational institution that forms the basis for the transmission of knowledge — namely, the *pesantren* network. With their own uniqueness and subculture, *pesantren* have proven that they are able to exist within a continually changing society. Although a lot of criticism has been aimed at this traditional educational institution regarding the charismatic *kiai* leadership, the lack of criticism amongst the *santri*, and no set teaching programme, the *pesantren* have their own strength and value that is not possessed by any other institution.

These aspects mentioned above have in turn crystallized and produced a certain religious understanding that has become a unique feature of NU; although when viewed in the larger context of the Islamic world, this religious understanding is not new, but could be described as an affirmation of Islamic traditionalism in general. This religious understanding rests on the ideology of *ahl al-sunnah wa al-jamâ'ah*, which within NU distinctly means that people in the field of fiqh follow one of the four schools of thought (Hanafi, Maliki, Syafi'i, and Hanbali), those within theology follow Abu Hasan al-Asy'âri and Abu Mansur al-Maturidî, and those within *tasawuf* follow Junaid al-Baghdâdî and al-Ghazâli.

This formulation of the *ahl al-sunnah wa al-jamâ'ah* ideology, which comes from KH Hasyim Asy'ari's *Qanun Asasi*, is rather simple, and in fact the aspects related to *tasawuf* and theology are not included at all.

Rather, these two aspects are highlighted in KH Bisri Musthafa's book, *Risalah Ahl al-Sunnah wa al-Jama'ah* (Kudus: Menara Kudus, 1966).[180] It is this understanding that NU classifies as pure Islam and not heresy.

Separately from this, the general conception within society is that the traditionalists are more backwards and tend to support the establishment (pro–status quo) in their understandings of society and Islamic thought. This, according to Abdurrahman Wahid, is because of their steadfast hold on tradition and orthodox Islam (fiqh), which leads them to reject modernity and a rational approach to life. Similarly in theology, they hold firmly to the scholastic theology of al-Asy'âri and al-Maturidî, which makes them fatalistic and prone to look down on rationalism (*ra'y*). In addition, the traditionalists are often accused of neglecting worldly issues in practising Islamic mysticism (*tasawuf*). Their activities within Sufi *tarekat* mean that they are considered indifferent to the dynamics of modernization and more defensive than offensive.

From this illustration, where NU has extraordinary socio-intellectual capital, the question arises as to why over a relatively long period of time (since the establishment of NU until the latter half of the 1980s) there have been very few developments in NU intellectualism, with NU instead becoming the guardian of orthodoxy. This question can be answered from several perspectives. First of all, over this period of time there was no intellectual mobilization within NU, in the sense that not many educated NU people continued on to higher education institutes. This did not only occur within NU, but was also common amongst Indonesian Muslims in general, although in contrast to other communities such as Muhammadiyah, NU was left further behind.

Secondly, as a result of this, the intellectual genealogy of NU ulama was almost homogenous, as there was no variation or diversification in the sources of their knowledge. This does not mean that NU ulama always held the same opinion on an issue. Although the intellectual genealogy was relatively similar, expression on a personal level was often different, in fact often in conflict with others. Thirdly, there had been no diversification of knowledge amongst the NU community. They had not yet made contact (or if they had, they had taken a defensive position) with the "secular sciences" from the West and used them as a new "tool" with which to "read" their religion. In fact, the majority of NU ulama in the 1970s and 1980s tended to be suspicious of that which they defined as Western, and thus adapted a defensive attitude.[181]

NU Intellectualism: Foundations

The intellectual mobility of the NU community only began in the latter half of the 1970s and the beginning of the 1980s, marked by an increasing number of NU youth who not only received education from various *pesantren* but also from universities or colleges. This was made possible after NU decided to no longer be institutionally involved in practical politics, following its fusion into the United Development Party (PPP) with other Islamic factions such as Parmusi, PSII, and Perti in 1973.[182] This forced fusion was not beneficial to society in general because it restricted their political rights. However, it contained a hidden blessing for NU. Through its small "fast" from politics, the NU community had more time to think about the education of the younger generation. *Pesantren* and other educational institutes, which had been neglected with the concentration on politics, started to receive attention. NU youth who had initially made politics their key ambition began to flock to higher education institutions.

The return of NU to the 1926 Khittah in 1984 was an important moment and the start of a new passion. KH Achmad Siddiq and KH Abdurrahman Wahid (respectively chairman and head of the executive council of NU [1984–89]) were determined and able to bring new intellectual passion to the organization. They both were an important part of the campaign for reformation within NU which marked the beginning of a new era for the traditional community. Interestingly, this intellectual enthusiasm which was signified by openness to all forms of religious fanaticism occurred at the same time that the Muslim world in general was undergoing a process of re-Islamization, if not "fundamentalization". As a result, on a macro-scale, the call for liberation by KH Achmad Siddiq and KH Abdrurrahman Wahid was barely a whisper in the midst of numerous Islamic movements.

The start of this scholarly tradition in turn gave birth to a new NU generation with an intellectual wealth that not only originated from *pesantren*, but also from universities. In short, this started a process of intellectual diversification within the NU community, in terms of intellectual genealogy, religious understanding, and the subjects that the NU youth chose to study.

During this time (the 1970s), the intellectual orientation of Indonesian Muslim students, including those with an NU cultural background, was still centred on the Middle East, as had been the case with the Indonesian ulama in the centuries before. Following this tradition, almost all senior

NU ulama, from KH Hasyim Asy'ari, KH Wahab Hasbullah, KH Bisri Syansuri, KH Achmad Siddiq, KH Ali Ma'shum to the new generation of KH Abdurrahman Wahid and KH Said Aqiel Siradj amongst others, studied in the Middle East. In the 1980s this tradition began to shift, with many NU youth not only going to the Middle East but also to the West, in accordance with a number of government policies to send Muslim youth to study overseas.[183] In addition to those who went overseas, many NU youth also enrolled in postgraduate programmes, both at IAIN and other higher education institutes.[184]

The NU youth who attended university (especially IAIN) as a continuation of their *pesantren* education were more able to critically reflect on their religious traditions. They had the courage to discuss the issues that had been considered taboo when they had been studying in *pesantren*. They could also discuss issues that had not been considered taboo, but that they had not been able to discuss previously due to a lack of critical awareness of the traditions and thought that they had inherited. Therefore, the doctrinal teachings they had received from their *pesantren* education were compared with and enriched by new knowledge and methodologies that they had obtained at university.

These two main currents of intellectualism (from the Middle East and the West/IAIN) in turn would form two kinds of thought in NU. Generally speaking, the NU generation that graduated from the Middle East would display a conservative nature, while graduates from the West were more liberal.[185] Meanwhile, graduates from IAIN or other PTAI tended to be split into one of the two, with some being conservative but also a significant number being progressive.

However, it must be highlighted that Western progressivism and Middle Eastern conservatism are not static, and on one level this classification is no longer valid as there are several NU figures who studied in the Middle East who are in fact very progressive. Figures like KH Abdurrahman Wahid (who studied in Cairo, Egypt and Baghdad, Iraq) and KH Said Aqiel Siradj (of Umm al-Qura, Mecca) are two such exceptions. More recently, NU youth who have studied in the Middle East, especially at al-Azhar in Egypt, have shown an extraordinary amount of progressivism. Nevertheless, the general tendency has not yet changed. The recent progressivism of those NU youth who studied in the Middle East is not purely a result of where they studied, but also due to other factors such as the current of progressivism within NU itself.[186]

On one level, this reality undermines Harun Nasution's theory on the Islamic reformation that places the West (the external factor) as the determining factor, while internal factors are more likely to lead to purification.[187] This theory is not relevant to the NU intellectual movement. Although it must be recognized that no movements occur without influence,[188] if this influence is always interpreted as originating from the West and that without it there would be no reformation, it is sure to contain a certain ideological bias. In the NU community, the revitalization of thought that has led to the birth of liberation was in many ways born out of its own traditionalism, although Western factors cannot be ignored either.

In comparison to those who studied in the West, more went to the Middle East. This is understandable, given that in addition to the Department of Religious Affairs, the prominent *pesantren* in Java often had their own networks with centres for Islamic Studies in the Middle East. These *pesantren* could send their senior students to a number of universities there. Meanwhile, not only were relations with the West relatively new, but they were purely facilitated through the Department of Religious Affairs. In addition, opportunities were difficult to find, although recently a number of funding agencies have sponsored studies in the West. Despite this, sending students to the West had a significant influence on the intellectual mobilization of *santri*.[189]

The next question then is: what role has this had in the formation of progressive discourse amongst the NU youth? Here it is necessary to divide, or more precisely differentiate, between NU progressivism at universities and outside of universities.[190] Rather surprisingly, progressive discourse within NU actually emerged amongst those who spent their time away from universities, either in *pesantren* or in NGOs; whereas the assumption is that campuses are academic fields that provide the best opportunity to cultivate liberal thought. This notion clearly requires further examination.

Several NU figures often identified as being progressive thinkers (the ideas of the following figures still require further examination), including Masdar F. Mas'udi, KH Mustofa Bisri, KH MA Sahal Mahfuz, and even KH Abdurrahman Wahid, all exist outside of universities. This differentiation (between those on campus and those from NGOs) may be biased because it gives excessive appreciation to those who have to date been underestimated. Meanwhile, on the other hand, campuses have become academic institutes where freedom of academic thought is guaranteed, and as such no matter how radical people's thoughts may be, they are considered quite normal. Indeed, several NU cadres on campus have written a number of books; however, their work has had no significance for the formation of progressive thought within NU. Their work seems average, they add little to the intellectual movement, and they do not question the fundamental aspects that have restricted NU thought. However, this does not mean that their work has no significance, as it suffices as an indicator of the emergence of the intellectual movement within NU.

In many ways, the progressive current in NU is represented by exponents who lead cultural movements off campus, although support of these movements from those at universities cannot be ignored either. The most prominent in all this, say the second carriage of Abdurrahman Wahid's locomotive, are the NU youth study groups that are developing progressive ideas.

NU's intellectual movement has shown increasing enthusiasm since the mid-1980s, when several NGOs began to emerge within the NU community (or NU youth). These NGOs were not just created for community empowerment, but also to promote fresh and progressive Islamic ideas and thought. This group of youth dared to break down and question several aspects of tradition, even doctrine, which had been accepted without question.

As mentioned in the previous section, this cannot be separated from the vertical and horizontal mobilization of a number of NU people, especially the youth, who had entered the world of modern education. In line with this, many NU youth lived in the cities and encountered modern studies that had not been available to them when they still lived and studied in villages. The consequence of this development was a change in and variation of thought, not just in order to adapt NU traditions and teachings to the reality of the outside world, but also to develop critical thinking concerning a number of religious doctrines.

This of course provoked a varied response from within NU, especially from the senior *kiai*. As a community, NU was split into two main groups: the conservatives who remained loyal to tradition with an exclusive and defensive face on the one hand, and the critical community that continued to question (develop) their doctrine and traditions on the other. In terms of quantity and traditional authority, the former group was by far the largest, though the latter has a quality of thought that is more structured and documented.

Notes

1. For more on this see Deliat Noer, *Gerakan Modern Islam di Indonesia 1900–1942* (Jakarta: LP3ES, 1980). Many people have criticized Deliat Noer's typology for being no longer relevant. Even if it is to be used, it needs at least qualification so as not to be misleading. However, it must be acknowledged that as a theory, his categories have had an enormous influence both in the academic world and in social life. More recently, his categories have not been used purely as an academic standard, but have become a basis on which to claim group identity, although within such claims there is a certain ideology that reduces the significance and role of one group over others. Such a tendency is not so healthy in either an academic context or social life in general.
2. Azyumardi Azra, "Islam di Asia Tenggara, Pengantar Pemikiran", in *Perspektif Islam Asia Tenggara*, edited by Azyumardi Azra (Jakarta: YOI, 1989), pp. xi–xiii.
3. Azyumardi Azra, *Jaringan Ulama Timur Tengah dan Kepulauan Nusantara Abad XVII–XVIII*, 3rd ed. (Bandung: Mizan, 1995), pp. 28–29.
4. Abdul Rahman Haji Abdullah, *Pemikiran Umat Islam di Nusantara, Sejarah dan Perkembangannya hingga Abad ke-19* (Kuala Lumpur: Dewan Bahasa dan Pustaka, 1990), pp. 24–30.
5. For more on historical evidence and the weaknesses of each theory, see Azyumardi Azra, *Jaringan Ulama*, pp. 24–36.
6. Azyumardi Azra, *Jaringan Ulama*, pp. 31–33.
7. Syncretic here can be seen from two different perspectives. First, it may be viewed as the mixing of Islamic teachings with local values that existed and were practised by society before the arrival of Islam, and secondly as Islamic doctrine that had already been mixed with the values and traditions of Persian and Indian trading communities who spread Islam. See Fachry Ali and Bahtiar Effendy, *Merambah Jalan Baru Islam, Rekonstruksi Pemikiran Islam Indonesia Masa Orde Baru* (Bandung: Mizan, 1990), p. 37.
8. Harry J. Benda, *Bulan Sabit dan Matahari Terbit* (Jakarta: Pustaka Jaya, 1980).
9. Clifford Geertz, *Abangan, Santri dan Priyayi dalam Masyarakat Jawa* (Jakarta: Pustaka Jaya, 1981).
10. W.F. Wertheim, *Indonesian Society in Transition* (Bandung: Sumur, 1956).
11. Robert Jay, *Santri and Abangan, Religious Schism in Rural Java* (Harvard: Harvard University, 1957).
12. Howard M. Federspiel, *Persatuan Islam, Pembaruan Islam Indonesia Abad XX* (Yogyakarta: Gadjah Mada University Press, 1996), pp. 1–3.
13. Martin van Bruinessen, "The Origin and Development of Sufi Order (Tarekat) in Southeast Asia", *Studia Islamika*, April–June 1994, pp. 3–23.
14. This "tension" between the two main currents in Islam (*tasawuf* and fiqh) was not typical of Islam in the archipelago, but was more of a continuation of the religious traditions in the Middle East. Within the *tasawuf* tradition there were two forms, Sunni mysticism and philosophical mysticism. Sunni

mysticism is the Sufi path where *ma'rifat* (internalization of God's knowledge and attributes) is the highest achievement. This kind of mysticism is accepted by al-Ghazâlî and acknowledged by those who believe in *ahl al-sunnah wa al-jamâ'ah*. Meanwhile, philosophical mysticism is the Sufi path which recognizes a level higher than *ma'rifat*, such as the *itti âd* (unity) of Abu Yazid al-Bustami (d. 947 CE), the *hulûl* (passivity) of al-Hallaj (d. 922 CE), and *wihdat al-wujûd* (pantheism) of Ibn al-'Arabi (d. 1240 CE). For a brief explanation see Harun Nasution, *Islam Ditinjau dari berbagai Aspeknya II* (Jakarta: UI Press, 1986), pp. 82–88.
15. Translated from the transliteration by S.M.N. al-Attas, *The Mysticism of Hamzah Fansuri* (Kuala Lumpur: University of Malaya, 1970), p. 489.
16. See S.M.N. al-Attas, *The Mysticism*, pp. 478–83.
17. Abdul Rahman Haji Abdullah, *Pemikiran Umat Islam*, pp. 157–58.
18. Ibid., p. 18. See also Ahmad Daudy, *Allah dan Manusia dalam Konsepsi Syeikh Nuruddin al-Raniry* (Jakarta: CV. Rajawali, 1983), p. 248.
19. Abdul Rahman Haji Abdullah, *Pemikiran Umat Islam*, p. 159. This book further details how al-Raniri believes that the *wujûdiyah* are heretics and deviant, basing his ideas on the arguments of Ibn Taimiyah, Ibn al-Qayyim, al-Sammani, Ibn Khaldun, and so on. He chose these figures because they were known to be strongly opposed to philosophical mysticism and pantheism, as interpreted by Ibn 'Arabi.
20. This is not intended to sharply polarize *tasawuf* and fiqh. However, it is necessary for theoretical needs despite the risk of simplification. In reality, although initially Islam tended towards mysticism, there have nevertheless been many *syari'ah*-minded Muslims who refused to make compromises with local traditions and customs in order to preserve fiqh orthodoxy, ever since the arrival of Islam in Southeast Asia. See Azyumardi Azra, "Islam di Asia Tenggara", p. xxii.
21. Martin van Bruinessen, *Kitab Kuning, Pesantren dan Tarekat* (Bandung: Mizan, 1994), p. 112. However, in accordance with Millner, this cannot be understood to mean that "heterodox" mysticism completely deviated from or neglected *syari'ah*. It is similarly erroneous to polarize the two, despite the tension between them being an undeniable historical reality.
22. Fazlur Rahman interprets neo-Sufism as mysticism that has been renewed or reformed, especially in the sense of being stripped of its ascetic features and contents as well as its metaphysics, and replacing them with Islamic orthodoxy. See Fazlur Rahman, *Islam* (Chicago: University of Chicago Press, 1979), pp. 205–6.
23. Azra suggests that it is possible that al-Palimbani died in 1789 after completing his final and most famous work, *Sayr al-Sâlikîn*, which means he was 85. *Tarikh Salasilah Negri Kedah* states that al-Palimbani was killed in a battle against Thailand in 1828. However, this is difficult to believe, besides not being

reinforced by other sources: 124 years old is too old to be going off to war. For further information, see Azyumardi Azra, *Jaringan Ulama*, p. 246.
24. Azyumardi Azra, *Jaringan Ulama*, especially Chapter 5.
25. Deliar Noer, *The Modernist Muslim Movement in Indonesia 1900–1942* (Singapore: Oxford University Press, 1973).
26. See also Djohan Effendi, "Progressive Traditionalist: The Emergence of a New Discourse in Indonesia's Nahdlatul Ulama during the Abdurrahman Wahid Era" (Dissertation, Deakin University, 2000), p. 72.
27. See for instance Rumadi, "Wacana Intelektualisme NU: Sebuah Potret Pemikiran", *Jurnal Tashwirul Afkar*, no. 6 (1999).
28. Zamakhsyari Dhofier, *Tradisi Pesantren, Studi tentang Pandangan Hidup Kyai*, 6th ed. (Jakarta: LP3ES, 1994), p. 1.
29. Fachry Ali and Bahtiar Effendy, *Merambah Jalan Baru Islam*, p. 50.
30. See KH Bisri Musthafa, *Risalah Ahlus Sunnah wal Jama'ah* (Kudus: Menara Kudus, 1967), p. 19.
31. Martin van Bruinessen, *NU: Tradisi, Relasi-Relasi Kuasa, Pencarian Wacana Baru* (Yogyakarta: LKiS, 1994).
32. Andree Feillard, *NU vis a vis Negara:Pencarian Bentuk, Isi dan Makna* (Yogyakarta: LKiS, 1999).
33. M. Ali Haidar, *Nahdlatul Ulama dan Islam di Indonesia, Pendekatan Fiqih dalam Politik* (Jakarta: Gramedia, 1998).
34. Choirul Anam, *Pertumbuhan dan Perkembangan Nahdlatul Ulama* (Sala: Jatayu, 1985).
35. Schrieke, "Ruler and Realm in Early Java", quoted from Howard M. Federspiel, *Persatuan Islam, Pembaruan Islam Indonesia Abad XX*, translated by Yudian W. Asmin and Affandi Mochtar (Yogyakarta: Gadjah Mada University Press, 1996), p. 6.
36. Faqih Hasjim was a student of Haji Rasul (Haji Abdul Karim Amrullah, father of Hamka), a reformer from Minangkabau. Faqih Hasjim arrived in Surabaya in the 1910s and preached in support of attacking the religious practices of local communities, such as *tahlilan* and grave visits. See Martin van Bruinessen, *NU*, p. 27.
37. Martin van Bruinessen, *NU*, p. 24.
38. G.F. Pijper, *Beberapa Studi tentang Sejarah Islam di Indonesia 1900–1950*, translated by Tudjiman and Yessy Agusdin (Jakarta: UI Press, 1984), p. 105.
39. M. Ali Haidar, *Nahdlatul Ulama*, p. 47. See also Choirul Anam, *Pertumbuhan dan Perkembangan*, pp. 44–45.
40. Kiai Wahab, as he is commonly known, is a very interesting traditional ulama. Although he was raised in a *pesantren* environment, he associated widely with people from all walks of life. Before establishing *Tashwirul Afkâr*, during his ten years in Mecca, Kiai Wahab was active in Sarikat Islam (SI), an association of Muslim merchants established in Surakarta in 1912 which was initially

aimed at warding off thieves through a patrol system and establishing a union of Javanese and Arab Muslim traders to compete with the Chinese. Wahab also worked with the nationalist figure Soetomo, who helped establish Budi Oetomo in 1908, in a discussion group known as Islam Studie Club. In 1916, Wahab founded a madrasah with the name Nahdlat al-Wathan in Surabaya, which later developed branches in Gresik, Lawang, Pasuruan, and so on. In 1918, Wahab also established the cooperation Nahdlat al-Tujjâr. See Andree Feillard, *NU vis a vis Negara*, pp. 8–9. See also Choirul Anam, *Pertumbuhan dan Perkembangan*, p. 43; and Saifuddin Zuhri, *Almaghfurlah K.H. Abdulwahab Chasbullah, Bapak dan Pendiri Nahdlatul-'Ulama* (Jakarta: Yamunu, 1972), p. 40.

41. Tashwir al-Afkâr was initially focused primarily on providing a place for children to study and learn religion. The institute, established by Kiai Abdul Wahab Hasbullah, Kiai Mas Mansur, and Kiai Ahmad Dahlan (head of a *pesantren* in Kebon Dalem, Surabaya) in Surabaya in 1918, later became a forum for the exchange of ideas, and even a means through which to defend the interests of traditional Islam. The group used the name Suryo Sumirat Afdeling Tashwîr al-Afkâr until 1929, after which it was officially recognized as a legal entity, and the Suryo Sumirat was lost. For further information see M. Ali Haidar, *Nahdlatul Ulama*, pp. 41–44.

42. Achmad Siddiq in *Khittah Nahdliyah* (Surabaya: Balai Buku, 1980), p. 27.

43. M. Ali Haidar, *Nahdlatul Ulama*, p. 57.

44. In the Congress in Bandung (6 February 1926), the delegation to Hijaz was finalized and represented by Tjokroaminoto (SI) and Mas Mansur (Muhammadiyah, previously a member of Tashwirul Afkâr with Kiai Wahab Chasbullah). In the previous congress, the fourth Islamic Congress in Yogyakarta (21–27 August 1925) also elected several delegates to go to Hijaz, namely Abdullah Siradj, Penghulu Pakualaman, and Soegeng (the latter was chosen for his ability to speak English). Both these congresses were largely controlled by non-*pesantren* groups. See Deliar Noer, *Gerakan Modern*, p. 243. See also M. Ali Haidar, *Nahdlatul Ulama*, p. 119.

45. This committee was chaired by Hasan Gipo, with Salih Sjamil as vice-chairman, Moehammad Shadiq Setijo as secretary, Abdul Halim as assistant secretary, and KH Abdul Wahab, KH Masjhoeri, and KH Khalil as advisors.

46. Initially the delegation to be sent included KH R. Asnawi (from Kudus) and KH Bisri (from Jombang), but this was changed to KH Khalil (from Lasem) and KH Abdul Wahab (from Surabaya).

47. Choirul Anam, *Pertumbuhan dan Perkembangan*, p. 54, as cited in KH Abdul Halim, *Sejarah Perjuangan Kyai Abdul Wahab Chasbullah* (Bandung: Penerbit Baru, 1970), p. 12. A slightly different version, quoted by Deliar Noer from the newspaper *Bintang Islam*, IV, 1926, states that the NU ulama asked King Ibn Sa'ûd:

...to not ban anyone from following the Syafi'i *madzhab*.

...to ban or torture anyone who interferes with, obstructs, or insults the Syafi'i *madzhab*.

...to assign set pilgrimages to Medina and pilgrimages to the graves of martyrs and their remains.

...to not obstruct people who practise *wirid zikir* (chanting the names of God) correctly or who recite *dalâil al-khairat* or *burdah* or study fiqh books from the Syafi'i *madzhab* such as *Tuhfah, Nihâyah, Bajah*.

...to continue to preserve the grave of the Prophet.

...to not destroy the tombstones of the martyrs... or the tombstones of the *auliya* (scholars) or ulama.

...to implement a tariff on goods or people entering Jeddah and a fee for those making the hajj in Mecca and Medina...

...to forbid Sheiks from Mecca from coming to Java in search of people ready to make the hajj because this would decrease the prominence of the land of Mecca and the nobility of the Sheiks in Mecca, and would increase the cost of the pilgrimage.... it is more important for the government to establish a hajj administrative committee in Mecca. See Deliar Noer, *Gerakan Modern*, p. 244. These two documents are not contradictory; rather, the source Noer cites is mixed with journalistic language and thus it prioritizes "provocative" issues. This is apparent in the issue of the schools of thought or *madzhab*, for instance, where the first document (KH Abdul Halim) speaks of the four *madzhab*, while the second document prioritizes the Syafi'i *madzhab*. This is understandable because although on a normative basis, NU and the *pesantren* community recognize the validity of all four schools of thought, in practice NU and the *pesantren* are identical to the Syafi'i *madzhab*.

48. Contrast this with Anam, *Pertumbuhan dan Perkembangan*, p. 55, who completely denies the role of the modernists in influencing the establishment of NU. This opinion is only correct if what is meant by "reaction to the modernist organizations" is a direct reaction. However, it must be recognized that the "modernist" organizations did "play a role" in motivating and crystallizing solidarity within the traditional *pesantren* community.

49. Martin van Bruinessen, *NU*, pp. 36–37.

50. *Statuten Perkoempoelan Nahdlatoel Oelama*, Rechpersoon, dated 6 February 1930 no. lx.

51. Ibid.

52. For a brief explanation see Rumadi, "Wacana Intelektualisme NU: Sebuah Potret Pemikiran", *Tashwirul Afkar*, no. 6 (1999).

53. For a comprehensive study, see Azyumardi Azra, *Jaringan Ulama Timur Tengah dan Kepulauan Nusantara Abad XVII dan XVIII, Melacak Akar-Akar Pembaruan Islam di Indonesia* (Bandung: Mizan, 1992). See also Abdul Rahman Haji Abdullah, *Pemikiran Umat Islam di Nusantara, Sejarah dan Perkembangannya*

hingga Abad ke-19 (Kuala Lumpur: Dewan Bahasa dan Pustaka Kementerian Pendidikan Malaysia, 1990).

54. Nurcholish Madjid describes this backwardness in an interesting way, using the following illustration: when al-Ghazâlî (d. 1111 CE) was preoccupied with the polemic over issues of philosophy with Ibnu Rusyd (d. 595 H/1198 CE), the Kediri kingdom in the archipelago ruled by Jayabaya was at its height. When al-Ghazâlî wrote philosophical works such as *Ihyâ' Ulûm al-Dîn*, *Tahâfut al-Falâsifah*, and *al-Munqiz min al-Dhalâl*, Jayabaya produced the *Jangka Jayabaya* which was more of a mystical work, if not a fantasy. However, al-Ghazâlî lived during the height of Islam; in fact, just at the time the Islamic Golden Age (*al-'ashr al-zahabi*) was about to decline. This reality, according to Nurcholish Madjid, brought about a cultural and intellectual discrepancy between Indonesian Islam and Islam in other parts of the world. See Nurcholish Madjid, *Tradisi Islam: Peran dan Fungsinya dalam Pembangunan di Indonesia* (Jakarta: Paramadina, 1997), pp. 3–11, 43–46. This sufficiently explains why the intellectual atmosphere in the archipelago was left behind other parts of the Islamic world, both in terms of discourse and productivity.

55. Ahmad Baso in his article "Kritik atas Nalar Melayu: Telaah atas Tradisi Intelektual Islam Indonesia dan Problem Rasionalitas", *Tashwirul Afkar*, no. 2 (1998), criticizes this theory. He argues that Azyumardi Azra's theory of a network of ulama neglects the role of figures such as Hamzah Fansuri, Syams al-Din al-Sumatrani, and Syekh Siti Jenar, as well as the Walisongo (Nine Saints) in Java. Such criticism contains some truth. It is not entirely accurate to argue that the roles of Hamzah Fansuri and Syams al-Din Sumatrani were neglected in Azyumardi Azra's theory; both were mentioned in proportion during Azra's discussion of Nûr al-Dîn al-Raniri, because both were involved in the debate over the *wujûdiah* belief. However, Ahmad Baso's criticism concerning the roles of Syekh Siti Jenar and the Walisongo who lived in the fifteenth century is valid. According to historians, the Walisongo played a large role in Islamizing Java in the fifteenth century, and many were of Arab descent. If this is true, then the question emerges as to whether there was an intellectual network with the centre of Islamic civilization. The answer remains quite "obscured" because there is very little data on Islam in Indonesia prior to the seventeenth century. Even if there were the Walisongo, the facts have been mixed with myths that are very difficult to prove empirically. See Martin van Bruinessen, *Kitab Kuning: Pesantren dan Tarekat* (Bandung: Mizan, 1995). See also M.C. Riflecks, *Sejarah Indonesia Modern* (Yogyakarta: Gadjah Mada University Press, 1991), pp. 13–14. See also Abdurrahman, "The Pesantren Architects and Their Socio-Religious Teachings (1850–1950)" (Dissertation, UCLA, 1997), pp. 45–58.

56. The term "*Jawi* Ulama" does not always refer to Java. In Javanese, the term "*Jawi*" is actually different from the term "*Jawa*/Java". However, in this context

the term refers to the ulama of the archipelago who lived in Mecca and Medina. This definition is also reflected in the book written by Mohd. Bin Nor Ngah, *Kitab Jawi: Islamic Thought of the Malay Muslim Scholars* (Singapore: Institute of Southeast Asian Studies, 1983).

57. See Azyumardi Azra, "Ulama Indonesia di Haramain: Pasang Surut Sebuah Wacana Keagamaan", *Jurnal Ulumul Quran* 3, no. 3 (1992): 76–85. This article was recently published in Azyumardi Azra, *Renaisans Islam Asia Tenggara: Sejarah Wacana & Kekuasaan* (Bandung: Rosdakarya, 1999), pp. 143–61.

58. As a reference for analysis, the NU can be categorized into several generations. The first generation consists of those who helped establish NU and who are represented by figures such as Hasyim Asyari, Wahab Hasbullah, and Bisri Syansuri. The second generation is represented by figures including Wahid Hasyim, Saefuddin Zuhri, Ahmad Siddiq, and As'ad Syamsul Arifin. The third generation is represented by figures such as Abdurrahman Wahid, Fahmi Saefuddin, and Mustafa Bisri. This categorization is by no means rigid, because figures such as Kiai Achmad Siddiq can be classified as either belonging to the second or third generations. Nevertheless, categorization based on generations is necessary as an analytical tool.

59. For more on the intellectual genealogy of NU ulama, see Zamakhsyari Dhofier, *Tradisi Pesantren*, pp. 85–96. See also Abdurrahman, *The Pesantren Architects*, p. 91.

60. For further information, see Karel A. Steenbrink, *Beberapa Aspek tentang Islam di Indonesia Abad ke-19* (Jakarta: Bulan Bintang, 1984), pp. 117–27. According to Martin, Nawawi produced no less than forty works, twenty-two of which are still circulating amongst the *pesantren*. See Martin van Bruinessen, *Pesantren dan Kitab Kuning*, p. 38.

61. Zamakhsyari Dhofier, "KH. Hasyim Asy'ari: Penggalang Islam Tradisional", in *Biografi 5 Rais 'Am Nahdlatul Ulama*, by Humaidy Abdussami and Ridwan Fakla AS (Yogyakarta: Pustaka Pelajar, 1995), p. 8.

62. For further information on the intellectual career and works of Mahfudz al-Tirmasi, see Abdurrahman Mas'ud, "Mahfuz al-Tirmasi (d. 1338/1919): An Intellectual Biography", *Studia Islamika* 5, no. 2 (1998): 29. Mahfudz's authority in the field of Hadith can be seen in the recognition given by ulama, especially Javanese *kiai*, of his position in the intellectual transmission of the Hadith. He is seen as being a strong link in the intellectual transmission of the Bukhari Hadith. He had the authority to grant a diploma to a student who successfully mastered the Bukhari Hadith. This diploma is believed to have come directly from Imam Bukhari himself and was written about a thousand years ago. It was passed down from generation to generation through twenty-three generations of ulama who mastered the Hadith. Mahfuz was the twenty-third ulama in the sequence.

63. See Zanakhsyari Dhofier, *Tradisi Pesantren*, pp. 26–27.

64. Ali As'ad, *K.H.M. Munawir Pendiri Pondok Pesantren Krapyak Yogyakarta* (Yogyakarta, 1975).
65. Chaidar, *Manaqib Mbah Maksum* (Kudus: Menara Kudus, 1972).
66. The majority of the NU ulama in Siddiq's family also studied in Mecca. For more, see Affan Ilman Huda, *Biografi Mbah Siddiq* (Jember: Pon-pes al-Fatah, n.d.).
67. Contrast this with Muhammadiyah's discontinuity in intellectualism due to the disowning of much of its intellectual wealth in the Middle Ages, because it was considered to have been tainted by heresy and superstition. Muhammadiyah's intellectual tradition was limited to the rule of the righteous predecessors or *salâf al-shâlih*, the time of Ibnu Taimiyah, and then the modern reformers such as Muhammad bin Abdul Wahab, Jamal al-Din al-Afgani, and Muhammad Abduh. This is often criticized even by those who are identified as being Muhammadiyah cadres, such as Azyumardi Azra. See Azyumardi Azra, "Mengkaji Ulang Modernisme Muhammadiyah", *Kompas*, 9 November 1990.
68. See Ibnu Majah, *Sunan Ibnu Majah*, vol. 2 (Beirut: Dâr al-Fikr, n.d.), p. 480 (Hadith no. 4057). See also al-Tirmizi, *al-Jamî' al-Sahih*, vol. 5 (Beirut: Dâr al-Ihyâ' al-Turâs al-'Arabî, n.d.), p. 26 (Hadith no. 2641).
69. This is not to say that the Islam that entered Indonesia was less "authentic", as is assumed by Western academics such as Clifford Geertz in his *Religion of Java*. The fragmentation of Islam into a number of schools of thought did not influence the authenticity of Islam, but on the contrary indicated continuity from the "centre of Islam" to the peripheral regions.
70. See Yusuf al-'Asy, *al-Daulat al-Umawiyat wa al-Ahdâs allatî Sabaqatuhâ wa Mahhadat lahâ Ibtidâ'an min Fitnati 'Usmân* (Damascus: Dâr al-Fikr, 1965), pp. 101–6. See also Hasan Ibrahin Hasan, *Târikh al-Islâmî: al-Siyâsî wa al-Dînî wa al-S|aqâfî wa al-Ijtimâ'î* (Cairo: Maktabah al-Nahdah al-Misriyyah, 1979), pp. 271–86. See also, Philip K. Hitti, *History of the Arabs* (New York: Macmillan, 1974), pp. 178–86.
71. The Kharijites are followers of Ali bin Abi Talib, who left and established his own group because he did not agree with the policy of accepting the peace offer from Mu'awiyah bin Abu Sufyan. This group in turn splintered into smaller groups, namely: (1) al-Muhakimah; (2) al-Azariqah; (3) al-Najdat; (4) al-Ajaridah; (5) al-Sufriah; and (6) al-Ibâdiah. See Ali Mustafa al-Gurabi, *Târîkh al-Fiq al-Islâmiyah wa Nasyat 'ilmu al-Kalâm 'inda al-Muslimîn* (Egypt: Maktabah wa Matba'ah Muhammad Ali Sabîh, 1959), pp. 277–82. Henceforth referred to as *Târîkh al-Firaq*.
72. The Murjiites emerged from the tension between the Kharijites and the fanatical followers of Ali, the Shi'ites. The tension led to the emergence of a new group that attempted to remain neutral and separate from the antagonism. The group was called Murhi'ah because its members refused to give an assessment of

what had happened at the time, preferring instead to delay resolution of the issue until the day they would be in the presence of God. See Harun Nasution, *Teologi Islam, Aliran-Aliran, Sejarah Analisa Perbandingan* (Jakarta: UI Press, 1986), pp. 22–30. Henceforth referred to as *Teologi Islam*.

73. For more information on these two groups, see 'Abd al-Qâhir bin Tâhir bin Muhammad al-Bagdâdî, *Al-Farqu bain al-Firâq* (Egypt: Maktabah Muhammad Sabih wa Auladuhu, n.d.), pp. 14–19.

74. His full name is Abû al-Hasan Ali ibn Isma'îl al-Asy'ari. He was born in Basrah in 270 H/873 CE and died in Bagdad in 330 H/935 CE. In his youth, he was a student of the prominent Mu'tazilite, Abu Ali Muhammad ibn Abd al-Wahab al-Juba`i. However, for some unknown reason al-Asy'ari, who had followed the Mu'tazilite understanding for decades, eventually left it. The exact reason is unknown because the explanations available in a number of books are less than convincing. The most common reason given is the inability of al-Juba'i to answer al-Asy'ari's questions when the two debated theological issues. For more on this debate, see Ahmad Mahmud Subhi, *Fî 'ilmi al-kalâm* (Cairo: Dâr al-Kutub al-Jamî'ah, 1969), p. 182. Commenting on the debate, Ali Mustafa al-Gurabi says that al-Asy'ari's forty-year adherence to the Mu'tazilite belief makes it difficult to believe that al-Asy'ari left the group only because al-Juba'i could not give him a satisfactory answer to his questions. See Ali Mustafa al-Gurabi, *Târîkh al-Firaq*, pp. 223–24. Separately from this, al-Asy'ari became a brilliant figure for his time. Amongst the works he produced are *al-Ibânah fî Usûl al-Diyânah, Risâlah fi Istihsân al-Khauz fi al-Kalâm, Kitâb Syarh wa al-Tafsîl, al-Luma', Mu'jaz, I'âdah al-Burhân,* and *Maqâlat al-Islâmiyyîn wa Ikhtilâf al-Musalliyyîn*. This last book is the most authentic source on al-Asy'ari's views on different religious doctrines and dogma.

75. His complete name is Abu Mansur Muhammad ibn Muhammad ibn Mahmud al-Maturidî al-Ansari al-Hanafi. He was born in a village close to Samarqand in about 238 H/853 CE and died in 333 H/944 CE. He taught many ulama, including Syaikh Abu Bakar Ahmad bin Ishaq, Abu Nasr Ahmad bin Abbas, Nusair ibn Yahya al-Balkhi (d. 268 H/881 CE), and Muhammad ibn Muqatil al-Râzi (d. 248 H/862 CE).

76. For information on the Qadarites and the Jabarites, see Muhammad Ibn 'Abd al-Karim al-Syahrastani, *al-Milal wa al-Nihâl*, vol. 1 (Beirut: al-Dâr al-Tsaqafiyah al-'Arabiyah, n.d.), pp. 85–90.

77. Anthropomorphism comes from the Hebrew word *antropos*, which refers to humankind or anything related to man, and *morphe*, which means form, shape, or figure. Anthropomorphism means: (1) describing the power of God, the gods, or nature in the form of or with the attributes possessed by humankind; (2) a belief that God or the gods possess characteristics that humankind possesses, such as consciousness, concern, intention, emotion, and sense. In its extreme form, anthropomorphism considers God's existence to be the same as human

existence, only more perfect and powerful. See Peter A. Angels, *Dictionary of Philosophy* (New York: Barnes & Noble, 1981), p. 13.
78. For further information see al-Gurabi, *Târîkh al-Firaq*, pp. 225–38. See also al-Bagdâdi, *Al-Farqu bain al-Firâq*, p. 337. See also al-Ghazâlî, *al-Iqtisâd wa al-I'tiqâd* (Ankara: Ankara University, 1962), pp. 138–39.
79. Al-Syahrastani, *al-Milal wa al-Nihâl*, pp. 97–98.
80. "Theologizing fiqh" is used to describe the religious process whereby fiqh, which regulates daily life, also has a theological dimension. This means that violation of a fiqh dictum is believed to also have a connection with theology.
81. Syncretism here can mean one of two things: first, a mixing of Islamic teachings with local values held by society before the arrival of Islam; or secondly, the mixing of Islamic teachings with the values and traditions held by the community of Indian and Persian traders who spread Islam to Indonesia. See Fachry Ali and Bahtiar Effendy, *Merambah Jalan Baru Islam, Rekonstruksi Pemikiran Islam Indonesia Masa Orde Baru*, 2nd ed. (Bandung: Mizan, 1990), p. 37.
82. Harry J. Benda, *Bulan Sabit dan Matahari Terbit* (Jakarta: Pustaka Jaya, 1980). Benda, for instance, differentiates between Javanese Islam and West Sumatran Islam. Javanese Islam, he argues, had mixed with local traditions and thus was no longer pure, while West Sumatran Islam was more pure because of the influence of the Wahabi movement in the Arabian Peninsula since 1773, whose main theme was the purification of the faith.
83. Clifford Geertz, *Abangan, Santri, Priyayi dalam Masyarakat Jawa* (Jakarta: Pustaka Jawa, 1981).
84. W.F. Wertheim, *Indonesian Society in Transition* (Bandung: Sumur, 1956).
85. Robert Jay, *Santri dan Abangan: Religious Schism in Rural Central Java* (Harvard: Harvard University, 1957).
86. Nikki R. Keddie, *Indonesia Trade and Society* (The Netherlands: Van Hoeve, 1967), p. 169.
87. Abdul Rahman Haji Abdullah, *Pemikiran Umat Islam di Nusantara, Sejarah dan Perkembangannya hingga Abad ke-19* (Kuala Lumpur: Dewan Bahasa dan Pustaka Kementerian Pendidikan Malaysia, 1990), p. 113.
88. Azyumardi Azra, *Renaisans Islam Asia Tenggara, Sejarah Wacana dan Kekuasaan* (Bandung: Rosda, 1999), pp. 6–8.
89. Abdul Rahman Haji Abdullah, *Pemikiran Umat Islam*, p. 98.
90. Ibid., pp. 99–100.
91. W.M. Watt, *Islamic Philosophy and Theology* (Edinburgh: Edinburgh University Press, 1979), p. 154.
92. Abdul Rahman Haji, *Pemikiran Umat Islam*, p. 108.
93. A. Hasymi, *Sejarah Kebudayaan Islam* (Jakarta: Bulan Bintang, 1975), p. 230. See also Azyumardi Azra, *Jaringan Ulama*, p. 261.

NU Intellectualism: Foundations 85

94. Snouck Hurgronje, *Mekka in the Latter Part of the 19th Century* (Leiden: Brill, 1970), pp. 268–72.
95. There is no certain date as to when al-Mutamakkin was born. According to Zainul Milal Bizawie, who undertook specific research on the figure, al-Mutamakkin was born around 1645. He was definitely born in Cabolek village, ten kilometres from Tuban. See Zainul Milal Bizawie, *Perlawanan Kultural Agama Rakyat, Pemikiran dan Paham Keagamaan Syekh Ahmad al-Mutamakkin dalam Pergumulan Islam dan Tradisi (1645–1740)* (Yogyakarta: Samha, 2002), p. 105. Ahmad al-Mutamakkin's teachings are detailed in his journal titled '*Arsy al-Muwahhidîn*, summarized by Zainul Milal Bizawie, pp. 146–75.
96. See Zainul Milal Bizawie, *Perlawanan Kultural Agama Rakyat*, pp. 115–34. See also Jajat Burhanuddin, "Tradisi Keilmuan dan Intelektual", in *Ensiklopedi Tematis Dunia Islam*, vol. 5 (Jakarta: Ichtiar Baru Van Hoeve, 2002), pp. 167–77.
97. It is known as the *Tarajumah* because the books are translations from Arabic books into Javanese. See Abdul Djamil, *Perlawanan Kiai Desa, Pemikiran dan Gerakan Islam KH. Ahmad Rifa'i Kalisalak* (Yogyakarta: LKiS, 2001), p. xvii.
98. According to Abdul Djamil's research, the exact number is not definite because another source places the figure at 69. This difference may be because of the existence of books that were discovered only recently that had been collected by his students and were seized by the Dutch colonial government.
99. For further explanation on these books, see Abdul Djamil, *Perlawanan Kiai Desa*, pp. 25–36.
100. Abdul Djamil, *Perlawanan Kiai Desa*, pp. 40–52.
101. Ibid., pp. 55–62.
102. Abdul Rahman Haji Abdullah, *Pemikiran Umat Islam*, p. 111.
103. See Martin van Bruinessen, *Kitab Kuning, Pesantren dan tarekat* (Bandung: Mizan, 1995), pp. 155–58.
104. A. Qodri Azizy gives an interesting though less than serious illustration of NU's fiqh-oriented perspective and compares it with Muhammadiyah. He describes NU as revolving around fiqh, while Muhammadiyah revolves around *tauhid* or the oneness of God. Thus, whenever NU interprets reality, the terms halal and haram (allowed and forbidden) are always used, while Muhammadiyah, with its project of purification, always views people in terms of their faith, and thus the term that surfaces is *musyrik* (idolator/idolatrous). See the interview of A. Qodri Azizy, "Mengibarkan Nalar *Ushûl al-Fiqh*", *Jurnal Gerbang* 6, no. 3 (2000): 140.
105. See M. Ali Haidar, *NU dan Islam di Indonesia: Pendekatan Fiqih dalam Politik* (Jakarta: Gramedia, 1994).
106. For more on this matter, see Abdul Rahman Haji Abdullah, *Pemikiran Umat Islam*, pp. 119–20. He argues that the first state to adhere to the Syafi'i school of thought was Samudra Pasai. However, Samudra Pasai had from the very beginning tended more towards the Shi'ia current. During the reign of Meurah

Silu (1261–89 CE), Syaikh Ismail bin al-Shiddiq came from Mecca, who then installed the Syafi'i school of thought and changed Meurah Silu's name to Malik al-Salih.
107. Martin van Bruinessen, *Kitab Kuning*, p. 23.
108. For an explanation of al-Raniri's books, see Ahmad Daudy, *Syekh Nuruddin al-Raniri* (Jakarta: Bulan Bintang, 1978), p. 9. Other data places the total of al-Raniri's works at 32. See Muhd. Saghir Abdullah, *Perkembangan Ilmu Fiqh dan Tokoh-Tokohnya di Asia Tenggara (1)* (Solo: Ramadhani, 1985), pp. 26–28.
109. For more information on the debate between al-Raniri and Hamzah Fansuri and Syams al-Din al-Sumatrani, see Ahmad Daudy, *Allah dan Manusia dalam Konsep Nuruddin al-Raniri* (Jakarta: Rajawali Press, 1983), pp. 201–39.
110. Muhd. Saghir Abdullah, *Perkembangan Ilmu Fiqh*, p. 26.
111. This kind of characteristic to mysticism was what figures such as al-Qusyairi and al-Ghazâlî were striving for when they attempted a rapprochement between the *syari'ah*-oriented (*ahl al-syarî'ah al-fiqh*) and the Sufi-oriented (*ahl al-haqîqah*) ulama. It was this effort that eventually led to the birth of the concept of neo-Sufism. See Azra, *Jaringan Ulama*, p. 109.
112. This book is now printed at the end of the book by Syekh Arsyad al-Banjari, *Sabîl al-Muhtadîn li Tafaqquh Amr fî al-Dîn* (Cairo: Dar al-Fikri, n.d.).
113. Abdul Rahman Haji Abdullah, *Pemikiran Umat Islam*, p. 127.
114. See Karel Steenbrink, *Kitab Suci atau Kertas Toilet? Nuruddin al-Raniri dan Agama Kristen* (Yogyakarta: IAIN Sunan Kalijaga Press, 1988), p. 5. A similar discussion can also be found in Steenbrink's other book, *Kawan dalam Pertikaian: Kaum Kolonial Belanda dan Islam di Indonesia (1596–1942)* (Bandung: Mizan, 1995), pp. 187–89.
115. Karel Steenbrink, *Kitab Suci atau Kertas Toilet?*, p. 29.
116. Muhd. Saghir Abdullah refers to him as Syekh Abd al-Rauf bin Ali al-Fansuri. There is uncertainty amongst historians as to whether Abd al-Rauf al-Sinkili and Abd al-Rauf bin Ali al-Fansuri are one or two people. Hamka in his book *Sejarah Umat Islam*, vol. 5, p. 879, for instance, states that there were two Syekh Abd al-Raufs in Aceh: one from Sinkel and one from Barus (Fansur). However, in other books, Hamka contradicts this when he writes: "I now proclaim to enthusiasts of history, that I have amended the negligence of Sejarah Umat Islam IV. And for the greatness of knowledge I now hold to the fact that Sheik Abd al-Rauf is only one man, but I will refer again to two men if someone finds reliable facts [to support such a claim]". See Hamka, *Antara Fakta dan Khayal Tuanku Rao* (Jakarta: Bulan Bintang, 1974), p. 195. This argument is also evident in A. Hasjmi's work that states that al-Sinkili is a Malaysian from Fansur, Sinkil, on the western coast of Aceh. Al-Sinkili's father is the older brother of Hamzah Fansuri. However, Azyumardi Azra doubts whether al-Sinkili is the nephew of Hamzah Fansuri, but does not ignore the possibility that they could be related. See Azra, *Jaringan Ulama*, pp. 189–90.

117. This is evident in the introduction to the book, as cited by A. Hasjmi, that reads: "The majesty said to me concerning the religion of God's Prophet, that Her Majesty wants a book in Javanese which will be distributed to the religious leaders specialised in Islamic law from the Syafi'i school of thought". See A. Hasjmi, *59 Tahun Aceh Merdeka di Bawah Pemerintah Ratu* (Jakarta: Bulan Bintang, 1977), p. 109.
118. Azra, *Jaringan Ulama*, p. 200.
119. Abdul Rahman Haji Abdillah, *Pemikiran Umat Islam*, p. 127.
120. Ibid., p. 160.
121. Ahmad Daudy, *Allah dan Manusia*, pp. 42–44.
122. Azra, *Jaringan Ulama*, pp. 212–32.
123. Ibid., pp. 232–39.
124. Karel Steenbrink, *Beberapa Aspek Islam Indonesia Abad ke-19* (Jakarta: Bulan Bintang, 1983), p. 100.
125. Anwar Harjono, *Hukum Islam Keluasan dan Keadilannya* (Jakarta: Bulan Bintang, 1987). p. 92.
126. Steenbrink, *Beberapa Aspek*, p. 91.
127. Ibid., pp. 254–55.
128. Muhd. Saghir Abdullah, *Perkembangan Ilmu Fiqh*, pp. 46–48.
129. For further information, see A. Hasjmi, *Sumbangan Kesusasteraan Aceh dalam Pembinaan Kesusasteraan Indonesia* (Jakarta: Bulan Bintang, 1977), pp. 48–57.
130. Quoted from Muhd. Saghir Abdullah, *Perkembangan Ilmu Fiqh*, pp. 59–60. The four pillars of *syahadat* are to believe in the Essence of God, the attributes of God, the acts of God, and the truth of the Prophet.
131. Muhd. Saghir Abdullah, *Perkembangan Ilmu Fiqh*, pp. 60–61.
132. Abdul Djamil, *Perlawanan Kiai Desa*, pp. 91–99.
133. See Ali Munhanif, "Islam dan Gerakan Petani", in *Ensiklopedi Dunia Islam*, vol. 5, pp. 238–42.
134. For a short biography of al-Nawawi, see Chaidar, *Sejarah Pujangga Islam, Syaikh Nawawi al-Bantani Indonesia* (Jakarta: Sinar Harapan, 1978).
135. For a review of *'Uqûd al-Lujain*, see Naqiyah Mukhtar, "Hak dan Kewajiban Suami-Isteri dalam pandangan Kitab Kuning: Studi terhadap kitab syarah *'Uqûd al-Lujain fi Bayân huqûq al-Zawjain* karya Muhammad Umar Nawawi al-Bantani", *Ulumul Qur'an* 7, no. 4 (1997): 26–34. The book *'Uqûd al-Lujain* has recently been criticized by a number of activists from the Forum for the Study of Classical Texts (Forum Kajian Kitab Kuning, FK3) in the book *Wajah Baru Relasi Suami-Isteri, Telaah Kitab 'Uqûd al-Lujjain* (Yogyakarta: LKiS, 2001). This book in turn was harshly criticized by several *santri* and *kiai* from Pasuruan *pesantren*, in the book titled *Menguak Kabatilan dan Kebohongan Sekte FK3 dalam Buku "Wajah Baru Relasi Suami-Isteri, Telaah Kitab 'Uqûd al-Lujjain* (Pasuruan: RMI Cab. Pasuruan, 2004).
136. Muhd. Saghir Abdullah, *Perkembangan Ilmu Fiqh*, p. 128.

137. Ibid., pp. 124, 138, 145.
138. Martin van Bruinessen, *Kitab Kuning*, p. 128.
139. For more on the politics of Islamic law in Indonesia, see Marzuki Wahid and Rumadi, *Fiqh Mazhab Negara, Kritik Atas Politik Hukum Islam di Indonesia* (Yogyakarta: LKiS, 2001).
140. KH MA Sahal Mahfudh, "Bahsul Masail dan Istinbath Hukum NU: Sebuah Catatan Pendek", in *Kritik Nalar Fiqih NU*, by M. Imdadun Rahmat (Jakarta: Lakpesdam NU, 2002), p. xiii.
141. NU's fiqh decisions through the *Bahts al-Masâil* Body have recently been compiled in the book by KH Aziz Masyhuri, *Ahkam al-Fuqaha: Masalah-Masalah Keagamaan Hasil Muktamar dan Munas Ulama NU 1926–1994* (Surabaya: Dinamika Press, 1997).
142. Abdurrahman Wahid, "Peranan Umat dalam Berbagai Pendekatan", in *Kontroversi Pemikiran Islam di Indonesia* (Bandung: Rosdakarya, 1990), p. 196.
143. KH Hasyim Asy'ari, *Tsalâts Munjiyât: Muqaddimah wa Khuthbah wa Risâlah* [The Three Saviours: Fundamental Law-Speech-Important Advice] (Jombang: Pondok Pesantren Tebu Ireng, 1994), p. 26. See also *Al-Qanûn al-Asâsi li Jam'iyyat al-Nahdlat al-'Ulamâ*, translated by KHA Abdul Hamid (Kudus: Menara Kudus, 1971), pp. 53–54.
144. KH Hasyim Asy'ari, *Tsalâts Munjiyât*, p. 22.
145. MA Sahal Mahfudh, *Nuansa Fiqih Sosial* (Yogyakarta: LKiS, 1994), p. 26.
146. *Taqrir jama'i* for NU ulama refers to the collective effort to select one of several *qawl*. See Aziz Masyhuri, *Ahkam al-Fuqaha*, p. 364.
147. *Ilhaq al-masâil bi nadhairihâ* is to generalize one legal case/issue that has not been resolved clearly in valid (*mu'tabar*) fiqh texts to a similar case that has been clearly resolved in valid fiqh texts. See Aziz Masyhuri, *Ahkam al-Fuqaha*, p. 364. This procedure is much the same as the *qiyas* (analogy) method known in *ushûl al-fiqh* (Islamic jurisprudential principles). The difference is that the former (*Ilhaq al-masâil bi nadhairihâ*) refers to valid explanations of texts, while the latter (*qiyâs*) uses the original laws found in the Qur'an and Hadith.
148. See *Keputusan Munas Alim Ulama dan Konbes Nahdlatul Ulama di Bandar Lampung* (Jakarta: LTN PB NU, 1992), pp. 5–6. Following the schools of thought by adhering to their *qawl* involves adhering to the opinions and explanations that have already been produced by that school of thought, while adhering to the schools in a *manhaji* manner involves adhering to the school's specific way of thought. *Qawl* are the opinions of the imams of each school of thought, while *wajh* are the opinions of the ulama of each school. *Ilhâq al-masâil bi nadhâirihâ* is to generalize one legal issue that has not been discussed in a text to a similar case that has been discussed.
149. Azis Masyhuri, *Ahkamul Fuqaha*, p. 367.
150. See A. Malik Madani, "Pola Penetapan Hukum Nahdlatul Ulama, antara Fakta dan Cita", in *Dialog Pemikiran Islam dan Realitas Empirik*, edited by

M. Masyhur Amin and Ismail S Ahmed (Yogyakarta: Pustaka Pelajar, 1993), p. 166.
151. MA Sahal Mahfudh, *Nuansa Fiqih Sosial*, pp. 45–46.
152. Ibid., p. 30.
153. KH Azis Masyhuri, *Ahkamul Fuqaha*, p. 301.
154. Martin van Bruinessen, *Kitab Kuning, Pesantren dan Tarekat* (Yogyakarta: LKiS, 1995), pp. 118–19.
155. Translated from Ch. M. Mahfoezh Siddieq, *Debat tentang Idjtihad dan Taqlied* (Soerabaia: H.B.N.O., n.d.), p. 36.
156. KH Hasyim Asy'ari, *Tsalâts Munjiyât*, p. 30.
157. Martin van Bruinessen, *Tarekat Naqsyabandiyah di Indonesia* (Bandung: Mizan, 1992), p. 47.
158. 'Abd al-Razaq al-Kasyani, *Ishtilâhât al-Shufiyyat* (Cairo: Dâr al-Ma'ârif, 1984), p. 84.
159. For further explanation of *maqâmât* and *ahwâl*, see Abu Nashr al-Sarrâj al-Thûsî, *al-Lumâ'* (Cairo: Maktabah al-Tsaqâfah al-Dîniyyah, n.d.), pp. 65–101. See also J. Spencer Trimingham, *The Sufi Orders in Islam* (London: Oxford University Press, 1973), pp. 3–4.
160. Martin van Bruinessen, *Tarekat Naqsyabandiyah di Indonesia*, p. 15.
161. For a more elaborate explanation of neo-Sufism, see Azyumardi Azra, *Jaringan Ulama*, p. 109.
162. Martin van Bruinessen, *Kitab Kuning*, p. 200.
163. For further information on this matter, see Fazlur Rahman, *Islam*, translated by Ahsin Mohammad (Bandung: Pustaka, 1984), pp. 201–2.
164. Thaha 'Abd al-Bâqi' Surûr, *Alam Pikiran al-Ghazâli* (Jakarta: Pustaka Mantiq, 1993), p. 64.
165. Al-Imâm Abi Hamid Muhammad Ibn Muhammad al-Ghazâlî, *Ihyâ 'Ulûm al-Dîn* (Dâr al-Ihyâ al-Kutub al-'Arabiyah, n.d.), p. 125.
166. Nevertheless, this "middle path" *tasawuf* is not without its critics. The liberal groups criticize it for its conservativeness, while the conservatives criticize al-Ghazâlî for being too liberal. The philosophers criticize it for its orthodoxy and the orthodox groups criticize it for its philosophy. However, it seems that these critics have not been able to alter the position of al-Ghazâlî as the "saviour" of Sunni *tasawuf*. For more see, M. Saeed Sheikh, "Influence of al-Gazâli", in *A History of Muslim Philosophy*, edited by M.M. Syarif (Weesbaden: Otto Harrasowits, 1963), p. 638.
167. The liberalism and radicalism of al-Bustami, al-Hallaj, and Ibn al-'Arabi's thinking denied the concrete reality of humankind in the *maqâmât* (tiers/levels) concept. The process of spiritual maturity, they argue, begins with denial or negation of concrete human consciousness (*fanâ'*) in order to attain an eternal consciousness (*baqâ'*) and then attain a higher level, in either the form of *ittihâd*, *hulûl*, or *wihdat al-wujûd*. Junaid al-Baghdâdî and al-Ghazâlî both

criticized these ideas based on the idea that the concrete reality of humankind through *maqâmât* could only be restricted at the levels of *mahabbah* and *ma'rîfat*. *Mahabbah* means love of God, while *ma'rîfah* is love of God through one's soul. Both are often seen as two *maqâmât* or levels that cannot be separated. There are at least seven *maqâmât* that have to be passed through, namely: *taubah*, *warâ'*, *zahud*, *faqir*, *shabar*, *tawakkal*, and *ridla*. Each *maqâm* is traversed through a winding struggle that requires spiritual perseverance. For more, see Abu Nashr al-Sarrâj al-Thûsî, *al-Lumâ'* (Cairo: Maktabah al-Tsaqâfah al-Dîniyyah, n.d.), pp. 65–101.

168. Dr. Lathiful Khuluq, MA, *Fajar Kebangunan Ulama, Biografi K.H. Hasyim Asy'ari* (Yogyakarta: LKiS, 2000), p. 50.
169. Ibid., p. 51. KH Hasyim Asy'ari's ban on celebrating the anniversary of his death did not have a significant influence on the attitudes of other NU ulama. In fact, the Second Congress of Jam'iyyah Ahl al-Thariqah al-Mu'tabarah decided that celebrating death anniversaries was allowed. This decision was reinforced by the decision of the Second Conference of the NU Central Board's Legislative Council in Jakarta in 1961, which acknowledged that the practice contained three aspects: (1) holding a pilgrimage to the grave and praying; (2) giving food to others on behalf of the deceased; (3) reading verses of the Qur'an and listening to *mau'idhah hasanah* (advice). This anniversary was held to model the figures being remembered. See Aziz Masyhuri, *Masalah Keagamaan Hasil Muktamar dan Munas Alim Ulama Nahdlatul Ulama ke Satu-1926 sampai ke Dua Puluh Sembilan 1994* (Surabaya: PP RMI and Dinamika Press, 1977), p. 233. NU ulama are of the opinion that such practices are allowed in Islam.
170. Dr. Lathiful Khuluq, MA, *Fajar Kebangunan Ulama*, p. 53.
171. The word "al-Nahdliyyah" at the end of the organization's name was only added in 1979 when conflict broke out during the meeting as a result of the political temptations of the New Order. When Golkar sought support from the Muslim community in the 1970s, the party paid special attention to *tarekat* teachers who had many obedient followers. A key figure that Golkar managed to seduce was KH Musta'in Ramli, who led a *pesantren* and the the *tarekat* network of Qadiriyah wa Naqsyabandiyah. In 1973, the organization had become a Golkar crony. The choice Kiai Musta'in Ramli had made inevitably provoked internal problems because of his persistance in campaigning for Golkar. The conflict peaked during the NU Congress of 1979, when the *tarekat kiai* elected new management and added the "al-Nahdliyyah" to signify that the organization chose NU as its parent organization and not Golkar. For more, see Bruinessen, *NU, Tradisi*, pp. 169–80. See also Bruinessen, *Kitab Kuning*, pp. 312–14.
172. Bruinessen, *NU, Tradisi*, p. 171.
173. Outside of these orders, there is in fact another, the Tijaniyah order, which is followed by many NU people; however, its validity is debatable. In the

lead-up to the 27th NU Congress in Situbondo in 1984, the Sixth Congress of Jam'iyyah ahl al-Thariqah al-Mu'tabarah al-Nahdliyyah was held in Nurul Qodim *pesantren* in Probolinggo, which questioned the veracity of the Tijaniyah order. However, the discussion, to which no Tijaniyah followers were invited, was unable to successfully agree about the order's validity or lack thereof. Controversy over the Tijaniyah order actually emerged as early as 1930 and was marked by hostility between Buntet *pesantren* in Cirebon, the centre of the Tijaniyah order, and Benda *pesantren* in Kerep, Cirebon, which still had family ties to Buntet *pesantren* but was anti-Tijaniyah.

174. See Martin van Bruinessen, *Kitab Kuning*, p. 308. The man known as the founder of this "new *tarekat*" was an Indonesian Sufi named Ahmad Khatib al-Sambasi (d. 1878 CE), who was born in Sambas, West Kalimantan, but lived and taught in Mecca in the middle of the nineteenth century. As a *khalîfah* (assistant sheik), he took the oaths of a number of students from Southeast Asia, the most famous of which was Abdul Karim. It is Abdul Karim who is mentioned in colonial literature as being involved in the peasants' revolt in Banten in 1888 CE.
175. For a more in-depth examination, see Fawaizul Umam, "Modal Sosial NU, Ekonomi Pemberdayaan Warga Nahdliyyin", *Gerbang* 5, no. 12 (2002).
176. For more on NU's other economic empowerment and social concern programmes (*syu'ûn ijtimâ'iyyah*), see Martin Van Bruinessen, *NU, Tradisi, Relasi Kuasa*, pp. 248–57.
177. Throughout the intellectual genealogy of NU ulama, especially in the first NU generation of figures such as KH Hasyim Asy'ari, KH Wahab Hasbullah, and KH. Bisri Syansuri, Mecca and Medina were seen as the centre of NU's intellectual orientation, as with the ulama before them. Almost all NU ulama have studied in Mecca. Research that proves this can be found in Abd. Rachman, "The Pesantren Architects and Their Socio-Religious Teachings (1850–1950)" (Dissertation, UCLA, 1997). In this dissertation, Abd. Rachman examines the intellectual genealogy of five key ulama who could be described as the foundation of NU intellectualism. They were Nawawi al-Bantani (d. 1897), Mahfuz al-Tirmasi (d. 1919), Khalil Bangkalan (d. 1925), Asnawi Kudus (d. 1959), and Hasyim Asy'ari (d. 1947). See also Zamakhsyari Dhofier, *Tradisi Pesantren: Studi tentang Pandangan Hidup Kyai* (Jakarta: LP3ES, 1982).
178. This phenomenon is not unique to NU. In fact, the tradition of Islamic scholarship has long experienced stagnation and standardization through orthodoxization since the third century of the Islamic calendar. In fact, the Islam that was brought to Indonesia and that spread through the archipelago in the twelfth and thirteenth centuries CE was an Islam that was already in decline. As such, developments in NU scholarship are fundamentally a continuation of the intellectual traditions in the wider Islamic world.
179. Mitsuo Nakamura, "Tradisionalisme Radikal, Catatan Muktamar Semarang

1979", in *Tradisionalisme Radikal*, edited by Greg Fealy and Greg Barton, p. 59. The result of this intellectual bias is a strong tendency amongst experts on Islam in Indonesia to pay more attention to "modernist" organizations. As a result, it is no surprise that organizations like Muhammadiyah are considered a more interesting object of study.
180. For a brief explanation, see Rumadi, "Wacana Intelektualisme NU: Sebuah Potret Pemikiran", *Tashwirul Afkar*, no. 6 (1999).
181. There are still remnants of this attitude. There are some conservative NU ulama who continue to pout over anything that smells slightly of the West, including sending (Muslim) students to study Islamic Studies at universities in the West. In the confrontation between "East" and "West", they view the West as the enemy of the East. However, this is not unique to NU. This attitude is rife throughout the Muslim world in general. There are at least three attitudes Muslims display when confronted with the West; that is, they are apologetic, identificative, and affirmative. First, some Muslims display an apologetic or self-defensive attitude by presenting the advantages of Islam, not only as a response to Western political hegemony but also to the challenges of Western intellectualism that question aspects of Islamic "teachings" such as jihad, polygamy, the position of women, and slavery. This response tends to be normative and idealistic, and as such, ignores reality. It is largely a defence mechanism against threats, challenges, and criticism from the outside world. Secondly, an identificative attitude is taken to identify the issues that are being faced and to formulate a response — and at the same time, an Islamic identity in the modern era. Thirdly, an affirmative approach is taken to reemphasize belief in Islam and reinforce the existence of the Muslim community itself. See Azyumardi Azra, *Pergolakan Politik Islam, dari Fundamentalisme, Modernisme hingga Posmodernisme* (Jakarta: Paramadina, 1996), pp. iii–vi.
182. The consolidation of a number of Islamic parties into the United Development Party (PPP) and the nationalist parties (Murba, PNI, IPKI, Parkindo, and the Catholic Party) into the Indonesian Democratic Party (PDI) was announced in 1973, but was only enacted in 1975 in Law No. 3/1975, in order to simplify political parties through the political restructuring programme of the New Order government. The government did so because many political parties were considered a source of political instability. See Syamsudin Haris, *PPP dan Politik Orde Baru* (Jakarta: PT. Grasindo, 1991), p. 158. See also Choirul Anam, *Pertumbuhan dan Perkembangan Nahdlatul Ulama*, pp. 266–68. Almost all books that discuss NU discuss this consolidation, as is the case with those written by Andree Feillard, Martin van Bruinessen, and A. Gaffar Karim.
183. The education of Muslim students in the West cannot be separated from the Indonesian Department of Religious Affairs' policy to cooperate with Western universities. This policy had been pioneered by H.A. Mukti Ali when he was Minister for Religious Affairs, but did not produce satisfactory results. When

Munawir Sjadzali was Minister for Religious Affairs for two periods (1983–93), he cooperated closely with Western universities, including McGill University in Canada; Leiden University in Holland; UCLA, Columbia, Chicago, and Harvard in America; Hamburg in Germany; and Monash University and Flinders University in Australia. Through this cooperation, many young IAIN lecturers from a wide range of backgrounds studied in these Western countries. For a full account, see "An Intellectual Engineering in IAIN", *Studia Islamika* 2, no. 1 (1995). See also Bahtiar Effendy, Hendro Prasetyo, and Arief Subhan, "Munawir Sjadzali: Pencairan Ketegangan Ideologis", in *Menteri-Menteri Agama RI, Biografi Sosial Politik*, edited by Azyumardi Azra and Saiful Umam (Jakarta: INIS, 1998), pp. 369–412. This policy was implemented until the period of Tarmizi Taher and Malik Fadjar, although after Indonesia was hit by the monetary crisis in 1998 the programme was somewhat hampered.

184. The distribution of NU youth who studied at these educational institutes mentioned above could not be tracked, and as such, there is no exact figure. In addition to the lack of data, there are also methodological difficulties in defining the "NU community". What or who is meant by the term? This question is asked because in the field there are some people who come from an NU background, but cannot be defined as playing a role in NU intellectualism.

185. This phenomenon or tendency is not unique to NU, but is a common symptom of Islamic scholarship in Indonesia. For more on these two orientations, see the various reports and articles in *Jurnal Ulumul Qur'an* 5, no. 3 (1994).

186. The intellectual dynamics of the NU youth in Egypt who are members of the Nahdlatul Ulama Students' Association (KMNU) are quite impressive. They cultivate the liberal thoughts of Hassan Hanafi, al-Jabiri, Jamal Banna, and so on, instead of Sayyid Qutub, Yusuf Qardhawi, Fathi Yakan, and the like. For an illustration of these dynamics, see for instance Arsyad Hidayat, "Mencari Islam Alternatif: Perjalanan Seorang Mahasiswa al-Azhar", *Tashwirul Afkar*, no. 8 (2000). See also M. Arif Hidayat, "KMNU, Al-Azhar, dan Generasi Baru", *Tashwirul Afkar*, no. 6 (1999). This enthusiasm for liberalism has recently not only spread to university students, but also into the world of *pesantren* which is often seen as the basis of NU conservatism.

187. See for instance Harun Nasution's inverview, "Antara Pembaharuan dan Pemurnian", *Pesantren* 5, no. 1 (1988): 30–36.

188. H.A.R. Gibb, *Aliran-Aliran Modern dalam Islam* [original title: *Modern Trends in Islam*] (Jakarta: Rajawali Press, 1990), p. 1.

189. Personal observations reveal that many NU youth followed IAIN's lecture training programme as initial training before studying overseas. These NU youth mainly originated from Walisongo IAIN in Semarang, Central Java; Sunan Ampel IAIN in Surabaya, East Java; Sunan Kalijaga IAIN in Yogyakarta, and several from Syarif Hidayatullah IAIN in Jakarta. The reason so many

came from Java is because NU is primarily based in this region. Though there were some students from outside of Java and West Java, there were only a few.
190. This distinction is perhaps not so accurate if the two communities are divided diametrically. It must be acknowledged that a large number of those active in the NU intellectual movement have studied at university. Rather, this distinction is only used as an analytical tool to examine the tendencies in the field.

3

NU AND THE ISLAMIC POST-TRADITIONALIST DISCOURSE

THE LANDSCAPE OF THE ISLAMIC POST-TRADITIONALIST DISCOURSE

Islamic post-traditionalism is still debated, both the term itself and the substance of the concept. The term "post-traditionalism" is uncommon; not only is it not found in the dictionary,[1] the prefix "post" attached to the term "tradition" suggests passing, surpassing, discarding, and abandoning tradition. However, the soul of the movement is actually about transforming and revitalizing tradition, not abandoning it. Meanwhile, the substance and discourse of thought that has developed is often considered unclear and as if to simply emphasize the traditional identity of the educated NU community.

The absence of the term in dictionaries is not a reason to not use the term. Dictionaries are constructions from reality, and thus the absence of a term from the dictionary is not a valid argument to suggest that the phenomenon it describes does not exist. In addition, if we interpret the term "post" as surpassing or abandoning tradition, this is not very satisfactory, because the term "post" also contains an understanding of continuity and change.[2] However, the accusation concerning the substance of the concept does indeed require serious thought. Those who coined the term must be able to prove that post-traditionalism is not just a continuation of the tension between the traditionalists and modernists using more sophisticated and theoretical tools, but is indeed the result of a long struggle of intellectual transformation. This community did not emerge out of the blue, but through an intellectual struggle with quite a deep traditional consciousness — traditional in both the sense of behaviour but also in the sense of a vast wealth of thought.

The emergence of this community can be traced back to when NU declared its return to the Khittah of 1926 in 1984. Besides the various interpretations of the Khittah of 1926, the moment opened up sufficient space for NU members to form a new group oriented more towards intellectual development.[3] Abdurrahman Wahid was the determining force behind this emerging passion of NU intellectualism.[4] Although this led to tension with senior ulama as a result of this group's intellectual "mischief", the presence of Abdurrahman Wahid with his intellectual capital and blue blood protected this "naughty" or "mischievous" group and eased tension. Nevertheless, in comparison to the number of NU members, this group was very small and often exposed to extraordinary political temptations.[5] Such temptations came largely during the reformation, which society welcomed, for instance, by forming political parties. NU, being a social force with a very real mass support base, was also tempted into establishing the National Awakening Party (PKB) on 23 July 1998.

The generation of NU youth who had made Abdurrahman Wahid the force behind the non-political NU movement were filled with much anxiety to see him establish a political party. Their anxiety stemmed from the dilemma of whether to stay true to their cultural convictions and the agenda of civil society empowerment and development of intellectualism by playing politics without a platform, or to enter the arena of practical politics by becoming activists of the party. The temptation became only more powerful when Abdurrahman Wahid was elected as the fourth President of the Republic of Indonesia in October 1999. Abdurrahman Wahid had his own reasons for changing the form his movement took. On the establishment of PKB, he argued that NU activists and sympathizers needed guidance with their electoral choices, a life and death issue for NU. After the reformation, he said, NU had to reconsider its political strategy.

Because of its mass power base, Abdurrahman Wahid argued for its own party so that NU could speak with one voice and avoid being used by other political parties whose interests were at odds with NU's interests.[6]

In this situation, many NU youth with potential eventually decided to become political activists of parties or of organizations under various parties, not only PKB but also other political parties that relied on support from NU, such as PKU, PNU, SUNI, and even PPP. The PKB youth figures such as Muhaimin Iskandar, Ali Masykur Musa, and Chotibul Umam Wiranu were people that had previously been known as the intellectual figures of the NU youth. Some, however, remained committed to the cultural-intellectual struggle and became NGO activists, academics, authors, and so on. They chose the cultural path and all the risks it entailed, despite the fact that they would receive less publicity and a much smaller income. Those who chose the former were indeed much more prosperous than those who chose the latter.

Without intending to polarize the two choices, the post-traditionalist community was born out of the struggle of the cultural group. It is this group that is often referred to by observers as the new layer in the NU intellectual movement. This occurred in nearly all large cities in Java and outside of Java, including Jakarta, Surabaya, Yogyakarta, Semarang, Malang, Bandung, and Lampung. More recently, this group became aware of the importance of synergizing its collective intellectual strength into a community that has started to refer to itself as the post-traditionalist community. This community is comprised of NGO activists who are culturally affiliated with NU, such as LKiS in Yogyakarta, eLSAD in Surabaya, PP Lakpesdam NU in Jakarta, P3M in Jakarta, Desantara in Jakarta, ISIS in Jakarta, Averos in Malang, and INCReS in Bandung.

The term post-traditionalism does not refer to their group identity, but to the way of thinking and the character of the movement. This becomes more evident in light of the reality that the involvement of the NU masses in practical politics has had an extraordinary effect on the lives of NU members. They were shaken when their political foundations were first uprooted, followed by the resignation of Abdurrahman Wahid from the presidency. In fact, Abdurrahman Wahid's resignation, with all the negative impacts it had within the NU community, further convinced the community that the cultural struggle was the right choice for NU and its members. Thus, the choice to continue to develop their cultural-intellectual work was not a mistake.

The term post-traditionalism first appeared when the Institute for Social and Institution Studies (ISIS), an NGO managed by NU youth in Jakarta, organized a discussion concerning the emergence of the new intellectual passion amongst NU youth on 27 May 2000 in Jakarta. The reverberations it caused spread widely, especially after LKiS made post-traditionalism its ideological basis in a strategic planning meeting in May 2000 in Kaliurang, Yogyakarta. It was this ideology that then became the title for Ahmad Baso's translations of a number of Muhammad Abed al-Jabiri's writings. Up to this point, although the term post-traditionalism had spread widely, there had been no academic exploration of the epistemological basis of the term. Although Ahmad Baso's translation used the phrase "Islamic Post-Traditionalism", it did not explain at all what it might mean. Several months later two ISIS activists, Muh. Hanif Dakhiri and Zaini Rahman, contributed a little with their book *Post-Tradisionalisme Islam, Menyingkap Corak Pemikiran dan Gerakan PMII* (Jakarta: Isisindo Mediatama, 2000). ISIS then published a bulletin under the title *Post-Traditionalism*. The post-traditionalist discourse continued to mature, and Lakpesdam NU undertook a rather serious study of the theme in the journal *Tashwirul Afkar* (no. 9, 2000). After this, post-traditionalism became a public discourse that featured in many discussions and seminars and received media coverage.[7]

The issue of *Tashwirul Afkar* mentioned above bore a front cover on which was written "Islamic Post Traditionalism: Ideology and Methodology". It contained a number of articles intended to provide a framework for the ideology and methodology of post-traditionalism. Generally speaking, the post-traditionalist community is aware that their emergence was due in part to the ingrained nature of the modernist–traditionalist dichotomy that has very strong roots in the history of Islam in Indonesia. This was not just the result of NU always claiming to be a traditionalist group, but also because of the feeling that a number of progressive-thinking NU figures were considered more modern than the modernists.

In irritation, Abdul Mun'im DZ, an NU youth leader who became a researcher at LP3ES, wrote:

> The comments of a number of modernist figures concerning the breakthrough in the thought of the NU youth, that they call more modern, are naive, because NU has never used a modernist paradigm, as have the modernists, in light of the fact that they prefer to use a Marxian paradigm or variations of other paradigms. This issue has increasingly found its form in the thought of Hassan Hanafi, Muhammad Arkoun, Nasr Hamid Abu

Zayd, and Muhammad 'Abid al-Jabiri. These thinkers not only have an appreciation for tradition, coupled with enthusiasm for renewal, but also have a high social commitment. It is for this reason that the community calls itself a post-traditionalist Islamic group.[8]

This quote gives a sufficient picture of the post-traditionalist struggle, both in relation to other Islamic communities and in relation to the intellectual interaction that inspired the community. Their struggle with other groups, such as the modernist groups which are largely represented by Muhammadiyah and the Islamic Students' Association (HMI), influenced the development of the intellectual movement of the NU youth. Meanwhile, their intellectual inspiration was more influenced by the progressive thought developing in the modern Arab world.

On the basis of the above illustration, there are several factors that influenced the intellectual movement of the NU youth which then crystallized into the post-traditionalist community. First, there was the factor of political developments. This factor was important because all dynamics throughout NU's history, both structural and cultural, were highly influenced and determined by political developments. The decision to return to the Khittah of 1926 in 1984, which was very much influenced by the New Order's project of political restructuring, had a significant impact on NU's socio-intellectual movement. The change to national politics in 1998 also had an impact on the NU community. On the one hand, there was a strong political movement which was marked by the establishment of PKB and several other political parties based on the NU masses; but on the other hand, a minority of youth, especially those who were NGO activists, maintained their distance from politics and continued their socio-intellectual movement.

Secondly, competition between the modernist and traditionalist groups, although unspoken, continued to exist within the psychology of the NU youth. However, this competition was very different from the competition within the first NU generation. While the competition of the first generation was more theologically nuanced and had an impact on political competition, the competition of the following generations was more intellectual, although the characteristics of the initial competition were not entirely lost. This competition was very much felt and was present within the discourse that then emerged.

Thirdly, the emergence of a progressive intellectual current in the Arab world helped motivate and give inspiration to the passion of post-traditionalist intellectualism. In fact, the discourse that developed and the themes that were taken and intellectually discussed were those found in the works of figures such as Nasr Hamid Abu Zayd, Hassan Hanafi, Muhammad Syahrur, and Muhammad 'Abed al-Jabiri.

In a more detailed examination, Laode Ida proposed four key factors that influenced the emergence of what he calls the progressive NU group.[9] The first factor was the presence of internal dynamics and conflict with NU tradition. This conflict was made possible as a result of an increasing number of NU youth (alumni of NU *pesantren*) entering the world of modern education and higher education institutes. This aided their vertical and horizontal mobility. As a result, variations and developments of thought occurred that had to come up against the traditions of the community itself. The meeting between old traditions and these new ones led to an extraordinary struggle that on one level divided the NU community. On the one hand there was a group who continued to criticize and wanted to change tradition, while on the other there was a group who fought to the death to preserve the traditions it had inherited from its predecessors.

The second factor concerned the influence and demands of modernization that came as a consequence of global developments. Modernization penetrated all aspects of social life, with all its pros and cons, requiring NU and its people to be aware of the developments so as not to be left behind. This development was in many ways in conflict with the tradition that had developed within NU, including traditions in behaviour, doctrine, and thought. In the world of education, for instance, the currents of modernization forced the NU community to adjust with a widespread modernization of education. As a result, although there were still *pesantren* that maintained their Salafi traditions, a number formed classical educational institutes with a more structured curriculum. Similarly, in organizational management, NU was required to introduce modern management principles.

The third factor was a concern over socio-political developments. Such concern emerged because NU was highly influenced by political developments. In fact, the change in NU's attitude towards the state and the system it had formed was a reflection of political change. There are several inherent problems here: (1) NU's adventure into politics ignored its primary function as a mass religious organization aimed at developing human resources, neglected its education programme, and so on. (2) As a result, NU became a mass organization controlled by politicians, where its people were exploited for the interests of the political elite.

The fourth factor was the development of human rights movements and democracy in several parts of the world. NU could not underestimate the value of human rights and democracy, which became the "new religion" of the international world, to the extent that NU had to critically review all doctrine and traditions concerned with this new thinking. It is thus understandable why a number of NU NGO programmes paid serious attention to the themes of democracy, gender, human rights, and civil society. This shows that the NU community made a serious effort to accelerate the development of doctrine, tradition and thought, both within the NU community and amongst the Muslim community in general.[10]

A more substantial element of modernization was the emergence of new critical thinking, largely from the West. This thinking was in many ways to counter the tradition of thought that had developed in the NU community. There is a specific note to make concerning the influence of critical thinking from the West. Indonesia's intellectual fever at the beginning of the 1990s over postmodernism, marked by the use of key terms such as deconstruction, *diff rance*, historical discontinuity, discourse, and decentring, had a significant impact on the passion for criticism of the NU youth. It was this passion which was used as a tool to read the doctrine and traditions they possessed. Their criticism itself was the child of the Enlightenment which Emmanuel Kant (1724–1804) saw as the way to free mankind from immaturity, a situation whereby mankind still depended on an authority outside of himself, in the form of tradition, religious dogma or the state. From here Kant formulated the concept of criticism, which in his eyes referred to the attempt to determine the limits and conditions of the likelihood of rationality, and with this determine what we might know, what we might do, and what we might expect.

According to Karl Marx (1818–83), this criticism did not only engage in dialectics of ideas, but was also relevant to emancipatory praxis; that is, the attempt to emancipate oneself from the oppression and alienation brought about by the power relations within society that are not emancipated, are sure to be distorted and biased, and as such are ideological and false. As a result, criticism must attempt to abolish power relationships within society that are reflected in the ownership of the means of production, so that knowledge and rational truth can be attained.[11]

From this illustration, it is clear that the emergence of a new critical layer in the NU community is influenced by many things. This group has certain tendencies which Laode Ida[12] examines. First, it is highly influenced by the progressive new thought that developed in other parts of the world, both in the West and in the Middle East. An intervention of thoughts from the outside world is necessary to renew the domestic traditions and culture of thought that are considered somewhat left behind. According to the theory of modernization, the traditions from outside that must be followed are those that come from developed countries. In this context, NU tradition and culture is considered backward and unable to be relied upon to lead the NU community forward. On this basis, although NU figures such as Abdurrahman Wahid and Masdar F. Mas'udi were very critical of the modernization project, in some respects they could not reject modernization outright.

Secondly, within the group there are figures and agents who pushed for change and had direct roles in the institutional structures that existed. This group not only possessed a good awareness of Islamic traditionalism, but its thinking had also been transformed and influenced by the wealth of other traditions. As such, this group made a significant leap from its old tradition to a new, slightly altered one after struggling intensely with other traditions.

Thirdly, the members of this new generation which had taken a giant leap in tradition were not only critical of other traditions, but were also critical of their own tradition and doctrine. As a result, they were not hesitant to criticize the *ahl al-sunnah wa al-jamâ'ah* doctrine — a doctrine that had never been touched, let alone questioned.[13] Until this point in time these teachings had been considered final; however, through the process of logical confirmation and a struggle with reality, they were now considered no longer able to respond to developments. On this basis, criticism and contextualization of doctrine could not be avoided.

The process of connecting religious doctrine and understanding led the community to continue to correct, criticize, evaluate, reflect on, and talk continuously about it, both individually and collectively. This community sought enlightenment and liberation for a more humane life, which was at times achieved through cultural rebellion and revolutions in thought.

This phenomenon almost became a general tendency for NU activists and several of its organizations, especially PMII (Indonesian Islamic Students' Movement), since the second half of the 1980s, particularly after Abdurrahman Wahid became chairman of NU's executive council. The tabloid *Warta NU* (9 May 1986) chronicled this tendency in a piece titled "Agama itu Dinamis" ("Religion is Dynamic"). Laode Ida directly quoted from this article:

> In reality we have never doubted the perfection of religion. However, religion as a manifestation of human experience and appreciation of the faith humankind holds dear must always be open to the question: is this indeed God's intention?
>
> As such, we understand how religion provides a set of obligations that must be adhered to *(awâmir)* as well as prohibitions that should be avoided *(nawâhi)*. We take both from the texts of the Qur'an and Hadith. What we then practice is a product of our understanding aided by explanations given by *ulama* in their various works, in the fields of *fiqh*, *tauhid*, faith, and so on.
>
> However, does this mean that everything is resolved? Does this mean that all of the problems we face in our everyday life have an answer? Do all *awâmir* reach into every aspect of life that requires regulation? If so, are all *nawâhi* also able to prevent everything that makes humans fall headfirst into the valley of misery?
>
> If textually examined, based only on the characters of the texts we have, we do not hesitate to say that not everything is covered.

This is intentionally quoted at length to show that several years after NU's return to the Khittah in 1984, a critical current began to emerge in the NU community which questioned several aspects of religious tradition and faith. For instance, the question "Is this indeed God's intention?" is a question that attempts to open up a space for dialectics between the holy texts and reality, so that God's intentions are never finalized or restricted in any one interpretation. This theme later received serious attention from NU youth intellectual development programmes concerning the critique of religious discourse.

Themes of progressive thought were initially developed by small academic communities which studied intensely a number of issues concerning religion, philosophy, and social theory. These small groups also provided guidance and advocacy, and helped mobilize action in opposition to injustice.[14] Martin van Bruinessen, a Dutch anthropologist heavily involved in these discussions, especially those by P3M through its *fiqh siyasah* (constitutional jurisprudence) programme, made the following comment:

> In discussions within the older *santri* circles and university students who come from an NU background, debate and the search for a new discourse is very much alive. Many among these youth have experience in a number

of community development activities, and have a concern for issues of social justice and the economy. The student organisation affiliated with NU, PMII, has over the last few years become a student organisation concerned with intellectual debate. In contrast with modern students, PMII members usually have a better grasp of traditional sciences, but they are usually more widely read than their purely traditional counterparts. While modernist students are still very much influenced by figures such as Maududi and Sayyid Qutb, PMII students display a big interest in more radical figures such as Hassan Hanafi, the Egyptian philosopher. Discussions in this community have recently turned to the issues of Third World underdevelopment, economic injustice, and human rights including women's rights in Islam. Such debate within this student community will increasingly place pressure on *ulama* who sit on the advisory council to highlight the same issues and rethink many of the established *fiqh* views.[15]

This statement of Martin's describes the psychological atmosphere of the NU community involved in the intellectual movement, the character of their thought, the inspiration of the movement, and the religious discourse that is being developed. This movement continues to progress and individual communities have their own ways of packaging the intellectual struggle. P3M for instance has developed a discourse of critical-transformative thought through *halaqah* (small study groups) within the *pesantren* circle, which is packaged into programmes such as Fiqih Siyâsah li Mashâlih al-Ra'iyyah (Islamic Politics for Strengthening the Political Rights of the People), Fiqh al-Nisâ' for strengthening the reproductive rights of women, Islamic *halaqah* and the concept of pluralism, *halaqah* on social ideologies, *santri* government, *halaqah* on emancipatory *tafsir* or exegesis, and more recently on emancipatory Islamic discourse.

LKiS has done so as well, in addition to publishing critical-transformative books such as *Kiri Islam/The Islamic Left* (Hassan Hanafi), *Islam dan Pembebasan/Islam and Liberation* (Asghar Ali Engineer), *Masyarakat Tak Bernegara/Stateless Societies* (Abdel Wahab el-Affendi), *Wahyu dan Revolusi/Revelation and Revolution* (Ziaul Haque), *Dekonstruksi Syari'ah/ Deconstructing Syari'ah* (Abdullahi Ahmed al-Na'im), *Tekstualitas al-Qur'an/ Textualising the Qur'an* (Nasr Hamid Abu Zayd), and *Post-Tradisionalisme Islam/Islamic Post-Traditionalism* (Muhammad 'Abed al-Jabiri). These published books imply the existence of a very strong vision of developing critical thinking and thought. They show a subversive spirit towards tradition and the environment within the community. The title *Dekonstruksi*

Syari'ah/Deconstructing Syari'ah for the translation of An-Na'im's book *Toward Islamic Reformation* shows that the enthusiasm for deconstruction that had developed in postmodernism has had a strong influence on this community.

In addition, LKiS also disseminates ideas through its Study Together programme which involves students from Yogyakarta, East Java, Central Java, and West Java. The programme emphasizes themes such as criticism of religious discourse, criticism of Islamic political discourse, criticism of gender discourse, and criticism of cultural discourse. Recently the community also started publishing about 30,000 prints of its Friday bulletin, *al-Ikhtilaf*, which is spread through the regions in which it has networks.

In addition, eLSAD also published Mahmud Mohammad Thoha's very provocative book *Syari'ah Demokratik/Democratic Syari'ah*, and publishes the journal *Gerbang* on themes related to religion and democracy. Lakpesdam NU also has similar programmes. Besides publishing the journal *Tashwirul Afkar* and holding the Education for Development of Ulama Awareness (PPWK) programme attended by young *kiai*, it also published the books *Civil Society versus Masyarakat Madani/Civil Society versus Civilised Society* (Ahmad Baso), *Kritik Nalar Fiqih NU/A Critique of NU Fiqh Reason* (Imdadun Rahmad, ed.), *Islam Pribumi/Pribumi Islam*, and so on.[16]

Desantara, which focuses on religious and cultural programmes, also has programmes for the intellectual development of youth activists. It runs the Emancipatory Madrasah programme, which is focused on criticism of religious discourse, criticism of gender discourse, and criticism of cultural discourse. It also runs cultural *halaqah* (study groups) in several cities, for periodic discussion of the indigenization (*pribumisasi*) of Islam. In addition, Desantara publishes the fortnightly magazine *Syir'ah*, the journal *Desantara*, and the journal *Srinthil*, the latter of which specifically discusses women's issues. Recently, Desantara has begun to publish books with a passion not far different from that of LKiS.

Outside of this community, there are several other groups such as LKPSM in Yogyakarta, an autonomous institute under the Yogyakarta chapter of NU which publishes books, journals, regular studies, research, and training. In addition, there is a group that calls itself Syarikat. It is a network of NU activists and youth from several regions who concentrate on conducting humanitarian research into the NU conflict with the Indonesian Communist Party (PKI), which took place from 1965 to 1966. They aim for reconciliation in order to realize a society that is just, peaceful, and that can come together to resolve humanitarian problems. The group works with YPKP 1965. This NU youth group that was established by Imam Azis, the founder of LKiS and LKPSM, also struggles persistently for equal rights for citizens of the nation, including former PKI members. Syarikat recommends revoking all forms of discriminative legislation, such as TAP MPRS Number XXV/MPRS/1966.[17]

Of course there was some resistance from within NU when these programmes were implemented; however, generally speaking, the young *kiai* who were invited to participate in forums could accept and express appreciation of the new ideas while continuing to hold to their own intellectual traditions. For ideas concerning human rights, gender rights, democratization, the environment, civil society, and so on, they were able to find comparisons with a number of their classical texts, known as the *kitab kuning*. They combined their own intellectual wealth in order to colour and also refine the new ideas, and they often used *pesantren* idioms when applying these ideas. They built a bridge of dialogue between their traditional wealth and the intellectual ideas from the outside world, and as such, there is clear continuity with the intellectual movement and the tradition and vision that they wish to create.[18]

As such, post-traditionalism in the NU community can be understood as a movement for the transformation of tradition. The movement is based on tradition that is continuously honed, renewed, and in dialogue with modernity. From there, tradition is reformed into a new tradition that is very different from the tradition before it. On the one hand there is indeed continuity, but on the other there is discontinuity from the previous tradition. The new tradition is usually accompanied by a liberalization of thought which often criticizes one's own tradition *(ego, al-âna)* and that of others *(al-âkhar)*.

In addition to these internal factors, there are several external conditions that led to the emergence of the post-traditionalist community. First, it was a response towards the development of Islamic thought in Indonesia which began to flare at the beginning of the 1970s. This response made the post-traditionalist community critical of modernity and tradition. Secondly, post-traditionalism emerged as a response to NU's efforts to empower society, led by Abdurrahman Wahid. This critical group of NU youth became supporters of Abdurrahman Wahid's ideas. Thirdly, post-traditionalism was a critical response to the NGO movement that was transforming social, political, economic, and cultural movements, as well as the reformation of Islamic thought.[19] Fourthly, post-traditionalism was a response to the development programme of the New Order government. This project not only prevented criticism or freedom of expression, but also put a stop to almost all humanitarian consciousness, requiring that every aspect of NU thought and thinking be devoted to the national project. The primary objective of the New Order modernization and development was the deification of stability, security, and economic growth. Dissatisfaction over the state development project made the post-traditionalist community critical of the state's power and ideological interests, which were increasingly dominating society's political power. With this motivation, they pursued social analyses to unpack the discourse and practices of the state (statism), which had been intervening in all aspects of society.

ISLAMIC POST-TRADITIONALISM: TRADITION AS THE BASIS FOR TRANSFORMATION

The spirit that rages through all intellectual activities of the post-traditionalist community is a passion to continue to question the established doctrine and tradition, based on ethical values obtained from struggling with several scientific traditions, through studies, research, and publication of books or journal articles. The community contests the validity of the various interpretations of the holy texts, traditions, and ideologies that do not serve the interests of humanity, or go so far as to defile humanity, both in terms of their relevance and in terms of the possibility of manipulation and politicization.[20]

One thing that needs to be noted is that the intellectual movement of the NU youth is based on an awareness to revitalize tradition, that is, an effort to make tradition (*turâts*) the basis for transformation. Here, the post-traditionalist community meets modern Arab thinkers, such as Muhammad Abed al-Jabiri and Hassan Hanafi, both of whom have a high appreciation of tradition as a basis for transformation. Through these figures, post-traditionalism found a starting point for its movement to make religion the spirit of freedom which prioritizes the oppressed, while continuing to see tradition as a point of departure.

As such, Islamic post-traditionalism made tradition its epistemological basis, which was transformed in leaps and bounds to produce a new tradition that had roots that stretched a very long way back to the original tradition, the distance between the two being necessary for a progressive ethos in self-transformation.[21] Tradition here refers to everything that is present and accompanies us here and now, that originates from the past, both our own (Muslim) past and the pasts of others (non-Muslims). This tradition encompasses: (1) meaningful traditions, in the form of cultural traditions or traditions of thought or thinking; (2) material traditions, such as monuments or objects from the past; (3) cultural traditions, or everything that we possess from our past; (4) universal humanitarian traditions, or everything present amongst us, but that comes from the pasts of others.[22] Taking this further, al-Jabiri states that tradition has had two opposing effects on the development of Islamic thought. On the one hand, tradition can promote a spirit to revive (*nahdlah*) or reform all forms of backwardness. Tradition is examined for the spirit of freedom and ability to leap towards a brighter future. On the other hand, tradition can become a mechanism for deflecting all the troubles from the outside world that it is unable to address.[23] In this context, tradition is only a place to seek refuge from the turmoil of the outside world that stuns, and occasionally criticizes, mocks, or humiliates tradition. Al-Jabiri labelled this phenomenon a traditionalistic understanding of tradition (*al-fahm al-turâts li al-turâts*).[24]

Hassan Hanafi also clearly recognizes that tradition is the doorway to, and basis of thought for, transformation and revolution. This is attained through continued criticism of the aspects of tradition that block progress. As a result, Hassan Hanafi proclaimed its influence on human liberation and history. However, like al-Jabiri, Hassan Hanafi also saw the negative side to tradition as well as its positive side. The positive side of tradition lay in interpretation and the benefits that could form the basis of social transformation, while the negative side was dogmatism, and resignation to *qadla'* and *qadar* (predestination or divine will and decree). Here the importance of revitalizing traditions that are considered irrelevant can in fact hinder transformation.[25]

Hassan Hanafi has paid serious enough attention to this transformation of tradition. This is apparent from his project on *al-Turâts wa al-Tajdîd* (Tradition and Renewal). He divides the project into three major agendas, each of which has elaborate and derivative sub-agendas. The first main agenda he mentions is *Mawqifunâ min al-Turâts al-Qadîm* (our attitude towards old tradition). The second agenda is *Mawqifunâ min al-Turâts al-Gharbî* (our attitude towards Western traditions), which is further elaborated in the book *Muqaddimah ilâ 'Ilmi al-Istighrâb* (An Introduction to the Science of Occidentalism). The third agenda is *Mawqifunâ min al-Wâqi'* (our attitude towards reality). Within these three agendas, Hanafi develops a paradigm of interpretation. Hanafi's three major agendas actually represent a dialectical process between the "ego" (*al-âna*) and "the others" (*al-âkhar*). Using this framework, we can see how important tradition is in building a civilization, and that it cannot just be ignored.

So far, it is clear that a critical attitude towards tradition is important to prevent being chained within the confines of the authority of tradition. This is achieved by objectifying (*maudlû'iyyah*) and rationalizing (*ma'qûliyyah*) tradition. Objectifying means contextualizing a tradition within tradition itself, while rationalizing means making tradition more contextualized to contemporary conditions.[26] With both these approaches, tradition no longer acts as something that is present as a part of our existence, which manifests as the subject, but as an object which exists outside of us and which deserves to be studied rationally and objectively.

Objectification and rationalization are possible through structural analysis, with the assumption that tradition is not dead, but is more a system and structure that is created. Structural analysis seeks to break down the structure by making the standardized system a constantly changing variable. This is also a means of liberation from all inherent authority, which in turn opens up the opportunity to establish our own authority. This kind of analysis is also known as deconstruction (*tafkik*), that is, breaking down the standardized and stagnant tradition, and seeing it not as a "structure", but as something that can change, so that tradition is not interpreted as being absolute, final, or ahistorical, but rather fluid, relative, temporal and historical.[27]

A rational, critical, and objective reading of tradition requires an ability to distance "us", as the subject, from tradition, as the object, which al-Jabiri refers to as *fashl al-maqrû' 'an al-qâri'* (separating [the object] which is being read from [the subject] which is doing the reading).[28] This attitude will lead to objectivity (*mawdlû'iyyah*) and a more historical perspective (*târîkhiyyah*) when viewing tradition. However, al-Jabiri also believes that there must be continuity (*istimrâriyah*) in viewing tradition, and as such, he also states that there is a required *washl al-qâri' bi al-maqrû'* (linking of the reader [subject] with the [object] that is being read).[29] Objectivism in this context means separating an object of study from the subject. On the other hand, it also relates the object with the subject, which is influenced by the factors discussed above. These two models are interrelated and interact with one another as intertwined networks, although the two must be separated methodologically.

Commenting on the processes of *fashl* (separating) and *washl* (linking) mentioned above, Ahmad Baso, an NU youth figure who has helped animate the post-traditionalist discourse, writes:

> Separating the reader and the object of said reading is aimed at placing tradition as an object of critical study. This is important for al-Jabiri because when reading its own tradition, the Muslim community often present its past traditions as "that which talks" about the present, as that which seems to have come back to the present with all its glory and brilliance, and without flaw. Muslims refer to their traditions not only to find what they desire, but also to resolve the issues they face in the contemporary era. This is not only so for the traditionalists and the salafis, but also in the modernist or "leftist" groups. While the modernists refer to Western traditions, the "leftists" search for justification of their "leftist" ideas in the Islamic tradition. What then emerges, according to al-Jabiri's observations, is not only this instrumentalist model, which finds "the good things" in tradition in accordance with what is desired, but also the "glorification" of tradition, which ignores criticism towards it.[30]

As such, objectivism represents the end of the reading of tradition. Al-Jabiri[31] offers three approaches that make it possible to attain a level of objectivism in studies of tradition. The first approach is the structural method of studying tradition, which is based on the texts as they are. Texts here are seen as a corpus, a unity, a system. The second approach is historical analysis. This is related to the effort to link the thoughts of the author of a text to his history, to the cultural, political, and sociological realms he exists in. This is important because besides being able to understand the genealogy (tradition) of the thoughts being studied, it also allows us to see the validity of the conclusions being drawn. Validity here is not always logical truth, but historical possibility (*al-imkân al-tarîkhî*), that is, the possibilities which enable us to clearly know what is said in a text, what is not said, and what is never said.

The third approach is ideological critique, which involves expressing the ideological and socio-political functions contained within a particular text, thought, and tradition. This is one way to contextualize a text, thought, or tradition in order to embed the historicity of a historical product. These three approaches are interrelated in the study of tradition.

Awareness of the significance of tradition has received serious attention amongst the NU youth, as they are very aware that their world has been highly influenced by traditions that are passed down from generation to generation. In the context of modernity and reformation, there have been two extreme tendencies in viewing tradition. First, there is the group that continues to deify tradition and does not see the empirical reality that has developed outside of its world. This group has never ideologically critiqued its tradition, and as such, tradition has been treated as one would treat a wildlife reserve. Tradition is never developed, and as a result, it is increasingly alienated from the reality around it and is unable to respond to the problems that arise in society. The second extreme tendency is for tradition to be considered as an obstacle in the way of progress, and as such, it must be sidelined and denied. Members of this group eventually become prisoners of their new tradition, unable to engage in dialogue and negotiations, and as such, they are no less fanatical than the first group in the way they grasp on to modernity. Modernity is not accepted rationally, but emotionally. As a result, they do not grasp the substance of modernity, only its outer layer. This view of modernity not only makes them very pragmatic, but also shallow in viewing and making sense of reality.[32]

In the midst of these two extremes, the post-traditionalist community sought to view tradition critically, historically, and objectively. The members of this community showed no hesitation in criticizing their own traditions, including religious doctrine that had until that time been accepted as it was. They began to question the *ahl al-sunnah wa al-jamâ'ah* doctrine that had been followed for years — both the doctrine itself and its capability and relevance to modern developments — and thus conceived a more transformative humanitarian theology. In the field of fiqh, they also conceived the contextualization of fiqh and the classical texts (*kitab kuning*), which produced fiqh of the people, fiqh of labour, social or *ijtimâ'iyyah* fiqh, political fiqh oriented towards the people, and so on. In the field of *ushûl al-fiqh* (Islamic jurisprudential principles), they also conceived a methodology considered fitting to the developments of the time by creating new principles.

This rethinking of a number of traditions was not undertaken out of an academic demand, but the demands of reality and social developments that necessitated intelligent answers. Had doctrine and tradition been left alone, they would have become increasingly isolated from reality, requiring a revitalization of tradition and its reconnection with reality. The ultimate objective of this movement to revitalize tradition was the attempt to liberate (free) the people from the shackles that bind, including tradition, orthodoxy, culture, and politics.[33]

As such, post-traditionalism is a critical awareness of going beyond tradition in order to give birth to a new tradition that accords with the demands of the present. Post-traditionalism also seeks to find a new way to think and liberate society which values difference, upholds the law, and develops a religious understanding that is inclusive, plural, and democratic. As a result, the post-traditionalist community is sure that analysing tradition critically is the best option in order to build a culture and tradition of thought which pushes for praxis-oriented social transformation.

In reconstructing a new tradition, post-traditionalism, which is inspired by modern thought developed in parts of the modern Arab world, especially by Jabir Ushfur in his book *Qirâ'ah al-Turâts al-Naqdî* (1992), there are three ideological and methodological branches. The first is the eclectic branch (*qirâ'ah al-intiqâiyah*), which requires a blend between originality (*al-ashâlah*) and modernity (*al-mu'âshirah*). Such a combination is necessary in order to remove the negative elements of tradition, while taking the positive ones to be used in responding to contemporary reality. The second branch is the revolutionary branch (*al-qirâ'ah al-tsawriyah*), which seeks to propose a new concept of thought that reflects revolution and liberation of religious thought. Tradition is seen as the door through which to bring alive a spirit of revolution in religion, as with Thayeb Tizinî's *min al-turâts ilâ al-tsawrah* (from tradition to revolution) project, Hassan Hanafi's *min al-'aqîdah ilâ al-tsawrah* (from faith to revolution), or Adones's *min al-tsâbit ila al-mutahawwil* (from absolutism to relativism). The third branch is the deconstructive branch (*al-qirâ'ah al-tafkîkiyah*), which seeks to comprehensively overhaul tradition. This may be attained through developing the epistemologies that developed in Europe, such as post-structuralism, postmodernism, semiotics, and hermeneutics.[34] The development of Western epistemology in Islamic thought has already produced several new ideas, such as the trilogy of Arab reason of Abed al-Jabiri,[35] Muhammad Arkoun's critique of Arab reason, Nasr Hamid Abu Zayd's conception of texts,[36] and Ali Harb's deconstruction of texts and their truth.

This illustration emphasizes that the post-traditionalist discourse that developed within the NU youth community was very much influenced by the development of modern Arabic thought, which was adopted as the eyes through which to read NU tradition and Islamic thought. The enthusiasm this brought with it was in the form of a critical awareness to question tradition and knowledge.[37]

Using these new eyes, the problem that post-traditionalism faces is how to go about reforming religious thought in a way that must critique tradition on the one hand, but on the other must depend on tradition as the basis for transformation. The ulama from the past have formulated an excellent principle, *al-muhâfadhah 'alâ al-qadîm al-shâlih, wa al-akhdzu bi al-jadîd al-ashlah* (maintaining the traditions of the past that are good, and adopting traditions that are new and better), but the problem is actually much more complicated than this formulated principle suggests. The complexity arises out of the tug of war between modernism and tradition.

Conflict between the two is also reflected in how modernity is viewed and responded to, with each presented as a choice, that is, a choice between accepting a Western paradigm of politics, economy, culture, and science; or choosing to maintain tradition, which is seen as an alternative, original model that is able to encompass all aspects of life. The first represents the attitude of the modernists (*ashraniyyûn, hadatsiyyûn*), while the second is clearly traditionalist (*salafiyyûn*). Amidst these assumed two extremes, a third, more eclectic (*intiqâ'î, tawfiqiyyûn*) group has emerged. It seeks to take the best elements, both from the modern Western model and from the Islamic past and traditions, and unite the two in a form that fulfils both these pre-existing models.

These three models have different ideological orientations and variations. Amongst the modernists for instance, there are some who promote liberal, socialist, and even Marxist–Leninist ideologies. There are also those that are narrow nationalists, although there are also some who are more flexible. Similarly in the *salafî* or traditional groups, there are members who are reactionaries and reject all forms of modernity because it is seen as a product of ignorance and infidelity, and thus they call for a pure and original Islam. There are also those who are more moderate and willing to accept elements of Western civilization as long as they do not deviate from Islamic doctrine. Amongst these, there is also a reformist *salafî* group in the sense that it tries to find elements and values in Islamic civilization that accord with the values and institutions of Western civilization. They are not shy in adopting such forms of modernity as new forms for the institutions and values that Islam is already familiar with and considers authentic; for instance, democracy is considered to correspond to the principle of *syûra,* and the system of socialism is related to the zakat (alms) institution, as both represent the needs of the poor. The political attitudes of the *salafîs* are also varied, as there are some who are nationalist, ultra-nationalist, or even pan-Islamist. Similarly, the eclectic group has a number of different expressions. There are some elements within it that are *salafi*-oriented but follow a liberal course, and there are those who are liberal but tend towards being *salafi*-traditionalist. There are international Marxists and nationalist Marxists, liberal nationalists and nationalist socialists, and so on.[38]

Muhammad Abed al-Jabiri asked an interesting question of all these choices: does the issue of Islam, tradition, and modernity represent an issue of choices? Is there indeed room to choose between what is known as the Western model and the authentic Islamic model? According to al-Jabiri,[39] in the context of modernism there actually is no room for such a choice. He argues that Western modernism forced its acceptance in other parts of the world with the launch of colonialism and occupation. On the other hand, the traditionalists also have no choice. We are not faced with a choice because tradition is inherited and we do not have the power to choose our own inheritance, as we do not have the power to choose our pasts. Our past is always a part of ourselves that is taken wherever we go.

Thus, the issue is not about choice, nor is it an issue of integrating the two models; instead it is about the divisions and ambiguities that always accompany life. In fact, more than this, the issue is one of ambiguity and ambivalence in responding to ambiguity itself. This situation of division transpires in almost all aspects of life: social, economic, political, cultural, and even educational. As a result, according to al-Jabiri, a more objective path must be found in order to respond to the issue.[40]

ISLAMIC POST-TRADITIONALISM IN THE CONSTELLATION OF INDONESIAN ISLAMIC THOUGHT

Researchers of Islamic thought in Indonesia — both indigenous researchers such as Bahtiar Effendy, Fachry Ali,[41] Syafi'i Anwar,[42] and Deliar Noer,[43] as well as foreign researchers such as Howard M. Federspiel,[44] Greg Barton,[45] and Kamal Hassan[46] — always use the fundamental categories of traditionalists and modernists as a starting point when mapping the movements of Islamic thought, although with varying explanations.[47] These two fundamental typologies then develop into new variants. From the traditionalists emerge the neo-traditionalists who seek to reform tradition, such as Abdurrahman Wahid, and the post-traditionalists who criticize tradition, by adopting a method of modern thought but continuing to use tradition as a basis for transformation. Meanwhile, the modernists gave birth to neo-modernism, represented by figures such as Nurcholish Madjid and Syafi'i Ma'arif, which then underwent a metamorphosis and became the liberal Islamic movement. However, this group also produced fundamentalist and neo-fundamentalist variants that tend to understand Islamic doctrine textually. This is more clearly represented in Figure 3.1.

In comparison to other movements of thought, the post-traditionalist movement is the youngest of all, in terms of its emergence and institutionalization of the ideas it developed, although sparks that bore the hallmarks of post-traditionalist thought had emerged sporadically well before such ideas were institutionalized. When the discourse of Islamic post-traditionalism stepped into the arena of Islamic thought in Indonesia, it received a variety of responses from several different circles, from the appreciative and the non-committal to the cynical. Some were appreciative because the discourse was perceived as a way to restimulate the dynamics of Islamic thought in Indonesia which, admittedly or not, was walking on the spot, producing no meaningful developments. Some were non-committal because post-traditionalism was seen as not yet having an established epistemological basis, or even not differing from other currents of thought. And lastly, some were cynical because the discourse was perceived as the NU youth's habit of imitation to emphasize their identity. In fact, in Robin Bush's dissertation on the development of thought amongst the NU youth which led to Islamic post-traditionalism and connected it to liberal Islam, she portrayed the development as little more than the continuation of the traditionalist–modernist conflict, just dressed in new clothing.[48]

The emergence of such varied reactions was only fitting, as the pioneers of post-traditionalism were themselves also not one-dimensional, allowing for a variety of motivations and possibilities. Nevertheless, to conclude that the discourse of post-traditionalism was purely to emphasize a certain identity, was old primordialism dressed in new clothes, an intellectual imitation, and so on, seems to be politically biased. Such arguments, although not entirely false, simplify the issue, as there is a more serious issue than simple competition between groups — namely, the way of viewing modernism, tradition, the holy texts, and so on. As such, it is not fitting to read this intellectual agenda through a political perspective

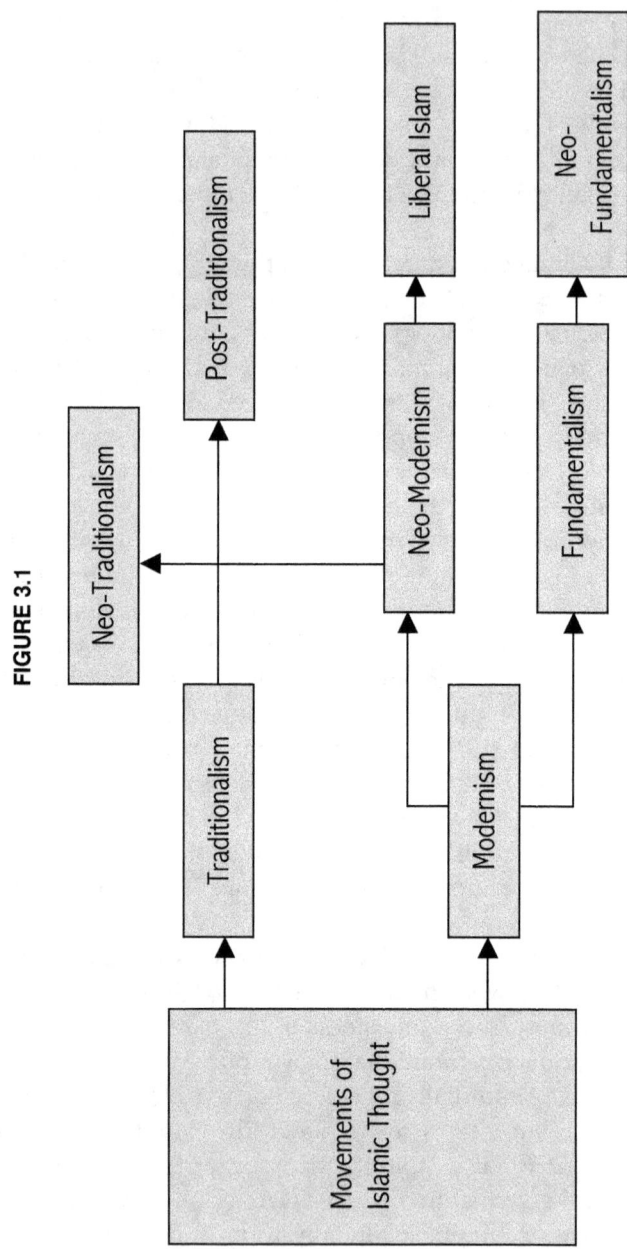

FIGURE 3.1

which only serves to politicize thought. Robin Bush's dissertation was indeed written for political science and, as such, it is understandable that it may contain political bias.

There are several reasons to support this argument. First, the post-traditionalist discourse is voiced largely by a community that is culturally affiliated with NU. NGOs that are concerned with development of thought and that have voiced post-traditionalist themes are also largely culturally affiliated with NU. Secondly, the term traditionalism has become a stamp of identity for NU with its variety of meanings. As such, when the term post-traditionalism emerged, people found it easy to identify it as belonging to NU, or at least to the agenda of the NU youth.[49] Thirdly, the post-traditionalist discourse emerged at the same time that the spirit of liberal Islam became the passion for Indonesian Islamic intellectualism with all its supporting activities, although the main supporter was Ulil Abshar-Abdalla, an intellectual NU youth figure and also head of Lakpesdam NU. Post-traditionalism gave the impression of wanting to be differentiated from liberal Islam, both in terms of epistemology and the basis of its movement. In fact, some people see post-traditionalism as being opposed to liberal Islam.[50] If liberal Islam is viewed as a continuation of the neo-modernism of Fazlur Rahman and Nurcholish Madjid, then post-traditionalism is seen as a continuation of the traditionalism of the NU community. Fourthly, the post-traditionalist theme came to the surface at a time when the political rivalry between the traditionalists and modernists was gaining momentum, that is, when Abdurrahman Wahid became president and the modernist groups sought to destabilize him. In this kind of political situation, a movement will always be viewed from the perspective of political interests.

It is difficult to accept Robin Bush's conclusion that post-traditionalism's connection with liberal Islam is no more than a continuation of the traditionalist–modernist conflict, for a number of reasons. First, examining exactly when the two communities were formed shows that post-traditionalism crystallized before liberal Islam. As mentioned above, post-traditionalism was first mentioned at the beginning of 2000 when ISIS held a discussion on the theme "Islamic Post-Traditionalism: The Intellectual Dialectics of the NU Youth". In the same year, LKiS undertook strategic planning on the theme "Islamic Post-Traditionalism". On the other hand, the liberal Islam community, whose headquarters are on 68H Utan Kayu Street, East Jakarta, only crystallized on 9 March 2011 when the Liberal

Islam mailing list emerged.[51] It is thus not possible that the discourse of post-traditionalism emerged out of rivalry with the modernist groups as represented by the Liberal Islamic Network (Jaringan Islam Liberal, JIL). Secondly, as Robin Bush acknowledges, several NU youth are part of JIL, or at least on their mailing list. In fact, Ulil Abshar-Abdalla, who is head of Lakpesdam NU, is also a JIL coordinator. It is thus not entirely correct to suggest that post-traditionalism and JIL are an evolution of the traditionalist–modernist conflict. Thirdly, the post-traditionalist community is also a form of cultural opposition to politicization within the NU elite. As a result, it has taken an apolitical attitude and maintained a distance from Abdurrahman Wahid's government. For these reasons, the post-traditionalist community was not intended to revive the old conflict by dressing it in "new clothes" as Robin suggests, although individuals from each community may have had such motivations.

Although concerning, this is the reality. The terms traditional and modern and all their derivatives are more than just academic categories; they have become group identities that allow members to differentiate between "us" (*al-âna*) and "others" (*al-âkhar*). Tradition is assumed to be a symbol of backwardness, conservativeness, and ignorance that is old-fashioned, closed off, and so on. Modernity on the other hand is imagined to be about progression, openness, dynamism, intelligence, and so on. These two currents were felt quite strongly when neo-modernism and liberal Islam arose on the one hand, and post-traditionalism emerged on the other. While the former were seen as being of the modernists, the latter was seen as being of the NU traditionalists. Admittedly, this is not healthy for the development of thought, because it encourages a particular way of thinking to become the identity of a group, and not a discourse that can belong to anyone. The question that arises of course is: was there a fundamental difference, especially at the epistemological level, between neo-modernism and liberal Islam on the one hand, and Islamic post-traditionalism on the other, which had become a discourse in Indonesia before either neo-modernism or liberal Islam?

Before further discussing post-traditionalism within the constellation of Islamic thought, it is necessary to examine the typology of Islamic renewal movements that Fazlur Rahman (d. 1989) proposed. Fazlur Rahman, a Pakistani intellectual who moved to Chicago, America, divided the movements of Islamic thought from the last two centuries into four categories.

First, there was the revivalist movement at the end of the eighteenth century, which was marked by the emergence of the Wahabi movement in Saudi Arabia, the Sanusi movement in North Africa, and the Fulani movement in West Africa. These movements did not make contact with the West, and had the following general characteristics:

1. Concern towards the socio-moral degeneration of the Muslim community and an attempt to change it.
2. The appeal to return to pure Islam by purging anything considered to be heretical, superstitious, or mythical as it was considered to defile belief. This movement called for a move away from the establishment and finality of the legal schools of thought and towards *ijtihad* or independent interpretation.
3. The appeal to undertake such renewal if necessary through armed struggle.

The second movement was classical modernism, which emerged in the middle of the nineteenth century and the beginning of the twentieth century and was highly influenced by Western ideas. This movement expanded the content of *ijtihad* to cover aspects such as the relationship between reason and divine revelation, social reform especially in the field of education, the status of women, political reform, and democratic forms of governance. This movement was pioneered by figures such as Sayyid Akhmad Khan (d. 1898) in India and Muhammad Abduh (d. 1905) in Egypt.

The third movement was the neo-revivalist movement. It based itself on the classical modernist basis that Islam encompasses all aspects of human life, both individual and collective. However, in order to differentiate itself from the West, the movement did not accept the method and spirit of classical modernism. However, it was also unable to develop any methodology to stress its own position. The best example of this movement is Abu al-A'la al-Maududi and his Jamâ'ati Islâmi in Pakistan.

The fourth movement was the neo-modernism movement, which sought out a progressive synthesis of modern rationality and interpretation of the classical tradition. According to Fazlur Rahman, although there was great passion for classical modernism, the movement had at least two fundamental weaknesses. First, it did not completely break down the method which was partially implicit in its handling of certain issues and the implications of its fundamental principles. Secondly, the movement unavoidably gave the impression of being an agent of Westernization. Rahman's neo-modernism developed a methodology deemed appropriate and logical that differentiated it from classical modernism.[52]

One very prominent thing that sticks out from Fazlur Rahman's typology is that it makes the West the determinant factor in all the changes that occurred. Harun Nasution also suggests likewise when he proposes that renewal in Islam only began in the eighteenth century, more precisely in 1798 when Napoleon Bonaparte went to Alexandria. From here, Harun Nasution then differentiates between the terms *renewal* and *purification*. While the first emerged because of external factors (Western progress), the second was more a result of internal factors along the theme of purifying the faith from deviance and impurity. While renewal was more oriented towards interpretation of the Islamic doctrine found in the Qur'an and the Hadith, purification was focused more on cleansing the faith from religious practices that had defiled it.[53] As such, Fazlur Rahman's neo-modernism continues to place Western modernism as the gateway to renewal. Meanwhile, tradition is seen both as the objective of renewal, and as the polish that refines modernism so that it smells like tradition. Charles Kurzman more explicitly acknowledged that liberal Islam, which was inspired by neo-modernism, brings tradition and the past back into the present for the interests of modernity, and not for tradition itself.[54]

As it developed, the neo-modernist Islamic movement in Indonesia, which according to Greg Barton was initiated by Nurcholish Madjid, morphed into liberal Islam. Thus, although the history behind their emergence and their genealogies are quite different, recently they have often been seen as identical, both epistemologically and in terms of their intellectual agendas. Greg Barton and Paramadina are the most authoritative on this, as they published the book *Gagasan Islam Liberal di Indonesia: Pemikiran Neo-Modernisme Nurcholish Madjid, Djohan Effendi, Ahmad Wahib dan Abdurrahman Wahid/Liberal Islamic Ideas in Indonesia / The Neo-Modernist Thinking of Nurcholish Madjid, Djohan Effendi, Ahmad Wahib and Abdurrahman Wahid*. Without sufficient explanation of methodology, liberal Islam featured in the main title on the book's cover, giving the clear impression that neo-modernism and liberal Islam were one and the same.[55] To date, no one has questioned this. As a result, this trend will be followed, with neo-modernism and liberal Islam being presented together, although personally I hope that protest arises over the equating of the two terms, especially from those groups that identify themselves with the liberal Islamic movement.

Ahmad Baso, although slightly bombastic, criticizes Greg Barton for placing Abdurrahman Wahid on the one hand and Nurcholish Madjid, Djohan Effendi and Ahmad Wahib on the other, into the same category of neo-modernism and liberal Islam. Of course there is no conflict between them, but they do have different agendas. According to Ahmad Baso, Barton's interpretation of liberal Islam, which allows him to place Abdurrahman Wahid and Nurcholis Madjid into the same group, fails to see the thoughts of the two intellectuals as a system whose elements are interrelated in their historicity and epistemology; rather, he sees them more as a pile of ideas and thoughts, a collection of quotes taken from here and there, without seeing the connections between one idea and the next. As a result, Abdurrahman Wahid's ideas on secularization, indigenization of Islam, and Islam as a social ethic escaped Barton's analysis. Even more scathingly, Ahmad Baso criticizes Islamists such as Barton for being poor in theory and methodology simply because of the ideological burden of orientalism that makes them want to see Islam in a positive light, and as worthy of praise; at the same time, this sacrifices the academic creativity and objectivity of Islamic scholarship.[56] Ahmad Baso's accusations sometimes contain some truth. The character, agenda, and implications of Nurcholish Madjid's thought were clearly different to those of Abdurrahman Wahid. However, with all their limitations, the studies of Greg Barton and other Islamists must be seen as a model, not as an ideology, as with the model Ahmad Baso presents that sees liberal Islam as an ideology.

That Abdurrahman Wahid and Nurcholish Madjid had different agendas, characters, and implications to their ideas is clear-cut. The starting point of Abdurrahman Wahid's thought was very different to that of Nurcholish Madjid. The Islamic neo-modernism that emerged from the tradition of Islamic modernism[57] was not a tradition that Abdurrahman Wahid adhered to. His thoughts were not based on an adoration of modernism, but on a critique of modernism which he universalized through traditionalism. In this context, John L. Esposito and John O. Voll's description of Abdurrahman Wahid as a "modern reformer but not [an] Islamic modernist"[58] is fitting. This sentence not only depicts Abdurrahman Wahid's cultural affiliation and social origins, but also illustrates the character and tradition of his thinking.

Zaini Rahman, an ISIS researcher, holds a similar opinion to Ahmad Baso. He argues that Greg Barton forgets that the modernist movement in Islam has its own history and context. The genealogy of modernist thought, and neo-modernist thought, can be traced back to the Wahabis and Ibnu Taimiyah who snubbed the traditionalists. In Indonesia, the same tendency is present, where the traditionalists and modernists both seek to discredit one another. It is thus irrelevant to say that the traditionalists are related to the modernists. The products of traditionalist thought are independent choices that attempt to radically cultivate and transform the wealth of tradition in response to challenges within society.[59]

Furthermore, there are several arguments used to reject the labelling of NU intellectualism, especially that of Abdurrahman Wahid, as neo-modernist. First, in terms of genealogy of thought and religious understanding, the NU community places more emphasis on continuity of tradition. It is highly resistant to modernist movements because they are considered a threat to tradition. If there are any liberal themes to its thought, it is in attempt to transform its tradition with more progressive thinking, so that such thinking becomes deeply rooted in its tradition and is wide-reaching. Secondly, in terms of the topic and choice of discourse, it seems that there is some resistance towards the phenomenon of symbolism and formalism in Islam, while (some) modernists actually promote Islamic formalism, which is considered unproductive for Islamic movements.[60]

In addition, Ahmad Baso,[61] quoting al-Jabiri's concept of tradition, criticizes the neo-modernist view of tradition. This is worth examining because it shows how post-traditionalism and neo-modernism view tradition. Islamic neo-modernist tradition refers only to Ibnu Taimiyah as its primary reference, and adds to this other traditions that support the authority of purification. This is evident for example in Fazlur Rahman and Nurcholish Madjid's view of Asy'ari's understanding. They read it as moderate Islam that supports social equilibrium, and read his theory on *kasb* (acquisition, a means between predestination and free will) as resembling the Protestant ethics that paved the way for capitalism. More explicitly, Ahmad Baso states that the movement to return to tradition within the Islamic neo-modernist groups is more of an effort to take some aspects of a particular way of thinking that are considered suitable to one's needs, while discarding parts which are irrelevant, or even a hindrance. For example, Asy'ari's theory of acquisition is quoted to show how Muslims have a high work ethic and thus cannot be called lazy, resigned to accept reality, old-fashioned, and opposed to progress.[62] Similarly, when the topic of civil society became a public discourse, the neo-modernists enthusiastically quoted al-Farabi's *al-Madînah al-Fadlîlah* or Ibnu Khaldun's theory on *madaniyah* to justify the concept of civil society.

In the context of vibrant Islamic thought in Indonesia, the emergence of the post-traditionalist discourse, both directly and indirectly, was in dialogue with the rising discourse of liberal Islam, which was deemed unable to accommodate the discourse of thought within the NU community. For more clarity, it is necessary to briefly examine the epistemology of liberal Islam. There are at least two books that elaborate greatly on the term, namely Leonard Binder's *Islamic Liberalism: A Critique of Development Ideologies* (Chicago: The University of Chicago Press, 1988); and Charles Kurzman's words in the introduction to *Liberal Islam, A Sourcebook* (Oxford: Oxford University Press, 1998). However, the term "liberal Islam" itself was first used by Asaf Ali Asghar Fyzee (India, 1899–1981),[63] although he never explained sufficiently what he meant by the term.

Leonard Binder's understanding of Islamic liberalism and Charles Kurzman's liberal Islam present different interpretations and perspectives of the concept. As Kurzman himself recognizes, Binder takes the point of view that Islam represents a subset of liberalism, while Kurzman takes the opposite approach and sees liberalism as a subset of Islam.[64] The consequence of this is that Binder seeks to view the dialogue between Islam and the West openly and allow the two to communicate in a series of give-and-take processes, including with local tradition (in this context Arab tradition). Meanwhile, Kurzman takes the opposite position, focusing more on the Islamic context by examining the thought of liberal Muslims as viewed from the perspective of Islamic tradition. This is why the introduction to his book is titled "Liberal Islam and Its Islamic Context". As such, Kurzman seeks to emphasize that those thoughts that are assumed to be liberal remain within the framework or bounds of Islam. This Islamic context is needed "to examine liberal Muslims in light of Islamic tradition".[65] As a result, while Binder examines how liberal Islamic liberalism is and whether liberal variants accord with Western standards, Kurzman questions whether liberal thought still exists within the Islamic context or not.[66] Kurzman's model of liberal Islam clearly coincides with Islamic modernism as explained at length by Barton.

In adopting Fazlur Rahman's typology, Barton explains that modernism is an open-minded approach to modern developments and rational studies that critically examines the history that has passed before it, but is different to the humanist rationalism which developed in the Christian world almost without restriction as a result of high criticism. Islamic modernism cannot be equated with neo-orthodox or liberal Christian theology, both of which are able to reject divine inspiration in the scriptures. Islamic modernism continues to acknowledge the authority of the Qur'an and argues its superiority over any human creation. As a result, Barton likens Islamic modernism to Protestant thought after the reformation movement, rather than to Christian neo-orthodoxy after the liberalism movement.[67] Barton's findings are identical to Kurzman's Islamic context, which sees the dynamics of Islamic thought always within the framework of doctrine, in the sense that Islamic thought — whatever its form — represents a reflection of religious doctrine, as if there were no other source of wealth that could influence Islamic thought.

The consequence of such a paradigm is that liberal Islam is less able to value local tradition, local beliefs, customs, and so on because they are considered heretical, syncretic, less Islamic, or even a deviation from Islam. This concept is clearly depicted in Islamic liberalist thought when it describes the series of events that led to the birth of liberal Islam. According to Kurzman, Islam's long history is coloured by three traditions. He labels the first tradition as customary Islam, which is marked by a combination between "little traditions" and "great traditions", the latter of which are assumed to be authentic and pure Islam. The Islam that has already been mixed with local or little traditions is considered to be an Islam full of heresy and superstition. This Islam is thus not pure and not authentic because it is deemed to be too accommodative towards local customs, which should have been the target of Islamization.

On this basis, the second tradition emerges, and is called revivalist Islam, which takes the form of fundamentalism and Wahabism. This tradition attempts to purify Islam which has been combined with un-Islamic local traditions that are deemed to have deviated from pure Islamic doctrine. It adopts the jargon of returning to the Qur'an and Hadith. The third tradition then is liberal Islam. According to Kurzman, as a supporter of revivalist Islam, liberal Islam defines itself differently in contrast to customary Islam and hails the primacy of Islam in the initial period in order to emphasize the invalidity of contemporary religious practices. Liberal Islam brings back the past for the sake of modernity, while revivalist Islam emphasizes modernity in the name of the past.[68]

Although it is recognized that there are many versions of Islamic liberalism, according to Kurzman there is a thread that unites them all —

namely, their criticism towards the traditions of customary and revivalist Islam. As such, liberal Islam is still concerned with finding the authentic Islam, the original Islam, as it is this Islam that it holds to be true. Authentic Islam in Kurzman's understanding is, to quote Mamadiou Dia (Senegal, b. 1911), as follows:

> Islamic authenticity requires a return to the sources, that is, to the Qur'an and to the sunna, not to take shelter there, to drown current cares there, but to draw from thence elements for the renovation and revitalization of Islamic philosophy.[69]

This paradigm of liberal Islam is thus not friendly towards local traditions, which are seen as being a less authentic form of Islam. It is this project that Islamic modernism has taken on in order to purify everything considered to defile the purity of Islam. As a result, Islamization is then seen as a process of purifying Islam from mixing with the perceived filth of local cultures.[70]

It was in this context that the discourse of post-traditionalism began to arise and then find both its similarities and differences with liberal Islam. The two both share an enthusiasm for liberal thought, secularization, pluralism, and de-formalization of Islamic law. They both want to avoid being trapped by orthodoxy, to be free from the confinement of religious texts, to struggle for democracy, and so on, although within each current there are glimpses of slightly different ideas. Meanwhile, they differ in terms of their views towards locality, grass-roots beliefs, grass-roots knowledge, and so on. Thus, while the liberal Islamic paradigm emphasizes authenticity,[71] originality, and genuineness, post-traditionalism has gone beyond all this. That is, it believes that Islamic authenticity cannot only be measured by measuring the level of "Arab-ness". Here, post-traditionalism coincides with modern Arab thought such as Nasr Hamid Abu Zayd's critique of religious discourse, Muhammad Shahrur's study of text, Mohammed 'Abed al-Jabiri's critique of Arab reason, and Hassan Hanafi's critique of Islamic reason. These figures' ideas are often used as the epistemological reference in critiques of religious discourse. As such, it can be said that Islamic post-traditionalism is "liberal Islam plus", that is, it is liberal Islam plus an appreciation of those things that are local and peripheral, and that work to free the oppressed.[72]

As it developed, post-traditionalist thought underwent changes, with the development of a discourse of emancipatory Islam by Masdar F. Mas'udi of P3M and Ahmad Baso of Desantara through the Emancipatory Madrasah programme. This discourse represented a paradigmatic elaboration of post-traditionalism amongst the hustle and bustle of Islamic movements in Indonesia. In exploring the paradigm and methodology of emancipatory Islam, Masdar F. Mas'udi mapped out several models of Islamic movements in order to position emancipatory Islam. According to him, the map of Islam that developed in Indonesia, especially related to the way religious texts are viewed, is as follows:[73]

1. **Scriptualistic, textualistic and formalistic Islam:** that is, an Islam that makes text both the start and end point of all thought. This means no matter how brilliant human reasoning is or how complicated social reality may be, they must both submit to the texts. This submission of reasoning and reality is often seen as a necessity of faith, to protect the holy texts as well as evidence of the truth of divine revelation. Such a perspective has implications for that which is called the truth, as there is only truth in the texts; there is no truth outside of the texts. Although through reasoning humans may discover the truth themselves, confirmation must be sought from the texts as proof of faith in this truth. If this process of confirmation fails, that which reasoning holds to be true fails too. In the tradition of Islamic scholarship, this is the standard model of understanding texts which has brought forth a number of scientific disciplines such as *'ulûm al-Qur'ân* (science of the Qur'an), *'ulûm al-hadîst* (science of the Hadith), exegesis, fiqh, theology and so on. It is this standard model that also shapes the Islamic community's structure of tradition. A number of these sciences have recently become key supporters of orthodoxy, where knowledge is restricted in such a way that Islamic studies may not step outside the guidelines that were erected by ulama in the past. Doing so could be considered a violation of Islam itself. This process has occurred over a relatively long period of time, to the extent that Islam has become a formal and closed discourse. The rules for thinking have been restricted so as not to damage or interfere with the purity of Islam. The long history of Islam begins and ends with the texts, which prompted Nasr Hamid Abu Zayd to call Arab-Islamic civilization a civilization of texts (*hadlârat al-nâsh*).[74] Texts of a variety of levels (primary, secondary and tertiary) underwent a process of widespread sacralization (*taqdîs al-nushûsh*).

2. **Ideological Islam:** that is, Islam that is not based on and does not worship the texts, but is based on its own ideal ideas and choices of truth. This form of Islam uses texts for justification. Ideological Islam tends to be sectarian, closed, and not interested in understanding others. It is the combination of scriptualist Islam and ideological Islam that forms the seeds of Islamic fundamentalism which holds its own opinion to be true and others to be wrong. This world view is highly susceptible to violence and politicization.
3. **Modernist Islam:** The vision of modernism in Islam is how to reconcile theology with modern reality. Modernity is viewed as a given, and society is left to accept it without contesting let alone rejecting it, so that theological convictions must be adjusted to the reality of modernity. The issues of modernist Islam are equivalent to the themes of modernism itself, while its enemy is anyone who opposes the dominant reality. Liberal Islam, on one level, as discussed earlier, was born of this modernist spirit.

According to Masdar F. Mas'udi, neither of the three groups are liberating or are able to resolve the real problems of humanity; and in fact, modernist Islam sometimes adopts Islamic fundamentalism exactly the same way as fundamentalist Islam does. The three are only out to destroy one another. On the basis of this, P3M developed an Islamic model that differs, by adopting the term emancipatory Islam. In essence, the term emancipatory cannot be separated from the history of critical theory, although within it there are many different currents. Criticism in this context involves two elements. The first is social reality, a way of thinking that questions the hegemonic ideology which runs contrary to real and material life. The second element is a transformative vision, or a commitment to change structures and relations, including power relations in the world of production (employer–employee), hegemonic relations between those who give and those who accept narratives (ulama–community), and political relations (those in power–the people). Moreover, in devising changes to be made, emancipatory Islam, in Masdar F. Mas'udi's view, follows the cycle given in Figure 3.2.

These four variables are interrelated. Emancipatory Islam is not based on the holy texts, as is the case with scriptualist, ideological, and modernist Islam, but on the very real problems of humanity. Holy texts here are not understood as laws but as inspiration that may be used as

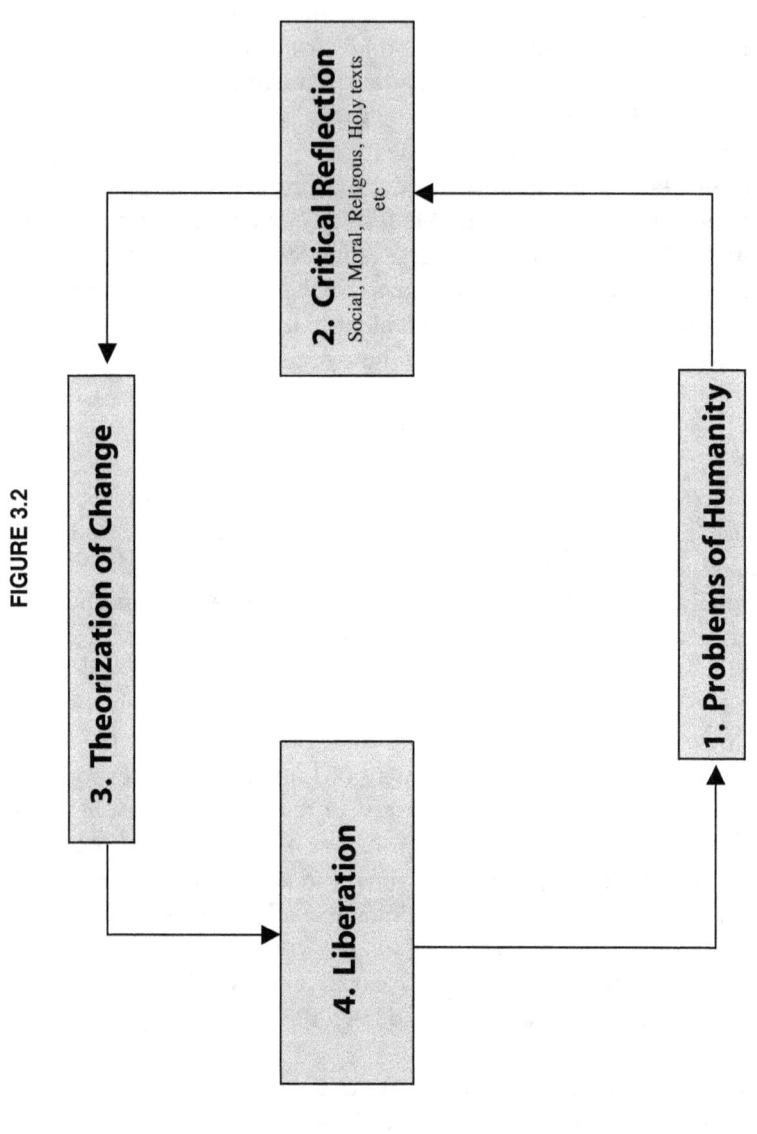

FIGURE 3.2

Adapted from *Panjimas* Magazine, no. 6/1, December 2002.

a reference for liberation, the ultimate aim of emancipatory Islam. Why inspiration? Because the Qur'an is viewed as a moral book whose values function to illuminate life, not a book required to explain everything that occurs in the world. As such, emancipatory Islam does not stop at a deconstruction of religious texts that can trap people in nihilism because they do not have their own stance, but rather deconstruction continues to be aimed at liberation.

Although the objective of emancipatory Islam is liberation, the issue of reading texts has received much attention. Why texts? Because texts are considered to be a serious problem that the religious (Islamic) community is currently facing. In fact, this different way of viewing texts often leads to exclusive and destructive attitudes.[75] This attitude towards texts is one aspect that differentiates emancipatory Islam from other Islamic models. Several differences are apparent in the following perspectives that emancipatory Islam has adopted:

1. **Perspective towards texts:** Emancipatory Islam pays particular attention to texts, because it is suspected that they are an arena of contestation between the various religious streams. On the one hand, there is an attempt to politicize texts, to make them legal and political documents that should be enforced as an alternative to change things for the better; but on the other hand, there is a tendency to use texts as a tool to justify liberalism. These two models have no set attitude towards the texts as they only use them for their own interests. As a result, the two are stuck in endless conflict, which has led to wars between texts. The first group uses texts as if they were the clothes of fundamentalism, while the second uses them as if they were the clothes of liberalism. Emancipatory Islam seeks to view texts as a part of reality that has limitations. These limitations do not indicate a weakness in texts, but are proof of the exceptional nature of humans to be able to respond to them. This is the importance of the perspective one takes towards a text. All readers of texts should wherever possible epistemologically deconstruct (*al-qathî'ah al-ma'rafiyah*) a text, but they must be able to contextualize (*al-tawâsul al-ma'rafî*) it too. This approach assumes that the fundamental issue is not situated in a text, but in empirical reality. As a result, this should lead to the growth of critical awareness towards social reality which is filled with oppression, discrimination, and domination, as well as a critical attitude towards

all forms of exploitation of texts that only lead to politicization and hegemony of exegesis.
2. **Attitude towards modernity:** Emancipatory Islam believes that oppression, discrimination, and domination are results of the particular system and ideology of modernity. Modernity on the one hand can be seen as a driving force for enlightenment, but on the other it is unable to push for equality and justice on a practical level. Modernity is the new colonial power which must be viewed critically, as it creates a positivistic attitude and moves further away from economic justice. This differs from the religious patterns that have been developing. Fundamentalist Islam and liberal Islam both depend on modernity. Fundamentalist Islam rejects modernity and proposes the alternative of returning to a *salafi* (pure) understanding, while liberal Islam makes modernity its only mechanism for social change. Both these movements are better described as urban movements. Here, emancipatory Islam seeks to establish itself as a popular movement which is always critical of all forms of oppression produced by modernity.
3. **Appreciation of local culture:** Emancipatory Islam has a strong commitment to local culture, so that transformation of society does not displace it from its roots. This is crucial in order to explore the local wisdoms that have to date been buried by other cultures. An appreciation of local culture is a form of acculturation of religion and culture that sees religion as not only formed by texts and divine revelation, but also by local culture. This is also necessary in order to realize diversity in religiosity.
4. **Emphasis on participation and action:** Emancipatory Islam believes that social change is not a top-down process, but one that grows from below. This is different from the view that has developed in both liberal Islam and fundamentalist Islam. Both believe that constitutional change is the only kind of social transformation and change. Emancipatory Islam is not so confident in the sophistication of texts, discourse, and the constitution (the Qur'an). No matter how sophisticated the texts, divine revelation, discourse, and the constitution (Qur'an) are, they cannot guarantee change. As a result, emancipatory Islam stresses the importance of participation and action on a practical level.[76]

Here, it is useful to compare emancipatory Islam with the Liberal Islamic Network's agenda. Luthfi Assyaukani, a pioneer of liberal Islam in

Indonesia, formulated four Islamic agendas that are liberating. First there is the political agenda, related to the attitudes of Muslims concerning a valid political system, particularly in connection to the form and system of governance. He argues that the form a state takes is a human choice, not a divine one. There is no verse in the Qur'an that defines one particular political system. God only suggests that it must be honest and fair. Secondly, there is the agenda that encompasses relations between Muslims. With the increasing complexity of community life in Muslim states, the search for a theology of pluralism is necessary. The problem is, in the Qur'an which is the religious reference for Muslims, besides those verses that support pluralism, there are more than a few that are often interpreted as obstacles to pluralism. Thirdly, there is the agenda inviting Muslims to rethink several religious doctrines that tend to disadvantage and discredit women. These doctrines contradict the fundamental spirit of Islam which recognizes equality and respect for all genders (QS. 33: 35; 49: 13; 4: 1). The fourth agenda involves freedom of opinion. This is vital in the modern world, especially as this issue is closely related to human rights. If Islam is to be described as a religion that has a high respect for human rights, then Islam must respect freedom of opinion. There is no excuse for Islam to be afraid of freedom of opinion. Every move by an individual, group, or the state to oppose this freedom must be contested, because this not only stunts the growth of humankind, but also of religion.[77] With these agendas, liberal Islam developed the following concept:

1. Opening of the door of *ijtihad* or interpretation in all fields of study. For liberal Islam groups, *ijtihad* or logical reasoning of religion is the main principle that allows Islam to survive in all climates. Closure of the door of *ijtihad*, either partially or completely, threatens Islam, because doing so will cause Islam to decay.
2. Emphasis on a religio-ethic spirit, not on the literal meaning of a text. The *ijtihad* developed by liberal Islam is based on the religio-ethic spirit of the Qur'an and Sunna, not on the literal meaning of a text.
3. Truth that is relative, open, and plural.
4. Advocation for minorities and the oppressed.
5. Freedom of religion and belief.
6. Separation of worldly and heavenly authority, of religious and political authority.[78]

The agendas of post-traditionalism and liberal Islam are not diametrically opposed, nor do they deny one another. The post-traditionalist community cannot reject a large part of the agenda that liberal Islam proposes, although at the derivative or detailed level there are some differences. However, each community has its own agenda and perspectives on individual issues. The perspective used to view an issue and the ability to define it both influence the formulation of these agendas. Separately from this, the emergence of these agendas is also related to the awareness that has emerged in each group, as well as the way they view and define problems of life. If this is taken to be true, then Jadul Maula, an activist of LKiS in Yogyakarta, is right when he says that the agenda and movements of the liberal Islamic community give the impression of being elitist and do not address the real problems in society.[79] Here, post-traditionalism with its various paradigmatic elaborations seeks to develop a populist religious concept related to the real problems in society. This means that all religious insight must be devoted to resolving the problems of humanity. No matter how sophisticated a methodology for understanding religion might be, it does not have the spirit to defend the oppressed and raise human dignity. In fact, it tends to side with oppressors and degrade human dignity and, as such, this kind of religious understanding deserves to be questioned.

THE INTELLECTUAL GENEALOGY OF ISLAMIC POST-TRADITIONALISM

Before discussing the genealogy of post-traditionalism, it is necessary to start with a discussion of the genealogy of neo-modernism and liberal Islam in order to clearly see the aspects of their genealogy that differentiate them from post-traditionalism. Liberal Islam, according to Kurzman, began with Syah Waliyullah (India, 1703–62 CE), although on a theological level he was very revivalist. However, because he developed a more humanistic response to local traditions compared to the Wahabis, Kurzman sees him as important. It was only in the nineteenth century that liberal Islam began to clearly differentiate itself from revivalism, both intellectually and institutionally. Intellectually, they differentiated between *ijtihad* and *taklid* (interpretation and imitation), reasoning and authority. Figures who voiced this theme include Jamâl al-Dîn al-Afgânî (Iran, 1838–97 CE), Sayyid Ahmad Khan (India, 1817–98 CE), and Muhammad Abduh (Egypt,

1849–1905 CE).⁸⁰ The main theme that these figures focused on was the issue of *taklid*. They sharply criticized the practice while calling for its opposite, *ijtihad,* to resolve problems in life. Ahmad Khan for example states:

> *Taqlid* is not incumbent (on the believer). Every person is entitled to *ijtihad* in those matters concerning which there is no explicitly revealed text in the Qur'an and *sunna* (the practice of the Prophet).⁸¹

Muhammad Abduh also writes:

> First, to liberate thought from the shackles of *taqlid*, and understand religion as it was understood by the elders of the community before dissension appeared; to return, in the acquisition of religious knowledge to its first source, and to weigh them in the scale of human reason, which God has created in order to prevent excess or adulteration in religion ... and to prove that, seen in this light, religion must be accounted a friend of science, pushing man to investigate the secrets of existence.⁸²

Entering the twentieth century, the *ijtihad* theme receded but was not entirely lost. Attention turned instead to the theme of Western education that was being adopted in the Muslim world. During this period, traditional education was faced with the difficult decision between maintaining tradition and adopting modern education. Educational institutes were eventually divided: some went to the extreme of adopting Western education systems, others entirely rejected it, and some tried to integrate the two. The feature of this movement was the introduction of Western education institutions and lessons to the traditional *pesantren* curriculum. When the revivalists tried to cure the ills of the Muslim world by stressing the importance of the seventeenth-century sources, the liberals tried to combine this emphasis with a different focus on the disciplines of Western science, such as engineering and military science, medicine and natural sciences, comparative studies of law and social sciences, and modern languages. With this attitude towards the West, Kurzman states that liberal Islam at this time was generally known as Islamic modernism.⁸³

As a result, it is not mistaken to suggest that neo-modernism and liberal Islam are both based on the paradigm of modernism. This intellectual genealogy is exactly the same as the genealogy of modernist groups such as Muhammadiyah. Muhammadiyah's intellectual genealogy was severed because it discarded the intellectual wealth that emerged during the *taklid* period. Azyumardi Azra states that Muhammadiyah's intellectual wealth was limited to the first generation of Muslims or righteous predecessors (*salâf al-shâlih*), before jumping (slightly) to Ibnu Taimiyah, and then in the seventeenth century started to adopt the ideas of reformers such as Syah Waliyullah, Muhammad bin Abd al-Wahhab, Jamâl al-Dîn al-Afgânî, Rasyid Ridla, and Muhammad Abduh.[84]

This is where the modernists differ most starkly from NU. The NU community greatly values its intellectual wealth from the *taklid* period that extended from about the tenth century to the beginning of the eighteenth century. During this period many significant works were produced by ulama, though many were commentaries (*syarah*) of revelations (*matan*), commentaries on commentaries (*hasyiyah*), and so on.[85] The modernists view this period as a dark period, a period of heresy full of superstitious practices. In fact, the modernist movement is oriented towards opposing such deviant practices, rejecting *taklid* and calling loudly for *ijtihad*.

Conversely, the NU community responds coldly towards the work and thoughts of reformers such as Muhammad Abduh, Jamâl al-Dîn al-Afgânî, and Rasyid Ridla. In various discussion forums, particularly the Bahts al-Masâil, the ideas of these figures are almost never referred to. As a result, NU's intellectual wealth has also been disrupted. While Muhammadiyah's was severed during the *taklid* period, NU's was severed during the period of renewal between the eighteenth century and the beginning of the twentieth century. It is not clear exactly what caused this, but further examination reveals that it cannot be separated from the tension between the traditionalists and modernists at the beginning of the twentieth century. At the time, the figures mentioned above were the primary reference for the modernists and were used as ammunition with which to attack the traditionalist perspective.

Thus, while Muhammadiyah is poor in classic intellectualism, NU has no intellectual background in renewal. With time, the two opposed entities started to move closer to one another. That is (parts of) the Muhammadiyah community started to pay attention to the classical traditions and local cultures that they had considered heretical and superstitious, while (parts of) the NU community also started to care about the ideas behind the renewal movement, although this was restricted to a very small community.

The issue then is how do we read liberal Islam? What are the parameters to measure liberalism in Islamic thought? As an academic framework, this is important to ensure that we are all on the same page. For this purpose Charles Kurzman is once again quoted, although every now and again criticized, as he suggests that there are several forms of liberal Islam, and also indicates which realms they exist in. The first is liberal *syari'ah*. This view assumes that *syari'ah* is fundamentally liberal if interpreted as it is. It is this model that most influences the liberalists. As such, Islamic liberalism is something that is inherent in the nature of Islam, not touched by outside elements. The existence of liberal *syari'ah* explains several things: (1) It avoids accusations that liberal Islam is not authentic; (2) The liberal position is not merely a choice but also God's order; (3) It is a source of pride because it means that liberalism in Islam developed far before liberalism in the West. These arguments are evidence of the fact that liberal Islam still needs Islamic legitimacy in forming its arguments. Furthermore, it also claims that Islamic liberalism is older than Western liberalism. In short, there is nothing to worry about with the development of liberal thought in the Islamic community.

The second form of liberal Islam is silent *syari'ah*. This means that liberal Islam arises out of specific issues that have no precedent in Islam, either normatively or historically. Although Muslims recognize that Islam is a universal religion, complete and perfect, this does not mean that everything is regulated in Islam (in the Qur'an and Sunna). Rather, there are many problems of humanity that are not explicitly addressed in the Qur'an. In fact, even those issues that are addressed explicitly are still discussed critically, in terms of their significance, the meaning of the text, and their historical background. Islam only regulates the fundamental principles in managing life. As such, the realm of silent *syari'ah* stretches far and wide, encompassing issues that have not been regulated, and dictums that have different contexts.

The third form of liberal Islam is interpreted *syari'ah,* which means that liberal Islam also arises out of issues which are multi-interpretable.[86] In *ushûl al-fiqh*, this is known as *zannî al-dalâlah*, or issues whose interpretations are still ambiguous and uncertain. Thus, although an issue may be addressed in a text, it is multi-interpretable and as such, liberal Islamic ideas exist in this realm.

Using this framework, liberal Islam has several important agendas which are also themes in its discourse, including the theme of democracy as a form of resistance to theocratic understandings that have developed in the Muslim world; struggling for the rights of women who have been subordinated in social structures which are supported by a certain theological understanding; campaigning for freedom of thought; and proposing an alternative way of thinking for the progression of Islam, although this requires going against the main current of thought. The objective of this discourse is respect of pluralism, acting in favour of the oppressed, and the destruction of hegemonic thought while avoiding — to borrow Arkoun's term — sacralizing thought (*taqdîs al-afkâr al-dînî*).

It is now time to turn to the genealogy of Islamic post-traditionalism. In the previous section, the genealogy of NU intellectualism and the tradition of thought that developed within the NU community was discussed. This was also contrasted with the wealth and tradition of thought that developed amongst the modernist community. The community of NU youth who developed an alternative way of thinking represents a continuation of the traditions that developed before their time, but with the application of a certain kind of criticism. There are a lot of similarities between post-traditionalism and liberal Islam in terms of the issues they take up, although every now and again there are differences in strategy and perspectives towards different issues. The various agendas that are the concern of liberal Islam are also the concern of the post-traditionalist community.

In tracking the genealogy of post-traditionalism, Ahmad Baso, in his post-traditionalist manifesto published in the journal *Tashwirul Afkar* (no. 10, 2001), describes the foundations, vision, and intellectual orientation of post-traditionalism, differentiating it from liberal Islam and neo-modernism. Ahmad Baso writes:

> The emergence of Muhammad Abid al-Jabiri's works in Indonesia signified the beginning of a phase to follow the initial phase pioneered by Abdurrahman Wahid. While Abdurrahman Wahid's thought started the post-traditionalist movement with a number of ideas, in al-Jabiri's hands the second phase was marked by a process of filling in its epistemological and methodological projections. It is this that is appreciated by those of the NU culture. The Abdurrahman Wahid phase, which included Hassan Hanafi and Fatima Mernissi, enriched the ideas behind the movement's thought and political actions, such as nationalism, indigenisation (*pribumisasi*), secularisation, and feminism. Meanwhile the phase now known as the phase of al-Jabiri, and also Mohammaed Arkoun and Nasr Hamid Abu Zayd, was the methodological phase of Islamic post-traditionalism.[87]

The names quoted above give a fair indication of post-traditionalism's intellectual orientation. Although Ahmad Baso does not explain how

Abdurrahman Wahid's ideas connected with al-Jabiri's methodology, we can nevertheless grasp how the post-traditionalist community appreciated liberal contemporary Arab thinkers. Within the internal NU community, Abdurrahman Wahid's name was held in high admiration (before he became president in 1999), not only because he embodied the charisma of NU blue blood, but also because of his intellectual capacity and wild streak. It is therefore true when Martin van Bruinessen states that progressive thinkers in NU almost always see Abdurrahman Wahid as their patron.[88] Perhaps the context changed a little after Abdurrahman Wahid became actively involved in politics as the chairman of PKB's advisory council; however, the majority of NU youth involved in the post-traditionalist network continue to respect the contributions he made towards opening up space for intellectual movements within the community.

Why were these names mentioned and not others? Ahmad Baso draws a line dividing neo-modernism and post-traditionalism. Neo-modernism traces its genealogy back to the Wahabi movement and its peak with Ibnu Taymiyah, while post-traditionalism draws its line of thought from those figures in dialogue with the tradition of Western enlightenment, from the generation of Abdullahi an-Na'im, Nawal Saadawi, Thariq al-Bisyri, Abdullah Laroui, and Muhammad Khafullah, to the generation of Michel Aflaq, Ali 'Abd al-Raziq, and eventually right back to Ibnu Rusyd. While neo-modernism embodies a spirit for purification of Islam, a search for the pure and original Islam, is anti-heresy, and has adopted the slogan of a return to the Qur'an and Sunna, post-traditionalism seeks new synthesis in its critical dialogue between Islamic tradition, Western tradition, and local culture.[89] In fact, Desantara for Culture Studies, a Depok-based NGO managed by NU youth such as Bisri Effendi, Nur Khoiron, and Ahmad Baso (not active in Desantara since the end of 2003), pays special attention to local culture.[90] Its project is a counter to the modernist politics of purification. In a wider context, this project is an expression of NU's intellectual responsibility, as a community that throughout history has been more accommodating towards local cultures and has been the target of some groups and their Islamization or conquest projects.

As such, post-traditionalism is an intellectual construct based on Indonesian local culture, and not pressure from outside (foreign projects), which interacts openly with a number of different social groups, from labourers to students, farmers, NGOs, *pesantren*, and so on. Post-traditionalism does not only accommodate liberal and radical thought from the likes of Hassan Hanafi, Mahmoud Mohammed Tahâ, Abdullahi Ahmed al-Na'im, Arkoun, Abu Zayd, Syahrour, and Khalil 'Abd al-Karîm, but also socialist–Marxist, post-structuralist, postmodernist, and feminist ideas, as well as ideas about civil society.

Ahmad Baso specifically mentions that post-traditionalist politics and its method of thought were constructed from al-Jabiri's ideas. This suggests that al-Jabiri's ideas in the *Critique of Arab Reason (Naqd al'Aql al-'Arâbî)* also hold an important position amongst the other names mentioned. Ahmad Baso argues in support of this:

> First of all Muhammad Abid al-Jabiri became known with his methodological project on *"Kritik Nalar Arab*/Critique of Arab Reason". This project offers two critiques: a critique of epistemological reason and a critique of political reason. The former is also known as "speculative reason", and takes an archaeological form to examine the mechanisms and means of reproduction of knowledge within the Muslim community until today. What is studied, for instance, is how *ushûl fiqih* shapes the way of thinking of Muslims with its methodology of *qiyas* (analogy) which can tend towards sacralisation, not only in issues of religious laws, but also across the entire spectrum of human culture, from language to arts theology, philosophy and politics (for instance, if discussing "Islamic" socialism). Meanwhile the critique of political reason, also known as "practical reason", emphasises praxis, with a critical focus on the means of power and control. This examines for example the connection between the emergence of the *siyâsah syar'iyyah* or *fiqh al-siyâsah* discipline (rules of governance) and the militaristic strategy the Caliphate adopted to subjugate its people.[91]

The significant impact of al-Jabiri, and the other names mentioned above, on NU thought is apparent in the fact that these figures' ideas are always present in youth discussions. The syllabuses of the programmes they run are very much inspired by these figures. For instance, the programme to develop Emancipatory *Tafsir* (Exegesis), held by the Jakarta chapter of P3M in September and October 2001, used Nasr Hamid Abu Zaid's *Mafhûm al-Nash, Dirâsah fî Ulûm al-Qur'ân* as the primary reference in every discussion. In addition, al-Jabiri's *Naqd al-'Aql al-'Arabi (Critique of Arab Reason)* trilogy was a primary reference, consisting of the three books *Takwîn al-'Aql al-'Arabi (Formation of Arab Reason,* 1982), *Bunyah al-'Aql al-'Arabi (Structure of Arab Reason,* 1986), and *al-'Aql al-Siyâsi al-'Arabi (Arab Political Reason,* 1990), all of which were published by Markaz Dirasah al-Wihdah al-Arabiyah, Beirut, Lebanon.[92] Hassan Hanafi's works such as *al-Turâst wa al-Tajdîd: Mawqifunâ min al-Turâst al-Qadîm* (Cairo: al-Markaz al-'Arabi, 1980); *Dirâsah al-Islâmiyah* (Cairo: Maktabah Anglo Misriyyah, 1980); *Qadlâyâ al-Mu'âshirah: Fî Fikrinâ al-Mu'âshir* (Beirut: Dâr al-Fikr, 1983); *Min al-'Aqîdah ilâ al-Tsawrah: al-Muqaddimah al-Nadhariyah* (Cairo: Maktabah al-Madbûlî, 1989), amongst others, were another important source. In fact, critique of religious discourse, which was inspired by Nasr Hamid Abu Zayd's book, *Naqd al-Khithâb al-Dînî* (Cairo: Sînâ li al-Nasr, 1994), is part of the course material of every study group programme held by LKiS, Desantara, and P3M, in addition to critique of political discourse, critique of gender discourse, and critique of cultural discourse. The first edition of the journal *Gerbang,* published by eLSAD Surabaya, also specifically focuses on a critique of religious discourse.

The project of post-traditionalist thought is criticism of all forms of religious doctrine that have become set in stone. Post-traditionalists dissect almost every aspect of religious awareness, which has until recently been both unquestionable and unthinkable. The *ahl al-sunnah wa al-jamâ'ah* theme which is at the very heart of NU's ideology, for instance, was approached through a critique of reason and a critique of religious discourse. Of course, they arrived at a different conclusion, because NU doctrine was deemed relative and no longer in accordance with modern developments. The most vocal NU figure to critique the *ahl al-sunnah wa al-jamâ'ah* doctrine was Said Agil Siradj,[93] who was then followed by other young figures.[94]

The NU youth who were involved intensively in the post-traditionalist discourse had no special network with these senior figures, although this does not mean they never communicated. Their appreciation towards these thinkers who helped form the post-traditionalist genealogy came more from their reading of these figures. The majority of this community, as explained in the previous chapter, were IAIN alumni. This is interesting because post-traditionalism was not propelled by NU cadres who had studied in the West such as Qodri Azizy, Masykuri Abdillah, Faisal Ismail, and Abdurrahman Mas'ud.

Here, Said Aqiel Siradj is an interesting figure to look at in greater depth, because the criticism he voiced, at least according to his own admission, was not inspired by liberal ideas that developed in the West, but was a result of his reading of Islamic tradition. In this sense, Said Agil undertook what al-Jabiri called *al-tajdîd min al-dâkhil*[95] (renewal from within). In an interview with *Tashwirul Afkar* he stated:

> I was educated in the Middle East and I read and mastered the Islamic schools of thought; from the ideas of the Kharijites, Shi'ites, Jabarites, Qadarites, Mu'tazilites, Murji'ites to the *ahl al-sunnah wa al-jamâ'ah* ideology, *tasawuf* (mysticism), the Islamic philosophy of Ibnu Rusyd, Ibnu Sina and so on. My way of thinking was formed from all these influences, the followers of the Islamic schools of thought.... Frankly speaking my way of thinking was not influenced by the West. My reading only looked at *'âlam fikr al-Islâmi* (the world of Islamic thought). This gave birth to my way of thinking.[96]

This quote emphasizes that critical and progressive thinking does not always have to come from the West. Western thinking here refers to modern thinking based on rationalism. Said Agil Siradj, however, shows that just reading classical works of Islam openly can lead an individual to think progressively and critically. The most determining factor is openness to all information without ideological bias, such as suspicion towards Shi'ite or Mu'tazilite ideas for instance.

There are several aspects that need to be underlined in the intellectual genealogy of the post-traditionalist community. First, the post-traditionalist community still sees the Middle East as the centre of its intellectual orientation, as did the previous NU generation of KH Hasyim Asy'ari, KH Bisri Syamsuri, KH Wahab Chasbullah, and so on. The only difference is that the post-traditionalist generation follows the intellectual path of those thinkers who are critically minded, as explained above. Secondly, post-traditionalists are also open to other sources of thought in addition to the Middle East in order to enrich their traditional wealth, including the Marxist, post-structuralist, and postmodernist traditions, as well as the tradition of critical philosophy that developed in Western countries such as France and Germany.[97] Using these other sources is very important, because it allows the post-traditionalists to take the traditional knowledge that they received from *pesantren*, and read it with new models that developed elsewhere in the world. This is where post-traditionalism receives its cosmopolitan face. Thirdly, a large part of the intellectual genealogy of post-traditionalism was not formed through teacher–student relations as with previous generations, but was formed through intellectual friction and reading the works of key figures. Quite differently from the intellectual genealogy of those ulama in the past who prioritized face-to-face meetings and teacher–student relations, modern developments have shaken this trend somewhat, though it has not completely disappeared.

In terms of struggling to achieve its agendas, there are several characteristics that define post-traditionalism. First, post-traditionalism is about escaping from the confines of tradition. For the post-traditionalist community, renewal must be based on tradition. Tradition becomes the point of departure for transformation. As such, post-traditionalism cannot reject tradition and also cannot just accept it at face value, but must cultivate it creatively and proportionally. Tradition here may mean religious practices, but what is more important is the tradition of thought. Secondly, post-traditionalism seeks to free itself from the historical burden whereby Muslims have tended to feel that they are not part of the universal history of humanity, but are a community that has its own history, and must therefore gather together and form their own tradition that differs from other communities. From here Muslims then wish to develop an Islamic culture according to the Prophet's example, with the ultimate goal of establishing an Islamic state. This burden must be released, because the demand is not for a hegemonic society where some reign over others, but a plural society that is egalitarian, democratic, and just. Thirdly, post-traditionalism seeks to escape from the literal meaning of texts when exploring religious messages.[98] Excessive ties to texts over a long period of time have already impeded Islamic thought.

CRITIQUE OF REASON AS THE PROJECT OF ISLAMIC POST-TRADITIONALIST THOUGHT

In recent times, criticism has been voiced that Islamic scholarship in Indonesia has no clear project, and as such, the direction in which Islamic thought is developing is also unclear. In fact, Indonesian intellectualism is often cynically referred to as seasonal intellectualism. During the season of postmodernism, everyone is talking about postmodernism, and discussions on the subject are held everywhere. When all of a sudden Mohammed Arkoun appeared amidst the paucity of Islamic thought in Indonesia, everyone was talking about Arkoun. The same thing happened with Hassan Hanafi and Abed al-Jabiri, as well as with themes such as civil society, human rights, democracy, and feminism. In short, there has been no collective project of Islamic thought, and as a result, Islamic thought in Indonesia has not been able to make an original contribution to the interests of the Muslim world in general. In actual fact, at the end of the 1980s and beginning of the 1990s, Islamic thought started to head in a positive direction — for instance, with the theme of transformative Islam — but unfortunately it receded without any clear reason. In fact, at the end of the 1990s and beginning of the new century, political affairs sucked up all of the nation's energy and as such, there was almost no meaningful development of thought.

The crisis of original Islamic thought is not specific to Indonesia, but is an issue in the Muslim world in general. This condition was caused amongst other things by the domination of the traditional-conservative Islamic perspective which dictated almost all aspects of Islamic thought. This perspective was formed gradually over the first four centuries of Islamic development, and had obtained a definite form by the twelfth century. After this point in time, Islamic science did not undergo any significant development. In fact, fragments of thoughts that tried to escape from the confines and domination found themselves faced by a great power that was difficult, if not impossible, to penetrate.

This kind of critique can be understood and interpreted as a form of restlessness to realize an Islam that cares for and has direct links to humanitarian projects. In order to head in this direction, it is necessary to review the Islamic research methods which are more likely to fall under the umbrella of orthodox understandings than the critical Islamic schools of thought. In this context, a research methodology that prioritizes *naqd al-'aqli* (critique of reason) is an alternative worth considering, although it must be admitted that this is only a temporary project and does not pretend to resolve all issues related to Islamic research methodology. Nevertheless, it does at least give direction to the development of new thought.

There are at least two terms that are usually linked to critique of reason: critique of Islamic reason, a term used by Mohammed Arkoun, and critique of Arab reason, the term used by Mohammed Abid al-Jabiri. We do not know exactly if the different terms indicate that they are motivated by different ideologies, or if they are just two different terms that share the same ontological basis. In this respect, Ahmad Baso's explanation of the linguistic tradition helps to clarify the problem, but is still less than satisfactory. He states that Arkoun used the term "critique of Islamic reason" in order to expand the scope of his critique to include non-Arab traditions of thought. Meanwhile, al-Jabiri's critique of Arab reason was to limit his critique to the tradition of thought that was expressed in Arabic and within a specific cultural geography. The critique of Arab reason was not projected to create a new science such as a new theology or *ilmu kalam*. Al-Jabiri's critique did not give much attention to issues of divinity, revelation, orthodoxy, and the various streams of scholastic theology; instead, it was more focused on the framework and mechanism of thought which dominated Arab culture at a certain period in time. Meanwhile, Arkoun's critique was aimed more at the concepts of orthodoxy, revelation, myth, imagination, symbols, and so on. [99]

The project of critiquing reason as introduced by al-Jabiri, Nasr Hamid Abu Zayd, and Mohammed Arkoun, generally shares the same agenda of escaping the shackles of tradition and text, despite their slightly different areas of concentration and ideas. The traditional way of viewing both tradition and text is the source of stagnation of Islamic thought.

There is not a long academic tradition of placing Islam as an object of scientific study, as there has been some reluctance to the extent that Islam is more often approached purely as a religion of divine revelation, where everything must go back to, and submit to, the revealed texts, period. On the other hand scientific research must situate Islam as a historical religion, rather than a religion of divine revelation, and as a historical religion it must be willing to be criticized.

Waardenburg (1973) explained that the difficulty in making religion a field of scientific research comes from two things. First, research means objectifying and standing at some distance from the object of said research. In researching religion, this objectification is not only of another party but also of one's self. Objectifying it is no easy task, as all humans have some connection to religion. Secondly, religion is traditionally understood as something holy, sacred, and exalted. Placing something so highly valued as a neutral object is generally considered to reduce, abuse, and even destroy the traditional values of religion.[100]

In this light, it is understandable that scientific research of Islam is difficult for those from within the Muslim community (insiders), and thus is much more frequently undertaken by those from outside the community (outsiders) who already possess a scientific tradition. There is a theological reluctance within the Muslim community to act impolitely towards their religion, while outsiders who are often called orientalists have no such burdens in regards to Islam. As a result, they can say anything about Islam, not just about religious practices as demonstrated throughout history, but they can also criticize fundamental elements of Islam such as the Qur'an and Hadith, although this is considered by some Muslims as interfering with and contradicting the basic values of Islamic theology. However, a new current has recently emerged amongst the insiders that dares to question several aspects of their religious beliefs that have always been considered final. This current is not only critical of outsiders and the West, but also critical of its own religious tradition and historical heritage.[101]

These two conventional approaches to Islam (insider and outsider) are based on different starting points and assumptions. The insiders see Islam as being based on the belief that Islam is a divine religion, its truth is absolute, it has universal values and is *shâlih li kulli zamân wa makân* (appropriate across all times and places). As a result, they cannot draw conclusions that contradict the basic values to which they already adhere. The conclusions drawn are often not based on fact, but on theological belief, because truth for them exists only insofar as facts accord with revelation, or more precisely, the divinely revealed text. As such, reality must submit and is subordinate to the revealed text.

In the tradition of Islamic scholarship, this kind of approach has produced a number of scientific studies such as *'Ulûm al-Qu'ân* (science of the Qur'an), *Ulûm al-Hadîst* (science of the Hadith), exegesis, fiqh, and theology, which in turn shaped the structure of tradition within the Islamic community. A number of these sciences have recently become the primary supporters of orthodoxy, where science is restricted and people are not allowed to venture outside of the guidelines that were established by the ulama of the past. The process of orthodoxization that began in the tenth century of the Muslim calendar has turned Islam into a formal and closed discourse, where the rules of thought are restricted so as to not damage or interfere with the purity of Islam as a divinely revealed religion.

Meanwhile, outsiders approach Islam as a historical phenomenon, that is, as a religion that has been practised by its people throughout history. Thus, the divine revelation that Muslims see as something to be respected and sanctified as part of religious purity is seen by outsiders as a history of humanity. At the moment the revelation was sent down to earth, it became part of history. As such, the divine text, although believed to be the word of God and the final divine word, still has a historical value because revelation (in the form of the holy text) always has a connection with reality.[102]

If this line of thought is agreed upon, then a scientific methodology must first be devised to rationally critique the structure of reason that has become the primary way of thinking for Muslims. In order to do so, there is a need to explain the concept of the critique of Islam or the critique of Islamic reason, so that there are no misunderstandings. The phrase "critique of Islam" in this context can be interpreted from at least two perspectives. First, the critique of Islam means placing Islam as a critical subject and an instrument in the reality of life that surrounds it. A critique of Islam in this sense is inspired by Islam's own mission from when it first emerged as a critique of the ignorance of the people of Mecca. This critique led to the passion to be liberated from all forms of restriction, both physical and psychological.[103] A critique of Islam (and all religions) in this understanding was examined well by Robert John Ackermann in his book *Religion as Critique* (1985).

Secondly, a critique of Islam can also mean placing Islam as an object of criticism. In this context, a critique of Islam is focused more on a number of traditions that have already become orthodox in almost all dimensions of Muslim life. This process whereby traditions become orthodox has meant that Islam has lost its vital spirit of criticism along with its spirit of liberalism. Because of this process, the religion that was once liberating developed into an idol that enslaved humankind. The religion that was sent down to elevate humankind to a higher level eventually used humans to elevate religion, and the religion that was initially for humankind made humankind exist for religion. As a result, the face of Islam changed, from reforming to established; from liberating to imprisonment; from justice to tyranny, and so on.

A critique of Islam here refers to the second understanding that places Islam (Islamic orthodoxy) as an object of criticism. In doing so, one must first agree to place Islam and all its elements on the altar of criticism, with all the consequences that entails. If this is achieved then the ontological critique of Islam is unlimited, extending even to those areas that have to date been considered part of the orthodox pillars of faith.

Part of the Muslim community (the conservatives) might consider this to be going too far, or even accuse it of sacrificing religion. This fear need not be an issue if Islam is seen not purely as a divine revelation but also as a historical reality. This contains both normative and historical aspects. However, it must be noted that Islamic normativity was born of a particular historical atmosphere. That is, the revelation that gave birth to normative aspects in Islam did not emerge in a vacuum, but in the surrounding historical atmosphere. If this line of logic is continued, one arrives at the conclusion that historicity can exceed normativity, and not the contrary, with normativity exceeding historicity.[104]

The tradition of critique in Islam is not actually a new thing, because the birth of Islam contained within it critical elements — namely, the critique of an ignorant Arab society that lived under the constraints of faith, economy, and culture.[105] Islamic scholarship has been familiar with the critical tradition for some time, since the third century of the Islamic calendar. It can be seen vaguely in the science of the Hadith which used standard methodologies to measure the quality of a hadith known as *'Ilmu Jarh wa Ta'dîl* (Criticism of the Narrators), *Ilmu Rijâl al-Hadîst* (Study of the Reporters of the Hadith), critique of the *sanad* (narrators), critique of the *matan* (reporters), and so on. These sciences discuss many issues related to the Hadith, such as the process of its transmission, the moral quality of those who transmit the Hadith, and the condition of the material of the Hadith. It is thus understandable why there is the potential for criticism in the tradition of Islamic scholarship. However, unfortunately this critical tradition did not develop; rather, it went from being an instrument for critique to the guardian of the orthodoxy of the Hadith.

In studies of the Qur'an there is also what is known as *asbâb al-nuzûl*, which discusses the reasons behind the revelation of the individual verses of the Qur'an. However, this science has almost been wiped out; it did not develop because it was deemed to have no relation to historiography, hermeneutics, critique of history, and so on. *Asbâb al-nuzûl* is considered only within the understanding that these events are contextual information related to the revelation of a verse. They are not the objective nor absolute reasons for the revelation. The understanding then emerges that the importance of the revelation lies in the generality of the words used, not in the event of its revelation, as stated by the principle *al-'ibrah bi 'umûm al-lafadh lâ bi khushûsh al-sabab*. The same thing occurred in the studies of theology, fiqh, and *tasawuf*. In short, the embryo of critical studies that existed in Islam did not develop because it became instead a part of the orthodoxization of religious studies. It is a rather sad reality.

This continued for quite some time throughout the history of Islamic scholarship and in turn led to naivety and a reverting back of the function of religion, as mentioned above. Islamic reason became stagnant and standardized. The Islamic texts that were initially alive, dynamic, and open to all forms of exegesis became closed, rigid, and fossilized. Religious issues that initially inhabited the thinkable realm moved into the unthinkable, and led to the sacralization of religious thought (*taqdîs al-afkâr al-dînî*). The holy texts that were initially open to all forms of exegesis became frozen through a hierarchical-authoritative process, both by the state and religion.

Given the state of Muslim society, it is not surprising that Mohammed Arkoun described Islamic reason in the following way: first, that it submitted to the orthodoxy of divine revelation. That is, Islamic reason had to submit and agree to only work in the area of knowledge that revelation had already determined. Secondly, Arkoun stated that Islamic reason respected authority and majesty and the obligation to submit to them. Authority that had to be obeyed was incarnate in the imam of the schools of thought, in fiqh, theology, and *tasawuf*. The decisions these imam made could not be debated or questioned because that would be regarded as straying from the correct guidelines. Thirdly, it played its role by adopting a particular perspective built on a medieval epistemology of the universe.[106] The construction of medieval knowledge was considered the end of Islamic scientific glory. The most concerning thing was that sometimes state reason interfered with religious reason; in fact, the two became one. As a result, opposing religious reason was seen as opposing state reason, and vice versa.

The initial standardizing of religious thought is understandable. The expansion of Islam to various parts of the world and the large number of new converts to Islam necessitated normative regulations in response to the variety of new issues that had never arisen before. The objective was clear: to prevent deviation in people's understanding of their newfound religion. However, this step was to have an extraordinary impact, not just for the laymen but also for the religious elite. That is, the religious elite who should have been free from orthodoxy became the most loyal protectors of orthodoxy. Just as medicine is taken to treat illness, orthodoxy and standardization of religious understanding acted as a medicine that proved too potent, and the body's cells that were not sick died as a result.[107]

A resolution for this reality is required in order to lift religion out of the mire of history. In order to do so, first of all a space must be provided for the growth of criticism within Islamic society. Islamic society is mentioned here to differentiate it from Islam itself. On a certain level, authentic Islam is different from historical Islam. Islamic society tends to be intolerant towards the growth of critical discourse because of the fear that it will damage its religion and faith. The experiences of a number of places and countries reveal this tendency. It has been written in history.

For instance, Fazlur Rahman had to leave Pakistan and settle in Chicago, and Nasr Hamid Abu Zayd had to leave Egypt and settle in Leiden after criticizing Imam Syafi'i.

The growth of a space for criticism must be immediately followed by dismantling the orthodoxy of thought or, at the very least, rationally critiquing Islamic thought to make it relevant to today. On one level this is already under way, begun by critical thinkers such as Arkoun, Mohammed 'Abid al-Jabiri, Nasr Hamid Abu Zayd, and Hassan Hanafi, although each one has different focuses and agendas. The problem then is how to foster this critical reasoning tradition so it becomes a new current in Islamic scholarship. This is of course no easy job, because the scientific community in higher education institutes has not accepted the ideas of these figures.

Relativization of religious thought requires a change in the way religious texts are viewed. To date, there is a mistaken view of religious texts, where texts become the ultimate aim, and force all reality to submit to them. This problem is only more complicated when linked with the very real silencing of the exegesis of texts, which produces monophonic exegesis through academic and religious authority. As a result, religious texts (especially the Qur'an) which were initially open corpuses are now closed corpuses. Religious texts must therefore be seen as products of history, and as such, they are inseparable from the laws of history.

At this point, Hassan Hanafi's cry is interesting for the ironies in religious history that it reveals. The studies of divinity, theology, fiqh, politics, and *tasawuf* are nothing more than a study of humankind. As a result, these sciences are not holy sciences that were simply given, but were constructed from humanitarian values and reflect events and conflicts in society. As such, God does not submit to the sciences created by humankind, and critiques of Islamic sciences are thus not always critiques of God.

Critique of reason in philosophy is also known as critique of epistemology,[108] that is, critique of the methodology that led to the birth of a science. As a result, the emergence of the critique of reason is a response to dissatisfaction with Islamic research methodology. The term critique of epistemology in this context is addressed to all Islamic scientific structures that are seen as products of the history of religious thought, which is deemed relative. Epistemological analysis that promotes criticism must be applied to the texts, both holy and profane, historical and philosophical, theological and juridical, sociological and anthropological, separately from their position or cognitive status in a tradition of belief, thought, or understanding.[109]

The main objective of this project is to break down the standardized religious postulates that existed within the realm of the unthought before moving to the realm of the unthinkable. Arkoun identifies these postulates as including, amongst other things: (1) historical continuity between the past and the present in the Muslim world, from the time of the Prophet until today; (2) Islam being equated to the state. In this matter Islam differs significantly from the other great religions; (3) Islam as a unifying force and provider of support. These postulates aim to stress that Islam is identical to religion, religion is identical to Islam, and Islam is identical to the Muslim world.[110]

These postulates ignore the scientific disciplines. Historical sociology will never accept that Islam is identical to the state, that Islam is the same as the Muslim community, and that Islam is a unifying force and a provider of support to the Muslim society. Social and cultural anthropology radically rejects equating Islam, religion, and the state in the postulates above. All religion is articulated in a number of myths, narratives, symbols, parables, rituals, and representations of collective dreams. These tools of articulation are not just used for religion, but also for all culture. In this perspective, culture cannot be separated from religion and politics, and it is also difficult to say that there is a stark difference between Islam and the other great religions. Philology — a fundamental discipline in critiquing all the traditions of exegesis of the Islamic, Christian and Jewish holy books — is also ignored by the postulates above.[111]

The question then emerges as to how the post-traditionalist community can go about a critique of Islamic scholarship. This question emerges because the critique of reason has so far not been viewed as an Islamic research method, since it does not yet have a standard structure to which to adhere. Post-traditionalism does not actually pretend to have established a new methodology in understanding Islam, but rather a critical framework for viewing the structures of orthodoxy which have not been questioned. In this sense, a critique of reason is part of this critical framework.

Criticism becomes very important if we examine the main trend in Islamic studies over a long period of time. Fazlur Rahman gives a good illustration in reviewing this general tendency. He writes:

> With the habit of writing commentaries for their own sake and the steady dwindling of original thought, the Muslim world witnessed the rise of [a] type of scholar who was truly encyclopedic in the scope of his learning but had little new to say on anything. This category of scholar-cum-commentator must be distinguished on the one hand from a very

different type of comprehensive thinker like Aristotle or even lesser figure like Ibnu Sina, who welded a variety of fields of inquiry into a unified system and coherent world view, and on [the] other hand from [a] modern type of specialist whose knowledge has extremely narrow confines. The later day medieval Muslim scholar I am talking about "studied" all the fields of knowledge available, but he did this mainly through commentaries and was himself a commentator and compiler.... One important but implicit assumption of this is that scholarship is not regarded as an active pursuit, a creative "reaching out" of the mind of the unknown — as is the case today — but rather as a more or less passive acquisition of already established knowledge.[112]

Fazlur Rahman's description above explains the general tendency for Islamic studies to preserve and guard the orthodoxy of Islamic scholarship, although that is not to say that there are not some thinkers who wish to escape this tendency. Slowly but surely, the realm of Islamic thought has narrowed through political processes, religious authority, or a synergy of the two. The space of the thinkable — to borrow Mohammed Arkoun's term — which was related to dogmatic debate in the classical period, became the space of the unthinkable, especially because of political control.

Arkoun also criticized the construction and content of Islamic thought:

Research on Islam as a religion is blocked because Muslims are becoming increasingly subject to the growing political, cultural and psychological constraints in their societies, while Islamologists, fascinated by the political effectiveness of "fundamentalists" give precedence to a combination of political science and political sociology in describing what they see as short-term trends, rather than have resource to the vitally necessary critical reappraisal of the epistemic framework of the Islamic cognitive system regarded long-term point of view.[113]

This issue can be narrowed down using a number of questions from the framework of contemporary philosophy, as proposed in the writings of Karl R. Popper, Thomas S. Kuhn, and Imre Lakatos. Using Karl R. Popper's philosophical framework, the question raised is: "Why do we find more things in the realm of justification of Islamic scholarship and very few related to new findings?"[114] If we use Thomas S. Kuhn's analytical terminology, then the question is: why in the discourse of Islamic thought is there a strong tendency to maintain "normal science" and no scientific pursuit of "revolutionary science"?[115] Or if we are using Imre Lakatos's framework: why is Islamic scholarship directed more towards "hard core" teachings that are desperately defended from intrusion to the extent that they cannot be refuted, than towards creative scholarship in the "protective belt" domain which can be clearly tested, reinforced, criticized, refuted, and corrected?[116]

These questions are intentionally strung together in order to show that there are still many things that should be debated in Islamic scholarship. This not only includes the material, but also the method used. In connection with this, I believe, there are at least two things that are both problems and agendas that must be resolved. The first problem is how to treat tradition, and the second is how to deal with religious texts, both those that are sacred because they originate from divine revelation or those that were produced by ulama in the past. These two agendas are interrelated, because an understanding of tradition greatly influences an understanding of the texts. Conversely, an understanding of the texts can influence the form that tradition takes.

Debating these two agendas using a critique of reason approach leads to two things: relativism of text and tradition on the one hand, and progressivism on the other. Relativism means negation of the texts (including divinely revealed texts) and tradition (including the traditions of the first Islamic generation, the Sunna) and as such, there is nothing to be sacralized from the two. Meanwhile, progressivism is a willingness to escape all shackles, including those of the texts and tradition. The emergence of the post-traditionalist discourse actually originated from the desire to be liberated from the religious understandings that had been made formal through orthodoxization.

So we come to the issue of tradition. Tradition here is interpreted as everything that is fundamentally related to the aspects of thought/thinking in Islamic civilization: doctrinal teachings, Islamic law, language, literature, art, scholastic theology, philosophy, and *tasawuf* or mysticism. On this matter, Mohammed Abed al-Jabiri[117] writes that there are at least two forms of knowledge (methodologies) concerning tradition which have become a corpus of knowledge in Islamic thought. The first method is the traditional method. This way of knowing about tradition, with all its aspects from religion to language and literature, holds to a literal model of understanding tradition (*al-fahm al-turâst li al-turâst*); that is, it is a form of understanding that refers to the views of the ulama from the past. The general features of this kind of approach lie in the issues that tradition faced in the past and its surrender to them. This approach, according to al-Jabiri, has two weaknesses, namely a lack of criticism due to the attitude of surrender, and a minimal historical awareness.

The second method is the orientalist approach. In this approach there are two aspects that must be read. The first aspect is the correlation between orientalism and imperialism that led to the Muslim–Christian conflict in the Middle Ages. This has had quite a large influence on the psychological atmosphere of the Muslim community, which feels inferior to the superior West. The second aspect concerns the objective conditions, both historical and methodological, that worked internally among European scholars and led to what Hassan Hanafi labels as Eurocentrism.[118] Both these approaches give rise to different characteristics in Islam.

Separately from this, in order to view an object of an academic study objectively, it is necessary to guard the distance between subject and object. It is necessary to maintain clarity of the research material, without it being influenced by feelings, emotions, or outside interests. This attitude is a significant problem for Muslim scholars who are supposed to be bound by religious dictums. Here al-Jabiri offers three approaches that allow for a level of objectivity in studies of tradition. The first approach is the structuralist method. Studying tradition using this method means studying the texts as they are, and situating them as a corpus, one unit of a system. First, the author of a text (writer, sect, or a particular current of thought) must be localized. This framework covers the various changes that motivate or restrict the thought of an author of a text. As a result, meaning cannot be grasped without first reading the expressions that represent a meaning, and this in turn can only be grasped through the reading of a text.

The second approach is historical analysis. This approach seeks to connect the thoughts of the author of a text to his historical, cultural, and political circles, amongst other things. This is important for at least two reasons: the necessity in understanding the historicity and genealogy of thought; and the necessity to test the validity and logical veracity of the conclusions reached through the structuralist approach. Validity here does not mean logical veracity, because this is already the objective of structuralism, but refers more to historical possibility (*imkân al-târikhî*), that is, the possibilities that allow us to know what is said in a text, what is not said, and what is never said.

The third approach is the critique of ideology. This approach is intended to express the ideological function, including the socio-political function, of a text of a particular system of thought (episteme). Revealing the ideological function of a classical text is a way to clearly situate it in a particular historical context.

These three approaches are interrelated, and insofar as they are related to tradition, they can be applied sequentially. However, when formulating a conclusion, the usual order used is to start with the historical analysis, then the critique of ideology, ending with the analysis of structuralism.[119] However, continuity must be maintained during the application of this methodology. Why? Because this issue is related to tradition as a part of our existence that must be expressed, not to be abandoned, to become a spectacle like a monument, and not as material for contemplation. Continuity is needed for several reasons: first, to reconstruct tradition in a new form with a new pattern of relationships; and secondly, to make tradition more contextual, especially at the level of rational understanding. As such, no matter how sophisticated an academic framework is, without being based on tradition, it will remain fragile and without grounding.

Besides the problem of methodology, other considerations that require attention in the critique of reason are the links between the approaches to Islamic scholarship that are linguistic–historic, theological–philosophical, and sociological–anthropological. It is important to recognize the different characteristics and forms of relations between text-based Islamic scholarship that uses the linguistic–philological approach, Islamic scholarship that is based on the products of thought, ideas, norms, concepts, and doctrines and uses a theological–philosophical approach, and Islamic scholarship related to social interaction that uses a sociological–anthropological approach.

In examining the relationships between these three approaches, Amin Abdullah[120] came up with a good analysis by questioning whether they were linear, parallel, or circular. Supporters of the linear model state the superiority of their own scholarly tradition and sometimes sneer at the other traditions of scholarship. As a result, they become less sensitive and pay less attention to the research results of those who use different approaches.

Those who adopt the parallel model are represented by Muslim historians who received academic training in the traditions of philosophy, philology, and socio-anthropology. However, they do not have a sufficient academic grounding to be able to gather each academic discourse into a comprehensive analysis. The difference between the linear and parallel models is that the former only involves mastering one academic tradition, while the latter involves mastering several traditions, but is unable to compile those traditions into an integrated analytical unit.

The solution to this weakness is the circular model, because adherents are aware of and consider all approaches in a multidimensional manner when studying Islamic scholarship as a comprehensive entity. Integrating these three approaches makes an individual more perceptive to the socio-anthropological dimension, while also paying attention to its philosophical and phenomenological aspects, as well as the linguistic-philological issues in Islamic tradition.

Using a critique of reason means that suspecting every product of thought and probing for the interests behind a thought is commonplace, even necessary. As a result, critique of reason is fundamentally opposed to the power of knowledge that slips into the subconscious and eliminates any awareness that everything we know to be neutral, essentialist, and substantialist, in truth contains interests. In this context, tradition can become an object of criticism, but at the same time can be the subject and tool of criticism. Criticism presupposes two elements. The first one is deconstruction (*tafkik*), that is, epistemological separation (*al-qathî'ah al-afistimalajiyah*) from all forms of authority that form (the tradition of) knowledge. This is done by remodelling the standardized system of relations into something fluid and dynamic, from absolute to relative, from ahistorical to historical. In the context of Islamic thought, authority of knowledge has a broad meaning, and it can take the form of culture, politics, history, social status, and so on. The second element is reconstruction, that is, the responsibility to insert reason into all problems.

In the context of deconstruction and reconstruction, the awareness that all traditions are invented and constructed is relevant. In the context of Islamic thought, we cannot simply refer blindly to the tradition of the Prophet Muhammad (Peace Be Upon Him, PBUH), to the Qur'an and Hadith, or to everything that occurred during the period of codification and consolidation (*'ashr al-tadwîn*), without passing through the perspective or "lens" constructed during this period. Is it not true that the history of Prophet Muhammad (PBUH) was only known after reading the books detailing the Prophet's history? Is not our understanding of the Qur'an also obtained through books of authoritative exegesis? This means that there was some authority that played a role in mobilizing knowledge. When speaking about fiqh, for instance, there is no way for people to free themselves from the authority of Imam Hanafi, Imam Malik, Imam

Syafi'i, Imam Hanbali, and so on. The same holds true for the Qur'an. The Qur'an cannot be seen purely as something transcendent, without influence from history and culture, but must be seen as a construct also formed by tradition and culture. That there are elements of tradition and culture in the Qur'an does not necessarily degrade the Qur'an and Islam, because when divine revelation comes into contact with anything outside of God it instantly becomes historical.

Up to this point, I have elaborated the concerns and characteristics of Islamic post-traditionalism. A strong feature of this community is the pattern of subversive thought through a critique of reason that continues to question and criticize the establishment. Will this model of thought endure, or will it simply follow the style because of political developments? History will be the test. It may well be that subversive thought is only a temporary response elicited when the post-traditionalists' socio-political position was under pressure from outside forces. Although this possibility cannot be ignored, it does not detract from the originality of post-traditionalist thought. Are not all products of thought influenced by, and products of, dialectics with developments occurring around them?

Notes

1. See for instance M.M. Billah's commentary on the term "Islamic post-traditionalism" in the paper "Kaum Muda NU: Hasil dari Pergeseran Struktural di Dalam Jama'ah Nahdliyyin". This paper was presented at "Post Tradisionalisme Islam: Dialektika Intelektual Kaum Muda NU/Islamic Post-Traditionalism: The Intellectual Dialect of the NU Youth", a discussion organized by ISIS on 27 March 2000. It was then published in *Bulletin Wacana Postra* (Jakarta: ISIS, 2001).
2. In the NU tradition, there is a famous saying or principle: *al-muhâfadhah 'alâ al-qadîm al-shâlih wa al-akhdzu bi al-jadîd al-ashlah* (maintaining the [traditions] of the past that are good, and adopting those that are new and better). Simply speaking, continuity is preserved in *al-muhâfadhah 'alâ al-qadîm al-shâlih*, while change comes from *al-akhdzu bi al-jadîd al-ashlah*. In the social sciences, this theory of "continuity and change" is applied largely by academics such as John O. Voll, *Islam Continuity and Change in the Modern World* (America: Westview Press, 1982); Azyumardi Azra, *Jaringan Ulama Timur Tengan dan Kepulauan Nusantara Abad XVII–XVII* (Bandung: Mizan, 1994); and Harry J. Benda, "Kontinuitas dan Perubahan dalam Islam di Indonesia", in *Sejarah dan Masyarakat, Lintasan Historis Islam di Indonesia*, edited by Taufik Abdullah (Jakarta: Pustaka Firdaus, 1987), pp. 26–41. The fundamental assumption of

this theory is that everything that occurs at a given point in time cannot be entirely separated from the past. No discourse or movement has ever appeared out of the blue. What actually happens is always a continuation of the past, albeit with elements of change. It is these aspects of change that cause life in society to continue to be dynamic.

3. For further information on these dynamics, see Andree Feillard, *NU vis-a-vis Negara, Pencarian Isi, Bentuk, dan Makna* (Yogyakarta: LKiS, 1999), pp. 364–411. See also Martin van Bruinessen, *NU, Tradisi, Relasi-Relasi Kuasa, Pencarian Wacana Baru* (Yogyakarta: LKiS, 1994), p. 1994.

4. Almost all observers acknowledge Abdurrahman Wahid's determining role in generating NU's spirit of intellectualism. Besides Martin van Bruinessen, Greg Barton, and Andree Feillard, see also John L. Esposito and John O. Voll, *Makers of Contemporary Islam* (Oxford: Oxford University Press, 2001), pp. 199–216.

5. In this context, foreign observers, and often indigenous ones too, are frequently deceived when examining NU, for two reasons. First, they often lack awareness that the educated members within NU still represent a very thin layer that can easily be crushed by the larger mainstream layer in NU. Secondly, they forget that the culture of the NU community is still paternalistic and oriented towards NU figures. This means that the charisma of a figure is still very influential in determining the direction the community moves in. Observations that tend to be instantaneous, that generalize things, and that forget NU's cultural anatomy have meant that they have had to correct their writing on civil society in NU, especially after the national political upheaval that forced Abdurrahman Wahid to step down from his presidency. However, to say that the theme of NU civil society is only a stepping stone to seize power is also not entirely true, because not all layers of NU civil society are involved in politics. It was the apolitical group that formed the community which developed the idea of post-traditionalism. When NU held its 30th Congress in Lirboyo, Kediri, East Java, the NU youth who were members of several NGOs held a "Congress of the Youth" to discuss the election of Abdurrahman Wahid as president, internal NU problems, empowerment of civil society, and national problems. This meeting was important because up to that point they had been engaged in empowering civil society as a counter and balance to the state; and as such, when the "golden child" of NU became president, they found themselves in a difficult position. For more on this matter, see Rumadi, "Civil Society dan NU Pasca Abdurrahman Wahid", *Kompas*, 5 November 1999.

6. Andree Feillard, *NU vis-a-vis Negara*, pp. 428–29. The developments within NU at the 30th Congress of 1999 in Lirboyo, Kediri and of PKB, especially concerning their respective ideological bases, were interesting because of a contradiction between the two. While in 1998, NU facilitated the establishment

of PKB based on the principle of nationalism and as a secular party that did not use Islam as an ideological basis, the NU Congress in Lirboyo brought NU back to an Islamic basis.
7. See for instance *Tempo*, editions 19–25 November 2001, within the rubric of religion.
8. Abdul Mun'im DZ, "Gerakan Liberalisme dalam NU" (paper presented at "Post-Tradisionalisme Islam: Dialektika Intelektual Kaum Muda NU", a discussion organized by ISIS on 27 March 2000).
9. The progressive NU group that Laode Ida refers to is oriented more towards the socio-political movement than the intellectual movement.
10. Laode Ida, *Gerakan Sosial Kelompok NU Progresif*, pp. 160–202.
11. See Franz Magnis-Suseno's introduction in Sindhunata, *Dilema Usaha Manusia Rasional*, 2nd ed. (Jakarta: PT. Gramedia, 1983).
12. Laode Ida, *Gerakan Sosial Kelompok NU Progresif*, pp. 172–74.
13. See for instance *Tashwirul Afkar*, no. 1 (1997), which specifically dismantles the *ahl al-sunnah wa al-jamâ'ah* doctrine.
14. For more on the struggle of the NU youth, both those active in the intellectual and social activist realms, see Hairus Salim HS and Muhammad Ridwan, eds., *Kultur Hibrida: Anak Muda di Jalur Kultural* (Yogyakarta: LKiS, 1999).
15. Martin van Bruinessen, *NU, Tradisi, Relasi-Relasi Kuasa, dan Pencarian Wacana Baru*, pp. 233–34.
16. See also Marzuki Wahid, "Post-Tradisionalisme Islam: Gairah Baru Pemikiran Islam di Indonesia", *Tashwirul Afkar*, no. 10 (2001): 16.
17. Marzuki Wahid, "Post-Tradisionalisme Islam", p. 17.
18. See Hairus Salim HS and Muhammad Ridwan, "Catatan Pendahuluan", in *Kultur Hibrida*, p. 7.
19. Muhammad Hormus, *Kritik Epistemologi LKiS terhadap Bangunan Keilmuan Islam dan Kemasyarakatan di Indonesia* (Yogyakarta: IAIN Sunan Kalijaga, 1998), pp. 62–63.
20. As a result, they are always suspicious of a number of major narratives — those produced by tradition, ideology, or the holy texts. For this community, the major narratives only seek to monopolize the truth. Global ideologies and dominant interpretations of religion also wish to monopolize the truth. On this basis, post-traditionalists reject all forms of this kind of unification, as it is unable to resolve problems. Here, Marzuki Wahid's notes on the 2001 "Manifesto Perang Kebudayaan/Cultural War Manifesto" for the NU youth of 2015 in Malang are interesting to consider. The manifesto suggests that the 2015 target of the NU youth movement is to: (1) Seize moral and intellectual leadership at all levels of social movements; (2) Remain consistent in extra-parliamentary politics based on multiculturalism by continuing to respect others as fellow citizens, complete with their own unique traditions and

culture; and (3) Seriously prepare for an economical society, by building an independent economic basis for the creation of a civil society. See Marzuki Wahid, "Post-Tradisionalisme Islam", p. 17.
21. Zaini Rahman, "Post-Tradisionalisme Islam: Epistemologi Peloncat Tangga", *Postra,* introductory edition, November 2001, p. 59.
22. Muhammad Abed al-Jabiri, *Post-Tradisionalisme Islam,* translated by Ahmad Baso (Yogyakarta: LKiS, 2000), pp. 24–25. See also Muhammad Abed al-Jabiri, *Nahnu wa al-Turâts, Qirâ'at Mu'âshirah fî Turâtsinâ al-Falsafî,* 5th ed. (Casablanca: al-Markaz al-Tsaqafi al-Arabi, 1986), pp. 11–19.
23. Muhammad Abed al-Jabiri, *Post-Tradisionalisme Islam,* p. 8.
24. Muhammad Abed al-Jabiri, *Nahnu wa al-Turâts,* p. 13.
25. For more, see the interview of Hassan Hanafi, "Mengkaji Tradisi untuk Transformasi dan Revolusi", *Tashwirul Afkar,* no. 10 (2001): 78–83.
26. Muhammad Abed al-Jabiri, *Post-Tradisionalisme Islam,* p. 28.
27. Ibid., pp. 29–30.
28. For more information, see Muhammad Abed al-Jabiri, *Nahnu wa al-Turâts,* pp. 21–24.
29. Ibid., pp. 25–26.
30. Ahmad Baso, "Postmodernisme sebagai Kritik Islam, Kontribusi Metodologis "Kritik Nalar" Muhammad Abed al-Jabiri", in the Translator's Introduction, Muhammad Abed al-Jabiri, *Post-Tradisionalisme Islam,* pp. xxii–xxiii.
31. Muhammad Abed al-Jabiri, *Post-Tradisionalisme Islam,* pp. 19–21.
32. Abdul Mun'im DZ, "Pembaruan Berbasis Tradisi, Sebuah Pengantar", in *Post-Tradisionalisme Islam, Menyingkap Corak Pemikiran dan Gerakan PMII,* by Muh. Hanif Dhakiri and Zaini Rahman (Jakarta: Isisindo Mediatama, 2000), p. viii.
33. Abdul Mun'im DZ, "Pembaruan Berbasis Tradisi, Sebuah Pengantar", pp. ix–x.
34. Zuhairi Misrawi, "Dari Tradisionalisme Menuju Post-Tradisionalisme", *Tashwirul Afkar,* no. 10 (2001): 58–59.
35. The *Naqd al-'Aql al-'Arabî* [Critique of Arab Reason] trilogy consists of three books: namely, *Takwîn al-'Aql al-'Arabî* [Formation of Arab Reason] (1982), *Bunyah al-'Aql al-'Arabî* [Structure of Arab Reason] (1986), and *al-'Aql al-Siyâsi al-'Arabî* [Arab Political Reasoning] (1990), all three of which were published by Markaz Dirâsah al-Wihdah al-Arabiyah in Beirut, Lebanon.
36. Nasr Hamid Abu Zayd, *Mafhûm al-Nâsh, Dirâsah fî 'Ulûm al-Qur'ân,* 3rd ed. (Beirut: Markaz al-S|aqafî al-'Arabi, 1996).
37. Historical references of this enthusiasm are easy enough to find. For instance, in Ibnu Khaldun's *Muqaddimah* he expresses concern over historical writing that has lost objectivity, and even history that is written chronologically and thus loses its sociological aspect. This is similar to when Imam al-Ghazâlî criticizes Ibnu Sina's philosophy in his work *Tahâfut al-Falâsifah* [Poisoned

[Minds] of the Philosophers], or when Ibnu Rusyd criticizes al-Ghazâlî in his book *Tahâfut al-Tahâfut* [Poisoned Poison]. Al-Ghazâlî criticized Aristotle's philosophy but accepted neo-Platonism, to the extent that he could be called a neo-platonic philosopher.

38. Muhammad Abed al-Jabiri, *Post-Tradisionalisme Islam*, pp. 186–88.
39. Ibid., p. 190.
40. Ibid., pp. 191–93.
41. Fachry Ali and Bahtiar Effendy, *Merambah Jalan Baru Islam, Rekonstruksi Pemikiran Islam Masa Orde Baru* (Bandung: Mizan, 1986).
42. M. Syafi'i Anwar, *Pemikiran dan Aksi Islam Indonesia, sebuah Kajian tentang Cendikiawan Muslim Orde Baru* (Jakarta: Paramadina, 1995).
43. Deliar Noer, *Gerakan Modern Islam di Indonesia 1900–1942* (Jakarta: LP3ES, 1996). This book was first printed in 1980, and by 1996 had been reprinted eight times.
44. Howard M. Federspiel, *Persatuan Islam, Pembaruan Islam Indonesia Abad XX* (Yogyakarta: Gadjah Mada University Press, 1996).
45. Greg Barton, *Gagasan Islam Liberal di Indonesia, Pemikiran Neo-Modernisme Nurcholish Madjid, Djohan Effendi, Ahmad Wahib dan Abdurrahman Wahid* (Jakarta: Paramadina, 1999).
46. Kamal Hassan, *Muslim Intellectual Response to New Order Modernization in Indonesia* (Kuala Lumpur: Dewan Bahasa, 1980).
47. For the general characteristics of these two groups, see Chapter 2.
48. In the conclusion of her dissertation, Robin Bush states:
"In spite of these instances of overlap and blurring of the divide between the Post-Traditionalists and *"Islam liberal,"* and in spite of Rumadi's attempts to argue that they are nearly identical save the "plus" element of attention to local tradition, evidence indicates that this is not so much a "new primordialism" but a very old primordialism dressed up in new clothing. *First*, the historical divide between the modernists and traditionalists has coloured Islamic relations in Indonesia since the modernist/revivalist emergence at the beginning of the 20th century, though it has certainly evolved along with the developments of neo-modernism and renewal of thought among traditionalist Muslims. The bitterness expressed on both sides about particular instances in history which were seen as betrayals is still very strong.

Second, the Post-Traditionalist/JIL split is driven by the same dynamic as the power struggle and contestation of territory as the earlier conflicts. That is while earlier modernist-traditionalist hostility erupted over such things as influence over voting patterns of grassroots followers, political power, positions in parliament, etc, the contemporary version of this conflict is a struggle over the territory of discourse. The activities of producing a discourse — publishing journal articles, holding seminars, training activists — are as much of a political terrain as partisan contestations within the DPR, and the territory of such discourse, its impact however indirect and elusively measured on a society, is the point of this contemporary conflict. In both cases, while the crux of the conflict was a territorial and political struggle of some kind, it was expressed in ideological terms. So while earlier modernist-traditionalist conflict may have been about a cabinet position or seats on a political party's executive board, it was expressed by the traditionalists of the time in terms of the modernists "lack of appreciation for the religious authority of the *kiai*", their "arrogance and derision of traditionalist Islam," or their "unwillingness to perform certain rituals." The contemporary version of the conflict, while about contestation over a discursive territory — specifically the "progressive" civil-society oriented discourse of moderate Islam, it is expressed in terms of "ahistoricity of texts" and "lack of attention to the marginalized and local tradition." There are substantial differences between these conflicts — ideologically speaking they are almost at opposite ends of a spectrum. At the same time, the dynamic of modernist-traditionalist struggle for power, couched, from the traditionalist perspective, in accusations of lack of respect for a particular set of beliefs and expression of Islam, remains a constant."

See Robin Bush, *Islam and Civil Society in Indonesia: The Case of The Nahdlatul Ulama* (Dissertation, University of Washington, 2002), pp. 202–3. (These page numbers may differ from the original dissertation, as I received a double-spaced copy but for economical reasons printed off a single-spaced hard copy. As such, the pages cited are from the latter.)

49. Zuhairi Misrawi told how when he was a researcher at Lakpesdam NU, he was once invited to join a Masjid al-Azhar discussion group, the Youth Islamic Study Club (YISC) of Kebayoran, Jakarta, on Islamic post-traditionalism, which was panelled by a Muhammadiyah figure, Dr Zainun Kamal. During the discussion, Dr Zainun Kamal stated clearly that post-traditionalism was a discourse of the NU youth (interview with Zuhairi Misrawi in Jakarta, 4 November 2002). These kinds of claims are not entirely correct, though to say that they are completely incorrect is also not true. Ulil Abshar-Abdalla, who is considered the most brilliant intellectual figure amongst the NU youth, spoke for example at the seminar on Bridging Islamic Post-Traditionalism and Liberal Islam in the New Passion for Indonesian Islamic Thought, which was held in the middle of November 2001 in Wisata International Hotel, Jakarta, by BEM IAIN Jakarta. Ulil Abshar-Abdalla, who was not involved in NU youth discussions concerning post-traditionalism, stated that post-traditionalism was a more advanced effort to preserve the conflict between PMII and HMI, or between NU and Muhammadiyah — the traditionalists versus the modernists. Post-traditionalism was more an effort to emphasize identity than to develop a discourse of thought. This suggests that post-traditionalism, both in the

sense of a community and a discourse of thought, cannot be separated from the NU youth.
50. See Rudhy Suharto, "Menimbang Pemikiran Islam Liberal", *Majalah Syi'ar*, July 2002, pp. 7–10.
51. See the materials of the JIL workshop, 1–2 March 2002, p. 1.
52. For more on this matter, see Fazlur Rahman, *Neo-Modernisme Islam, Metode dan Alternatif*, 2nd ed., edited by Taufik Adnan Amal (Bandung: Mizan, 1989), pp. 17– 21.
53. See Harun Nasution, *Pembaruan dalam Islam, Sejarah Pemikiran dan Gerakan*, 9th ed. (Jakarta: Bulan Bintang, 1992), pp. 28–33. See also Harun Nasution, "Antara Pembaruan dan Pemurnian", interview in *Pesantren* 5, no. 1 (1988): 30–36.
54. Charles Kurzman, *Liberal Islam, A Sourcebook* (Oxford: Oxford University Press, 1998), p. 5.
55. A little of Barton's explanation that equates the two terms states: "Neo-modernist Islamic thought in Indonesia is a profound movement of liberal thought, both in its general understanding and in its more specific understanding as referred to by political theorists such as Leonard Binder". See Greg Barton, *Gagasan Islam Liberal di Indonesia, Pemikiran Neo-Modernisme Nurcholish Madjid, Djohan Effendi, Ahmad Wahib dan Abdurrahman Wahid* (Jakarta: Paramadina, 1999), pp. 519–20.
56. See Ahmad Baso, "Islam Liberal sebagai Ideologi, Nurcholish Madjid *versus* Abdurrahman Wahid", *Gerbang* 6, no. 3 (February–April 2000). He wrote the same thing in "PMII, dari 'Islam Liberal' ke 'Post-Tradisionalisme Islam' " in the epilogue of Muh. Hanif Dhakiri and Zaini Rahman, *Post-Tradisionalisme Islam*, pp. 95–111.
57. Greg Barton, *Gagasan Islam Liberal di Indonesia*, p. 8.
58. John L. Esposito and John O. Voll, *Makers of Contemporary Islam*, p. 202.
59. Zaini Rahman, "Post-Tradisionalisme Islam: Epistemologi Peloncat Tangga", *Postra*, introductory edition, November 2001, p. 58.
60. Zaini Rahman, "Post-Tradisionalisme Islam", p. 58.
61. Ahmad Baso, "Modernisme Islam vs Post-Tradisionalisme Islam", pp. 37–38.
62. See Nurcholish Madjid, *Islam, Doktrin, Peradaban: Sebuah Telaah Kritis tentang Masalah Keimanan, Kemanusiaan, dan Kemodernan* (Jakarta: Paramadina, 1992), pp. 598–607.
63. On this, Fyzee writes: "We need not bother about nomenclature, but if some name has to be given, let us call it *'liberal Islam'* ". See A.A. Fyzee, "The Reinterpretation of Islam", in *Islam in Transition: Muslim Perspectives*, edited by John J. Donohue and John L. Esposito (New York: Oxford University Press, 1982), p. 193.
64. See Charles Kurzman, *Liberal Islam*, p. 13.

65. Ibid., p. 13.
66. The superiority of Kurzman's book in comparison to Binder's is in the variations of the themes he discusses. While Binder only emphasizes liberalism in the context of political thought, Kurzman is more varied, discussing themes from politics and democracy, women's rights, the rights of non-Muslims, and freedom of thought, to ideas about modernity.
67. Greg Barton, *Gagasan Islam Liberal di Indonesia*, pp. 43–45.
68. Kurzman notes that liberal Islam and revivalist Islam often clash, sometimes quite violently. In such clashes, the liberalists are almost always the victims, especially if the state or those in power side with the revivalists. Several cases are relevant, including: Mahmoud Muhamed Thaha (Sudan, 1910–85) who opposed the Sudanese government's understanding of Islamic law, and was executed for being deemed an apostate; Subhi al-Salih (Lebanon, d. 1986) who opened all doors to *ijtihad* or interpretation, and was shot dead by a Shia in 1986; Farag Fuda (Egypt, 1945–92), a liberal politician and columnist who criticized Islamic extremism and was killed in 1992; and Maulvi Farook (India, 1945–90) and Qazi Nissar Ahmed (India, 1948–94), who were killed respectively in 1990 and 1994 because they opposed the violence of the Islamic separatists in Kashmir, India. For more, see Charles Kurzman, *Liberal Islam*, p. 12.
69. Charles Kurzman, *Liberal Islam*, p. 13.
70. This perspective colours the way modernists view Islam's struggle with local culture. The purity of Islam is interpreted as its ability to tame objects. See for instance Taufik Abdullah, "Pengantar: Islam, Sejarah dan Masyarakat", in *Sejarah dan Masyarakat, Lintasan Historis Islam di Indonesia*, edited by Taufik Abdullah (Jakarta: YOI, 1987), p. 3.
71. Contrast this with Robert D. Lee, who attempts to identify the authentic aspects of Islamic thought in his book *Mencari Islam Auntentik, Dari Nalar Puitis Iqbal hingga Nalar Kritis Arkoun* (Bandung: Mizan, 2000).
72. See the short article by Rumadi, "Islam Liberal 'Plus'=Post-Tradisionalisme Islam", *Kompas*, 23 November 2001.
73. See *Laporan Hasil Kegiatan Workshop dan Need Assessment Jaringan Islam Emansipatoris* in Ciloto, 21–24 July 2002, in cooperation with P3M and the Ford Foundation, pp. 9–12.
74. See Nasr Hamid Abu Zayd, *Tekstualitas Al-Qur'an, Kritik terhadap Ulumul Qur'an* [original title: *Mafhûm al-Nâsh: Dirâsah fî 'Ulûm al-Qur'ân*], translated by Khoiron Nahdliyyin (Yogyakarta: LKiS, 2001), p. 1.
75. Conversation with Zuhairi Misrawi (Coordinator of the Emancipatory Islam Program, P3M) on 21 July 2002. Zuhairi Misrawi repeated this argument several times on a number of different occasions.
76. Profile of the Emancipatory Islamic Network, P3M Jakarta.

77. See Luthfi Assyaukani, "Empat Agenda Islam yang Membebaskan", *Koran Tempo*, 13 July 2001.
78. Material from JIL Workshop, 1–2 March 2002.
79. Interview with M. Jadul Maula, 23 December 2002.
80. I do not agree with Charles Kurzman's theory that sees liberal Islam more in the context of "religious practice" and aligns it with customary Islam and revivalist (puritan) Islam. I would rather situate liberal Islam in the context of a religious discourse that provides a counter discourse to those that have become orthodox, pro-status quo, that do not side with the oppressed and minorities but side with those in power, and so on. The discourse of liberal Islam seeks to revive the liberating spirit of Islam that has almost become extinct, consumed by the processes of orthodoxy.
81. Charles Kurzman, *Liberal Islam*, p. 8.
82. Albert Hourani, *Arabic Thought in the Liberal Age, 1798–1939* (London: Oxford University Press, 1962), pp. 140–41.
83. Charles Kurzman, *Liberal Islam*, p. 9.
84. Azyumardi Azra, "Mengkaji Ulang Modernisme Muhammadiyah", *Kompas*, 9 November 1990.
85. See Manna' al-Qaththan, *Târikh Tasyrî' al-Islâmî* (Egypt: Muassasah al-Risâlah, 1992), pp. 331–32. Elsewhere, I have presented a more comprehensive classification of Islamic thought into various periods, especially concerning the field of fiqh. See Rumadi, "al-Maslahat al-Mursalah dalam Pembaruan Hukum Islam di Indonesia" (MA thesis, IAIN Imam Bonjol), pp. 86–132.
86. Charles Kurzman, *Liberal Islam*, pp. 13–17. Kurzman's categories are still problematic. The question could be posed: what are the areas which liberal Islam is unable to reach? This is a fair question because using Kurzman's categories means that liberal Islam is able to reach almost all religious areas, except for those matters that are — to borrow from Imam Syafi'i (d. 204 H) — *ma'lûm min al-dîn bi al-dlarûrah* (agreed on), such as the obligation to pray, the number of prayer cycles, and other personal religious issues. Almost all public issues fall within the realm of liberal Islam. Kurzman does not explicitly explain this, but in light of the works he has edited and categorized as liberal Islam, it seems that Kurzman uses a very minimal standard in determining the extent of an individual's liberalism. It is thus understandable why he groups Yusuf Qardhawi and M. Natsir with the liberal Islam community. In actual fact, these two figures give the impression of believing more in fanatical (conservative, fundamentalist?) Islam than liberal Islam, though this is not to rule out any possibility of either of the two possessing a liberal side to their thinking. In addition, Kurzman's liberal Islam paradigm is too oriented towards the texts. This may mean that liberal Islam is only understood on a normative level, its dialectics being normative, not historical. In actual fact, liberal Islam is more

historical than normative, although liberalism itself cannot be separated from its normative aspects.

87. Ahmad Baso, "Neo-Modernisme Islam vs Post-Tradisionalisme Islam", *Tashwirul Afkar*, no. 10 (2001), p. 32. Mentioning these names does not mean that they all shared the same ideas. For instance, Muhammad Abed al-Jabiri and Nasr Hamid Abu Zayd both accentuated different aspects.
88. See Martin van Bruinessen, *NU, Tradisi, Relasi-Relasi Kuasa*, p. 221.
89. Ahmad Baso, "Neo-Modernisme Islam vs Post-Tradisionalisme Islam", p. 32.
90. Desantara runs study groups or *halaqah* in a number of regions, including West Java, Central Java, and Sulawesi, to discuss Islam and local culture. It also holds a series of discussions in Jakarta to further elaborate on the idea of Islamic *pribumisasi* (indigenization) that Abdurrahman Wahid once raised at the end of the 1980s and beginning of the 1990s. Ahmad Baso reflects positively on this series of discussions in his book *Plesetan Lokalitas, Politik Pribumisasi Islam* (Jakarta: Desantara and The Asia Foundation, 2002).
91. Ahmad Baso, "Neo-Modernisme Islam vs Post-Tradisionalisme Islam", p. 33.
92. See P3M Jakarta's report on Emancipatory *Tafsir* Study Groups held in September 2001 at the PKK guest house in Jakarta, and in October in al-Hikam *pesantren*, Malang. There were two intakes, each consisting of two rounds. The first was a methodological exploration, and the second for *bahts al-masâil*. The first intake was in Jakarta, and the second in East Java. Participants were young *kiai*, NGO activists, students, and *pesantren* leaders from a variety of areas, including Lampung, Central Java, East Java, Jakarta, and West Nusa Tenggara.
93. See "*Ahl al-Sunnah wa al-Jamâ'ah*, Asal-Usul, Perkembangan, Epistemologi, dan Doktrin-Doktrinnya" (paper presented in the *halaqah* on *Ahl al-Sunnah wa al-Jamâ'ah*, held by the Bahstul Masail forum and NU's Central Advisory board, 19–29 October 1996). This paper was a modified version of "Mengembalikan Aswaja sebagai *Manhaj al-Fikr* dalam Memahami Islam" (paper presented at the *Ahl al-Sunnah wa al-Jamâ'ah* Workshop, PMII Central Board in Tulungagung, 20 October 1995).
94. See for instance *Tashwirul Afkar*, no. 1 (1997), which specifically addresses the theme, "Menafsir Ulang *Ahl al-Sunnah wa al-Jamâ'ah*/Reinterpreting *Ahl al-Sunnah wa al-Jamâ'ah*".
95. Muhammad Abid al-Jabiri, *al-Mas'alah al-Tsaqâfiyah* (Beirut: Markaz Dirâsah al-Wihdah al-Arabiyah, 1994).
96. See *Tashwirul Afkar*, no. 6 (1999), especially pp. 96–97.
97. On this, see the interview with KH Mustofa Bisri, "Berpijak Tradisi, Mengkaji Hasanah Lain", *Tashwirul Afkar*, no. 9 (2000): 123–28.

98. Abdul Mun'im DZ, "Gerakan Liberalisme dalam NU" (paper presented in a discussion at the Institute for Social Institutions Studies [ISIS], Hotel Mega Matra, Jakarta, 27 March 2000).
99. For more, see Ahmad Baso, "Pengantar Penerjemah: Post-Tradisionalisme sebagai Kritik Islam, Kontribusi Metodologis "Kritik Nalar" Muhammed Abed al-Jabiri", in *Post-Tradisionalisme Islam*, by Muhammaed Abed al-Jabiri (Yogyakarta: LKiS, 2000), pp. xxix–xxx. I am not too concerned with the difference between these two terms because the two have no principle differences. As evidenced by history, "Islamic reason" has been highly influenced by Arab reason, especially translated through the structure of language, as language is a structure of reason. Adam Schaff (1967) notes that a language system (not only its lexicon but also its semantic system) has a large impact on the way its speakers see the world, including the way they interpret and break it down, which in turn influences the way they think.
100. Jacques Waardenburg, *Classical Approach to the Study of Religion* (London: The Hague, 1973), p. 2.
101. One other matter that is very prominent in contemporary studies of Islam in various parts of the Muslim world is the emergence of a new tradition whereby Muslims are beginning to treat Islam more liberally, in an attempt to escape from the shackles of tradition, the texts, and so on. They do not hesitate to critique those religious traditions that have always been understood and accepted at face value without question. See Nashr Hamid Abu Zayd, *Mafhûm al-Nash, Dirâsat fî 'Ulûm al-Qur'ân* (Egypt: al-Hai'ah al-Mishriyah al-'mmah li al-Kitâb, 1993), which not only critiques the foundations of the understandings of the Qur'an, but also questions the process of revelation which possibly involved reductions. This is of course a highly sensitive issue in Islam because it can lead to conclusions about the relativism of the Qur'an. The same observation can be made of another of Abu Zayd's books, *Naqd al-Khithâb al-Dînî* (Cairo: Sînâ li al-Nasyr, 1993), and those of thinkers such as Muhammad Abed al-Jabiri with his *Critique of Arab Reason*, Hassan Hanafi's *Critique of Islamic Reason*, and Mohammed Arkoun's *Applied Islamology*.
102. For a good account of the relations between text and reality, and the claim that the Qur'an can be interpreted openly, see Nasr Hamid Abu Zayd, *Mafhûm al-Nash*. In this book, he concludes that the Qur'an is more of a cultural product (*muntaj al-tsaqafî*), although its ideas are divine revelation. However, the elements that give shape to this revelation, such as language, the text, and other historical processes, are a result of the dialectics of Islamic culture.
103. On the elements of liberation in Islam, see Farid Essack, *Qur'an, Liberation and Pluralism* (Oxford: Oneworld Oxford, 1997). See also Ali Asghar Engineer, *Islam dan Teologi Pembebasan* (Yogyakarta: Pustaka Pelajar, 1999).

104. To date, conventional studies of Islam have tended to emphasize normativity over historicity, in the sense that historical reality must submit to the normative provisions found in the text of the Qur'an and Hadith. Although it might seem like there is freedom of thought, that freedom must also submit to the text, and may not go beyond the text. As a result, although in fiqh and *ushûl al-fiqh* there is the understanding that in application of law the objectives of Islamic law or *maqâshid al-syarî'ah* must be prioritized, in practice, when establishing laws, attention is paid primarily to *maqâshid al-lughah* (objectives of philology). That is, as long as a legal dictum can be accounted for normatively it is deemed complete, regardless of whether it is of benefit to the prosperity of humankind or not. As such, the benefits sought are not for the prosperity of humankind but for the texts, because benefiting the texts is considered a benefit to humankind.

105. The birth of Islam as a critique of reality was later seen as the embryo of the theology of liberation in Islam. For further argumentation on this matter, see Asghar Ali Engineer, *Islam dan Teologi Pembebasan* [original title: *Islam and Liberation Theology: Essay on Liberative Elements in Islam*], translated by Agung Prihantoro (Yogyakarta: Pustaka Pelajar, 1999).

106. Muhammad Arkoun, *Al-Fikr al-Islâm: Naqd wa ijtihâd*, translated by Hasyim Salih (London: Dâr al-Sâqi, 1990).

107. This kind of atmosphere in turn produced authoritative webs of power in the form of Islamic research structures that promoted "obedience" over "criticism". In the view of the structuralists, these kinds of research structures then produce subjects (the researcher, society, the Muslim community), and not the other way around. On the relationship between text and reality, this perspective argues that it was reality that formed the religious texts and not the texts that formed reality. If this structuralist view is correct, then it is no longer relevant to talk about the subject in Islamic research, because the above reality unconsciously proclaims the death of the subject. Researchers are no longer a subject, but become the "object" of the religious structure that the Islamic community created itself through the process of orthodoxy. In rather unadorned language, "The Islamic community was locked in a prison that it created itself." Yet strangely, this "prison" is often deemed the "saviour" that will lead people to happiness.

108. Epistemology is one of the branches of philosophy that talks about the methods used to obtain and arrange a structure of knowledge. As such, epistemology talks about the structures of reason that form knowledge. When explaining Arab reason (*al-aql al-'arabî*), Al-Jabiri stated that reason (*al-'aql*) was the set of rules and laws of thought determined by a particular culture (Arab) as a foundation to obtain knowledge. These laws of thought are often imposed as the episteme by a particular culture (Arab). See Muhammad 'Abid al-

Jabiri, *Takwîn al-'Aql al-'Arabî*, 5th ed. (Beirut: Markaz al-Dirâsah al-Wihdah al-'Arabiyah, 1991), p. 15.
109. Mohammed Arkoun, "Kritik Konsep Reformasi Islam", in *Dekonstruksi Syari'ah II, Kritik Konsep dan Penjelajahan Lain* [original title: *Islamic Law Reform and Human Right Challenges and Rejoinders*], by Abdullahi Ahmed an-Na'im et al., translated by Farid Wajidi (Yogyakarta: LKiS, 1996), p. 13.
110. Mohammed Arkoun, "Kritik Konsep Reformasi Islam", p. 14.
111. Ibid., pp. 15–16.
112. Fazlur Rahman, *Islam and Modernity: Transformation of an Intellectual Tradition* (Chicago: University of Chicago Press, 1982), p. 38.
113. Mohammed Arkoun, "Topicality of the Problem of the Person in Islamic Thought", *International Social Science Journal* (August 1988): 420–21. See also Robert D. Lee, *Mencari Islam Autentik: Dari Nalar Puitis Iqbal hingga Nalar Kritis Arkoun* [original title: *Overcoming Tradition and Modernity: The Search of Islamic Authenticity*], translated by Ahmad Baiquni (Bandung: Mizan, 2000), pp. 165–98.
114. Karl R. Popper, *The Logic of Scientific Discovery* (London: Unwin Hymann, 1987).
115. Thomas S. Kuhn, *The Structure of Scientific Revolution* (Chicago: University of Chicago Press, 1970).
116. Imre Lakatos, "Falsification and the Methodology of Scientific Research Program", in *Criticism and the Growth of Knowledge*, edited by Imre Lakatos and Alan Musgrave (Cambridge: Cambridge University Press, 1970), pp. 132–38.
117. Mohammed Abed al-Jabiri, *Post-Tradisionalisme Islam*, pp. 9–11.
118. Eurocentrism from the orientalist project inspired Hassan Hanafi to develop its opposite, occidentalism (*'ilm al-istighrâb*). Although there are several aspects to this concept that need to be challenged, it does have the ability to create a new awareness of the backwardness of the Muslim community in comparison to other civilizations. On occidentalism, see Hassan Hanafi, *Oksidentalisme, Sikap Kita terhadap Tradisi Barat* [original title: *Muqaddimah fî 'Ilmi al-Istighrâb*], translated by M. Najib Bukhori (Jakarta: Paramadina, 2000). For a comparison, see also Asaf Husein, Robert Olson, and Jamil Qureshi, eds., *Orientalism, Islam and Islamist* (Amana Books, 1984). See also Mohammed Abed al-Jabiri, "al-Istisyrâq fi al-Falsafah: Manhaj wa Ru'yah" in *al-Turats wa al-Hadâtsah: Dirâsah wa Munâqasyah*, by Mohammed Abed al-Jabiri (Beirut: Markaz al-S|aqafi al-'Arabi, 1991), pp. 63–94.
119. For further information, see al-Jabiri, *Post-Tradisionalisme Islam*, pp. 19–21. More technically speaking, structural analysis seeks to remodel the structures that have always been viewed as standardized, and see them as changing variables. The consequence of this is liberation from all authority inherent in these structures, which in turn allows us to plant our own authority in them.

This analytical model is also known as deconstruction (*tafkik*), that is, breaking down the standardized and stagnant system of relations and making it a "non structure", changing and fluid; in other words, shifting it from absolute to relative, from something ahistorical to something more historical, from absolute to temporal.

120. Amien Abdullah, "Pendekatan dan Kajian Islam: Normatif atau Historis Membangun Kerangka Dasar Filsafat Ilmu-Ilmu Keislaman" (unpublished paper prepared for the compilation of the book on Methodology of Islamic Scholarship by the PPSDM of Syarif Hidayatullah UIN, Jakarta).

4

ISLAMIC POST-TRADITIONALISM AND THE FUTURE OF NU INTELLECTUALISM

HALAQAH: SOCIALIZATION OF THE ISLAMIC POST-TRADITIONALIST IDEA

In this section, I will examine several of the activities that the post-traditionalist community undertakes to improve and make public its ideas. I will do so by looking at a number of institutes that run *halaqah* (religious study groups), Study Together programmes, Bahts al-Masâil (forums),[1] and so on as a way of spreading Islamic post-traditionalist ideas. The critical ideas of the post-traditionalist community are socialized through a variety of methods and strategies. Besides publication and public discussions, *halaqah*[2] and Study Together programmes and all their variations are common methods. *Halaqah* are essentially seminar forums, in the broad sense of the term, which discuss religious issues related to contemporary demands according to a set curriculum.

They pay significant attention to religious discourse that is progressive, liberal, enlightening, not conservative, and anti-textual/scriptural. The focus of their attention is no longer on Islam as a religion that must be taken for granted, but has shifted to the significance and function of religion in life in response to fast-paced social change. They frequently undertake studies of and criticism towards religious doctrine that is considered imprisoning, oppressive, and not in line with humanitarian values. In fact, they do not hesitate to enter the most sensitive areas of religious thought and doctrine to deconstruct and expose the ideological preconditions, culture, and myths hidden behind the sacred religious texts.

Within this critical NU community, LKiS (Lembaga Kajian Islam dan Sosial/The Institute for Islamic and Social Studies) in Yogyakarta[3] is the most remarkable group.[4] The institute was established at the beginning of the 1990s by progressive figures such as M. Imam Azis, M. Jadul Maula, Nuruddin Amin, and Hairussalim HS, and could be described as the driving force behind NGOs who work actively to study, introduce, and disseminate progressive ideas. Recently, many groups have claimed that LKiS is developing leftist ideas. This claim emerged largely after LKiS published Kazuo Shimogaki's *Kiri Islam, Telaah Kritis atas Pemikiran Hassan Hanafi/The Islamic Left, A Critical Study of Hassan Hanafi's Thought* in 1993. The book included a copy of Hassan Hanafi's left-wing Islam manifesto (*al-Yasar al-Islâmî*).[5] The LKiS community is often suspected of promoting a form of communism dressed in Islamic clothing because its progressive ideas often go beyond rigid religious understandings and inspire populist sentiments.[6]

Many people believe that Hassan Hanafi's concept of the Islamic left was influenced by Marxism, even communism. As a result, NU youth who appreciate Hassan Hanafi's ideas are often accused of being communist–Marxist. In an interview with *Tempo* on a visit to Indonesia, Hassan Hanafi denied the accusation that the Islamic left was influenced by Marxism. He stated in full:

> Not at all. The left is a social science concept. The left is the power for change. The Islamic revolution, Islamic justice, Islamic jihad, are all concepts of the Islamic left. I am prepared to change the use of the Islamic left as a concept if I can find a better concept. The Islamic left continues to see Islam as its primary reference. The Islamic left means that I am an agent of change in the Islamic community, and I take Islam as an ideology. The Islamic left has not been influenced by Marxism or socialism, because my thoughts are based on the social situation in Islamic countries, the majority of which are still dominated by poverty and high unemployment, such as Indonesia. We do not need to become Marxists to see the issue of social justice here. Why do people who talk about social justice have to be Marxist?[7]

I myself believe that it is possible that there were outside influences, including Marxism, that shaped Hassan Hanafi's very open concept of the Islamic left, either directly or indirectly, because in general no current of thought exists without influence. Abdurrahman Wahid analysed this with more clarity. He argued that Hassan Hanafi's Islamic left referred to a class analysis that was dominated by socialism, including forms of socialism that were not Marxist–Leninist. Hassan Hanafi chose socialism based on Marxism–Leninism, which he modified because he rejected the idea that the materialism of historical determinism would predict the downfall of capitalism and feudalism and the victory of the proletariat. By following this historical determinism model, Hassan Hanafi took a leftist position (*al-mawqif al-yasâri*). This was due to the fact that he adopted the idea of liberation by deconstructing the old construct that was reactionary to capitalistic feudalism. Because the reactionaries were considered right-wing, their opponents, including those who were not communist, were deemed left-wing. As such, the views of the Islamic left are, generally speaking, rejected by the communist left.[8]

Aside from this controversial and simplistic way of viewing the issue, since the publication of this book, the LKiS community has been identified as the Islamic left,[9] which in turn has influenced the NU youth communities in a number of areas. This is apparent at least in the studies and books they have published, which address Islam and liberation, Islam and democracy, deconstruction of *syari'ah* and people's fiqh, amongst other themes, which characterize the strength of the LKiS vision of liberation, democracy, tolerance, and transformation.

Kazuo Shimogaki's *Kiri Islam*, which presented Hassan Hanafi's thought, deserves a special mention here. Hassan Hanafi's inspiration to give Islam a leftist identity became the ideological basis of the NU youth at the time. The book was quite popular and was a core reading for NU youth activists. Akhmad Fikri AF, the publishing director of LkiS, explains several aspects to this. First, the socio-political situation in Indonesia at the time showed symptoms of repression. Freedom of opinion and expression were restricted to the extent that voicing an opinion required courage and carried with it no small political risk. Secondly, the discourse of Islamic thought at the time was dominated by modernist thought that tended to be positivistic. Whatever direction the national development policy moved in, Islamic thought also moved in the same direction.[10] It was no simple thing for LKiS to dare to publish such a book in the repressive era of the New Order.

As it developed, LKiS was significantly influenced by left-wing Islamic sentiments. It also criticized the authority of the ulama as the group with the greatest right to interpret Islam, in addition to the hegemony of power that restricted freedom of expression in interpreting religion.[11] It must be acknowledged that these themes were foreign to the NU community, and as such often produced less than welcoming responses, not just from the NU community but also from non-NU groups.

Before LKiS was established, P3M had already been formed. However, when it was first established, P3M was not completely an NU cultural movement, because those involved were from a variety of backgrounds, from Abdurrahman Wahid to Dawam Rahardjo and Adi Sasono, the last two of whom are identified as modernists. Moreover, P3M represented a division in LP3ES of Jakarta. In time, P3M gradually revealed itself to be a vehicle for NU cadres, especially after Masdar F. Mas'udi took the reins as director. The youth recruited were largely progressive NU youth, and the programmes developed were typical of NU, such as contextualization of the *kitab kuning* (classical texts), *fiqh al-siyâsah* (fiqh on governance), and *fiqh al-nisâ'* (fiqh on women), although they then went on to explore other issues such as religious pluralism, democracy, civil society, and human rights.

It was a similar story for Lakpesdam NU, which was established in 1985. Initially, the institute did not develop a very critical religious discourse, although it ran activities oriented towards social change, especially within the NU community. Lakpesdam NU seems to have started developing a critical discourse when it held the Education for Development of Awareness amongst the Ulama (PPWK) event in 1992 for *kiai* from a number of regions.

In addition, since 1997, LKiS has run a programme called "Study Transformative and Tolerant Islam Together". This programme is an alternative critical education programme for youth in an attempt to strengthen civil society by developing a discourse of criticism towards religious texts, tradition, and so on. With this Study Together model, LKiS has successfully developed a network of progressive intellectual youth who have helped spread the idea and discourse of tolerant and transformative Islam across a number of areas and universities. Another benefit is that those who are targeted by this programme are those who are also targeted by radical Islamic groups such as Jamâ'ah Tablig and Dâr al-Arqâm, which are popular with first semester students, especially at public universities.

This programme began with the simple desire of LKiS managers to gather enthusiasts and readers of the books that LKiS had published into a forum where they could freely discuss the religious and social issues of the day. In addition, the programme grew out of the concern of LKiS managers that religion was being used purely as a tool for mobilization in the interests of the state and for reinforcing the legitimacy of the state to oppress the people. Furthermore, many religious understandings had arisen in society that were not in accordance with the true function of religion as the liberator of people from oppression, discrimination, and tyranny. As a result, LKiS sought to oppose this socio-religious condition by promoting a religious understanding that was liberating, transformative, and tolerant. LKiS felt this was important because it was rare to find an Islamic educational institute that dared to introduce alternative and critical Islamic discourses.[12] On this last matter, it could be said that the Study Together programme was a direct criticism of the method of teaching that had been considered unsuccessful in displaying religion's liberating function for humankind.[13]

The Study Together programme was not only received enthusiastically within the educated (student) circles, but it also became a strategic medium for the emergence of progressive and inclusive Islamic thought. Those involved in the LKiS Study Together programme generally felt privileged to be given the space to think freely about and accept Islamic discourses that were not available at their universities.

There are four subversive elements that the Study Together programme adopts, namely a Critique of Religious Discourse, Feminism and Religion, Religious Dialogue, and Islamic Political Awareness. Each of these themes has its own unique characteristics, in addition to the universal feature whereby they all seek to find a connection between knowledge, power, ideology, and society.

Simply speaking, the Critique of Religious Discourse programme is an experiment to employ a discourse analysis methodology and perspective in order to answer how religion (Islam) is used these days to create human beings, create subjects, create reason, or to shape the actions of those that adhere to religion (Islam). And given this, the programme then aims to question how to create diversity in a creative and true manner.

The theme Feminism and Religion discusses the politics of female identity. As is known, the patriarchal structure that has been embedded in the human consciousness for centuries, with all the ideological and religious packaging that justifies and strengthens it, has made women bewildered by the very existence of humanity itself. The critical questions that are usually proposed when addressing the issue are: how is the identity of women formed, and who really forms it? What is the role of religion in forming the identity of women?

The theme of Religious Dialogue examines and identifies the influence of pluralism in religious life. The theme is directed towards further analysing the implications of interreligious interdependence in a plural society. It also critically examines how far interreligious dialogue, both theoretical and practical, can be offered as a creative and productive way to accommodate and anticipate pluralism.

The theme of Islamic Political Awareness discusses the latest theoretical and practical issues in Indonesian politics. Discussions begin with the fundamentals, including political philosophy, especially on justice, freedom, and empowerment of civil society. It is also aware that the landscape of thought in political philosophy not only swings between the left and right, between equality and freedom, but that there are rich variations in the middle of this pendulum. This programme aims to establish a more realistic plain in which to theorize about citizenship and to study crucial cases in contemporary Indonesia.

Lately, five years after its establishment, the idea emerged that spreading an alternative religious discourse was part of a more real social movement.[14] As a result, LKiS managers expanded the Study Together programme so that it no longer just provided space for the will to think, but also for the will to act. There was thus synthesis between discourse and action. In other words, the results gained from this process of knowing were then questioned in relation to the real problems in Indonesian society, both on a national and local scale. This is important because although the concept of civil society has long been touted, in reality society is rarely the victor in confrontation with the state, the military, and the market.

The significance of the shift in the Study Together programme towards a more social movement was that it motivated and strengthened the emergence of pluralistic, tolerant, and transformative Islamic cadres in society at the same time that the government issued the policy on regional autonomy. The Study Together programme was then further expanded to include three main themes, namely Islam and Interreligious Relations, Islam and the Women's Movement, and Islam and the Politics of Citizenship. Critique of Religious Discourse was intentionally not included as a theme because it was considered to be a basic perspective in reading social problems. As such, a critique of religious discourse became the soul and perspective of all discussions concerning the above three themes.

LKiS activists designed the programme for NGO activists, students, and young *kiai*. The main aims of the Study Transformative and Tolerant Islam Together programme were: first, to provide a forum for organizers of movements in society to share experiences in advocacy and to reflect together on the social problems they faced in the field; secondly, to undertake a critique of religious discourse together that would form the basis of the perspective they would use in viewing reality and the social problems taken from cases they experienced on a daily basis in the field; thirdly, to learn from fellow participants, from facilitators, or from keynote speakers about the issues currently being faced by society concerning the relation between community, culture, locality, state, and capitalism; and fourthly, to attempt to collectively find a groundbreaking discourse and a model for future movements to strengthen civil society.

The Study Together programme has already produced a new element in local communities that now has a prominent capacity for critical thinking and is highly resistant to several forms of oppression towards the people, whether it is by the state or by economic conglomerates. This element has become the new layer in the NU social structure, with knowledge that differs from the organization's traditional community.

An examination of the curriculum shows that the Study Together programme is indeed intended to present a number of scientific tools that teach individuals to always be critical of reality — both social reality and the reality of knowledge. The curriculum of the LKiS Study Together programme can be found below.

The curriculum of Islam and Interreligious Relations includes:

1. "Islam" and "The Other"
2. Ideology and Political Policies of the New Order
3. Muslim–Christian Contestation
4. Study of Religious Policy
5. Religious Conflict in Indonesian History
6. Reconciliation between "Islam" and "The Other"
7. Exploration of the Film *Nyadran* (tradition of cleansing)
8. Field Trip to Yogyakarta Department of Religious Affairs and the Sapta Dharma Sect

9. Presentation of Field Trip Results
10. The New World Order and the Role of Religion in the Global Order
11. Formulating a Counter Global Movement
12. Construction of Religious Discourse and Contemporary Interreligious Relations
13. Deconstruction of Religious Discourse and Contemporary Interreligious Relations
14. Exploration of the Film *Joan of Arc*
15. The History of Orthodoxy (Islamic Reason and Power): Construction of Religion and Interreligious Relations in the Formative Era of Islam
16. Prophet Muhammad's (PBUH) Experience: the Context behind the Birth of Islam as a New Religion
17. The Qur'an, Mass Culture, Religious Pluralism, and Social Movements in Indonesia
18. Participants' Workshop: Religion, Pluralism, and Social Movements
19. Social Organization
20. Searching for the Root of a Problem and Strategies to Achieve an Objective
21. Community Participatory Action Research
22. Policy Advocacy
23. Plans for Follow-Up Action

The curriculum for Islam and the Women's Movement includes:

1. Group Discussion on Gender Issues in Communities
2. Sex and Gender
3. Sex, Gender, and Sexuality
4. Institutionalization of Gender
5. Gender Injustice, Perpetrators, and the Apparatus
6. Perpetrators of Gender Injustice: Individuals and the State
7. Religion as an Apparatus for Perpetrators of Gender Injustice
8. Women in Fiqh
9. Women's Movements in Indonesia
10. Feminism and the Women's Movement
11. Islam, Feminism, and the Women's Movement
12. Three Phases of the Feminist Movement in the Indonesian Context
13. Islam and Indonesian Feminism (Influence of the Islamic Revitalization Movement, Beginning of the Twentieth Century)

14. Islam and Indonesian Feminism (Influence of the New Order)
15. Islam and Indonesian Feminism (Influence of Regional Autonomy)
16. New Social Movements
17. Critique of Religious Discourse
18. Social Organization
19. Searching for the Root of a Problem and Strategies to Achieve an Objective
20. Community Participatory Action Research
21. Policy Advocacy
22. Plans for Follow-Up Action

The curriculum for Islam and the Politics of Citizenship includes:

1. Individuals, Society, and the State
2. Field Trip to the Justice Party and the Mujahideen Council (*Majlis Mujahidin*)
3. Geo-Politics and its Impact on Individuals, Society, and the State
4. Geo-Economics and Creation of Dependence on Global Capitalism
5. Construction of Democracy and Development in Indonesia
6. Regional Autonomy in the Context of Citizenship Politics
7. The Civil Movement and the Politics of Citizenship in Indonesia
8. Critique of Religious Discourse
9. Analysis of Political Policies
10. Methodology of Policy Analysis
11. Social Organization
12. Searching for the Root of a Problem and Strategies to Achieve an Objective
13. Community Participatory Action Research
14. Policy Advocacy
15. Plans for Follow-Up Action

In addition to LKiS, P3M in Jakarta,[15] from its establishment to the mid-1990s, developed a populist discourse using religious tradition as a basis for transformation. It promoted themes based on transformative ideas using traditional terminology such as *fiqh al-nisâ'* and *fiqh al-siyâsah*. P3M is indeed known to be caring, not just towards the *pesantren* community but also towards the scientific wealth that the *pesantren* possess. As a result, the *halaqah* that P3M started to run intensively at the end of the 1980s for *kiai* were based on themes well known within the *pesantren* community because they used the same terminology.[16] In addition to these themes, P3M also held *halaqah* on the major world ideologies, Islam and democracy, *pesantren* democracy, and so on.

A significant part of the development of the post-traditionalist discourse was P3M's Emancipatory Islam programme. As briefly mentioned in the previous chapter, this programme was a further elaboration of the post-traditionalist discourse. The Emancipatory Islam programme has three main activities: (1) education (*Ma'had al-Islâm al-Taharruri*); (2) radio and television talk shows; and (3) publication of the Friday bulletin *Al-Nadhar* and its website (www.p3m.or.id, which recently changed to www.islamemansipatoris.com).

Before further discussing the Emancipatory Islam programme, I feel it is necessary to first elaborate on the concept of emancipation itself. The term "emancipatory" attached to the word "Islam" is actually taken from the Frankfurt School's concept of critical theory. The most popular keyword is emancipatory praxis, and the obsession to achieve *aufklarung* (enlightenment), which means exposing and breaking down the ideological veils that cover the inhumane reality of consciousness. By unmasking the ideology behind all matters, including the structure of critical theory itself, critical theory seeks to promote the freedom of humankind from all forms of oppression and exploitation, as Karl Marx once dreamed of. The critical theory proposed by the Frankfurt School sharply criticized modernity, particularly the process of rationalization within modernity. In the history of philosophy, critical theory pertained to the neo-Marxist school of thought that was developed in Frankfurt University by Horkheimer, Marcuse, and Theodor W. Adorno (first generation), and later by Jurgen Habermas (second generation). The social context in which critical theory emerged was the modern world that at the time was coloured by Stalin's totalitarianism, Hitler's Nazi fascism and authoritarianism, and the new barbarianism of the war.[17]

The first generation of critical theory was disappointed with the modern rationality of the era, which was deemed to have lost its criticism, which meant that it deviated from the spirit of enlightenment. As a result of deifying rationality, which was initially believed to lead to autonomy and freedom, modern humankind became trapped in a closed system that was irrational and devoid of meaning. There was not even the smallest of spaces for criticism, unless that criticism further strengthened the system.

In this modern society all contradictions, oppression, frustration, and alienation became invisible. It seemed as if all aspects of life ran smoothly, efficiently, and productively. What was actually occurring was a process of dehumanization. When critics sought to expose this false impression, they discovered that the irrational system was precisely the result of the human attempt to be rational. Rationality, which was once very critical of traditional myths, in turn became a new myth in the form of science and technology. It was on this basis that the first generation of critical theorists took a pessimistic attitude towards rationality, tending to withdraw or resign themselves so as not to be swallowed up by the system, and in fact, eventually giving the impression of being anti-praxis.[18]

In later developments, the pessimism of the first Frankfurt generation was revised by Jurgen Habermas. Habermas loudly defended the claim of the universality of rationalism, and argued that his ancestors in Frankfurt had wrongly read the characteristics of modern enlightenment. He sought to save the elements of emancipatory criticism from critical theory by assuming that Western enlightenment not only led to pathology, but also to self-improvement and maturation of social life. The mistake of the initial Frankfurt generation, according to Habermas, was that modern rationality was only understood as subjective rationality, that is, solely related to the ability of reason to control objective processes of the universe through work.

This was not necessarily a valid reason to become pessimistic and consider criticism to have been lost. Rather, modernization has other types of rationality that were neglected by Marx and the initial Frankfurt generation — namely, inter-subjective rationality or communicative rationality, or the ability of reason to understand the intentions of other people or groups on a reciprocal basis. The process of rationalization need not be ultimately aimed at domination and oppression whenever it is understood as the result of argumentative discourse, where the argument that makes a more superior claim to validity is received by consensus. Rational criticism begins to function when communication is distorted or punctuated by coercion, when consensus is only a pseudo-communication, in order to remove these distortions.[19]

Using this critical theory perspective, the term "emancipatory" is presented as a choice for how to undertake the Islamic movement. From this perspective, it is understandable why P3M activists suggested the need to more closely link ideas of liberation or emancipation in Islam with praxis. This is apparent in the vision they developed, as follows:

1. **Humanistic**: to promote a humanitarian vision in viewing all issues and situate humankind as the subject of change, with social reality as the object. This is based on the idea that human welfare is the objective of religion and, as such, improving the quality of life is the primary commitment of religion.
2. **Critical**: to accept or reject anything with full awareness of the consequences, after having undertaken a complete examination of the issues. This process of critical reflection necessitates a long process of continuity and, as such, diversity in religion is only natural.
3. **Transformative**: to direct and make change become the vehicle in realizing the humanitarian commitment of religion. The birth of religion is always preceded by the emergence of humanitarian problems. As a result, the significance of religion is equal to its ability to resolve the problems of humanity.
4. **Praxis**: to assume the integration of thought, expression, and action. The commitment of Emancipatory Islam not only stops at the level of ideas or discourse, but works towards achieving change in concrete reality. Praxis thus represents the middle path so as to avoid the two religious extremes of either deification of reflection (sacrifice of action), or deification of action (sacrifice of verbalism).[20]

In running the Emancipatory Islam programme, P3M activists are very aware that sacralized religious texts (on a variety of levels) pose an extraordinary problem. As a result, the programme pays serious attention to this problem, which has become petrified and is rarely ever touched. Before the programme was established, P3M already held several Emancipatory Exegesis *halaqah* that specifically discussed the exegesis of the Qur'an. In this sense, the Emancipatory Islam programme is a continuation of the Emancipatory Exegesis programme, and thus it is understandable that the former continues to view religious texts as a problem that requires serious attention. The profile of the Emancipatory Islam Network states:

> Understanding and appreciating texts is a serious problem facing the religious community at the present time, in fact it is not uncommon that different perspectives on a text result in exclusive attitudes and destructive behaviour. What is equally alarming is that such religious understandings can then lead to claims to truth that only exacerbate interreligious relations. This causes texts to exist only in a partial form, and to lose their primary

vision as open and liberating texts. Texts become the most lively arena for conflict in revealing the truth.[21]

The phrase "open and liberating texts" is interesting to highlight because it actually implies an awareness for undertaking liberating actions using religious instruments. The question is, does religion (Islam) have enough components to achieve liberation? The normative–theological response would be that Islam is a liberating religion. This claim is vaguely apparent in the Prophet's spirit of struggle and in several normative foundations in Islam. However, over the course of history this spirit faded, until it was eventually completely lost. The following section of the Emancipatory Islam profile states:

> It is as if texts exist purely to give rise to problems, rather than prosperity or wellbeing. The consequence is that the critique of texts is a phenomenon that can no longer be avoided. As a result, it is apparent here how important a methodological framework is in order to understand the texts, which is expected to be able to create a new paradigm, one of justice, humanity, politeness, equality, pluralism and liberation. Understanding of the texts is not purely a literal understanding, but sees all its other dimensions.[22]

With this paradigm, Emancipatory Islam exists to give new meaning to religion by emphasizing the social responsibilities of religion in resolving the very real problems of humanity. The liberation theology developed in Latin America had a rather strong influence on the programme; and in fact, liberation theology is specifically discussed in *halaqah*.

The Emancipatory Islam Network profile mentions three important matters in integrating religion and humanitarian issues:

> First, Emancipatory Islam seeks to give a new perspective to the texts. There is the impression that understanding of the texts is only possible through the use of other 'original' texts, both primary and secondary texts. Emancipatory Islam attempts to see texts through the context and problems of humanity. Because in reality the texts were born out of the socio-cultural context and society of their time. Secondly, Emancipatory Islam places humans as the subject of religious exegesis. This is in order to decrease the distance between text and reality, which has to date been far too great. Almost all of the religious understandings that are present within society are based on the texts, which are then made into legal products so as to give legal status to reality. As a result, not only do the texts lose their transformative spirit, but worse: the texts

become increasingly distanced from reality. Third, Emancipatory Islam is concerned with humanitarian issues more than with theological issues. Emancipatory Islam seeks to shift religious attention from issues in the sky (theocentrism) to real issues faced by humans (anthropocentrism). Emphasis is on praxis, so that religion is not only understood as ritualism but as liberation of society from all oppression.[23]

These three points explain how important it is to reel in the problems from the "sky" that receive the attention of most religious scholars and bring them back down to earth. Islam cares more for problems concerning God and divinity than those concerning humanity. As a result, Muslims have become highly sensitive towards any affront to religion, rather than towards the abuse of humanitarian values. In actual fact, Islam was sent to the world not to defend the majesty of God, but to elevate the dignity and prestige of humankind. The sentence "Emancipatory Islam is concerned with humanitarian issues more than with theological issues" implies a deep awareness of this problem.

The question that then emerges is: how is emancipatory Islam positioned within the Islamic movement and thought in Indonesia? In the previous chapter I lightly touched on the position of post-traditionalism within the constellation of Islamic thought in Indonesia. As a part of the post-traditionalist community, emancipatory Islam sneaks in between the tough competition between fundamentalist Islam and liberal Islam. On a number of different occasions, Masdar F. Mas'udi talked about how both groups were equally biased towards religious texts. Fundamentalist Islam believes that the texts are the final word and that they are able to resolve all problems of humanity, and as such, reality must (be forced to) submit to (and by) the texts. Meanwhile, liberal Islam holds that the religious texts can no longer deal with such rapidly changing reality. As a result, if we want to progress, we must leave the texts and look towards the Western nations.

Both currents are equally extreme in their religious views, and as such, it is necessary to show that the Islamic community has many nuances and is not black and white. Although the religious texts are limited and are not always able to answer the problems we face, neglecting them outright is also not realistic, because Islamic civilization, as recognised by Nasr Hamid Abu Zayd, is a civilization shaped by the texts (*hadlârat al-nash*).

It is here that emancipatory Islam has a commitment to and perspective on several issues. It is this commitment that differentiates it from other Islamic movements. Each of these perspectives is as follows:

1. **Perspective towards the texts:** Emancipatory Islam pays specific attention to the texts, because the texts have become the arena of conflict between a number of religious currents. On the one hand, there has been an effort to politicize the texts, that is, to make them legal and political documents that would be implemented as an alternative for change for the better; but on the other hand, there is the tendency to use the texts as a justification of liberalism. Neither of these models has a firm attitude towards the texts and only uses them in accordance with its interests. As a result, both become trapped in endless conflict, which results in a "war between texts". The former sees texts as the "clothes of fundamentalism", while the latter sees them as the "clothes of liberalism". Emancipatory Islam attempts to see the texts as a part of reality that has its limits. These limitations do not indicate a weakness in the texts, but are proof of the exceptional nature of humans to be able to respond to them. This is the importance of the perspective one takes towards a text. All readers of texts should wherever possible epistemologically deconstruct (*al-qatî'ah al-ma'rafiyah*) a text, but they must be able to contextualize (*al-tawâsul al-ma'rafî*) it too. This approach assumes that the fundamental issue is not situated in a text, but in empirical reality. As a result, this should lead to the growth of critical awareness towards social reality which is filled with oppression, discrimination, and domination, as well as a critical attitude towards all forms of exploitation of texts that only lead to politicization and hegemony of exegesis.
2. **Attitude towards modernity:** Emancipatory Islam believes that oppression, discrimination, and domination are a result of the particular system and ideology of modernity. Modernity on the one hand can be seen as a driving force for enlightenment, but on the other, it is unable to push for equality and justice on a practical level. Modernity is the new colonial power which must be viewed critically, as it creates a positivistic attitude and moves further away from economic justice. This differs from the religious patterns that have otherwise been developing. Fundamentalist Islam and liberal Islam both depend on modernity. Fundamentalist Islam rejects modernity and proposes the alternative of returning to a *salafi* (pure) understanding, while liberal Islam makes modernity its only mechanism for social change. Both these movements are better described as urban movements. Here, emancipatory Islam seeks to establish itself as a popular movement which is always critical of all forms of oppression, both those produced

by the texts and by modernity, but without disregarding the positive aspects of modernity.
3. **Appreciation of local culture:** Emancipatory Islam has a strong commitment to local culture, so that transformation of society does not displace it from its roots. This is crucial in order to explore the local wisdoms that have to date been buried by other cultures. An appreciation of local culture is a form of acculturation of religion and culture that sees religion as not only formed by the texts and divine revelation, but also by local culture. This is also necessary in order to realize cultural diversity in religiosity.
4. **Emphasis on participation and action:** Emancipatory Islam believes that social change is not a top-down process, but a bottom-up one. This is different from the view that has developed in both liberal Islam and fundamentalist Islam. Both believe that constitutional change is the only kind of social transformation and change. Emancipatory Islam is not so confident in the sophistication of texts, discourse, and the constitution (the Qur'an). No matter how sophisticated the texts, divine revelation, discourse, and the constitution are, they cannot guarantee change. As a result, emancipatory Islam stresses the importance of participation and action on a practical level.[24]

In line with this commitment and perspective, P3M runs a series of *halaqah* and *bahst al-masâil* with a curriculum that combines Islamic traditional wealth with modern science, especially hermeneutics as a means of reading the holy texts, and discourse analysis to see the relationship between knowledge and power. This awareness emerged because on the one hand, religious doctrine has moved increasingly further from the source of humanitarian problems, but on the other hand, pressure is placed on religion to appear to be helping resolve humanitarian problems.

The introduction to the module on emancipatory Islamic education explains that studies of religion have developed in three directions. First, religion began to be seen as a social reality. Religion is not a foreign creature that emerged on earth out of the blue, but rather has always been in dialogue with social reality. Thus, an understanding of religion cannot be separated from social reality; in fact, religious messages are closely related to social and cultural messages. It cannot be denied that the presence of religion cannot be separated from the historical process. Besides being formed by history, the presence of religion also forms history.

The dialectic of religion and reality is a necessity, and has led to a process of acculturation between the two. In light of this, studying religion is not purely a study of divine revelation, but also a study of how revelation was formed by and formed history.

Secondly, a critique of religious discourse developed. Religion, which was initially perceived as a path to salvation and truth, in reality often became an obstacle to and challenge for the realization of salvation and truth. In the name of religion, an individual could be justified for taking actions that harmed others and society. This of course begs the question: why does religion always appear to be stiff, hard, and rigid? If this is the reality, is it true that religion is the path to salvation? The normative–theological response would be "yes"; however, this answer is not satisfying on a socio-intellectual basis.

Thirdly, religious doctrines have been reinterpreted. The failure of religion to respond to humanitarian problems signified the need for new meaning that would bring alive the essence of religion, so that religion was not only a tool for justification and a vehicle for the interests of particular groups. Religion should actually be understood as the way to reinforce values of humanity, justice, welfare, and equality. An exegesis of religious doctrines should not only position the texts as central and see them as the objective of social transformation and change, but should seek to seat them as the foundation of universal morals and ethics that encourages equality, diversity, and justice. A willingness to reinterpret religious texts and doctrine is necessary when religion is placed in a situation that demands that it dynamically interact with a continually changing reality. This requires religion to be brought down to earth in a liberating and enlightening manner.[25]

It is clear that emancipatory Islam wishes to escape from the tug of war between fundamentalist and liberal Islam, neither of which cares directly about real problems. Although it pays more attention to problems of praxis, this does not mean that emancipatory Islam neglects philosophical reflection and debate. Philosophical reflection is required so that the Islamic community is not trapped in work that is void of theory. On this basis, there are at least two requirements. First, the anthropocentric dimensions of religious doctrine must be revealed. Religion can be used as a tool of resistance against the authority of religious leaders and the state. Religion can become the foundation of civil society, which has its own standards of rationality and local dimensions. Secondly, the liberalism and pluralism of religious doctrines must be revealed. Here, religion is interpreted not in its capacity as a set of symbols, but as a set of values that appreciates diversity and sides with the weak, so that religion is therefore not taken out of context, nor does it become trapped in latent and useless debate. As a result, exegesis of religious doctrine does not stop at the cognitive–theoretical level, but becomes inspiration for change on the level of praxis.

In order to obtain a more complete picture of the emancipatory Islamic *halaqah*, I feel it is necessary to outline their curriculum, so that the tendencies and passion that brings them alive can be seen. The curriculum includes:

1. **Historicity of Exegesis**

    This material introduces participants to the diversity of exegesis and the differences between exegeses and their historicity. This is in order to critically examine various interpretations, and realize that every interpretation reflects the historical experiences of the interpreter. Looking back at several of the classical books on exegesis, the differences between those authors who lived in palaces and those who lived amongst the common people are clearly apparent in their work. The ideological dispositions of an interpretation become more apparent if studied from the interpretations of the *âyat al-ahkâm* (legal verses) of the Islamic schools of thought. In general, these exegeses or interpretations are closely related to the mainstream ideology of their time, and as such, the political and ideological struggles that developed during the writing of these interpretations influenced the way the holy texts were interpreted. This material is thus aimed at cultivating the awareness that exegeses are always contextual (closely linked to the situation in which they were compiled) and full of interests (ideological, political, or economic); therefore, every one of these exegeses is relative and historical.

2. **Historicity of the Holy Text (*Târikhiyat al-Nushûsh al-Muqaddasah*)**

    This material seeks to develop an awareness that the holy text (the Qur'an) as a text was formed through a historical and cultural process. As a result it is not everything, as there are many of God's ideas that are not recorded in the sacred text (the Qur'an). This hopes to desacralize the text. In addition, the material presented also explains that all texts (or at least most of them, I suggest) are formed through historical and cultural processes. As a historical reality, the holy text (the Qur'an) was sent to a particular group, at a particular time, through a particular Prophet, and in a particular language. On this basis, the view that texts are a cultural product needs to be developed into a "new theology" in order to cultivate an understanding of the historicity of texts. This material also explains the process of codification of texts that is still debated and that involved political struggles in its time.

3. Discourse Analysis

The material for discourse analysis is aimed at developing a critical attitude towards discourse, particularly religious discourse, both that which has been handed down through the generations and that which continues to develop in Indonesia and in other parts of the world. In addition, the material analyses discourse and the factors that encourage the birth of a discourse. In real life, religion was internalized by its adherents through thought processes until a variety of discourses emerged. Consciously or not, throughout the course of his life, an adherent of a religion inherits certain religious discourses that he then internalizes and practises. As with discourse in general, religious discourse, including contemporary religious discourse, has a particular history behind its emergence; and as such, it is necessary to be critical of what is behind this discourse so that religious adherents are not trapped into claims about the truth, or exclusive attitudes that deny the existence of those who adhere to different religious discourses.

4. Social Analysis

This material seeks to foster a critical awareness that the context of human life is always changing and that behind these changes there are many actors, including state actors, economic actors, and ideological actors (including religious figures). In addition, change is not always in the interests of the people. As a result, this material hopes to give a kind of analytical framework through which to read social reality, especially in relation to humanitarian problems, both those related to structures (economy/capitalism, the state, culture, social relations) and superstructures (ideology, world view). As such, social analysis explains that the method of analysing social reality is by understanding the humanitarian problems that emerge in society, who the actors behind change are, and how social relations are formed. Here, it becomes increasingly apparent that social reality cannot be understood purely through a natural reading of society by observing, listening, reading, and feeling. Not only does this kind of natural reading have limitations, but reality also often hides things behind what appears on the surface. As a result, an analytical framework is needed to be able to penetrate reality and examine what is hidden behind the reality we see at a glance. This framework is important because the process and result of a reading of reality determines the conclusion arrived at.

5. **Hermeneutics (*al-Qirâ'ah al-Jadîdah*)**
This material seeks to give an understanding of the religious texts through hermeneutic reading tools, which means religious texts never stop producing new meaning. Limiting the meaning of the texts is to deny the very nature of the texts. This material explains that every exegesis involves the dimensions of the author, the text, and the reader. The process of finding meaning in the texts must be in open dialogue with these elements. As a result, a religious text never stops producing new meaning, because meaning is a construction from the ever increasing knowledge that surrounds the text and the reader. Meanwhile, the author's role is complete when his ideas have been expressed in the form of a text. In this light, texts are actually open and dynamic. Knowledge about the principles of hermeneutics and the process of exegesis of texts is needed in order to be able to discover new meaning.[26]

The willingness of the traditional Islamic community to accept new reading tools from foreign sciences that were, until now, not known within the NU traditional community, is increasingly apparent. A progressive and open attitude is also evident amongst the NU youth community active in the Desantara Institute for Cultural Studies, an NGO specifically concerned with Islam and culture that uses a cultural studies framework as its reading tool. Besides regularly holding *halaqah* on Islam and local culture in several provinces and a series of discussions on indigenization or *pribumisasi* of Islam, Desantara also regularly runs study packages under the title Emancipatory Madrasah.

The term "emancipatory" contains much of the same argument and spirit as that of P3M. More explicitly, the mention of the term indicates that its activities are directed towards the liberation of awareness and behaviour from the shackles of domination and the hegemony of the modern powers of religion and the state. The Emancipatory Madrasah profile shows a very strong spirit of opposition to modernization and all its effects, such as the domination and hegemony of interpretations of reality. For instance, the section on its background states:

> The modernisation implemented by the New Order (and the "reformation" regimes after it) created dominance in areas such as economics, politics and culture. In the economy, individuals and communities are the subjects of capitalism. In politics, they are the subjects of the state. In culture they are the subjects of that which is called the nation. In capitalism, humans are measured by their achievements and entrepreneurship in accordance with economic requirements. The state requires political subjects that can submit to party bureaucracy. Meanwhile in culture subjects are organised and guided in order to realise a single homogenous nation.[27]

This declaration indicates that there is no neutral space in which individuals as subjects can make their own choices freely. All spaces have been hijacked by interests: political interests, economic/capitalistic interests, or cultural interests. All individuals must go with the flow if they do not want to be considered primitive or left behind. The profile continues:

> Moreover, the regimes of modernity have given birth to the production of knowledge and truth. This includes the constructs of religion, gender and culture. The modern construct of religion is a religious form that is authentic, valid, textual and substantialistic. The slogan "return to the Qur'an and Hadith" is one form of the modernist construct that marginalises local creativity in religiosity. It is these kinds of constructs that give rise to a puritan, if not fundamentalist, religiosity.[28]

This indicates how fed up the community is with the "regime of meaning" created by the ruling power (authority), which has robbed people of their right to create new meaning. The spirit to rebel against the establishment is even more evident in the discussion curriculum and agenda, which is as follows:

1. Critique of Religious Discourse class
   - Overview of religion:
     a. Constructs of religion
     b. Religion and the construct of culture
     c. Religion: Power and cultural citizenship
     d. Historicity of the holy texts and exegesis

- Formation of religious texts and religious truth (the Christian and Islamic cases)
- Religion as resistance
  a. Strategies of local religions
  b. NU as a "post-colonial" religion
  c. Religion and multiculturalism
2. Critique of Gender Discourse class
   - Evaluation and review of women and modernity
     a. Gender in the cultural studies perspective
     b. Religious construct of women
     c. Capitalistic construct of women
     d. State construct of women
     e. History of women's movements and thought in Indonesia
   - Women and multiculturalism
     a. Women and traditional art
     b. Women and traditional rites
     c. Women and economic activity
   - Women and resistance
3. Critique of Cultural Discourse class
   - Construct of culture
     a. Cultural theories
     b. Construct of national culture
     c. Actors behind cultural constructs (the market, official religions, the state)
     d. Cultural strategies, negotiation, and resistance
   - Cultural studies concepts: constructs, resistance, power relations, contestation
   - Cultural resistance and cultural studies methodology (ethnography and semiotics)[29]

Without intending to diminish the roles of other institutes, institutes like LKiS, P3M, Lakpesdam NU, and Desantara represent the very heart of post-traditionalist intellectualism amongst NU activists, each with their own unique emphasis. The intellectual agendas that are apparent in their education syllabuses and choice of publications strongly mark the post-traditionalist discourse as a "subversive discourse". This subversive discourse was greatly inspired by postmodernism, which rejected the existence of centralism (decentring) and all forms of hegemony.

In the broader context, the post-traditionalist community is also inspired by the postcolonial passion that sought to oppose the discursive constructs of colonialism. Colonialism was, in this context, initially orientalism, but can be more loosely interpreted as any power that is able to force its wishes on others. Simply speaking, post-colonial studies passionately criticized the establishment of central power, both in the sense of political power and cultural power. These studies contained a spirit of resistance of the marginalized against those of the metropolises, those of the periphery against those of the centre. It was a spirit to deconstruct the dominant and hegemonic narratives.[30]

ISSUES IN THE RELIGIOUS THOUGHT OF ISLAMIC POST-TRADITIONALISM

Critique of Religious Discourse as a Perspective for Reading Islam

As discussed above, the post-traditionalist community pays serious attention to the critique of religious discourse. The basic assumption of a critique of religious discourse is that not one single religion was born in a vacuum. On the contrary, every religion was born into a certain historical context. Without a historical context religion would have no meaning, and its existence would be a non-existence. This also proves that religion is in dialogue with the era in which it exists, and it is through this dialogue that religion finds its significance in society. Through dialogue, it is believed that religion can change the reality surrounding it; and at the same time, this reality also influences religion.

Although it teaches universal humanitarian values, religion can (often) be an effective tool for the interests of those in power. This is possible because of its dogmatic characteristic that implies that religion could not possibly be wrong, and its openness to all kinds of interpretation. As a result, a critique of religious discourse strongly assumes that there is no single interpretation of religion. The critique of religious discourse seeks to develop critical awareness at least in the following areas: (1) awareness of interreligious relations; (2) awareness of gender relations; (3) awareness of socio-political relations, which includes the relationship between individuals and society, people and rulers, and primordial/ ideological groups. A critical awareness in these areas can be cultivated if the dominant religious discourse that tends to be legitimizing becomes a critical, inclusive, and tolerant discourse. This kind of discourse can be built through:

1. Critical analysis of the religious texts that includes context as an important factor in understanding texts.
2. Critical analysis of religion as dogma and discourse (interpretation). Religion, which has to date been understood as dogma in its practice, is now powerless in the face of demands for social change, and as such, religious groups often develop reactionary thoughts or movements.
3. Critical analysis of the relationship between knowledge (truth) and power (power relations) in forming the dominant religious discourse. Each discourse or interpretation of religion that emerges is somehow related to the power where the interpreter/commentator or his supporters live. As a result, the veracity of a religious interpretation must (also) be viewed in terms of its power relations. As such, there is no sacralization of religious interpretation/exegesis.[31]

The perspective that the critique of religious discourse has towards religion can be depicted as in Figure 4.1.

This diagram describes how religion (Islam) originates from God's revelation. As a revelation, it is both immortal and universal. Nevertheless, religion does not exist in a vacuum. In its existence, religion comes into contact with tradition and local beliefs. Islam is often interpreted in a number of different ways. There are some groups who interpret Islam with their own ideology and interests. This kind of interpretation usually functions to legitimize ideological agendas and interests. There is also a model of interpretation that is aimed at transformation. The LKiS group that developed this programme of course wishes to place itself in this final category, which seeks to discover how best to make religion a basis for social transformation.

The emergence of the critique of religious discourse within the NU community cannot be separated from the influence of Nasr Hamid Abu Zayd's book *Naqd al-Khithâb al-Dînî*. This book, in addition to Nasr Hamid's other books, is almost always the primary reference in *halaqah*. His critique of contemporary religious discourse was the starting point of the NU youth's project on the critique of religious discourse. This current became the new trend for the Study Together programmes run by NU youth in several places. As such, the new intellectual trend amongst the NU youth

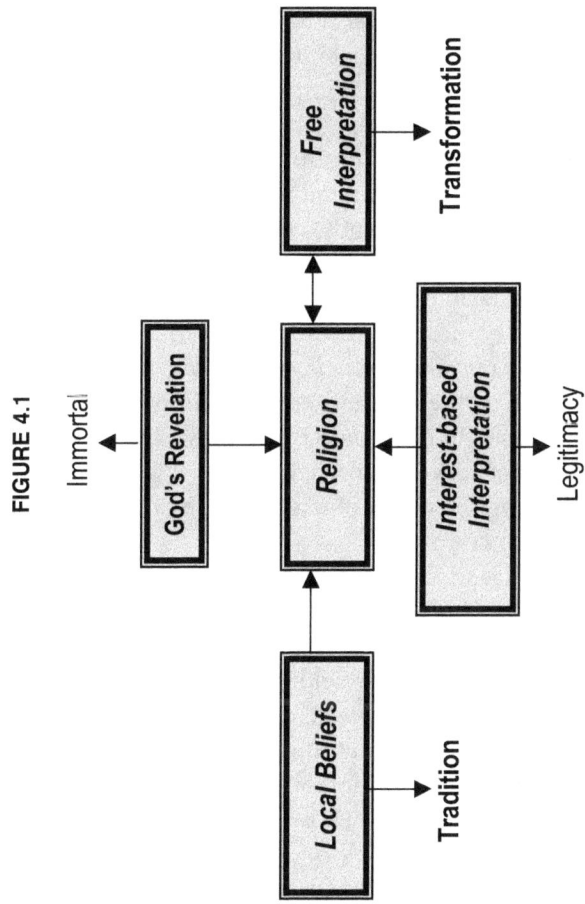

FIGURE 4.1

is due to the influence from the critique of religious discourse project, which has been used to read their own traditions and other traditions in Islam in general.

Nasr Hamid Abu Zayd[32] developed several harsh critiques of the mainstream mechanisms in Islam behind the formulation of contemporary religious discourse. First, he criticized the tendency to see religious thought as religion itself (*al-tawhîd bayn al-fikr wa al-dîn*). The implication of this perspective is not only that it neglects the epistemological distance between subject and object, but it implicitly claims to be able to resolve all conditions and existential and epistemological obstacles. The mechanisms behind religious discourse also produce claims of absolute truth. From this perspective, any interpretation of religion is positioned as being equivalent to religion itself, and consequently, criticism of religious interpretation is often considered to be a criticism of religion.

Secondly, Nasr Hamid Abu Zayd criticized interpreting all phenomena, whether social or natural, by reverting everything back to the primary principle or cause (*radd al-dhawâhir ilâ mubtada' wâhid*). This mechanism of discourse relies on the religious emotions of the laymen, and makes it difficult to discuss anything as everything is reverted back to The Absolute. This denies human existence and negates the laws of nature and society, as well as depriving the world of any knowledge that is not based on the official religious discourse.

Thirdly, Nasr Hamid Abu Zayd criticized the dependence on the authority of the *salaf* (the texts) or *turâst* (tradition), otherwise known as *al-i'timâd 'alâ sulthati al-turâst wa al-salaf*. This is achieved by shifting the *turâst* texts, which should be secondary texts, and making them primary texts that are tied to the sacredness and authority of power. The implication of this religious discourse is that interpretation is equated with religion, as with the first mechanism. Moreover, this mechanism holds too much to the formal forms of religion, while ignoring the fundamental principles of religion (*maqâshid al-syarîah*).

Fourthly, he criticized the finality of intellectual certainty and mental belief (*al-yaqînu al-dzuhni wa al-hismi al-fikr*). This kind of belief rejects all difference of thought, except in those areas that are considered peripheral or branches of the fundamental issues (*furû'*), not in fundamental issues themselves or their roots (*al-ashl*). *Al-ashl* are deemed to be fixed, unchanging, and single. Any change or diversification of *al-ashl* is viewed as an attempt to undermine the sanctity of religion.

Fifthly, Nasr Hamid Abu Zayd criticized the neglect of the historical dimension (*ihdâr al-bu'di al-târikhî*). This is very apparent in the romanticism of the past, which is seen as the golden age of Islam (*al-'ashr al-dzahabi*). The mechanisms of this discourse coincide with the other mechanisms, in that they directly equate thought and religion, which results in a sacralizing of the temporal and humane.

It is this awareness that was used as the starting point in discussions of the critique of religious discourse. It requires that the set of rules and system of values that exist within religion be re-examined and broken down in order to situate them in the historical context in which they were formed and established. This is important because the system of values is in contact with and is constructed by the system of values that exists outside of religion. In other words, it is a necessity to return the system of values that religion or any product of religious interpretation (religious thought) claims to possess to its historical dimensions.

Refusing to do so not only makes religion and religious interpretations ahistorical, but also distances them from reality. If it is ahistorical, religion can no longer be an open system of values, in the sense that it is open to be understood and interpreted in accordance with the demands of the time, and thus it becomes a system of rules that binds and traps. The main consequence is that humans who are social actors are no longer able to be creative, to act, or to regulate the world in which they live. Rather, they must submit to a system of values or rules that is considered final, because it is not their right to make innovations in that system of values for the benefit and needs of the world that they live in and will continue to live in.

In essence, that which is considered the truth in the system of values (rules) of religion or valid in religious exegesis (not religion itself) is little more than an ideological construct. Religious texts or products of religious exegesis are a discourse that is a representation of a particular ideology: the context that surrounds the birth and development of a text or thought. This ideology is formed continually through various social practices, for instance through religious sermons or speeches, until it becomes a part of what defines daily life and legitimizes and maintains social, political, cultural, or economic domination.[33]

In relation to religious exegesis, each group in Islam develops an ideological articulation of its religious discourse. All these groups compete for the authority of religious truth. They try to dominate other groups through political power (state control) and cultural systems which they declare to be universal. Through this process, interpretation of religious truth is produced and reproduced continually, written and read over and over, and re-expressed in the social realm that continues to change, both by individuals and in collective memory.

Ideals about religious (Islamic) truth are formed by the system of linguistic signs that are standardized in religious discourse. Linguistic signs are a social convention. Meaning is not built through direct relationships between signs and signifiers: there is no direct relationship between the real world and language. Rather, meaning emerges as a result of signifying practices. For instance, to say that something is "black" is not because it is naturally black, but the colour black exists because there are other signs that do not signify black: they may signify yellow, green, red, white, and so on.[34]

At this point, there are no systems of values in religion, including in religious belief or religion itself, that are free of language signs. They are all constructed in and through linguistic signs. As such, religious belief or faith that is believed to have come from heaven does not escape linguistic constructions. Humans cannot access (read, understand, and interpret) religion without these linguistic signs. This is what is meant by religion as a discourse.

The point of this perspective is to stir up a construct that is considered neutral, objective, without flaw, sacred, and presented as the truth. Religion as a discourse must be broken down so that it does not become rigid, by revealing its ambiguous, confusing face and the hierarchy of concepts which have been received at face value.

Several concepts in religion (Islam for instance), before they were rigidified and made sacred and then became the basic practices in life, were produced through logocentric procedures for formation of meaning. Meaning is created through linguistic signs that are given different statuses: one is considered normal while the other is considered abnormal, of less value, less civilized, or assigned other negative attributes. Meaning is produced through differentiation and stigmatization in a system of binary oppositions.[35]

In a binary opposition system, relations are oppositional relations, with one defeating and/or controlling the other. This power relation, according to Michel Foucault, does not work to oppress and repress, but to normalize and regulate. It is not negative and repressive, but positive and productive. Power produces reality, domains of objects, and rituals of truth. It is channelled through social relations, where it categorizes actions as good or bad as a way of controlling behaviour.

A clear example of this is knowledge about pure (Arab) Islam and *kejawen* Islam. The category of pure (Arab) Islam was produced to define teachings that accord with the Islamic teachings that were sent to earth in the Arab world fifteen centuries ago. Meanwhile, the category of *kejawen* Islam was produced to define those teachings that do not accord with — or in fact, which deviate from — those teachings of fifteen centuries ago. The first kind of Islam is identified as the original and true Islam, while the latter is identified as fake Islam, which has deviated from its original form, which has been changed and contaminated by local cultural value systems (in this case Javanese), and thus must be rejected. One is elevated, while the other is denigrated; one is deemed normal, while the other is deemed deviant.

In society, this discourse of pure Islam (Arab versus *kejawen* Islam) is accepted and circulated as something wrong or right through knowledge and discourse. The definitions of pure (Arab) Islam and *kejawen* Islam shape individuals as to how to be true Muslims, and how not to be. Being a true Muslim means observing and practising teachings and rituals in their original form, while the wrong way of practising Islam is by practising teachings and rituals by adding to, taking from, and/or reformulating them in accordance with cultural systems or values from outside of the Arab world. This way of thinking has significant implications for the construction of religious understanding, to the extent that religious ritual practices that cannot be found in their original form are considered deviant practices.[36]

The effect of these two discourses can be seen in the social relations within religious communities. In order for religious (Islamic) practices to proceed correctly in accordance with how they were when Islam was sent down to the Arab world, all forms of religious (Islamic) rituals, teachings, and practices that stray or deviate from their original form must be prevented and opposed. The discourse of pure (Arab) Islam is normalized (made to be the norm), while the discourse of *kejawen* Islam is stigmatized and negative attributes are attached to it, such as heresy and syncretism. As a result, the discourse of pure (Arab) Islam which is considered normal is chosen and believed by the majority of Muslim society to be the true Islam, and as such, it is the dominant discourse. Meanwhile, the discourse of *kejawen* Islam is marginalized. From this perspective, it is thus understandable that a number of Islamic movements have tried to make spiritual connections by using Islamic symbols from the past because they are deemed more Islamic.

This pure Islamic construction does indeed dominate the religious awareness of Muslims. According to Michel Foucault, the dominant discourse has two consequences. First, the dominant discourse provides directions as to how an object should be read and understood. Secondly, the discursive structure created about an object is not necessarily the truth.[37] In the case of the two discourses above, the dominant pure (Arab) discourse marginalizes the other reality that *kejawen* Islam is part of Islam itself, and that the essence of its teachings and rituals is the same as that of so-called authentic Islam. This dominant discourse also ignores attempts at understanding and reading as a form of Islamic exegesis that originated from the Arab world itself and is a profound expression of religious experience. Anything that emerges is deviant and must be purged simply because it emerges under *kejawen* Islam, even though in religion, interpretation or attempts at understanding religion are a part of religious practice itself.

This kind of critical reading model in discourse theory is known as discourse analysis. This critical reading model is then used as a perspective to read social reality, because social reality takes place in and is formed by a network of relations where everyone seeks to dominate everyone else. In this context, religion has an important role in accumulating power in the reality of social, cultural, and political life. Here, religion seems to play with its own power. As a result, it is important to read how discourses are produced, and how groups or elements in society, especially religion, make this reproduction. It is this reading that is known as a critique of religious discourse.

The question is: why use discourse analysis to read religion? The *Terms of Reference* of the LKiS Study Together programme explains that the perspective of discourse theory is based on a very radical concern for the process of the formation of the human self. This perspective expects to be able to produce:

1. Human beings who dare in contemporary times to seek breakthroughs in understanding that enable new directions in competing with the persisting standardization of truth.
2. Human beings who are always able to undertake ascetic self- discovery.

3. Human beings who are always able to discover novel emotions that can help them live authentic lives.
4. Adventurous human beings who continue to search for truth for the creation of an autonomous self.
5. Human beings who are permanently able to critique themselves and to create, transform, and transfigure themselves to achieve autonomy.[38]

What needs to be stressed here is that the signs of discourse theory are a path leading to the desire to find spaces for other perspectives on self-formation outside of the dominant mass perspective on self-formation. Discourse is any expression of meaning in accordance with:

1. The unique constraints of a certain situation and a certain level of language.
2. Pressure from the selection of elements of knowledge that affect every speaker-writer, who are members of certain groups which in turn are tied to particular chronological histories.
3. The various passions, instincts, protests, or creation of subjects that are involved in a unique existential experience.[39]

So, although the primary materials of analysis are the texts (textuality), it is the very complex process of expression that analysis seeks to capture. As such, analysis forces any reading of the texts to be related to other sciences which claim to be based on reality, such as history, anthropology, politics, and economics.

Are these sciences then neutral and objective? Not at all, because there are interests in every science or field of knowledge. As a result, what is emphasized here is bias. Reading religious (Islamic) discourse should be based on the principles of re-reading, which are aimed at accepting the discontinuity, denial, and inconsistency that are imposed on a daily basis by contemporary action theory in Islamic states. The principles for accepting this reality are:

1. Humans are a concrete problem for humans.
2. It is the responsibility of humans to have sufficient knowledge about reality (the world, life, meaning, and so on).
3. This knowledge is an attempt to overcome the biophysical, economic, political, and language pressures that restrict life (and therefore make

life mortal), speech, politics, history, and economics (and therefore work).
4. Knowledge is a continually repeated way out (and as such is a permanent risk) from the confines that tend to engulf all cultural traditions after a phase of deep cultivation.
5. This way out is in accordance with the spiritual actions of the Sufis who never became established at any stage throughout their journeys (*sulûk*) towards God; and with the epistemological rejection of serious scholars who know that all scientific discourse is temporary.[40]

With this model of knowledge on the critique of discourse, the post-traditional community criticized all the doctrines and traditions that it had adhered to. This criticism brought with it a passion to reject single interpretations of religion, tradition, and reality. A critique of singular interpretations can be read in "Dari Redaksi/From the Editor" in the journal *Gerbang* which was published by the NU youth of eLSAD, Surabaya, as follows:

> At its most fundamental value, religion represents the human spirit of liberation from all forms of slavery, whether it is slavery to nature or to other humans. However as it developed, religion often became an idol that enslaved humankind itself. The religion that was initially sent down to elevate humankind eventually positioned humankind to elevate religion. This occurred because "religion" was no longer full of the values that were essentially a reflection of human nature.... The reversal of the function of religion cannot be separated from the excessive standardisation of Islamic reason, which ultimately led to petrifaction. This excessive standardisation led to the development of one singular interpretation. The Islamic texts that were once alive, dynamic and open to any interpretation became rigid, static and fossilised. The holy book that was once open to all forms of interpretation became unyielding through hierarchical authority: of religion and/or state institutions.[41]

This quote indicates that the problem of religious authority (religious, cultural, and political), which then produced Islamic orthodoxy, had a serious impact on the history of the development of Islamic thought. On the one hand, unity of thought did indeed avoid chaos and diversity, and allowed the Muslim community to appear in harmony and without turmoil. On the other hand, behind this harmony, something very valuable in religion had been sacrificed — namely, the dynamics of thought which had actually made Islam valuable in history. The ideology of harmony in religious thought is very dangerous if it collaborates with and/or is sustained by the system of power, because those who oppose this harmony can be accused of opposing both religion and the state.[42]

New Interpretation of *Ahl al-Sunnah wa al-Jamâ'ah*

One passion that has grown within the post-traditionalist community is the spirit to destroy the "centre" which is considered to have hegemony over the interpretation of Islam. This passion for decentring is used to re-read the *ahl al-sunnah wa al-jamâ'ah* doctrine, which is the doctrine and "ideology" of NU. Criticism of this doctrine not only relates to the content of the doctrine, but also questions how far the doctrine is able to respond to the continually changing times. The *ahl al-sunnah wa al-jamâ'ah* theology is also criticized for being overly elitist and far from popular visions. The first edition of *Tashwirul Afkar* in 1997 specifically adopted the theme "Reinterpreting *Ahl al-Sunnah wa al-Jamâ'ah*", an audacious act that had actually begun with Said Aqiel Siradj when he critically read the *ahl al-sunnah wa al-jamâ'ah* doctrine. Criticism has been undertaken because the doctrine is considered too narrow to accommodate the social and intellectual movements of the NU youth community. In fact, the *ahl al-sunnah wa al-jamâ'ah* doctrine has been likened to a stuffy, airless room[43] that is not comfortable to inhabit.

Said Aqiel Siradj struggled hard to give new meaning to the NU *ahl al-sunnah wa al-jamâ'ah* doctrine by not simply adopting the doctrine at face value, but by dismantling its methodology of thought (*manhaj al-fikr*). After an examination of history, he explained that the *manhaj al-fikr* of the doctrine was to hold to the principles of *tawassuth* (moderation), *tawâzun* (balance), and *i'tidâl* (justice).[44] These principles were believed to be able to lead individuals to a non-extreme religious perspective (*gayr tatharruf*).

Laode Ida mapped out several aspects that differentiate between the conventional understanding of the *ahl al-sunnah wa al-jamâ'ah* doctrine in the NU community and the "new" understanding developed by the young generation and pioneered by Said Aqiel Siradj.

In the eyes of several NU *kiai*, Said Aqiel's ideas are considered excessive and harmful to NU ideology. Nevertheless, his ideas were enthusiastically welcomed by the NU youth. His thoughts represented a space for their spiritual turmoil. The youth always questioned why *ahl*

TABLE 4.1

Aspect	Conventional Understanding	"New" Understanding
Position of *ahl al-sunnah wa al-jamâ'ah*	*Ahl al-sunnah wa al-jamâ'ah* is seen as a school of thought that follows a specific doctrine: in the field of fiqh it follows one of the four schools of thought (Hanafi, Maliki, Syafi'i, and Hanbali); in the field of *tasawuf* it follows Junaid al-Baghdâdî and al-Ghazali; and in the field of theology it follows Abu Hasan al-Asy'âri and Abu Mansur al-Maturidî.	*Ahl al-sunnah wa al-jamâ'ah* is not seen as a school of thought but as a method of thought (*manhaj al-fikr*) that encompasses all aspects of life based on the principles of *tawassuth* (moderation), *tawâzun* (balance), and *i'tidâl* (justice).
Value of truth	Exclusive, strict, absolute, and tends to be textual. Something can be called true if it can be accounted for textually.	Inclusive, flexible, and relative. Truth does not have to be accounted for textually, but more importantly must be relevant to the main spirit of Islam.
Fundamental Understanding	*Ahl al-sunnah wa al-jamâ'ah* is a doctrine used to differentiate between Sunni and non-Sunni groups. It is believed that Sunnis will enter paradise while non-Sunnis will not.	*Ahl al-sunnah wa al-jamâ'ah* cannot purely be seen as a doctrine as if to be Islam itself, but has a vast and tolerant understanding.
Orientation	Traditional-conservative, theocentric, and tends to submit to reality because everything that occurs in the world is seen as the will of God.	Rational-progressive, anthropocentric, and active in addressing the realities of life.
Political stance	Rulers have a central position and can do as they please to their people. Meanwhile the people are apolitical, because politics is seen to be monopolized by the government. The people have no control over themselves because power originates from God, not from the people.	The people have a central position. All policies must be oriented towards the welfare of the people. As a result, the people can criticize and control what the rulers do.

Source: Laode Ida, *NU Muda, Kaum Progresif, dan Sekularisme Baru* (Jakarta: Erlangga, 2004), pp. 153–56.

al-sunnah wa al-jamâ'ah, which dogmatically follows Imam Abu Hasan al-Asy'âri and Abu Mansur al-Maturidî in theology, follows one of the four schools of thought, follows al-Ghazâlî and al-Baghdâdî in mysticism, and is seen as the truth that will allow them to enter paradise or heaven. What about those who adhere to other understandings, or are non-Muslim? Does this mean that the gate to paradise is always closed to them? These critical questions formed the agenda for their discussions.

This problem arose because, like it or not, NU was faced with pluralism. NU has a principle that is often put forward in response to new developments, which reads as *al-muhâfadhah 'alâ al-qadîm al-shâlih wa al-akhdzu bi al-jadîd al-ashlah* (maintaining old norms that are good, and adopting new norms that are better), and is a principle that actually suggests elasticity. The problem is, what *al-jadîd al-ashlah* (new and better norms) should be accommodated? This is where different opinions began to emerge. Do pluralism, freedom of thought, respect of human rights, egalitarianism, democracy, and so on represent *al-jadîd al-ashlah* that must be accepted? This is where the problem really lies. In this context, there is an ambiguous attitude in the NU community, especially amongst the ulama, in defining *al-jadîd al-ashlah*. Although the doctrine is open and willing to accept new norms, the response to new demands has been hesitant. In fact, Said Aqiel Siradj has often said on a number of occasions that NU should not just take new and better things (*akhdzu bi al-jadîd al-ashlah*) in a passive manner, but must actively search for those new things (*al-îjâd bi al-jadîd al-ashlah*). This is of course much more difficult.

The journal *Tashwirul Afkar*, which is published by Lakpesdam NU, is highly influenced by the philosophy of structuralism which is used as a tool through which to read the emergence of the *ahl al-sunnah wa al-jamâ'ah* group. This is apparent in the concepts used, such as the collapse of the grand narrative and the emergence of smaller narratives, as evident in the following quote:

> From the perspective of structuralism, the rise of the Asy'arites to overthrow the Mu'tazilites represents the rise of small narratives against the grand narrative which at that time was represented by the Mu'tazilites. The Asy'arites decentred the Mu'tazilite discourse. This was because as a discourse the Mu'tazilites had become the central determinant of existing discourses. The Mu'tazilites in this sense were the dominant discourse that marginalised other discourses. Like a circle, the Mu'tazilites represented the centre of the circle.[45]

As such, the deconstruction of the *ahl al-sunnah wa al-jamâ'ah* doctrine can on the one hand be seen as signifying a new scientific framework that has existed side-by-side with Islamic sciences; but on the other hand, it can be seen as signifying the existence of real humanitarian challenges that must be resolved immediately, where the *ahl al-sunnah wa al-jamâ'ah* doctrine seems to be trapped amidst the flood of humanitarian problems. More explicitly, the NU *ahl al-sunnah wa al-jamâ'ah* doctrine currently faces two challenges. First, it faces a challenge from within the NU community itself, with the emergence of the new wave of thought and a new scholarly tradition that is unfamiliar to the *pesantren* scholarly tradition. Secondly, it faces challenges from outside of NU that take a number of forms, including the challenge of religious pluralism. How does the *ahl al-sunnah wa al-jamâ'ah* doctrine respond to the issue of national pluralism? This problem is quite difficult to resolve using this conventional doctrine, in light of the fact that the *ahl al-sunnah wa al-jamâ'ah* doctrine is fundamentally a sect doctrine that emerged out of the endless internal conflict in Islam. The still very prominent discourse in the NU community is how to differentiate between those groups who are correct and those who are not. Religious pluralism is not only related to non-Muslims, but also encompasses the plurality of religious understandings within Islam, such as *ahl al-sunnah wa al-jamâ'ah* versus the Mu'tazilites and the Shi'ites. This is a crucial issue that must be resolved, considering that inter-sect competition in Islam is so strong that Sunnis do not hesitate to say *la'anahum Allâh* (May God's wrath be upon them) when talking about the Mu'tazilites. Another external issue is the challenge of democracy. Democracy has become a new religion that creatures of the earth find difficult to reject. The problem is that democracy as a discourse often touches on religious concepts, such as sovereignty in a state. In the democratic concept of state, the highest authority lies in the hands of (the majority of) the people who are represented by the people's representative councils. In the *ahl al-sunnah wa al-jamâ'ah* concept, in accordance with the beliefs of Sunni fiqh experts, a good state is a state that is based on Islam, the Qur'an, and Hadith. Human authority must submit to religious authority. The final challenge is the challenge of human rights, that is, all those matters that the *ahl al-sunnah wa al-jamâ'ah* doctrine must face concerning the fundamental rights of humans and the attempt to respect those rights. This demand arose after the *Universal Declaration of Human Rights* by the United Nations (UN) in 1948. The *ahl al-sunnah wa al-jamâ'ah* tradition actually has a concept of *dlarûriyyat al-khams* (five fundamental rights), including *hifdh al-dîn* (maintaining religion), *hifdh al-nafs* (maintaining life), *hifdh al-'aql* (maintaining mind/intellect), *hifdh al-nasl* (maintaining lineage), and *hifdh al-mâl* (maintaining property),[46] which are seen as the fundamental human rights principles in Islam. However, the problem is that these noble principles are still narrowly understood purely to maintain the interests of Islam, not the interests of humankind.

This awareness is very evident for instance in the following statement:

> The issue is, is the NU *ahl al-sunnah wa al-jamâ'ah* theological construction able to respond to the demands made by the newly developing religious thought that has recently become increasingly progressive and complex? Perhaps for *fiqh* constructions NU's *ahl al-sunnah wa al-jamâ'ah* doctrine can still "survive" and respond to social change. However we need to look at the theological doctrine that is used as the reference for NU's *ahl al-sunnah wa al-jamâ'ah* doctrine. We must honestly acknowledge that this theological doctrine is a domain that is not flexible like *fiqh*. Theology is full of claims of truth and infidelity. The characteristic of all theological doctrine is its inflexibility in maintaining the idea that the theological system itself is most correct. Acknowledging this is necessary to defend a specific ideology.[47]

This statement is an explicit recognition of the NU youth community's concern for its theological doctrine. There are two choices in this situation: will NU continue to hold to the conventional *ahl al-sunnah wa al-jamâ'ah* formulation, or will it critique the concept that has to date been valid? The post-traditionalist community has clearly chosen the latter option. Post-traditionalists not only critique but also reorient their theological doctrine, changing it from a theocentric doctrine only concerned with elite problems concerning God, the holy text, the angels, heaven, rulers, and so on, into a more anthropocentric doctrine that is populist, and which is then called a humanitarian theology.[48]

The term humanitarian theology is not often heard, because the term theology is related to God, theology of divinity, and is not related to humans. Humans in this sense are the objects, even though it was humans who formulated theology, not God. As a result, humanitarian theology is a contradiction in terms. Theology itself indeed means the science of God (*theo* means God, and *logos* means science); it discusses God and all His omnipotence, the Creator, the Essence that is Most High, absolute, unlimited, and so on. Meanwhile, humanity is quite the opposite: it is limited, an identity of creation, lowly, and dependent on God.

This kind of contradiction is also found in the term liberation theology, which has of late caught the interest of a number of Muslim intellectuals. In fact, Farid Essack, an activist and thinker from South Africa, seriously studied the dimensions of liberation in the Qur'an in his excellent book, *Qur'an, Liberation and Pluralism* (Oxford: Oneworld Oxford, 1997). Theology fundamentally requires humans to submit to the convictions that are considered to be the pillars of faith of a religion. Thus, humans are bound, must submit without question, and are consequently not free. Meanwhile, the term liberation signifies the opposite: freedom from all kinds of shackles and from structural and cultural bonds, including attachment to certain beliefs or rules. On this basis, theology is fundamentally unable to liberate humans from the bonds that tie them down, although some Muslims state that Islam (Islamic theology) is a liberating religion.

In the midst of these norms of understanding there is an attempt to shift the focus of theology, which is too oriented towards God, towards humans. Of course, this is rather rare (or non-existent) in the tradition of Islamic theology. Nevertheless, it is important not to lower the greatness of God (because without being elevated at all, God is already the Most High); but this effort is more to formulate a theology that has a social vision, that is transformative, a theology with a humanitarian vision, although I am aware that this is no easy thing to do in the Islamic tradition.

Despite the significant challenges, formulating a theology with a social and humanitarian vision is necessary, because the idea is almost completely free of the thoughts of the Islamic theologians from the past. It is thus not strange that it is currently difficult to find a socio-humanitarian vision in the theology developed so far, including in NU's *ahl al-sunnah wa al-jamâ'ah* doctrine. Theological convictions and social reality seem to be completely separate, as if there is no relationship at all between them. Theology is in one place *(fî wâdin)*, and humanitarian problems are somewhere else entirely *(fî wâdin âkhar)*. Following this line of thought means that there is no connection between theology and social transformation, and if someone wanted to use theology as a basis for social transformation it would be like trying to find a needle in a very large haystack. Here lies the importance of humanizing theology and theologizing humans. Humanizing theology requires theology to adopt a vision and orientation towards humans; while theologizing humans means situating humans as the basis for theological understanding. In Sunni theology, this is achieved not simply by replacing old Sunni theology with a new Sunni theology, but rather by giving a social perspective to theological convictions. As a result, fears that the quite well-established Sunni theology will be lost need not emerge.

Fulton J. Sheen (1928), in his provocatively titled book *Religion Without God*, discussed an interesting new conception of religion: "What is this new idea of religion? It is briefly a religion without God, that is, God as traditionally understood. Religion centres not about God but man. It is man first, not God." This statement is a criticism of a formal religion that cares more about the religious institution, and whose adherents have actually forgotten God because their behaviour often betrays religious values.[49] Differing from this, people like Karen Armstrong[50] who claim to be free monotheists do not care so much for formal religious institutions but believe in God.

If this way of thought is accepted, then the NU community is in a period of theological transition. The NU theological structure which is based on the Sunni tradition does not have a social framework to respond to a number of humanitarian problems, is unable to wrestle with the wild anarchy of meaning, fails to accommodate rapidly changing social dynamics, and is too fragile to be the foundation for social empowerment towards a more social, humanitarian, and democratic society. This kind of critique is not without basis, and represents the restlessness of many who are aware of the importance of theology in the transformation and empowerment of the people — something which is not present in conventional theology.

This kind of theology influences the way social reality is interpreted through a top-to-bottom framework. The "top" has the connotation of being good and pure/holy, and can also mean the elite that are in power, while the "bottom" is related to all things popular, decadent, lowly, and profane; it may also refer to the masses, who tend to be anarchic, and as such, should be regulated and governed over. Unconsciously, social stratification is legitimized through hierarchical realities: God—the angels—humans—things.[51] In fact, theology is an ideology that becomes the foundation, or at least the inspiration, for individuals or communities in their social interactions and transformations. Thus, it is understandable that the process of social transformation in the Islamic community, especially NU, could be described as having no grasp, no direction, and being disoriented.[52]

Therefore, a review of the doctrinal aspects of Sunni theology, in the view of the progressive NU youth, is an inevitable necessity, especially in relation to *tasawuf*, which tends to be theocentric, metaphysical, fatalistic, and which places excessive emphasis on eschatology. In terms of doctrine,

NU theology follows the understandings of Abu Hasan al-Asy'âri (d. 324 H/936 CE) and Abu Mansur al-Maturidî (d. 944 H), while in *tasawuf* it follows Abu Hamid al-Ghazâlî (d. 505 H/1111 CE) and Junaid al-Baghdâdî (d. 429 H).[53] A close examination of the content of these figures' teachings, which are all grouped together, raises a lot of questions.[54] How could al-Asy'âri and al-Baghdâdî' be grouped together when their theologies are very different, if not contrary to one another, especially in regard to reason and revelation? The same could be said for al-Ghazâlî and al-Baghdâdî. How could al-Ghazâlî and al-Baghdâdî, who have different traditions of thought, be grouped together? Al-Ghazâlî was an ulama who loved the *bayâni* tradition of thought, while al-Baghdâdî was a great figure in the *irfânî* tradition of thought.[55]

Even today, no explanation has been put forward to explain why al-Asy'âri's teachings are placed together with those of al-Maturidî. If the choice of al-Maturidî to accompany al-Asy'âri was projected to strengthen the *ahl al-sunnah wa al-jamâ'ah* doctrine that was too al-Asy'âri oriented, then it was not the best choice, because al-Maturidî's thoughts did not develop greatly in the Sunni world. However, if it was intended as another door to views outside of al-Asy'âri's Sunnism, then we can appreciate the insight of the first generation of NU ulama. As a result, the following generation should not have become trapped in claims about the truth, justifying its own theology while faulting that of others.

Another problem emerges if we trace the emergence of the theological sects in Islam historically. The emergence of these sects indicates the presence of an intense intellectual struggle that was able to temporarily respond to the theological issues that emerged at the time. On this basis, it is only fitting that the relevance of these ideas should be questioned of late, because theological thought is deemed to no longer have enough energy to respond to contemporary humanitarian problems.

Classical theology was indeed successful in responding to the questions that plagued humans who always thought about God. Here, theology was used to find eschatological certainty. As such, it is not surprising that classical theology, which was also maintained by NU, was more theocentric in that it made God the centre of all thought. In divine issues for instance, theological debate always dwelled on the issue of God and His attributes. These debates focused on whether God had attributes or not, if the attributes of God were within or outside of His Essence, and so on. If justice was discussed in classical theology, it was limited to God's justice in responding to human behaviour in the hereafter. Thoughts about aspects of humanity concerning whether or not there was such a thing as human free will also ultimately discussed God's response in the hereafter. In short, all aspects of theological thought made God the centre of discussion: they were theocentric. Meanwhile, humans were only part of a mosaic that had no meaning whatsoever.

Practical matters were not discussed because they were considered part of other areas of science, such as fiqh, morality, and *tasawuf*. This is understandable because the science of dialectical theology (*ilmu kalam*) is the science of *aqidah* (faith), with *aqidah* referring to those things that bind the human heart and conscience. The problem is: why is it not possible to question why *aqidah* exists? *Aqidah* was formulated as a guide to actions. *Aqidah* was not just something to be stored in one's heart but to be manifested in real life. As a result, the science of *aqidah* must also speak about the realities of human action, and the realities of life. This science thus has a practical characteristic, although not at the same level as that of the science of fiqh, which deals with the physical rules between fellow humans, between humans and their environment, and between humans and God. The practical nature of theology exists in the realm of the mind/mentality and the heart, and in the spiritual passion, belief, and attachment that directs and influences action.[56]

Hassan Hanafi also criticized classical theology for always subordinating humankind when he wrote a commentary on the *ushûl al-dîn* texts of the ulama from the past. These texts continually praised God and the Prophet. According to Hassan Hanafi, praising God and stating the weakness of humankind in the face of His greatness created a psychological condition that was unable to change the situation. The souls of Muslims were stunted and weakened by the continual reminder that God is great, while humankind is weak and needs help. This kind of attitude was so entrenched in the psyche that it made people less confident and lacking power when dealing with temporal rulers: political, cultural, or religious.[57]

As such, theological debate and thought did not greatly explore issues of humanity. With time, theology seemed to move further away from social issues and from its objective of raising universal human dignity without discrimination. The emergence of several theological currents in Islam was born out of the conviction of each current that it represented the truth and that all others were wrong.

The same thing is apparent in Sunni theology, which initially sought compromise with a number of extreme thoughts on the principles of *tawassuth* (moderation), *tawâzun* (balance), and *i'tidâl* (justice). It was hoped that these principles would lead to a less extreme religious attitude in viewing reality. However, as Sunni theology developed, especially the theology NU believed in, it became trapped in making ideological claims of being the group that was most safe and that had the most authority to enter paradise, while denying the opportunity of salvation to other groups.

As such, although Sunni theology initially contained principles of moderation, in practice it became trapped in extremism, or at least was no longer maintaining a middle path between the two extremes. Sunni theology was inclined to choose one of the extremes, either to the right or to the left. This is very apparent if we examine the struggle of theological thought.

Let's take for example the theory of human action, which split theological thought into two major groups, each with its own minor variations. The Qadarites believed that all aspects of human action, including will (*al-masyî'ah*), power (*al-istithâ'ah*), and the action itself (*al-fi'il*), originated from humans themselves. Meanwhile, the Jabarites believed the opposite: that all the elements that make up an action originate from God. Somewhere in the middle of these two extremes was Sunni theology, with Abu Hasan al-Asy'âri's theory of *kasb* which was actually intended to mediate between the Qadarite extreme on the one hand and the Jabarite extreme on the other. However, al-Asy'âri's *kasb* theory did not mean that human efforts actually determined the occurrence of an action, but remained in subordination to God. As a result, al-Asy'âri's *kasb* is interpreted less as a human effort, and more as a gift from God.[58] Consequently, al-Asy'âri's theory was not effective in shaping change.

In addition to human action, this is also apparent in the argument over reason and revelation. In order to obtain a complete picture of the matter, it is necessary to first illustrate the issue. Theological discourse on reason and revelation revolves around four matters, namely: (1) knowing God; (2) the obligation to know God; (3) knowing right from wrong; (4) the obligation to do good and avoid evil. For al-Asy'âri, logical reason (without divine revelation) could only provide the answer to one of these issues — namely, knowing God. That is, without divine revelation, humans could use their logic and would be capable of knowing that there is a God. However, the other three aspects could only be known through divine revelation.[59]

Reason could not lead to the knowledge that there are obligations to knowing God, to knowing right from wrong, or the obligation to do good deeds and avoid evil. Thus, stealing, murdering, or gambling could not be deemed wrong if there was no divine revelation to that effect.

This opinion is different from al-Maturidî's, where reason, he argues, could reveal the first three aspects (knowing God, the obligation to know God, and knowing right from wrong). Divine revelation was only necessary to know the obligation to do good deeds and avoid evil, while reason could already decide what was right and what was wrong. Thus, according to al-Maturidî, a deed could be called right or wrong if it was substantially right or wrong.[60] Al-Maturidî's conviction was very similar to that of the Mu'tazilites, who reckoned that logical reasoning could reveal all four aspects mentioned above. Their opinion on reason and divine revelation has recently influenced theories on human action. While al-Asy'âri's stance was closer to the Jabarites, al-Maturidî and the Mu'tazilites were closer to the Qadarites.

These kinds of theological themes colour the entire theological discourse in Islam. Theological discussions almost never depart from these conventional themes. It represents the wealth of Islamic thought that we have inherited. The important agenda for the following generation is not just to know, preserve, and defend to the death this theological thought, let alone to continue the claims about who is Muslim and who is kafir (infidel), but also to figure out how to transform this way of thinking.

Criticism of Sunni theology leads to the question: is a blind defence of theological doctrine still relevant in today's world where theological barriers should have dissolved? There are at least two answers to this question: relevant and irrelevant. The first response usually argues that theology is the foundation to the formation of religious structures. As a result, without theological convictions, Islam will never stand strong. Meanwhile, those who answer that it is irrelevant argue that theological debate should be left alone to be recorded in history as the wealth and treasure of Islamic intellectuality, while we, a generation significantly distanced from the birth of theological thought, have no interest in theological thought any more.

The majority of the NU community follows the first argument, although recently there has been a shift in thought that likens defending certain theological currents to a wager between heaven and hell, which will only be a hindrance as entering heaven or hell has no relation to the theological system an individual follows. This idea may be rather radical, unpopular, or even a violation of a most fundamental aspect in the NU community, because NU has always held to a specific interpretation of Sunni theology.

Critical NU youth often find it difficult to escape from this pressure and the stuffy room of theological thought. Nevertheless, they are becoming aware that now, consciously or not, they have become the victims of the history of past theological disputes. This awareness incorporates, for instance, the awareness that to date they have continued to preserve the theological conflict they inherited from their ancestors, although this can be seen as an ordinary intellectual dynamic. The problem is if this theological conflict involves the masses as both supporters and opponents, as has happened in history. They appear to fight for the only path to salvation, when what they are struggling for is no more than one slice of truth from many slices.

This controversy is further complicated because politics or the state become involved, as occurred historically with the *mihnah* or inquisition during the governance of al-Makmun (813–33 CE), a caliph of the Abbasid dynasty. In this position, people can no longer differentiate between religious and political reason because the two are so intertwined. Something that should exist in the secular realm (political reason) was not infrequently sacralized as a religious opinion. There were many other similar cases in Islamic history in addition to the inquisition. Another famous case is how Mu'awiya used the Jabarite theology to support his regime. Mu'awiya used the Jabarite theology to legitimize his politics by stating: "If God was not willing, I could not have become Caliph; if God hated me, God would have replaced me with someone else."[61]

It is understandable that rulers preferred to feed their people the Jabarite theology, because it allowed them to easily manipulate their power as the will of God that could not be opposed. As a result, rulers of the past became very uneasy when the Qadarite understanding developed in society, because it could potentially be used as a tool to rebel against the rulers. A similar thing occurred during the reign of Caliph 'Abd al-Mâlik (685–705 CE). One day, the caliph sent a letter to Hasan al-Basri, who was seen to be developing and teaching the doctrine of free will and free action for humans. The letter stated, amongst other things:

> *Amîr al-mu'minîn* (the leader of the faithful) has received a report about your views pertaining to independence of humans (*qadar*) that was not heard of in the previous generation. *Amîr al-Mu'minîn* does not know of a single person of those he has met including those who were friends of

the Prophet that holds the same opinion as people say you have on this issue.... As a result, it is hoped that you write a letter to him about this opinion, explaining whether it is a verbal transmission *(riwâyah)* from one of the friends of God's Prophet, or your own opinion *(ra'y)* or something else that is reinforced in the Qur'an.[62]

This quote indicates how state intervention in religious thought has become a part of Islamic history. Here, the state positions itself as the censorship institute of all religious thought in order to determine which ideas are allowed to develop and which are forbidden. In the above case, the Umayyad dynasty clearly had interests in the Jabarite theology to legitimize its power. By accepting the Jabarite doctrine, the Umayyad regime, which initially made no theological claim to legitimize its power, became legitimate in the eyes of religion. In this case, it was not religious authority, but political authority wrapped in a religious message that was operating. Those who dared to oppose the formal religious current would be tried and sentenced because politically they endangered and threatened the stability of power. This was the case with Ma'bad al-Juhani, the pioneer of the Qadarite understanding, who was beheaded by the Umayyad regime in 80 H/699 CE under the order of Caliph 'Abd al-Mâlik bin Marwan because he taught about the independence of humans. A similar fate befell Ghilan al-Dimsyâqî, who was sentenced to death by the Umayyad Caliph, Hisyâm bin Mâlik, in 105 H/723 CE.[63]

The above illustration provides a sufficient picture of how the segregation of theology contributed significantly to the rise of violence — both physical violence and in the form of depriving creative thought. As a result, the task of the current generation of Muslims is not to preserve and perpetuate this theological conflict, but to discover how to defuse this tension, while at the same time continuing to preserve intellectual dynamics.

Methodologically speaking, this structural way of thinking is used to change the structures that are well established and very rarely questioned. Al-Jabiri more assertively proposed that the structural model of thought was intended to remodel the standardized structure as a variable that was changing and dynamic. Doing so means that individuals must be able to liberate themselves from all authority, which in turn opens up the opportunity to establish their own authority. In the postmodernist tradition, this kind of analysis is also known as deconstruction *(tafkik)*, that is, breaking down the standardized (and stagnant) tradition in a particular structure, and seeing it not as a "structure", but as something that changes and is fluid. This involves changing it from being absolute to being relative, from being ahistorical to historical, from being absolute to being temporal, and so on.[64]

One prominent thing in theological debate is the restriction in making claims about the truth. In comparison to differences in the field of fiqh, claims in theology are much harsher, and as such, polarization is much sharper between those who are kafir and those who are Muslim, between unbelievers and believers. In fiqh, no matter how harsh a difference of opinion is, it does not lead to claims of infidelity; the claims are much more moderate. As a result, we must first agree on how to treat theological thought. This is important not only to ensure that we are all on the same page, but also to reconstruct the theological views that tend to be black and white. Using the method explained above, it is hoped that theology will have grey areas: areas between the black and white that become areas for dialogue.

Situating theology as a problem of tradition carries a number of consequences. First, theology has to be placed in the secular realm, or in other words it must be secularized.[65] The question is: how is it possible to secularize theology? Does theology not always emphasize transcendence, as it talks about the "heavens", the Essence Above, and so on? It is only fitting that this question should emerge, because conventional theology indeed gives that impression. Secularization of theology — if one agrees with the term — is the attempt to bring theology closer to worldly, lowly, human issues. As such, formulating a theology with humanistic inspiration is a necessity, although many consider this strange. Secularization of theology also means making theological debate more sublime by adopting humanitarian and social issues. Theology will then become a true power for humans, not just to believe in religion, but — more importantly — to become an inspiration and foundation for thinking about a life that liberates humans from various forms of oppression.

Secondly, seeing theology as a problem of tradition also means distancing theology from claims about who is Muslim and who is kafir, who is a believer and who is a non-believer, heaven and hell, and so on. This is a logical consequence of the process of theological desacralization described above. The ultimate aim of the desacralization of theology is the relativism of theology, where the science of theology — as with other sciences — must be placed upon the altar of relativism. That is, those truths assumed to be theological truths are not always absolute, valid throughout all time, and unable to accept change, because even in theology the laws of relativism are still valid.

Therefore, although we believe in the truth of a particular theological doctrine, this does not prevent us from confirming other people's theologies. In fact, if the boundaries segregating theology become truly fluid, then people no longer need to be identified on the basis of their theological convictions. An individual would also no longer need to identify him or herself as a follower of a particular theology, and thus may be at one time a Shi'a and at another a Sunni; at one point he may be an Asy'arite, and at another a Mu'tazilite; at one time she may follow the Qadarites and at another she may follow the Jabarites, and so on. This phenomenon is unconsciously present in everyday life, although if pointed out many people reject the idea. The most evident example in the NU tradition, which follows Sunni theology, is the presence of several Shi'a elements in NU society's religious traditions. In fact, Abdurrahman Wahid once stated that, culturally speaking, NU was Shi'a. There are several indicators of this, such as a number of *shlawat* or prayers to Muhammad (PBUH) that are specific to the Shi'a tradition and that are practised in *pesantren*; certain *wirid* (additional prayers after standard prayers) that state the five descendants of the *ahl al-bayt* (family of the Prophet Muhammad, PBUH); the tradition of visiting graves; building a roof over graves; prayers for the dead; anniversaries for the dead; and reading the *diba'* prayer.[66]

Thirdly, seeing theology as a problem of tradition also requires the reconstruction of theological understandings. This reconstruction requires an open attitude to accept changes to what has always been believed in as the only truth. On this, Hassan Hanafi offered a theology that understood movement in all fields. This reconstruction involves many things, including: changing the perspective towards texts from one which is less aggressive to one which is more aggressive, and being rational and open to the framework of modern science when viewing religious texts.

With these three basic frameworks, it is urgent that the paradigm of theology be changed. This change in paradigm involves several things. First, there must be a change in theological paradigm from being theocentric (God at the centre of everything) to more anthropocentric (humankind at the centre of everything). While the former paradigm sees worldly affairs as God's affairs, the latter sees worldly affairs as the affairs of humankind. Secondly, the way the world is viewed must be changed. While conventional theology saw the world as something united with God so that it was always approached through a divine/godly perspective, a change would mean that theology would view the world as something separate from God. As a result, the world is viewed from a worldly perspective, and is not always approached through a divine/godly perspective, although its divine nature cannot be completely rejected. Thirdly, the way of viewing nature must be altered from being seen as a sign of God's presence to being seen as a means or instrument to worship the divine. Fourthly, the theological perspective that makes individuals the focus in viewing the realities of life must shift to place communities at the centre of focus in viewing the realities of life. The consequence of this is that the concept of piety will change itself, from ritual–individual piety to social piety. As such, a pious individual is not necessarily one who worships with dedication despite oppressing other humans, but rather one who is highly committed, not just in avoiding behaving in such a way that oppresses others, but also in enforcing humanitarian values and liberating humans from various shackles — whether it be the shackles of politics, culture, poverty, or even the shackles of religion (the religious elite). These changes to the paradigm of theology can be seen in more detail in Table 4.2.

There is actually quite a strong foundation in Islam for a change in the orientation and paradigm of theology. Normatively speaking, we are familiar with the Sufistic Hadith which is the reference for human self-definition, and which states: *man 'arafa nafsahu faqad 'arafa rabbahu* (people who know themselves will know their God). This Hadith positions humans as both the subject and object in understanding themselves and God.

As the subject, humans are required to be wise in understanding themselves in their capacity as humans who have both strengths and weaknesses without involving any attributes from outside of themselves. This Hadith reveals how physical human beings are one with God, who is non-physical; or at least, there are elements of God (God's *nasût* characteristics) that are integrated in human beings (human's *lahût* characteristics). As a result, when humans think about themselves they are basically thinking about God; humans who defend humanitarian values and rights are basically defending divine values and rights. It is here that we can understand the words of God: "And I (God) am closer to people than their own jugular vein" (Qur'an, 50: 16).

It is this that allows Sufis to unite with God and immerse themselves in the sea of God (*istigraq fî bahr al-wihdah*) to the extent that they sometimes produce expressions that according to fiqh are apostate, such as al-Hallaj's

TABLE 4.2
Change in the Paradigm of Theology

Conventional Theology	Humanitarian Theology
• Situates God as the centre of orientation (theocentric). Everything is left to God, including worldly affairs.	• Makes humans the centre of orientation (anthropocentric). Worldly affairs are left to humans.
• Themes discussed are always on a higher level, such as God, the angels, the holy book, heaven, and hell.	• Themes discussed are on a lower level, such as humankind, the earth, and society.
• World reality is viewed as something united with God and is thus always approached from a divine perspective.	• World reality is viewed as something different from the Divine and thus is not always approached from a divine perspective, although that which is Divine cannot be rejected either.
• Nature is viewed as a sign of Divine presence. Elements of nature and our perspective of nature can be a divine experience.	• Nature is a means of worshipping God. Humans, regardless of elements or perspective, control and manage nature in obedience to God.
• Individuals are the focus and orientation in viewing the realities of life.	• Community is the focus and orientation in viewing the realities of life.
• Emphasizes individual piety.	• Emphasizes individual and society piety.
• An individual's piety is measured based on his or her ritual worship.	• An individual's piety is measured based on his or her involvement in upholding social-humanitarian values.
• The virtue of human dignity and rights is measured and understood on an individual basis.	• The virtue of human dignity is understood as a part of the responsibility to help preserve the universe.
• The whole is equal to the sum of its parts. Every system or structure is an isolated part, autonomous and not interrelated.	• The whole is bigger than the sum of its parts. Everything is a part that is always interrelated with other parts, is interdependent, and reciprocally cooperates.

Source: Adapted, with a number of modifications, from the journal *Gerbang*, no. 2 (1999).

anâ al-haqq (I am the creative Truth), Abu Yazid al-Bustami's *subhânî-subhânî mâ a'dama sya'nî, mâ fî* (Glory be to me, how great is My majesty), and Abu Ali al-Firasi's *jubbatî illâ Allâh* (within this robe is nought but God). This fusion of human beings with God must be broadened to encompass all humanitarian–religious work that is able to be undertaken in accordance with the laws of space and time. This kind of behaviour directly benefits and is felt by other people, in contrast to the contemplation of *fanâ'* (extinction), which is exclusive and limited.

As such, humans no longer need to decline into an animalistic lustful life which has indeed been within humankind from the very beginning, but are slowly able to balance the real world with their ideal world. This kind of human is known in *tasawuf* as the perfect human (*al-insân al-kâmil*) who is able to define him or herself and is able to respond to the demands of the time according to his or her theological convictions.[67]

Changing the theological paradigm, as explained above, is not an easy task to undertake in the tradition of Islamic thought. The difficulty largely lies in the assumption that theology is fundamental to religion. As a result, changing aspects in theology is often seen as a threat to religion because those changes are seen more as an attempt to undermine religion itself.

Therefore, changing the theological paradigm must first be accompanied by an awareness that theology is a product of thought that is not immune from change, criticism, and correction. This avoids what Mohammed Arkoun calls *taqdîs al-afkâr al-dînî* (sacralization of religious thought), including theological thought. Adopting this perspective means that we face no barriers in rethinking what we have always held to be true.

Restlessness has already formed a particular self-identity amongst the NU youth. They are restless not only in the realm of theology but also in that of fiqh. There is a difference in the way fiqh is viewed according to the conventional understanding and the understanding the NU youth are developing. While the former sees fiqh as the truth of orthodoxy, the latter situates fiqh as a paradigm for social interpretation. As a result, while the former always subjugates reality to the truth of fiqh, the latter uses fiqh as a counter discourse in the midst of competing political discourses. While the former appears black and white in the way it views reality, the latter is nuanced, and occasionally complex in the way it responds to reality.[68]

The discussions from the *halaqah* of NU ulama, run by RMI and P3M from 1988 to 1990, revealed five characteristics of this "new fiqh" paradigm. First, it always involves reinterpretation by studying fiqh texts and searching for new contexts. Secondly, the meaning of adhering to a school of thought was changed from textual schools of thought (*madzhab qawli*) to methodological schools of thought (*madzhab manhaji*). Thirdly, it involves a fundamental verification of which teachings were primary (*ushûl*) and which were secondary, or branches (*furû*). Fourthly, fiqh is presented as a social ethic, not as the positive law of the state. Fifthly, it introduced the methodology of philosophical thought, particularly in cultural and social issues.[69] Given these characteristics, post-traditionalism can no longer question from where a thought originated — whether it was from the Mu'tazilites, Kharijites, Shi'ites, or anywhere else. Rather, post-traditionalists turn their attention to how far those ideas can be implemented in reality and benefit humankind universally. On this basis, they still consider the Mu'tazilite understanding as a reflection of the movement for human liberation and rationalism. Similarly, they elaborate the Kharijite doctrine because the Kharijites inspired people to seize their rights and were firm in restoring their dignity. Post-traditionalism also considers Shi'ism because of its persistence in opposing neo-colonialism and Zionism.[70]

With this perspective, several aspects of the *ahl al-sunnah wa al-jamâ'ah* doctrine, especially in fiqh, such as the obligation to follow one of the four schools of thought (in its standard meaning) and the restriction against *talfiq* (practice of selecting different opinions on any one issue from different schools of thought and combining them), become fluid. There is an interesting study in relation to this by Badrun Alaena on the NU youth in Yogyakarta and the shift in meaning of the *ahl al-sunnah wa al-jamâ'ah* doctrine. He surveyed 120 respondents from various organizations, including Ansor, LKPSM, IPNU, IPPNU, Fatayat, PMII, FKGMNU, and LKiS. He examined three issues, namely, the importance of adhering to a school of thought, methodological schools of thought (*madzhab manhaji*), and the *talfiq* method. The results were as shown in Table 4.3.[71]

This data indicates the presence of an extraordinary change in current, with very few respondents seeking to maintain the old concept of the schools of thought. All three areas — adhering to a school of thought, *madzhab manhaji*, and use of the *talfiq* method — reveal a criticism of conventional understandings, which are perceived as being less able to give "space" for social experimentation.

The purpose of this change in orientation is how to make religion and all systems within it the spirit for liberation, which is actualized by

TABLE 4.3

Question Variables	Category	Total	Percentage
Society adhering to a school of thought	Important	17	14.16%
	Unimportant	97	80.83%
	Unsure	6	5%
Ahl al-sunnah wa al-jamâ'ah as a method of thought (manhaj al-fikr)	Agree	103	85.83%
	Disagree	15	12.5%
	Unsure	2	1.66%
Method of talfiq	Allowed	78	65%
	Not allowed	30	25%
	Unsure	12	10%

rejecting singular interpretations of religious doctrine. The question that arises is: can religion be a liberating critical paradigm for social dynamics and change? This question can only be answered positively if theological doctrine is more grounded and oriented towards humanity. In doing so, religion does not lose its liberating and humanitarian dimension.

Islam and the Politics of Citizenship

One focus of the post-traditionalist community is the theme of Islam and the politics of citizenship. In this context, civil society is made a prominent theme as the way to obtain rights as citizens of the state. P3M's *halaqah* on *"Fiqh al-Siyâsah li Mashâlih al-Ra'iyyah"* or "Islamic Politics for Strengthening the Political Rights of the People" is one attempt to cultivate awareness of people's rights as citizens. From 1996 to 2000, P3M implemented a training series in *fiqh siyâsah* (fiqh on governance), with several variations in the material used and the names of activities. The activities it encompassed included:

1. **Socialization *Halaqah*:** This was aimed at introducing the fundamental thoughts and objectives of *fiqh siyâsah* to *pesantren* leaders, particularly the elders. There were fifty to sixty participants who took specific themes in accordance with the issues relevant to the areas in which the activity was held. Ideas were gathered for the compilation of a training curriculum.

2. **Training in *Fiqh Siyâsah*:** This activity was aimed at discussing several key issues in Islam, democracy and human rights, and reflecting on daily life. It involved a number of experts and activists familiar with the material. The training lasted a week, and was implemented twelve times in Java, West Nusa Tenggara, Lampung, East Kalimantan, and South Sulawesi. Each intake included between thirty-five and forty participants.

3. **Follow-up *Halaqah*:** This activity was held to resolve a number of problems present in society, after the alumni from the training had implemented activities related to democratization, including social advocacy and formation of discussion groups (*bahts al-masâil*). Education on *fiqh siyâsah* was intended to facilitate the alumni in follow-up discussions on topics relevant to the needs of the areas in which the alumni resided.

4. **Research:** In order to develop ideas from and evaluate the activities held, research was undertaken to discuss the ideas developing amongst *kiai/nyai* (male/female religious teachers), both those involved in the *fiqih siyâsah* education and those who were not involved. This activity sought to map the issues and ideas developing in *pesantren* related to democracy and enforcement of human rights. The research adopted the theme: "*Pesantren* and Democracy: The Views of *Kiai/Nyai* on Pluralism, Tolerance, the State, Political Parties and General Elections."

5. **Publication and Seminars:** Publication of the *Halqah* magazine, once every two months as a vehicle for discussion and exchange of information amongst alumni, *kiai/nyai*, *santri*, and society in general.[72] Seminars were conducted to discuss current events related to Islam and democracy in Indonesia.

Besides P3M, LKiS also ran a programme that was much the same, under the name "Training in Islam and Enforcement of *al-Dlarûriyyât al-Khams* (The Five Necessities)". The activity was held in 2001 in several regions, including Aceh, Makassar, and Java, and was a political training model, not just for the NU community but for society in general. The introduction to the programme noted that it was inspired by the reality where:

> *Civil society* is a discourse developing in Indonesia. This concept of civil society or empowered society can be understood as a society (citizens) which is able to formulate its rights and obligations independently and

> responsibly. It is understood as possessing the ability to maintain and struggle for public interests and express them in concrete steps. In order to realise this condition, there needs to be a tolerant, critical and open culture. In the context of Indonesia, civil society as described above is not yet something concrete. The state still dominates all aspects of social life. This is because, amongst other things, society's perspective of religion tends to be rigid. Islam teaches its adherents to understand their rights and responsibilities proportionately. In several Qur'ânic verses and the Hadith, Islam teaches about liberation of humankind, justice and struggling for the right to (state) power so that social mechanisms run as they should. However religious values and teachings that are loaded with humanitarian messages and which should be used as a basis to develop a civil society are reduced into purely ritual symbols. This attitude is apparent in the sacralisation of the profane, in an attempt to excessively purify religious symbols. As a result religion legitimises undemocratic attitudes. Religious symbols and interpretation are controlled by the state and religious elite and are used to protect their interests.[73]

This quote indicates that something is wrong with developing religious expression, which is caused by religious bureaucratization. On the one hand, religious bureaucratization directs people towards following one religious understanding controlled by the elite; but on the other, it makes religion increasingly insensitive to socio-political problems in society. As a result, the spirit of religion is increasingly foreign to the very soul of life, and understandings of religion are thus distorted and values are reduced. This leads to symbolic religious thought and behaviour, and as such, the assumption emerges that realizing a civil society is not a religious struggle. The report continues:

> In light of the values contained in religious teachings and the sociological condition of Indonesian society which is highly religious, religion (Islam) in Indonesia has great potential to become the foundation on which to develop civil society. This is possible through a reinterpretation of religious teachings which have been reduced by the state and the interests of the religious elite. On this basis, activities are required to cultivate religious awareness that cares about the effort to develop civil society. The effort to develop civil society can be begun, for instance, by promoting studies of the position of the people in the context of state discrimination, examining the values and views of the state/society towards public interests, expanding the space for community participation in and control of the government, spreading alternative visions and actions for the state (cultural politics), and critically studying the normative aspects of religious teachings.[74]

In this view, civil society is a key word in the struggle for democracy in any country.[75] One pillar in the struggle to empower civil society is to increase social control of all forms of state management and public policy as a form of political participation. Through political participation, the issue of citizenship and democratic mechanisms can run openly. Although hated, the existence of state institutions with all their characteristics cannot be rejected. As a result, the agenda is not one of how to ignore state institutions, but how to control the state by creating a system that is just and open. Creation of a just and open state system cannot be left just to the state, but requires maximum participation of the people. It requires that the state be commandeered so that it actually serves society. Here it is significant that society becomes involved in making public policy.[76]

The NU youth have firmly chosen civil society, which is translated as empowered society/community, as a movement that should be actualized in Indonesia. If not translated, they prefer to simply use the term civil society. They do not like the term "civilized society" (*masyarakat madani*) that was introduced by the modernists, particularly Nurcholish Madjid. This rejection is not purely a result of the new rivalry between the traditionalists and modernists, but also because the two terms presuppose different historical references and concepts.

Their rejection lies in the understanding that civilized society places religion as the centre of social change, while civil society seeks to place religion on the same level as other social institutions. The choice of civil society is deemed fitting because it is felt to be the most adaptive to the cultural and religious pluralism of Indonesia. Ahmad Baso put forward the most provocative view on this issue in his work *Civil Society versus Masyarakat Madani, Arkeologi Pemikiran "Civil Society" dalam Islam Indonesia/ Civil Society versus Civilised Society, The Archaeology of "Civil Society" Thought in Indonesian Islam* (Bandung: Pustaka Hidayah, 1999). Broadly speaking, Ahmad Baso concluded that the political issues proposed by Indonesian Muslim scholars concerning the discourse of Islam and civil society were not concrete. As a result, contemporary political problems — such as political legitimacy, centrality of power, and balance of power between society and the state — seemed to be overlooked in the concept of civilized society as civil society. The invention of the concept of civilized society, a political concept, has become a religious concept.[77]

As a political concept, civil society is a non-state actor with an interest in forming a historic bloc through which to face state hegemony, and it generally displays the following characteristics. First, civil society is a form of societal self-organization that allows every individual to actualize his or her political aspirations without intervention from outside parties. Secondly, it is free from excessive control of individuals and restriction of moral autonomy. In other words, civil society does not tolerate authoritarianism, anarchism, tyranny, and other forms of violence. Thirdly, it always permits and accepts plurality. Fourthly, as a result of its emphasis on individual independence, individual membership to social groups is voluntary. That means that individuals cannot be forced to do anything if it is not in line with their aspirations. Fifthly, civil society is not identical to civil administration.

Civil society is a concept in response to the political reality where the state becomes a scary monster, so powerful that it can dominate all aspects of human life. Although it originates from the context of Western society during the shift to capitalism and the implementation of bourgeois democracy, the theory developed as a counter to state domination and hegemony. The concept of civil society is a formulation from Western political society, which moved from being a natural society to a political society. A natural society is one that is not familiar with systems or law and as such, represents a society of anarchy (marked for instance by the presence of slavery and abuse). Meanwhile, a political society is a society in which politics is the authority, and there is the rule of law.

Civil society is a society that knows, respects, and protects the human rights of its people, which are known as civil rights. Meanwhile, civilized society (*masyarakat madani*) is a new concept developed by Muslim scholars in Indonesia, and largely introduced by Nurcholish Madjid, as the equivalent of civil society. The term *madani* in this context was inspired by a number of matters. First, it was taken from the concept of al-Farabi (d. 339 H/950 CE) who wrote the book *al-Siyâsah al-Madâniyah* (Civil Politics). From here, civil society was translated in Arabic as *al-mujtama' al-madanî*, which was then "Indonesianized" to become *masyarakat madani*. Secondly, it refers to the Prophet Muhammad's (PBUH) life in Medina. This period is considered the most ideal era in Islamic history, because of the Prophet Muhammad's (PBUH) success in building and guiding a plural, democratic, peaceful, and mutually respectful society based on law, rights, and collective responsibility. Thirdly, *madani* is considered ideal in the sociological context of the Arab world, where the city (Medina) is considered more important than the peripheral or rural areas. As a result, the term *madinah* refers to urban society that understands the law, has a high quality of life, and a progressive way of thinking and insight.[78]

The concept of civilized society (*masyarakat madani*) contains a number of problems which differentiate it from the character of civil society. First, there seems to be a dichotomy between Mecca (symbolizing rural society) and Medina (symbolizing urban society). For a Muslim, this perspective is problematic because it means the Prophet Muhammad's (PBUH) life is restricted to his life in Medina. However, of the 114 chapters of the Qur'an, 91 were revealed in Mecca, and only 23 were revealed in Medina. Admittedly, the Mecca chapters are short in comparison to the Medina ones, and are more related to faith and moral teachings. However, one must remember that it was in Mecca that teachings on equality, mutual respect, and justice without one group feeling more important than others, began to emerge. This was different from the Medina period where Muslims felt superior to other religious groups.

As such, it is impossible to state that Mecca was void of an ideal social life. The principle of justice, which is highly relevant to modern life, was one of the teachings struggled for in Mecca. This argument intends to assert that the term *madani*, which was elaborated from the life of the Prophet Muhammad (PBUH) in Medina, tends to minimize the role of Mecca, and prioritize the centre over the periphery (regions). This is of course rejected by the civil society concept, which views the centre and regions not in dichotomy but as variants that form a united synergy that is able to counter the hegemony of the state.

Secondly, while in Medina, the Prophet Muhammad (PBUH) began to introduce a way of life that led to the creation of a class structure in society. This was very evident in the initial era after the death of Prophet Muhammad (PBUH) with the emergence of the famous adage *al-'aimmah min quraisy* (the leader was from the Quraysh tribe). The public at the time said that the Quraysh was a very prestigious tribe, a first-class tribe, and as such, had privileges that other tribes did not have, namely the right to lead. This has, throughout history, been the cause of many problems, as occurred at the Tsaqifah Bani Saidah,[79] where one group felt it was superior and able to dominate over others. This is of course not an ideal condition in which to develop civil society, because of the inequality between elements and groups fighting in a social and political contest.[80]

Using this perspective, the NU youth have questioned Nurcholish Madjid's use and praise of the Medina period as a reference for civilized society. Nurcholish Madjid stated, for instance:

> As a participative egalitarian society, the classical Islamic period resembles a society which is just, open and democratic as in modern socio-political concepts. This egalitarian and participative characteristic was apparent in the Prophet's own examples, likewise with the examples of the wise Caliphs *(al-khulafâ' al-rasyidun)*.[81]

In addition to differences in the substance of the terms and their interpretation, there is also a significant difference in the positions each concept takes in dealing with the state's authority. In the NU and activist communities, civil society is a power outside of the state which functions to control the political system of governance. In this context, NU remained outside of the state structure, as a peripheral community, during the New Order regime.[82] As a result, it is very understandable that NU civil society takes a position opposite to, rather than working with, the state. In addition, the majority of the NU community live in villages in rural areas with all the characteristics and limitations this entails. It is also understandable that NU activists adopt this rural spirit to give a unique meaning to civil society in light of their competition with other groups. With this rural spirit, and in order to strengthen civil society, NU activists adopted the issue of empowerment and strengthening of grass-roots society to give it a bargaining position vis-à-vis the government.

From this perspective, it makes sense that the modernists have preferred to position themselves as a supplement to and component of government programmes rather than in opposition to the state, because their interests were better accommodated by the New Order government. Nurcholish Madjid's political modernization slogan, "Islam: yes!, Islamic party: no!", can easily be used as justification of the New Order's political restructuring, which not only restricted the number of political parties, but also required all to adopt Pancasila (the five principles) as their one and only foundation. As a result, the New Order's political accommodation of Islam[83] was actually an accommodation of the political interests of the modernists, because it excluded NU. That is, NU's political interests were never accommodated by the New Order government.

It is clear from this illustration that Islamic post-traditionalist political praxis is the strengthening and empowerment of civil society.[84] That is, post-traditionalists are more interested in people's movements, liberation, or other ideas that contain a transformative and revolutionary ethos.[85] As a result, the post-traditionalists pay serious attention to social and political ethics that accord with humanitarian values, the role of society in implementation of power, participation of minorities in politics, control mechanisms and monitoring of the state, accountability of power holders to the public, balance and division of power, and other issues.

Theoretically, Islamic post-traditionalism would like political issues to be key religious issues (*ashl min ushûl al-dîn*) and not just branches of fiqh (*far' min furû' al-fiqh*), as many *ahl al-sunnah wa al-jamâ'ah* followers hold to. However, this does not mean that Islamic post-traditionalism wants Islam to be a political ideology, as do the Kharijites and Shi'ites. On the contrary, what post-traditionalism means by seeing politics as *ashl min ushûl al-dîn* is to see religion as a way to control political life in civil society. This kind of Islamic post-traditionalist political reasoning is obtained from philosophy, more precisely, Averroism.[86]

However, Islamic post-traditionalism is unique in its attitude towards the system of government. Islamic post-traditionalism does not agree with the two contemporary currents of thought concerning the relationship between religion and state, the first stating that Islam provides a clear system of governance, and the second that Islam only regulates social systems. Rather, post-traditionalists argue that the issue does not lie in these two stances, but in whether we are able to produce a social and state system that actually represents the real aspirations of citizens concerning more evident social justice. As such, they reject liberal Islam's model of the privatization of religion. The liberal Islam community is not aware that it is not the state that controls the public realm, but market mechanisms that are unjust, exploitative, and oppressive. If liberal Islam cares about justice, it should not fight to cleanse the public realm of religious elements, but should fight unjust market mechanisms, because those individuals who wish to bring religion to the public realm do so because they feel their aspirations for justice are not accommodated in the public space that exists. Thus, the public realm is actually owned by market mechanisms. In other words, there is a suggestion that it is not religion that disrupts the public realm, but the market.

Here, the Prophet Muhammad's (PBUH) experiences both in Mecca and Medina show how religion is oriented towards, cares about, and is intensely involved in forming society and even states. As a result, the two main currents of thought concerning the relationship between religion and the state are equally devoid of real substance, because both discourses do not allow us to engage in dialogue with reality. Religion should be a real experience for individuals and society. In the language of contemporary social sciences, religion actually fights against alienation. The belief that religion must leave the public realm is erroneous, because religion is basically a mechanism to liberate humankind from alienation.[87]

Masdar F. Mas'udi also proposed this idea in slightly different language. He contended that making religion a purely private affair was an irresponsible form of religiosity, because the humanitarian problems that demand religious responsibility exist in the public realm. In the daily paper *Kompas*, he stated:

> What is the meaning of this continuously chaotic religious life? Its significance, I believe, in so far as religion continues to refuse being defined as a public affair, is that there is only potential for conflict, nothing more. Not only between different religions, but within the one religion too. Because private religion is in practice a symbolic religion, religion as a group identity, which is irrational and closed. This kind of religiosity only increases problems for humankind rather than helping solve them. This does not mean that private religiosity must be rejected. Religiosity is, first and foremost, personal and private submission to God. But the authenticity of this personal claim can only be proven through public actions of piety in collective life. Like a coin, religion has two inseparable sides; the private and the public, the vertical and the horizontal. If the private side is submission to God *(habl min Allâh)* in symbolism of personal piety, then the public side *(habl min al-nâs)*, in the language of the Qur'ân, is the commitment to love and liberate one another, especially the weak and hungry *(al-Ma'ûn*: 1, 2, 3).[88]

The following part reads:

> The current issue is, how should the liberating message of the public realm of religion be spread? Of course, it cannot purely be preached in mosques, or in churches. It cannot just be translated into either individual or group charitable actions. In fact the latter, although significant, can if we are not careful lead to collective self-interest and eventually raise the suspicion of other groups. The public religious message of liberation must be enforced, and can only be enforced elegantly and effectively through advocacy of policy in legislation, or other state regulations.... The intense struggle *(jihad)* of religious and spiritual experts from amongst the *ulama*, priests, pastors, monks and so on, to advocate for public policy that sides with the people, especially the weak at all levels, is the most sacred, in fact more sacred in comparison to the role of the private religiosity they currently practice. I do not care if when the state develops this mandate of

public religion to liberate the weak it violates the principle of separation between religion and the state (secularism). For me, absolute secularism is necessary to free the state from the shackles of private religion which is closed, dogmatic and narrow. However, it is scandalous to suggest that secularism is intended to liberate the state from the transcendental moral message, the public religious message of liberating the weak, because this kind of state is none other than a tool for the strong to blackmail and defile the weak.[89]

This stance clearly rejects the two simplistic political stances: one that desires the privatization of religion, and the other that seeks the opposite. Choices in social life cannot be black and white, or a simple matter of choosing one thing and rejecting the other. In the context of civic life, the state should not be given the opportunity to control or force a belief on its people. However, it is not so easy to simply strip the arena of public life of the spirit and morals of religion. The struggle to enforce religious morals and ethics must not be trapped by symbolism, but must be concerned with how the spirit of justice, advocacy for the oppressed, and equality, which is indeed the spirit of religion, can become inspiration for the management of socio-political life. The issue of the formalization of Islamic *syari'ah* must also be placed in this context. That is, the debate is not about whether Islamic law needs to be formalized or not, but about which legal system can guarantee justice, egalitarianism, and equality. These values can come from a number of sources, including Islamic *syari'ah*, other traditions, and culture itself.

Generally speaking, the post-traditionalist community rejects the formalization of Islamic *syari'ah*. Lakpesdam NU addressed this theme in *Taswirul Afkar* No. 12, 2002, which sported a very striking cover proclaiming "*Deformalisasi Syariat*/Deformalisation of Islamic Law". Although the issue also featured an article by Adian Husaini, the secretary general of KISDI, who is known to be pro-formalization of Islamic law, the general spirit of the issue was a rejection of the movement to formalize Islamic law in the nation-state.[90]

The debate over Islamic *syari'ah* is always accompanied by debate over space and the role played by the public realm and the private realm in the relationship between religion and the state. Both realms are assumed to be in a situation of constant tension and seek to deny one another. Here, religion is seen as a private affair and the state as a public affair. The state, which exists in the public realm, may not intervene in the private lives of society, including forcing society to observe or not observe religion. Despite its simplicity, this reality is indeed true, although it still requires explanation and elaboration so as not to fall into the trap of simplicity. Given this context, the first question that emerges is what is actually meant by the private and public realms.

The public realm is the space where all people, regardless of religion, ethnicity, race, or group can be in open and free contest. The key word in the public realm is equality — equality of the relationships between the parties involved in contest. As such, in political contest, the public realm can be understood as the realm for citizens, for individuals who are seen not as members of a particular race, religion, or ethnicity, but as members of a political party or society. The public realm is not an institution or organization, but — as Habermas argued — is more like a rather complex network through which to communicate ideas, opinions, and aspirations. Every community in which public norms are discussed will result in a public realm. As a result, in a democratic state there is a large public realm. In this context, the meaning of public space can be vague: it can be full of competition, even anarchic, although this does not mean it is without rules. The public selects the themes and rational reasons itself.

Meanwhile, the private realm is the space where an individual can live within him or herself without interference from other parties. This is the independent realm where individuals can freely make choices (or choose not to choose) about anything and everything. It allows individuals to develop and perfect themselves away from interference by outside institutions. As a result of the separation between religion and state, religion is situated in the private realm. Privacy here is interpreted as religious and moral values. Concepts such as the meaning of life, religious conviction, world view, and perfection of life are areas that must be returned to individuals or groups in society. This gives birth to the awareness of individual rights and private ownership rights, which in turn leads to a free market economy, where the state is forbidden to intervene in the free enterprise of its citizens. As it developed, the concept of the private realm also referred to the intimate sphere which incorporated the realm of the household, satisfaction of daily needs, reproduction, and sexuality.

The state, as a political institution in the public realm, should be the guardian of the independence of each of these realms. In this context, the state functions to publicize the public and privatize the private.

Dictatorships emerge because of the expansion of the private realm into the public realm, where the latter is eventually eliminated. This is the privatization of the state where the state, which should belong to all people, becomes the possession of a group of people who use its power to do as they please.

The need to separate the two realms, the public and private, is related to the need to secularize political life so as to avoid an overlap between the function of religion and the state, which leads to the "religiousization" of politics and the politicization of religion. This is by no means absurd. In pre-modern societies where religion was a complete institution that had not been differentiated, all aspects of political, economic, and cultural life were addressed by religion. As a result, society could not differentiate between the profane and the sacred. Individuals had no rights, the physical was interpreted as divine, and so on.

Although theoretically speaking, the separation between the private and public realms is clear-cut, in reality it is difficult to find something that is purely private or purely public. The question then is, can this binary opposition way of thinking resolve issues? In reality, something that is private contains within it public elements, and vice versa. The desire to observe or not observe a religion, which is actually a private right of any religious adherent, in reality often becomes the affair of other people or groups outside of the involved individual. In addition, religion not only calls for individual piety, but also discusses social issues that go beyond the boundaries of the individual. It not only talks about the internalization of religious values, but also about externalization or expression as a form of religious observance. On this level of externalization, religion is often asked to play a role in building a more democratic and civilized society. How can religion play a role in building society if it is only allowed to be a purely private affair?

José Casanova identified several reasons why religion continually appears in the public realm. First, religious doctrine pushes people to express their convictions in public; it is not only personal but also social. Secondly, the revitalization and reformation of old traditions that are still alive allow religion to exist in the public realm. Thirdly, global factors also push religion into the public realm. On this basis, Casanova proposes the concept of religious deprivatization.[91]

He argues that religious deprivatization takes at least three forms. First, it takes the form of a religious mobilization to maintain traditions from the onslaught of the state and market. An example is the mobilization by the Protestant and Catholic fundamentalists in opposition to the practice of abortion. With this mobilization, religion motivated the public to debate the moral and ethical values of society, although in the end these morals and values were not those of a particular religion, but those of society in general. Secondly, religion enters the public realm to question the system of state and society so that it functions according to intrinsic norms. Thirdly, it exists in the compulsion to maintain traditional values that are deemed good by the majority of society and by opposing those things that could reduce these values.[92]

One thing that needs to be underlined in José Casanova's concept of deprivatization is that the concept only exists on the level of morality and the common good, and not in the context of highlighting a particular religious teaching, or in fighting for religious symbols in the state structure and legislation. The concept of religious deprivatization, I believe, cannot be used as an argument to endorse religion roaming freely in the public space. In the public space, religion only talks about collective morality, as the guardian of morality and ethics, and nothing more. Of course morality here means morality that has been objectified, where all people, regardless of their religion, can objectively judge something as good or bad. As such, in the public realm, the claim of religious universality is no longer absolute, but relative, because each religion can make different claims.

ISLAM AND FEMINISM

Religion is often used as a reason to subordinate women in a number of aspects in life. This is evident, for instance, in the concept of the hijab, where the ideal place for women is in the house. In the concept of *imâmah*, women are not allowed to be involved in politics. In regard to inheritance, females receive half of what a male receives. Females are also not allowed to lead prayers (as imam) attended by male congregants. These are just a few examples of how religious doctrine has played a role in subordinating women. Of course, there are still many other attributes that religious exegesis assigns to females, from issues of sexuality to political roles.

Islamic post-traditionalism considers this kind of religious doctrine and interpretation a detriment and discredit to women. Further, religious exegesis that does not side with women is contrary to the fundamental spirit of Islam, which acknowledges equality between men and women.

In this sense, Islamic post-traditionalism, as with feminist movements in Islam in general, suggests the need to critically re-read religious doctrine, thought, and texts.[93] This must be undertaken with respect based on a humanitarian spirit.

Why is interpretation of the Qur'an considered to have a role in forming opinions that discredit women? This is for no other reason than that the majority of interpreters apply a textual interpretation to Qur'anic verses which is often biased in favour of the interests of men and disregards social conditions. So long as these verses are interpreted textually, the narrowing (to say nothing of discrimination) of the roles and subordination of women is not a form of theological (religious) discrimination, but a construction by religious leaders about reality related to the texts.

Textual exegesis increasingly reveals its bias when faced with other verses which suggest equality between men and women. As a result, interpretation of the Qur'an must move from being textual to contextual, without leaving the text. Times continue to change and develop dynamically, and it is necessary that Qur'anic exegesis also be dynamic. On this matter, almost all ulama agree that the Qur'an is too open to interpretation.

Within the NU community, the discourse on women has flourished. Autonomous NU bodies, especially Fatayat and Muslimat, have placed women's issues at the core of their programmes. Several NGOs within the NU environment, or those managed by NU youth, are also concerned with women's issues, although their cadres differ. P3M, for instance, during the 1990s had a programme on fiqh on women (*fiqh al-nisâ'*), which was continued by Rahima, a splinter NGO from P3M from the *fiqh al-nisâ'* dimension, although Rahima is not entirely an NU youth movement.

The Fahmina Institute in Cirebon, which was established in the 2000s as a forum for the cultural expression of the NU youth and *pesantren* alumni, also seriously addresses the issue of Islam and gender. It does so through a variety of methods and strategies. Besides publishing books, bulletins, training modules, a website, and cassette recordings, Fahmina also addresses the issue by strengthening knowledge in *pesantren*, amongst activists, and in the government. LKiS also discusses gender issues in its Study Together programme. Similarly, Desantara has a critique of gender discourse as one of its points of discussion in its Emancipatory Madrasah programme. Separately from this, several NU youth such as KH Husein Muhammad, Siti Musdah Mulia, Syafiq Hasyim, Faqihuddin Abd. Kodir, Marzuki Wahid, Badriyah Fayumi, Abd. Moqsith Ghazali, Maria Ulfah

Anshor, and Ala'i Najib have also paid specific attention to women's issues, in addition to other activists from a variety of different regions.

Robin L. Bush asks why the gender discourse flourished in the NU community. She argues that it was because women were still seen as a symbol of identity who carried with them the purity of religion; she also states that it was for nationalist reasons, in addition to the manifestation of the attempt to confront modernity while continuing to hold to traditional principles.[94] In light of this argument, it is not surprising that the feminist discourse became a source of contestation between the NU community and the Islamic community in general.

Nevertheless, the gender discourse within NU was not singular. Generally speaking, the gender issues that developed revolved around how to lift women out of oppression, how to seize the public space controlled by men (or at least offset male domination), and how to oppose discrimination in all dimensions of life. They were not only social issues, but also issues related to religion such as polygamy, inheritance, providing testimony, and being the imam leading prayers. The main priority amongst Islamic feminists, including the NU activists in the women's movement, was how to reinterpret religious doctrine and practices that were detrimental to women.

Outside of this current, a new, but still soft-spoken current has emerged — that of post-colonial feminism. The fundamental assumption of post-colonial feminism is that, to date, feminists have existed within a colonial framework. The public realm that feminists are trying to control is the colonial world. In the context of Islamic post-traditionalism in NU, Desantara activists are campaigning for this idea, which has seeped into the female activist community as they struggle for a larger public space for women so that they are not confined to the domestic realm. Through the journal *Srinthil*, Desantara addresses local feminist issues that do not gain the attention of the women's movement in general.

This is achieved by making post-colonialism a spirit to oppose the hegemony of those groups who exploit women. Quoting the post-colonial intellectual Franz Fanon, Ahmad Baso states that it is time for women of the Third World to free themselves from the grip of the public realm by resisting colonialism from within the private realm, the domestic realm. This is necessary because the public realm is already controlled by the powers of colonialism and the only medium through which women can resist is in the private realm.[95]

Of course, the post-colonial feminist appeal has contrasting implications with the conventional Islamic feminist movement. Issues that were once criticized because they were considered symbolic of the oppression of women — such as the *jilbab*, *burqa*, polygamy, and domestic affairs — are redefined as an arena of contestation in which women demonstrate their ability to strategize against and resist the hegemony of colonial power.

Post-colonial feminists with their multicultural agenda question the women's or feminist movement in Indonesia, which is always in tension between tradition and modernity, between a universal female identity and local resistance. The question they ask is: to what extent have feminist activists formulated their movement to attain an ideal direction, including formulations about female identity, and in what direction do they intend to move? From here, post-colonial feminism takes local voices as criticism of the current feminist agenda, which is largely dominated by the urban middle class and focuses on issues such as quotas in political parties, parliament, bureaucracy, and protection of women at the state level. In criticism of the Indonesian feminist agenda, the post-colonial feminists direct their attention to criticize the theoretical agenda of mainstream feminism which is oriented more towards Western feminism, and to offer a new and more relevant agenda with a local voice, that is, a multicultural agenda.[96]

In relation to this, post-traditional feminism is equated to the post-colonial feminist identity. The themes discussed are no longer concerned with the process of naturalization of the female subject, nor the victimization of women which would justify the empowerment project, but are concerned more with the identity of women as something different, as a contradiction, as a different experience which is both related and sensitive to the asymmetry between gender, class, race, and ethnicity. More specifically, it addresses the voice of subaltern women who exist outside of the "formal" feminist construct.[97] With this focus, post-traditional feminism takes up these subaltern voices which have to date symbolized the backwardness of the female bourgeoisie.

RELIGIOUS DIALOGUE FOR JUSTICE

Every human has the same fundamental rights that all people must respect. Islam is believed to be a religion that guarantees respect of these basic rights. The Qur'an itself never advocates discrimination against non-Muslims. On the contrary, Islam always demands its people to get to know, to respect, and to cooperate with others. As a result, a Muslim is not allowed to violate the absolute basic rights of other humans, including non-Muslims. Every religious individual believes that religion is the path to salvation and eschatological happiness. Religion not only integrates society, but also plays a sociological role in triggering disintegration and social conflict. Both directly and indirectly, religion has played a role in igniting various conflicts in Indonesia.

This occurs because of suspicion and misunderstanding between two different religious groups. The relationship between the majority and the minorities is still coloured by mutual distrust. There are several issues that feature here. First, each religious group is negatively prejudiced (suspicious) and applies particular labels (stereotypes) out of jealousy. Secondly, minority groups feel that they are marginalized in the state bureaucracy and the private sector, although according to the majority they already have greater representation than they should in comparison to their numbers. Thirdly, there is discrimination in social life, especially concerning civil rights, based on religion. As a result, social groups that do not formally follow a religion recognized by the government do not have access to services such as the marriage registry, national identity cards (KTP), and birth certificates. Fourthly, public law policies are biased in favour of the Muslim majority. This is not only for state policy, but also for collective policy at the lower levels of housing, establishment of houses of worship and so on.[98]

The inequality in the relationship between Muslims and non-Muslims is caused by a number of issues. First of all, it is caused by intolerant religious understandings. This is a result of the theological doctrine that was planted in society, which is one that promotes closed exclusivity. This kind of theology is more likely to promote claims of truth and finds it difficult to accept truth outside of itself. The second issue is the lack of an open interreligious relationship. Although interreligious dialogue is often undertaken, the network is still rather limited, if not to say elitist. The third issue concerns discriminative political policy and legal products. The fourth issue is the presence of groups that benefit from tension between religious adherents. The first two factors are more a result of religious discursive practice, while the latter two are a result of the interference of power and the interests of those involved.

In order to overcome this, the post-traditionalist community feels that several agendas are important. First, religious teachings must be reinterpreted in order to produce a more tolerant and open theological teaching. This is important because theological understanding has a significant influence on determining the religious characteristics of an individual. Secondly, dialogue forums between Muslims and non-Muslims need to be established in order to promote honesty. This is crucial as religious dialogue is often held purely as a formality, without honesty and willingness on behalf of each side to mutually give and take. Thirdly, it is important to have real and intense cooperation between Muslims and non-Muslims in public services. Fourthly, the political system and legal products that are discriminative must be made tolerant and open.[99]

On the level of religious discursive practice, the Prophet Muhammad's (PBUH) experience as a Muslim in the midst of several other (religious) teachings that existed before Islam needs to be re-read. At the very least, there are five principles that can be taken from Prophet Muhammad's (PBUH) experience in managing religious life which are reflected in the verses of the Qur'an. First, there was the principle of plurality: several religious variants were given the freedom to exist, and in fact, Prophet Muhammad (PBUH) identified the adherents of some of these religious variants as having the same beliefs as he did. The second principle was inclusivity, that is, the recognition of truth outside the religious group one adheres to, and being critical of others in terms of theology, economics, and politics. The Prophet Muhammad (PBUH) was critical of others in order to establish a certain dynamic within society so that the oppressed would have hope.

The third principle concerned local identity, which became an icon for one aspect of community identification. Without this local identity, the Arab nation would not have discovered its self-worth. The fourth principle was vision, which involved developing society with a new morality and spirit. The fifth principle was hegemony, in the sense that one people (society) must have self-worth or self-esteem. A people without abundant self-esteem cannot grow into a strong nation.[100]

These five principles that can be gleaned from the Prophet's experience in managing interreligious relations suggest the existence of a relationship pattern that is free and flexible. Islam, which is now believed by its adherents to be a religion, was at the time not a defined entity. The general tendency for Muslims is to view Islam as a defined religion so that it is felt to be the most true and final religion, while all other religions are not true and must be fought against. This kind of understanding is dangerous and will lead to religious conflict that ends with the desire to mutually deny and destroy one another.

In Indonesia, religion has already been defined by the government in several policies, such as the Presidential Decree No. 1/1965 on prevention of the abuse or desecration of religion, the Instruction of the Minister of Religious Affairs No. 4/1978 on religious sects that are not religions, and the Decree of the Minister for Religious Affairs No. 70/1978 on a guide to religious propagation (monitoring missionaries). The Instruction of the Minister of Religious Affairs No. 4/1978 in particular meant that followers of religious sects or cults had to adhere to one of the official religions recognized by the state.

Several problems arose from this in the context of interreligious relations in Indonesia, which are depicted in Figure 4.2.

This figure shows the complexity of religious life in Indonesia. This is not purely related to the religious community itself, but also to state intervention. Indeed, this intervention is not entirely to blame, because it is the religious community itself that invites the state to act because of its inability to resolve issues. On one level, this intervention is dangerous because the state is indeed interventionist and, as a result, religion is subordinated and loses its independence. Religion, which should be the moral guide for those running the state, instead becomes controlled by the state. Furthermore, religion can be used by the state for its political interests.

An awareness and spirit to restore religion's independence needs to be cultivated in the midst of these problems plaguing religious life. In doing so, a strategic effort is needed to follow up on the matters above. First, reconciliation is needed, or a process to restore social harmony based on religious awareness and sincerity. Reconciliation must be undertaken in the context of changing the social order which has been torn apart as a result of social conflict. Secondly, advocacy of policy is needed. This is necessary to prevent the government from creating policies that damage social life, and to assist and empower society to confront government policies that have already been implemented at the expense of society. As such, elements within society, particularly religion and the government, will be in balance. A change in relations occurs between (1) the state and society, and (2) formal religions, local religions, and other minority groups. Thirdly, meaningful and independent social groups need to be formed. This is not only necessary to respond to local issues, but also as a means to respond to global issues.

FIGURE 4.2

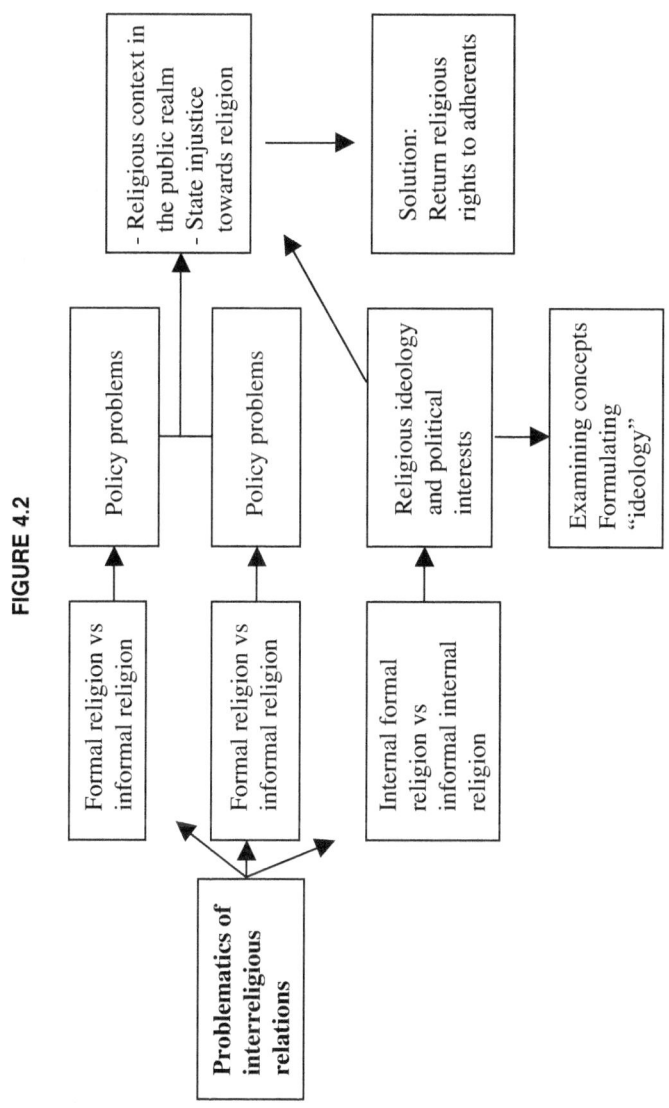

The need for dialogue is not merely to foster tolerance and peaceful coexistence, but is directed more at the aspiration to form a plural society, not only to point out the fact that plurality exists, but that there is active involvement in this plural reality. As such, pluralism is not the same as cosmopolitanism, which indicates the presence of people from diverse religions, races, and nations who live side by side in one region, but do not positively interact with one another.

It must be recognized that interreligious dialogue, which is now nearly three decades old, has been undertaken without reflection. Reflection in interreligious dialogue is very important to improve the substance of the dialogue itself. Reflection is needed to understand to what extent dialogue has been undertaken, what theoretical or practical frameworks are needed, what aspects should be included, and so on. Without reflection, dialogue is mere improvization. In short, reflection is self-criticism for the improvement of dialogue.

The lack of reflection has meant that many of those undertaking religious dialogue often become pessimistic or depressed. This is not merely because they feel that dialogue goes nowhere, like walking on the spot, but also because of the many paradoxes and ironies in interreligious relations. While religious dialogue continues to be pursued, religious violence and unrest continue to occur. All previous dialogue seems irrelevant.

Therefore, interreligious dialogue should not be isolated from the social, economic, and political problems of society. If it is, then interreligious dialogue only becomes an elitist commodity.[101] The objective of interreligious dialogue is to contribute ideas towards resolving humanitarian crises. Through dialogue, religion discusses its perspective on a just and prosperous future order for society.

ISLAM AND LOCAL CULTURE

Many within the NU community are deeply concerned with the existence of local culture in the religious context, as evidenced by Desantara's projects on Islam and local culture, *pribumisasi* (indigenization) of Islam, and lately, Lakpesdam NU's ideas on *"Islam Pribumi*/Indigenous Islam".[102] Abdurrahman Wahid proposed the idea of the indigenization of Islam at the beginning of the 1980s, which was then simplified by changing the greeting *assalamu'alaikum* to good morning (*selamat pagi*), good afternoon (*selamat siang*), or good evening (*selamat sore*).

In a discussion on *pribumi* Islam through the "emancipatory mailing list" managed by P3M, Ulil Abshar-Abdalla wrote:

> What is unique about this proposal [pribumi Islam] is not merely that it encourages pribumisasi of Islam, that is bringing Islam down from the "sky" of its claimed universality to the concrete "earth" where it gains a foothold, and must deal with a number of plural realities; but that it also recognises that Islam has already set foot on the plain of concrete reality in the lives of Muslims across the world. I believe that pribumi Islam, although it has been allowed to exist in social reality, has not had its theological and epistemological status recognised. Thus acquiescence must be distinguished from recognition. If we want to use a multicultural perspective there is a fundamental difference between acquiescence and recognition. NU does indeed allow elements in pribumi culture to exist, but perhaps the theological status of those elements, and the status of Islam that has combined with them, is not viewed on the same level as the Islam of the Arabic language classical texts that come from the Arab world and are heavily influenced by Arab culture.[103]

This statement implies there is a struggle between that which is regarded as Islam and that originates from a particular place and time, and societies that live in a different place or time. The post-traditionalist community has an interest in discussing this issue because NU has been accused by other groups of being too lenient in accepting local culture. In many cases, NU indigenizes Islam by compromising between Islamic teachings and local culture. However, it is largely a unilateral and one-way process, where Islam appropriates local cultural forms and then injects the spirit of Islam into them.

Would Islam à la NU tolerate *pribumi* culture appropriating Islamic ritual forms and filling them with the spirit and divine insight of the indigenous inhabitants (*pribumi*)? There is no clear answer to this, because within NU there is a group that is highly critical of local religious practices. Abdul Mun'im DZ, editor of the journal *Tashwirul Afkar*, stated in a discussion on *pribumi* Islam at Lakpesdam NU's headquarters that the key issue is the triumphant mentality or rather arrogant perspective of divine religions that see themselves as religions sent by God, and see the earth as the creation of human culture. Does Islam, through its claim of being *rahmatan li al-'âlamîn* (a blessing for all creation), have the right to go and conquer other beliefs as it pleases?

So, the concept of *pribumi* Islam has a significant meaning because it forces us to go further than just allowing *pribumi* elements to exist and to actually recognize those elements. Moving from acquiescence to recognition requires a theological leap that is by no means easy. Further, according to Ulil Abshar-Abdalla, there is a more important step than either acquiescence or recognition. Ulil states:

> However, there is a step that I believe is much more crucial and important, and it is here that the visibility of the concept of pribumi Islam is tested. Recognition is not yet sufficient, but important. More central is how these local elements have not died out with the descent of universal religions like Islam. However we must not also fall into the dangerous trap of believing that all things pribumi are necessarily glorious and noble. There are also elements that must be criticised in those things "pribumi". My hypothesis is that there is nothing that is not pribumi. Even the Islam of the Prophet's time was an Islam that was born into a pribumi context (Mecca and Medina). Islam is always embedded in the culture of the place where it sets foot. There is no Islam that is like cotton, floating in the air, with no known place, like spirits and ghosts.[104]

Ulil Abshar further states that universalization is always based on something particular. The process of universalization presupposes two things: first, the distillation and abstraction of universal abstract values in Islam; and secondly, re-contextualizing and concretizing those values into the contemporary context. Therefore, there are three processes: embedding, disembedding and re-embedding. These three processes can be illustrated as follows: Islam comes from the Arab world, embedded in Arab culture (embedment); this Islam is taken, its Arab elements removed, so that its essence remains (disembedment); then this essence is planted into our own world (re-embedment). Islamic universalization can be accepted if it follows this cycle. Islamic universalization is rejected if it jumps from the Arab world to Java, Sumatra, Madura, or Makassar, without undergoing the process where the Arab elements are removed.[105]

Khamami Zada, the coordinator for Lakpesdam NU studies, writes that *pribumi* Islam as a response to authentic Islam assumes three things. First, *pribumi* Islam is contextual, that is, it is an Islam that is understood as a teaching related to a particular time and place. Change over time and difference across regions is the key to interpreting teachings. As such, Islam undergoes change and dynamics in responding to changing times. Secondly, *pribumi* Islam is progressive, in that the progression of time is not seen as a potential deviation from the fundamental teachings of religion

(Islam), but is seen as a trigger for intense creative responses. Thirdly, *pribumi* Islam is liberating. In this understanding, Islam is a teaching that universally answers the problems of humanity, disregarding religious and ethnic differences. As such, Islam is not stiff and rigid in responding to the constantly changing social reality.[106]

Based on this illustration, the NU post-traditionalist community believes that in the name of purification and universalization of religion, locality has been used as a pretext for marginalizing, even eliminating, certain Islamic communities by labelling their religious beliefs as local Islam, traditional Islam, cultural Islam, syncretic Islam and *zindiq* (heretical), amongst other things. Even worse, this process of elimination does not allow that which is labelled local Islam the space to appear completely, but forces it to appear as a collection of stereotypes that is shallow and without context. This Islamic tradition is immediately boxed up, in order to protect the purity and universalism of Islam. In fact, as a result, it is often not called an Islamic tradition, but a local deviation.[107]

This kind of marginalization of local culture was non-existent in Islam during the time of the Prophet Muhammad (PBUH). At this time, Islam existed in dialogue with the local Arab culture, and as a result it did not stand alone. It was the historical background and social context of Arab society that made Islam develop at the time. Local engagement was significant for the Islamic movement and the ancestors of the Arabs, namely Abraham and Ismail, became the historical basis on which the Prophet Muhammad (PBUH) accepted Arab society and developed it. A number of religious practices, such as the *istisqâ'* prayer (asking for rain) and the practice of *tawâf* (circling the Kaaba), were Arab traditions from before the Prophet Muhammad's (PBUH) time. From here Islam grew out of locality. One could go to the extreme and say that Islam and locality must be married.

This defence of local Islam is clearly very different from pure Islamic ideology and liberal Islamic ideology. Pure Islam identifies itself with the experiences of the Prophet Muhammad (PBUH), and because of its purity it claims to be universal. Meanwhile, liberal Islam follows the ideas of pure Islam which emphasize Western liberalism. This is clearly evident in its findings that discuss matters from anti-theocracy to religious dialogue and freedom of thought, without ever entering the realm of or caring about the damage done to local Islamic constructions as a result of the purification era. In the end, liberal Islam only believes in universal values, although universal values are a product of Western civilization.

What must be emphasized is that when Arab locality was formed, competition emerged between different Arab social groups. The Prophet Muhammad (PBUH) managed to stand in the midst of this local competition and maintain harmony by offering a perspective beyond his time, where there was culture that had to be maintained and there was culture that had to be developed in order to deal with newer challenges. Jadul called this a dynamic equilibrium.[108]

In Mecca and Medina the Prophet Muhammad (PBUH) did not begin with a name (that the religion he brought was Islam), but by taking action that liberated humans from all forms of oppression. Everything he did was directed towards the liberation of Arab society at the time, by managing everything that existed and empowering it to build a new social order. He did not start something new that then oppressed what already existed.

Islam, insofar as it can be understood from the experience of Prophet Muhammad (PBUH), was an open movement that gave hope to all social groups — including religious, class, ethnic, and gender groups that existed within a particular socio-cultural region — to critically confirm their self-identification with their locality and manage differences that emerged as a consequence, and that directed these different groups to always look to more distant ambitions in order to fulfil the potential of their own human dignity.[109]

These ideas ultimately aim to avoid claims of authenticity so that religious (Islamic) patterns can be created according to a local context. Appreciation of locality is followed by recognition of diversity in the interpretation of religious (Islamic) practices in different regions. As such, Islam is no longer viewed as singular, but heterogeneous. There is no longer the view that the Islam of the Middle East is the pure and most true Islam, because Islam as a religion continues to exist throughout history.

Hairus Salim HS, an icon who helped guide the establishment of LKiS, stated firmly that it was time for post-traditionalism to celebrate locality because there is rationality in locality. Thus, the belief that Islam is a universal religion must be re-examined.[110]

RENEWAL OF FIQH AND *QAWÂ'ID AL-USHÛL*

As explained in the second chapter, fiqh (Islamic jurisprudence) is an important part of the *ahl al-sunnah wa al-jamâ'ah* discourse in NU. In fact, *pesantren*, as the heart of NU, cannot be separated from fiqh. NU's political decisions throughout history can also not be separated from fiqh arguments.¹¹¹ As such, it is not going too far to say that Islamic reason in the NU community is equivalent to fiqh reason. Meanwhile, *ushûl al-fiqh*, the principles of Islamic jurisprudence and the methodological foundation on which fiqh laws are based, has not received as much attention or developed as quickly as has fiqh itself within the NU community. The community would rather wrestle with finished legal products (fiqh) than with methodology (*ushûl al-fiqh*).

Nevertheless, this does not mean that *ushûl al-fiqh* is not studied in *pesantren*. A number of *pesantren* continue to pay attention to *ushûl al-fiqh*, although with different levels of intensity. More recently, the Salafiyah Syafi'iyah *pesantren* in Situbondo paid special attention to the development of fiqh and *ushûl al-fiqh* through the establishment of the Ma'had Aly University. Ma'had Aly was intentionally designed to create fiqh cadres who could not only master fiqh documents, but who also had a good control of *ushûl al-fiqh*.

In this regard, I pay particular attention to Ma'had Aly in Situbondo as the vehicle for renewal of fiqh[112] and *ushûl al-fiqh*. Abd. Moqsith Ghazali, an important exponent who helped drive the Islamic thought at Ma'had 'Aly in Situbondo (although he has not been a lecturer there since 2004), analysed the importance of renewing fiqh by considering the Indonesian social context. In his view, Islamic fiqh has been dominated by the following characteristics:[113]

a. Exclusive Fiqh

The exclusivity of Islamic fiqh is largely apparent when dealing with non-Muslims. Through fiqh, non-Muslims are always seen as a threat, and as such cannot be positioned equally with Muslims. In fact, *dzimmi* (protected) infidels, infidels who submitted to Islamic governance, were ordered to wear certain symbols to differentiate themselves from Muslims. They were forbidden from constructing houses with roofs that were higher than those of their Muslim neighbours; they were required to wear blue or yellow clothing, a thick belt over their clothes, and torn and perforated caps, all of which symbolized the inferiority of the *dzimmi* infidels in regard to Muslims.[114] This exclusive perspective led to exclusive fiqh products. Fiqh exclusivity then influenced and shaped fiqh structures. This is evident in bans on marriage across religions, bans against inheritance going to heirs of different religious orientation, the ban on religious conversion punished by death, and other regulations.

b. Racial Fiqh

Bias based on the race, ethnicity, or origin of Islamic jurists has greatly influenced the nature of fiqh. One example here is the difference between Imam Syafi'i and Imam Abu Hanifah. Imam Syafi'i was of Arab ethnicity and Quraysh descent, while Abu Hanifah was a Farsi. Imam Syafi'i believed that the al-Fatihah must be read in Arabic during prayer, while Imam Abu Hanifah allowed it to be read in Farsi for those who were unable to read Arabic. Similarly, there were differing opinions about whether or not Arabic had to be used in Friday gatherings. The Syafi'i supporters, such as Ibnu Hajar al-Haitami, said that using Arabic was obligatory, even with congregations that did not understand Arabic. Meanwhile, Hanafi followers believed the opposite, that the sermon could be read in other languages.[115] This was also apparent in discussions on *thayyib* (good) or *khabîst* (bad or dirty) animals, which influenced whether or not their meat was halal (allowed to be eaten). The Syafi'i's referred the standard of *thayyib* and *khabîst* to the Arabs, as discussed in the book *Taqrib* by Abu Syuja'.

c. Patriarchal Fiqh

One often criticized issue is the patriarchal nature of fiqh. This is a result, amongst other things, of the fact that the large majority of ulama who formulate fiqh are men and exist in male dominant cultures, and as such it is not surprising that the fiqh they produce has a male bias. In almost all aspects, males are positioned above women: the value and weight of one man is equal to that of two women; a husband is free to divorce a wife suspected of adultery (*li'ân*) but a wife has no such right; women are forbidden to lead prayers if there are males in the congregation, and so on.

d. Agrarian–Traditional Fiqh

Conventional fiqh is that which is formulated in the context of agrarian society. This is very noticeable, especially when conventional fiqh discusses the objects on which *zakat* (alms) must be paid, which are largely agrarian products, particularly those in the Arab world. Although fiqh discusses *zakat* on products of mining, wealth, and so on, it does not dominate the discussion. Similarly, in the section on *mu'amalah* (financial transactions), especially in the discussion of business (trade), the jurists' imagination is of simple and traditional agricultural produce. A transaction, for instance, is assumed to be a meeting between two individuals who are bound by a contract. As a result, conventional–traditional fiqh must revise a number of its concepts so that fast-paced social changes are not always addressed by the imaginations of ulama from the past.

e. Local–Arab Fiqh

It cannot be denied that Arab culture is dominant in the fiqh works of the past. In fact, the standard to determine whether something is halal (allowed) or haram (forbidden) uses the Arab standard. This is apparent for instance in determining whether animals are *thayyib* or *khabist*, as explained above.

This criticism is not all new. Much criticism has been directed at the characteristics of fiqh, although with varying emphases. I also do not seek to deny the veracity of this criticism, although it attacks the entirety of fiqh. In specific instances, there are elements of fiqh that do not have the features described above. As a result, this criticism must be interpreted as criticism of the general characteristics of fiqh.

A much more important matter is the criticism of conventional *ushûl al-fiqh* which in many instances is no longer in accordance with the development of new methodologies. Abd. Moqsith Ghazali raises several critical points. First, old *ushûl al-fiqh* methodology underestimates the ability of public reason to select the legal–formalistic provisions in Islam which are deemed no longer relevant. As a result, when there is conflict between public reality and the literal meaning of the texts, public reason must submit to legal–formalistic provisions. Secondly, classical methodology does not pay enough attention to the ability of humans to formulate the concept of welfare, although it is the welfare of humans themselves that is in question. Humans are in this sense mere objects and are thus referred to as *mukallaf* (people who are accountable). Thirdly, there is a tendency towards idolatry of texts and neglect of reality. Interpretation is always text driven, and as such, any exegesis that does not have textual support is deemed illegal. Texts are viewed as manifestations of truth itself, and there is no truth outside of the texts.[116]

Although he did not offer an entirely new *ushûl al-fiqh*, Abd. Moqsith Ghazali proposed a number of *qawâ'id al-ushûl* (rules for the principles) developed from old *qawâ'id al-ushûl*. The rules he proposed as an alternative to old principles are as follows:

1. *Al-'Ibrah bi al-maqâshid lâ bi al-alfâdh*

This principle means that what an interpreter holds to in undertaking *istinbâth* (inferring laws from texts) is not the characters and text of the Qur'an and Sunna, but the *maqâshid* (intrinsic meaning) contained within it. The moral aspirations and ethical values of the Qur'an must be prioritized over specific legal provisions. *Maqâshid* can be understood not merely through understanding the particular personal context but also the universal context (*kulli*). Understanding the context is not for the context itself, but to draw out the fundamental Islamic principles that are known as *maqâshid al-syarî'ah*. When these fundamental principles are found, then the text must be stripped of its initial context (decontextualized) to then be reconstructed in accordance with the conditions it currently faces.

This principle is the antithesis of the old principle *al-'ibrah bi 'umûm al-lafdh lâ bi khushûsh al-sabab*. This old principle was generally held by ulama in interpreting verses of the Qur'an, stating that the generality of the text was to be held to, and not the particularities. As a result, if a text is of a general nature, then there is no choice but to uphold that text as an example, although the text was revealed in response to a specific case. As such, there is a general belief that the closer an interpretation is to the literal meaning of a text, the closer it is to the truth. The further it is from the meaning of a text, the further it is from the truth.

2. *Jawâz naskh al-nushûsh bi al-mashlahah*

This principle means that serious benefit can outweigh the specific provisions of a text. This principle emerges from the assumption that Islamic law was revealed for no other reason than the welfare of universal humanity (*jalb al-mashâlih*). Therefore, in order to realize universal well-being, specific legal provisions of the texts can be "ignored".

Those who devised this principle were aware of the ontological questions of *ushûl al-fiqh* concerning who had the right and the authority to formulate well-being, and if there was conflict between the texts and well-being, which one would be victorious. Abd. Moqsith Ghazali touched on this matter, and even quoted Najm al-Dîn al-Thûfi (716 H), a follower of the Hanbali school of thought, who stated that it was impossible for there to be conflict between the texts and well-being, because the texts taught well-being itself.[117] While humans assume well-being to be superficial and relative, the well-being determined by God through the texts is intrinsic and objective. Humans do not have the authority to question and criticize the literal well-being in the texts.

This principle that Abd. Moqsith Ghazali proposed is based on a different paradigm from mainstream opinions that place the texts above reason. Mainstream opinions argue that that which a text views as good, must also be considered good by humankind. However, this principle assumes that it is possible for there to be a difference between the textual and human views of well-being. If this occurs, according to this principle, then human well-being can annul specific provisions of the texts. This is possible because well-being is the primary spirit of the texts, and thus may outweigh a number of specific provisions of the texts that are deemed irrelevant.

The holy texts without well-being, according to Moqsith, have no function for humankind, except for the text itself. Texts only have meaning if they also benefit humankind. Abd. Moqsith Ghazali reinforced his argument by quoting Ibn Rusyd, who stated that wisdom (well-being) was the sibling of the *syari'ah* established by God.[118] Similarly, Izz al-Dîn Ibn Abd al-Salâm stated: *innamâ al-takâlif kulluhâ râji'atun ilâ al-mashâlih al-'ibâd* (the entire objective of religion is human well-being).[119]

In addition to this, he also quoted Ibnu Muqaffa', as cited in Adonis, who divided the verses of the Qur'an into two categories: *ushûl* and *fushûl*. *Ushûl* referred to those verses that did not change, and which were fundamental and universal. There are not many of these kinds of verses, because they represent the moral spirit which is valid across all time and space. Meanwhile, the *fushûl* verses referred to particular verses that can change with the times, although behind *fushûl* provisions there is an unwritten *ushûl* spirit. Unfortunately, Ibnu Muqaffa' said, the majority of Muslims were trapped in the *fushûl* (particular) verses to the neglect of the *ushûl* (universal) verses.[120]

3. *Tanqîh al-nushûsh bi al-'aql al-mujtama' yajûzu*
This principle is actually similar to the previous one, insofar as it grants a larger role to humans to determine good from bad. This principle states that public reason has the authority to "amend" religious dogmatic provisions concerning public issues, both in the Qur'an and Sunna. If there is conflict between public reason and the literal meaning of the texts, then public reasoning has the authority to edit, perfect, and modify these provisions. Abd. Moqsith Ghazali presented several examples that are often discussed

publicly, such as the verses on *'uqûbât* (legal punishment) and *hudûd* (limits), *qishâsh* (equal retaliation, an eye for an eye), and inheritance. The provisions of these kinds of verses can be corrected through *tanqîh* procedures in the form of *taqyîd bi al-'aql* (restriction through reason), *takhshîsh bi al-'aql* (specialization through reason), and *tabyîn bi al-'aql* (clarification through reason). This is possible, Abd. Moqsith Ghazali argued, because these verses are of the *fushûl* category and it is thus possible to restrict, specialize or clarify them using reason. As such, this procedure means that *fushûl* verses are not annulled, but restricted, specialized, or clarified through reason.

This opinion is very different from the mainstream views of ulama, both from the classical and contemporary eras, who always subordinate reason to the power of the texts. The Mu'tazilites were the only theological group in Islam that elevated the role of reason, but continued to see the texts as the source of absolute truth. As a result, when reason meets the texts, reason only rationalizes what the texts say, especially the verses categorized as *qath'î* (eternal and unchanging). In this latter case, reason cannot go beyond or question the texts. It is only useful to interpret the *mutasyâbih* (ambiguous) verses.

These principles represent the furthest point in the development of thought of the NU youth. Indeed, not all NU people, especially the senior *kiai*, agree with these daring principles because of the frightening consequences they entail. These principles will be judged, not only for elevating the position of reason, but also for overturning Islamic teachings that are felt to be well established. As a result, they will be quickly accused of being an infiltration of liberal ideas into NU.

Nevertheless, I feel that the reach of the intellectual developments in the NU community, as reflected in these principles, indicates the presence of dynamic thoughts that reach deep into the heart of NU. The tradition of *ushûl al-fiqh* has not developed nearly as much as fiqh, but has been used as a traditional basis on which to liberate thought. As a result, although seeming rather liberal, the NU aspiration to use tradition as a basis for liberation is felt.

RESPONSE TO POST-TRADITIONALISM AND THE FUTURE OF NU INTELLECTUALISM

In the magazine *Panjimas* (No. 20, February 2003), a Paramadina researcher from Jakarta wrote an interesting article about the tendencies of the NU youth intellectual movement. He argued that their intellectual energy was spent on sharpening the traditionalist–modernist dichotomy that many people had walked away from. They did so by holding a number of scientific activities mixed with the contemporary Islamic thought of Nasr Hamid Abu Zayd, Hassan Hanafi, 'Abid al-Jabiri, Mohammad Arkoun, and so on, only to eliminate the modernist thoughts of figures such as Nurcholish Madjid and Dawam Rahardjo.[121] Continuing his criticism, the researcher argued that a new intellectual movement had emerged in the NU youth community, which published journals, books and so on, but these journals and books were always oriented towards purging the modernists. As a result, journals such as *Tashwirul Afkar* (Lakpesdam NU), *Gerbang* (eLSAD, Surabaya), and *Postra* (ISIS) could be called sectarian journals, because they have always been managed with a sectarian perspective and spirit.

This criticism, I believe, is important to address, not by arguing or apologizing, but by seeing it as a starting point to continually critique the intellectual agenda being developed. Will any good come out of the NU intellectual movement by asking whether what they have been doing is merely in opposition to the intellectual movement of other communities? It must be acknowledged that NU youth such as Ahmad Baso and Nur Kholik Ridwan enthusiastically criticize the thought of Nurcholish Madjid, who is considered the driving force behind Islamic modernism in Indonesia, in their work. However, it must be immediately noted that this tendency is not the only one developing. Outside of this, they also pay much attention to other Islamic thought. As a result, to say that the intellectual energy of the NU youth is exhausted on criticizing Nurcholish Madjid is not entirely true, although it cannot be completely denied.

Ulil Abshar-Abdalla also raised this issue in a seminar on "Islamic Post-Traditionalism and Liberal Islam". A key figure in the Liberal Islamic Network (JIL), Ulil Abshar-Abdalla argued that the emergence of the Islamic post-traditionalist community represented the failure of the NU youth to establish dialogue with the outside reality, as well as their disappointment and jealousy towards other communities. Post-traditionalism, in Ulil's view, is a more sophisticated method to preserve the conflict between PMII and HMI, between NU and Muhammadiyah, and between the modernists and the traditionalists. Thus, post-traditionalism is more of an effort to emphasize group identity than to develop a discourse of thought.[122] Robin L. Bush proposed a similar argument in her dissertation as discussed earlier

— namely, that post-traditionalism was no more than the preservation of the traditionalist–modernist conflict in "new clothing". This perspective is not entirely misguided, but it is unconsciously trapped in the dichotomy that always places the NU community second, so that when a new twist or turn emerges, it is always viewed as a form of rivalry and not a natural phenomenon due to the educational mobility of the NU youth.

In addition, this criticism contains the assumption and supposition that the intellectualism of the NU youth is singular and monolithic. This assumption is actually far from reality, because the intellectual thought of the younger generation in NU is actually quite varied and far from monolithic. It is not rare for members of this generation to sharply debate issues with one another, both through official forums such as *halaqah*, seminars, and discussions, and in unofficial forums. In fact, within the progressive current of NU youth, there are groups with their own particular social ties. There is often intellectual tension between these groups. Although it is difficult to map them into distinct entities, the phenomenon can be felt by anyone delving into the intellectual dynamics of the NU community. Tension is not only present in rivalry over thought; sometimes even personal relations become strained.

This atmosphere is not often grasped by observers of NU who are not intensely involved in its intellectual struggle. This is apparent from the observations of scholars who concluded that NU's *bahst al-masâil* or discussion forum seemed simple and only a way of finding *'ibârah-'ibârah* (announced or literary expressions) in the *al-kutub al-mu'tabarah* (standard books recognized and used in religious cases), as if there were no intellectual debate. This assumption becomes increasingly misleading when observers view documents from the NU *bahst al-masâil* that only detail the questions and answers to a particular religious or fiqh problem, referring to the *'ibarah* of the standard fiqh texts to support their arguments. At a quick glance, it seems as if there is no intellectual debate to the process. In fact, the *bahst al-masâil* forum is one of very academic debate. Reference to the fiqh texts is one tradition in the intellectual wealth that has been preserved by NU and passed down over the generations. However, reference to the *'ibârah* of the classical texts during every *bahst al-masâil* does not occur randomly, but through intense discussion; and, in fact, different opinions are often voiced because different *'ibârah* are cited as the foundation for arguments. This reveals the importance of being deeply involved in every change that occurs in the NU community.

Islamic Post-traditionalism and the Future of NU Intellectualism 253

As touched on in the previous section, the emergence of the new intellectual NU generation and the socialization of their ideas through a number of forums and NGO programmes have prompted varied responses from different social circles. I feel it is necessary to make a specific note concerning the *kiai* and *pesantren* community. It is important because the implications and the future of intellectualism depend on how this community responds to these dynamics. The role and response of the university campus community to these dynamics cannot be disregarded either. This differentiation (between the *kiai/pesantren* community and the campus community) is only a simple categorization, and is not intended to polarize one with the other. If simplified, the varying relations that illustrate the dynamics of NU intellectualism can be depicted as in Figure 4.3.

Explanation:
1. The NGO community that is culturally linked to NU includes NGOs, study groups, and other associations run by youth that are culturally associated with NU. They consciously use NU and all its culture as the social capital and spirit of their movements. As such, they feel they are a part of NU.
2. The *kiai/pesantren* community is a social group in NU which is given the label *kiai* because of its role and social status. In a *pesantren*, the *kiai* are the most essential elements. In this context, the title *kiai* is awarded in respect of an individual's depth of knowledge.[123] A number of *kiai* are formal NU leaders, while others are informal leaders.
3. The higher education community refers to the NU generation that primarily has its basis in the *pesantren* tradition, which enrolled in higher education institutes, and eventually made careers in these institutes. Some also became bureaucrats, especially in the Department of Religious Affairs.
4. Structural NU encompasses formal NU leaders who occupy positions in the NU structure, in the Advisory or Executive branches, autonomous bodies, or committees.

Figure 4.3 illustrates the circular interaction in the dynamic process of renewal of Islamic thought. The separation of these four communities is perhaps not realistic, and therefore they cannot be understood as black and white categories. The large majority of those in the NU NGO community come from the *pesantren* tradition or are alumni of higher

FIGURE 4.3

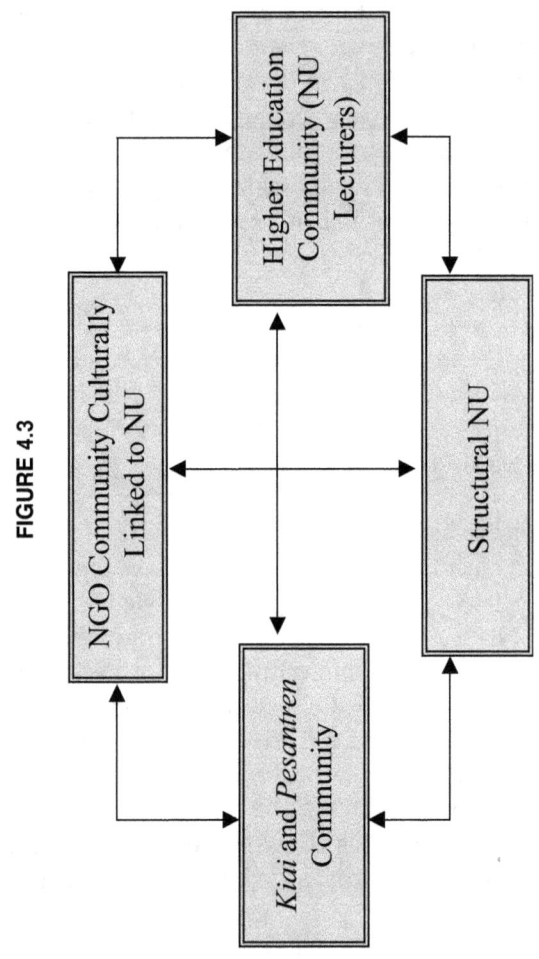

education institutes. However, their formation and intellectual struggle occurred within the NGO environment. As a result, the *pesantren* and higher education institutes have contributed greatly to the growth of NU intellectualism in the NGO environment. Similarly, overlap is apparent in a number of NU activists who hold positions in the NU structure or its autonomous bodies. It is sometimes difficult to differentiate between the NGO community and NU autonomous bodies. Therefore, once again, this categorization must be viewed as a tool to simplify reality, not as a depiction of reality itself.

In the context of this research, the NGO community is positioned as the centre of liberation of NU intellectualism. Doing so is not an exaggeration because the community is the driving force behind the intellectual dynamics through more structured programmes. This is understandable because the NGO world gives freedom to its activists to develop religious thought and ideas. This space is difficult to obtain in the *pesantren* world, which has its own subculture, and also at higher education institutes, which are so rigid with methodology. It is thus understandable that alternative thought often emerges in NGOs rather than in *pesantren* or universities, especially NU universities.

On the basis of this illustration, I believe that the NGO community managed by NU youth can be said to be the subject that drives the dynamics of NU thought. Meanwhile, the other communities (the *pesantren* and university communities) are the "objects" and targets of NGO movements. This is evident in that almost all the training programmes related to the development of Islamic thought which are run by NU youth in NGOs target *kiai* (especially young *kiai*), *pesantren*, and campus communities (both lecturers and students). Almost all community empowerment and development of Islamic thought programmes target *pesantren, kiai*, and students. On one level, the NU generation that developed careers in universities is often a counterbalance, if not an opponent of NGO intellectual movements, particularly on certain issues.

This explains some of the responses of different communities to the NU youth dynamics. Both internally and externally, the responses are never singular. First, there are those groups who do not mind the movements and actions of the NU youth. Although these groups do not necessarily agree entirely with their ideas, they are accepting, and even on some level protective, of the NU youth. Figures such as KH MA Sahal Mahfudz, KH Muchith Muzadi, KH A. Musthafa Bisri — to mention a few names

— are NU *kiai* who fit into this group. Of course KH Abdurrahman Wahid cannot be forgotten, as both the initiator and protector of the movement. The NU youth often communicate with these *kiai* about their movements, although these *kiai* do not necessarily agree with all the ideas they develop. The NU youth, many of whom came from *pesantren*, are aware of the importance of protection from these *kiai* in making way for their programmes. Failure to culturally communicate with *kiai* is often an obstacle in the way of entering the *pesantren* community. As a result, before running a programme, NU youth usually communicate with *kiai*. In fact, these *kiai* are often involved in opening or speaking at activities that promote progressive Islamic ideas. This cultural strategy is very important in NU, because failure to communicate with prominent *kiai* can threaten total failure.

Secondly, there are groups who respond harshly and tend to oppose the critical religious ideas developed by NU youth through their NGOs. They do so because these new religious ideas are deemed to have gone beyond the boundaries of the NU *ahl al-sunnah wa al-jamâah* doctrine. KH Masduqi Mahfudh, chairman of the East Java Advisory branch of NU, has repeatedly expressed his restlessness with the NU youth. In his speech at the opening of the East Java NU Conference from 11 to 13 October 2002 at Pondok Pesantren Miftahul Ulum al-Yasini in Pasuruan, KH Masduqi Mahfudh expressed his agitation at seeing the development of liberal thought amongst the young NU generation and called on the East Java NU branch to instruct NU members to be aware of and prevent liberal Islamic thought[124] from spreading in society. He stated: "If liberal Islamic thought is exhibited by NU officials (at all levels) they will be severely rebuked (*istitâbah*) or receive a sanction such as being removed from NU management."[125] This agitation is not only felt by KH Masduqi Mahfudh, but is certainly also felt by many NU *kiai* and officials.

The managers of the Lasem chapter of NU in Central Java once sent a letter to NU headquarters[126] in response to the controversy over Ulil Abshar's article, "Menyegarkan Kembali Pemahaman Islam/ Reinvigorating Islamic Understanding" (*Kompas*, 18 November 2002), and several of Masdar F. Mas'udi's ideas that were deemed improper. Although the letter addressed a specific issue, the controversy over Ulil's article, it was only the tip of the iceberg concerning the restlessness of several NU figures. Several points highlighted in the letter are relevant here, including that it:

1. Deplored NU headquarters' silence over the controversy of Ulil Abshar's article, even though the Forum Umat Islam Indonesia (FUII, Indonesian Muslim Forum) had reacted strongly with a "death fatwa". The Lasem chapter requested that NU headquarters issue a formal statement declaring that JIL's ideas (the letter grouped Masdar as being a part of JIL) were *bid'ah dlalâlah* (deviant) and strayed from the *ahl al-sunnah wa al-jamâah* understanding.
2. Requested that NU headquarters sanction Ulil Abshar and Masdar F. Mas'udi (expelling them from NU membership/management) if they were not prepared to *rujû' ila al-haqq* (return to Islam), because they were believed to be JIL figures who were deviant and misleading (NU Charter, Chapter II, Article 4, Verse 3). At the same time, they requested that NU headquarters always be on the alert for all deviant understandings, both from within and outside of NU.
3. Disagreed with Masdar F. Mas'udi's activities that were run in the name of the NU branch and that used the NU stamp for his own interests.[127]

In addition, restlessness emerged amongst senior NU ulama. There was a meeting held in Buntet, Cirebon, on 10 March 2004, attended by several senior *kiai* such as KH Abdullah Faqih (Tuban, East Java), KH Abdullah Abbas (Buntet, Cirebon), KH Fachruddin Masturo (Sukabumi), KH Muhaiminan Gunardo (Parakan, Temanggung), and KH A.R. Ibnu Ubaidillah Syathori (Arjawinangun, Cirebon). It was held in response to the national political development surrounding KH Abdurrahman Wahid's presidential candidacy for the 2004 election, although the effort eventually failed because the General Election Commission (KPU) felt that he did not meet the necessary health requirements. One decision reached in the meeting was that in response to the concern of NU members over the new religious thought of the NU intellectual youth that was considered contradictory to the *ahl al-sunnah wa al-jamâ'ah* doctrine, the NU community was advised not to adopt such thoughts and to consider them as not being a part of NU.[128]

This clearly indicates the deep worries amongst many senior NU *kiai* concerning the ideas and movements developed by the youth. In fact, even when they were discussing a very real political problem, they were reminded of the issue. It was clearly a considerable concern that never left their thoughts. Unfortunately, these senior *kiai* did not respond more substantially to the specific issues related to those ideas and thoughts considered deviant, leaving the public to examine them themselves.

Concern was also apparent in the opening speech of KH Hasyim Muzadi, general chairman of the NU Central Executive Board at the "Muktamar Pemikiran Islam NU/Congress on NU Islamic Thought" at PP Salafiyah Syafi'iyah, in Asembagus, Situbondo, East Java.[129] KH Hasyim Muzadi, who is known for being relatively moderate, was clearly not thrilled with the signs of liberalism in the Islamic thought of the NU younger generation. In his speech, Hasyim Muzadi specifically asked Ulil Abshar-Abdalla to not act in the name of NU, because if his thoughts were not controlled it could have negative consequences for the very diverse NU community, which ranged from being highly conservative to very liberal. Nevertheless, Hasyim Muzadi continued, this did not mean that liberal thought would be denied. They would devote a forum to debating arguments over controversial thought in the community. If these thoughts were just allowed to run rampant, however, the impact would not be good for NU. However, Hasyim Muzadi expressed his awareness that NU could not ban a thought, no matter how strange it might seem to NU, because it was a human right. Not permitting Ulil to use the NU label was purely to avoid unwanted side effects.[130]

Here, Hasyim Muzadi did not specifically explain what he meant by "will have a negative impact on the NU community" and "unwanted side effects". Nevertheless, the statement was made as a balance and control so that wild thoughts did not provoke conflict amongst sacred religious dimensions. It can also be viewed as a way of calming the anger of several *kiai* who were agitated by the boldness of the younger generation. On the other hand, this statement can also be interpreted as an attempt by the NU institution to wash its hands and not be responsible for the developing thought, as explained in the previous chapter. If this is true, then the NU institution has been left behind by the developments of its own people.

This phenomenon can actually be read as the gap between NU as a formal institution which must obey organizational rules and principles, and the NU that is understood and internalized by activists outside of this structure. This gap is not a new phenomenon, but an old tendency that has never been resolved. As with other sectors, such as in the education sector, change through the formal NU structure is always constrained because of the complexity of interests within the structure, and thus, development of thought through the formal NU structure is often sluggish.

The asymmetry between the NU institution and structures outside NU in regard to Islamic thought peaked at the 31st NU Congress at the Donohudan Lodge for Pilgrims in Boyolali, Central Java, from 28 November to 2 December 2004. One important theme that was discussed concerned the opposition to the development of liberal thought by NU youth.

The emergence of the liberal Islam issue in the lead-up to the congress began with a declaration by KH Mas Subadar, an ulama from Pasuruan, in which he stated firmly: "The most pressing issue to be decided immediately in this congress will be to cleanse JIL people from within NU. There must not be any JIL members in NU!"[131] This harsh declaration coming from a rather influential figure was aimed at Ulil Abshar-Abdalla, coordinator of JIL, and KH Masdar F. Mas'udi, who was mistakenly considered part of JIL even though he was discussed as being a possible candidate to become the chairman of the NU Central Executive Board (although this was not actualized).

Hasyim Muzadi repeated this declaration in his introduction to the accountability report at the 31st Congress. He proposed the redefinition of NU, as a moderate Islamic social organization. Hasyim Muzadi interpreted the term "moderate" as being not radical, and not liberal. In fact, he emphasized that liberal Islam did not fit with NU because the term "liberal" meant a "tendency to permit (make halal) all things". This was not a new stance for Hasyim Muzadi, who had made more or less the same comment when opening the Congress on Islamic Thought in NU in October 2003 in Situbondo.

In addition, during the 31st Congress, I found a number of brochures opposing JIL. They rejected the possibility of allowing individuals stigmatized as being liberal Muslims into NU management positions, and were indicative of the rather serious resistance to liberal Islam within NU. Nineteen elderly *kiai* such as KH M.A. Sahal Mahfudh, KH Mas Subadar, KH Muhaiminan Gunardo, and KH Masruri Mughni signed a pledge rejecting liberal Islam. "NU must oppose the liberal way of thinking that deviates from *ahl al-sunnah wa al-jama'ah*", read the pledge.[132]

During the official forums of the 31st Congress, similar statements were made in several commissions, including the Bahst al-Masâil Mawdhû'iyyah Commission and the Tawshiyah Commission. The Bahst al-Masâil Mawdhû'iyyah (Thematic Forum) Commission, one session of which discussed the theme of hermeneutics, became an arena of resistance against what was defined as the project of liberal Islamic thought. This was reflected for instance in participants' rejection of hermeneutics as a method of Qur'anic interpretation, because it was feared that it would give rise to liberal Islamic groups in NU and would rock NU thought. Several NU exponents who were uncomfortable with the development of new thought in the NU community, which they recklessly labelled as liberal Islam, eventually took their concerns to the Tawshiyah (Advice) Commission. This commission then recommended that in accordance with the principles of *ahl al-sunnah wa al-jamâ'ah*, NU reject all forms of fundamentalism, extremism, liberalism, and other deviant currents of thought. As a consequence, NU management at various levels, including NU autonomous bodies, had to be cleansed of liberal individuals. It was thus clear that directly or indirectly, liberal thought was considered a form of "deviation" that had to be watched out for, and rejected.[133]

Meanwhile, the progressive NU youth at the 31st Congress were largely outside this arena, promoting the issue of politicization of NU by Hasyim Muzadi rather than the new current of thought. They are often aware that the NU Congress does not belong to them, but is the arena of the NU conservatives, so that there is little point in contesting anything in the forum. In fact, presenting opposing ideas in the congress is seen as counterproductive, as it only increases the hatred of the conservatives. As a result, it is not an exaggeration to say that the congress became a court to try progressive liberal thought *in absentia*.

Outside the formal arena of the 31st Congress, debate over liberal Islamic thought occurred in several informal discussions. This current of thought always receives much blasphemy and insults. I was present at two discussions, both book reviews: one on a book written by KH Sahal Mahfudh, with KH Husein Muhammad and Syafiq Hasyim as keynote speakers; the other on a book by Hilmy Muhammadiyah and Sulthan Fathoni,[134] with Hilmy Muhammadiyah and Ahmad Baso as speakers. They both became arenas in which liberal Islam was put on "trial" by the audience. I was not too surprised by the lambasting participants gave; in fact, I had expected as much, including the criticism aimed at KH Husein Muhammad, who is often categorized as an "eccentric *kiai*" because his progressive ideas tend to be liberal.[135] The most surprising statement actually came from Ahmad Baso, who has always been identified as a progressive NU youth thinker. While criticizing liberal Islam, which he said was anti-tradition and anti-local culture, Ahmad Baso stated that "our task is to '*ahl-al-sunnah-wa-al-jamâ'ah*-ize' liberal Islam (JIL), not liberalize *ahl al-sunnah wa al-jamâ'ah*".

I do know what the motivation behind this statement was, but it can be simplistically interpreted in two ways. On the one hand, Ahmad Baso may have wanted to be in a safe position because he knew that the audience he faced was not happy with liberal Islam, but on the other hand he wanted to emphasize again that the Islamic post-traditionalism of a number of NU youth was not the same as liberal Islam. The difference between the two, for Ahmad Baso, lies in respect of *turâst* or local tradition. However, this is a unilateral assessment with which liberal Islamic activists do not necessarily concur.[136]

After the 31st Congress, Ahmad Baso's attack of liberal Islamic groups increased. In a cultural discussion on the formal NU website, *NU-Online*, Ahmad Baso linked his criticism of liberal Islam to the strength with which the orientalists culturally dominate by presenting themselves as modern and NU as traditional. Baso also began to attack liberal Islam saying:

> The Liberal Islamic Network (JIL) always sees tradition as problematic, as Ulil Abshar-Abdalla wrote after the 31st NU Congress, that the rejection of hermeneutics by congress participants was evidence of a shift from NU being critical to being "right-wing". JIL never read the rejection as a counter discourse, a result of how NU portrays itself as not accepting of anything and everything orientalism offers just in order to be called modern or critical of historical constructions. In fact in the most recent Congress NU offered a better approach to making legal decisions.[137]

In relation to this, Ahmad Baso had a different view of what occurred in the 31st Congress, especially in relation to the rejection of hermeneutics as a method for Qur'anic exegesis. Ahmad Baso suggested that hermeneutics was a product of Western social studies, which were pulled into the struggle of natural sciences in interpreting the truth of the world. However, the internal struggle in Western cosmology became problematic when Europe began its economic and physical expansion into the East. Natural sciences, which are known for their positivist traditions, did not only plunder the wealth of the East, but also the entire realm of Eastern thought and culture. Hermeneutics followed afterwards. Initially riding on the "train" of philology which revealed the secrets of the Eastern texts, hermeneutics was then involved in all projects and works to disclose the meaning of texts, both profane and sacred. Hermeneutics was even involved in efforts to reinterpret Islamic texts.

When the 31st Congress discussed the possibility of using hermeneutics to read and interpret religious texts, it raised suspicion. Participants viewed hermeneutics as being the driving force behind liberal Islam, which had always been problematic. The rejection of hermeneutics by the majority of participants at the congress was because it placed tradition as an object to be dissected, while hermeneutics was the subject doing the dissecting. However, Baso said, when the congress agreed that hermeneutics should be rejected, reality was reversed: hermeneutics became the object under scrutiny, and the participants of the 2004 NU Congress became the subject scrutinizing it. In fact, when hermeneutics was introduced, the assumption was that NU needed to be enlightened in assessing tradition, and that it needed to be freed from all conservative interpretation, in order to become moderate and liberal.[138]

The struggle that took place in the 31st Congress reflected the numerous variations and changing dynamics in developing religious thought. This can be interpreted in several ways. First, sowing liberal progressive thought in the formal NU environment is no easy thing. In fact, at the 31st NU Congress there was extraordinary resistance from those who controlled the formal NU structure, and they have since become highly sensitive to all forms of renewal of thought. They easily label anyone they consider an opponent as adhering to liberal Islam. This is not a healthy situation for the development of NU intellectualism because too much sensitivity can lead to childish thinking. Secondly, this issue, once again, indicates that within the NU youth community there are differing opinions and critiques of the various tendencies of thought. This was clearly apparent in Ahmad Baso's critique of the liberal Islam project of Ulil Abshar-Abdalla, even though liberal Islam is not entirely an NU current of thought because its activists come from a variety of social backgrounds. Generally, the progressive Islamic thought that signifies Islamic post-traditionalism within NU tends to be varied.

Thirdly, this also suggests that although observers argue that over the last two decades NU has shown extraordinary intellectual zest which, amongst other things, has been marked by an increasing number of NU youth thinking progressively and entering higher education institutes, it is still just a thin layer and is thus easily expelled from NU. Instead of occupying positions in the NU structure, progressive NU youth are often not considered to be a part of NU. This progressive group is often considered a thorn in the flesh which causes only pain, not pride. Fourthly, in terms of the substance of the religious thought being developed, the NU youth are admittedly consumers of the currents of thought that develop outside

Indonesia, both in the Middle East and the West. They do not have truly original thoughts. They also still need a centre of orientation for their thoughts, although it is no longer singular as occurred in previous centuries, when the Haramain, Mecca, and Medina functioned as the centre of their intellectual orientation.[139]

In light of this, the future of NU intellectualism, besides revealing an increasingly dynamic face, will also be coloured by increasing pressure from those within the NU structure. Although the NU structure does not directly control thought that develops, the *kiai* who are known to be conservative will always monitor those individuals deemed a danger to NU. If this occurs, then NGO activists in the NU community who are developing progressive Islamic thought will face an increasing number of obstacles, particularly from those within the NU structure and the *kiai*. Nevertheless, it will never be able to completely kill off the progressive movement. Not only are progressive NU youth spread relatively evenly throughout NU, they are also increasingly attending higher education institutes.

There are still two questions to answer. Can these NU youth who attend higher education institutes still be considered as a part of NU? This question is related to how far the flexibility of NU's *ahl al-sunnah wa al-jamâ'ah* ideology can accept different currents of thought. The second question is: in this constellation and tension, how and in what direction will the future configuration of Islamic thought in NU progress?

The first question is important to discuss in light of the many people who feel that the thought developed by the NU youth is outside of the real *ahl al-sunnah wa al-jamâ'ah* ideology. As a result, it is difficult to see them as a part of the NU movement of thought. To answer this question, we must first answer what actually makes an individual a part of NU. I believe that NU identity is first and foremost determined by culture, not by a particular current of thought. This can be traced back to the initial founding of NU. Before it was established in 1926, NU was initially a *jamâ'ah*, a group of people or community which possessed and practised a particular religious culture. This culture was then later structured into a *jam'iyyah*, or organization. This process not only involved institutional arrangements, but also framing the cultural practices in formulations of religious understanding. This meant that cultural identity and feeling became a part of the NU organization and the deepest part of NU identity itself.

This process of cultural structuring always has a two-sided effect. On the one hand it is a reinforcing process, because scattered cultural elements can be organized into a strong body that allows culture to survive. On the other hand, it can also lead to tension because the structure often feels it has the authority to regulate culture. Religious formulations in the structure are often considered final. As a result, they are used to measure whether an individual's religious understandings exist within the framework of religious understandings that are recognized or not.

Structuring religious understandings through institutions often makes it difficult for NU to accelerate. Doctrine also becomes less flexible in facing change. NU becomes like tight-fitting clothing, especially when those steering the organization have narrow religious understandings. Lately this has been increasingly felt, especially as NU has had to face the rapid flow of scientific information which has forced NU to review a number of its religious doctrines. The hardening of the attitudes of the NU elite, both formal and informal, towards the movements of the NU youth can be seen from the perspective of the limitations of doctrine to accommodate development.

Based on this discussion, I wish to emphasize that culturally the NU identity cannot be eliminated, even with the NU structural strength, so long as these individuals still feel that they are a part of NU. Similarly, wild religious thought cannot damage the NU identity, although such thoughts are not entirely NU's religious products. NU's identity can only fail if these individuals no longer feel that they are a part of NU or become active in other organizations. As a result, NU's identity is actually determined by this cultural community itself.

I believe that recently there has been an effort to delegitimize the NU identity through organizational procedures. These organizational procedures also incorporate formulations of theological doctrine. As a result, those managing the NU structure have become the wielders of authority who probe into whether an individual can still be called NU or not. Here, analysis about the concept of authority and its connection with the formation of knowledge in Islam is necessary to discuss.

Khaled Aboe el-Fadl,[140] an expert in Islamic law from Kuwait, differentiates between two forms of authority — namely, coercive authority and persuasive authority. Coercive authority is the ability to direct another person's behaviour by influencing, taking advantage, threatening, or punishing him so that he is forced to obey. Meanwhile, persuasive authority involves normative power. It is the ability to direct an individual's convictions or behaviour on the basis of faith. Quoting R.B. Friedman, Aboe el-Fadl differentiates between the two terms "being in authority" and "being an authority". Being *in* authority means occupying an official or structural position that gives an individual the power to issue orders or directions. An individual who is *in* authority seeks the obedience of others by displaying symbols of authority that send a message that the individual *in* authority has the right to issue orders. Here, there is no freedom to make private decisions, because an individual may have a different opinion to the person in authority, but he has no choice other than to obey.

Meanwhile, obeying *an* authority involves a different spirit entirely. Here, an individual leaves his personal opinions because he submits to the authority which possesses better knowledge, wisdom, or understanding. As a result, submission to a person *in* authority involves submitting to the formal position or capacity of an individual, but submitting to *an* authority is done out of the belief that said authority has unique abilities or skills.

The above explanation can be used as a lens through which to view NU dynamics. Formal NU managers want to control the knowledge of their people because they are *in* authority. However, the problem is that NU has already been a cultural movement and thus has always submitted to *the* authority, not those *in* authority. In many cases, those *in* authority have to submit to *the* authority, that is, the ulama and *kiai*, the majority of whom are not part of the NU management structure.

In NU, these two authorities cannot be viewed dichotomously, because many exponents in NU who were initially *an* authority have become *in* authority. As a result, the two authorities exist in one individual. This actually gives them an extraordinary power, because individuals who are *an* authority can change their character to being *in* authority. Pressure to submit to NU regulations increases because of the combination of these two authorities. This is a double-edged knife. On the one hand it is a force that can be used to improve NU, but on the other it can be a hindrance if authority is used for narrow and short-term political interests.

I now turn to a discussion of the second question, concerning the future configuration of NU intellectualism. I believe that in the midst of the sharp polarization and quite strong pressure placed on the intellectual movement of the NU youth as described previously, there are several possibilities. First, polarization will continue and this critical group will always exist at the periphery of the NU community. This possibility could occur if the Islamic movement in Indonesia is increasingly dominated by the fundamentalist/conservative current and the NU structure also falls under the control of this current. Secondly, the NU youth's current of thought will dominate NU developments. This possibility could occur if progressive NU youth take control of the NU structure with the full support of the *kiai*. However, this possibility seems small in light of the current development of Islamic movements. In addition, the NU youth who represent this progressive force are not entirely unified. Thus, although a number of NU youth have secured management positions in the NU structure, it is difficult for them to implement their ideas through the NU structure.

Thirdly, there will be convergences that allow both to exist in synergy. This is the more likely possibility. NU as a mass organization cannot ignore the potential of its young cadres, because they are NU's investment for the future. Convergence may occur at the level of religious ideas or on a more personal level. Convergence at the level of ideas will be marked by the ability of progressive ideas and agendas to influence NU movements. Meanwhile, personal convergence will be marked by personal accommodation in the NU structure. The entrenchment of several figures such as Masdar F. Mas'udi and Nasaruddin Umar in the elite ranks of NU Central management is a form of this accommodation, but still in a very limited sense.

This convergence is determined more by how the youth can communicate with the various groups and currents within NU. In NU culture, no matter how radical an individual's thoughts, if he can establish cultural communication with NU figures, both formal and informal, then accommodation is easy. Therefore, cultural communication is the keyword to resolving the polarization in NU.

Another matter that deserves attention concerning the development of NU youth intellectualism is the stamina of the movement. It must be admitted that expanding the NU youth movement is aided greatly by international funding agencies. The NU youth are highly aware of this. In meetings, they often discuss ways of freeing themselves from their dependency on these funding agencies. In the initial periods they did not have this dependency, and the emergence of study groups at the beginning of the 1990s that became the embryo of their current movement was out of pure idealism. Recently, their movement has received support from outside Indonesia so that it can become a larger movement that utilizes a variety of media.

This issue is like a double-edged sword. On the one hand the funding strengthens the movement, yet on the other it becomes ammunition with which to attack the NU youth, for becoming foreign agents. When promoting pluralism, democracy, human rights, gender, and so on, they are often accused of being agents campaigning for Western ideas. The NU youth are aware of this, and as such they continue to try to be critical of the West and its agenda of modernization. The awareness to use Islamic tradition as the basis for transformation is part of this effort to distance themselves from the possibility of becoming lost in a Western agenda.

This funding agency problem has caught the attention of many. NU headquarters, through its general chairman KH Hasyim Muzadi, once bemoaned the critical and seemingly oppositional NU youth as being funding cadres, and not NU cadres. KH Hasyim Muzadi expressed these feelings in an NU plenary meeting. In fact, the official NU website (www.nu.or.id) published an analysis in its editorial section on "Dikader Funding/Caderised by Funding". The analysis reads:

> A serious matter to be emphasised is the development of dynamic thought within our *ulama* community. But unfortunately in rice there are worms, in amongst NU thinkers there is a group that thinks and behaves in a way contrary to the NU Sunni-Syafii tradition. According to the indications of the general chairman of NU, this has occurred because currently many NU youth are caderised by funding, which has been training and financing their activities, so that they think more like westerners in viewing Islam and tradition than like NU people who maintain and develop their own traditions. The most salient aspect highlighted by the *ulama* is their daring to deconstruct *syariah* and the Qur'an.[141]

Elsewhere it states:

> In general they view funding as a kind-hearted humanitarian institution, whose entire activities are aimed at improving human dignity. They never see that these funding agencies are inseparable from capitalism and global imperialism. Indeed their social organisational activities are aimed entirely at defending the interests of the people, but their movement is very limited, so that no matter how radical they may be, they can still be controlled, and will never disrupt the structure of global capitalism that is so strongly entrenched here. Moreover, these activists do not usually question the fundamental structure of this imperialism, that is intervention in states and nations. On the contrary, these cadres have more or less been perceived to be like the West, with an excessively liberal and permissive attitude in the name of tolerance.[142]

This quote depicts how NU headquarters feels about its own youth. However, this accusation about funding caderization is interesting in light of the fact that NU headquarters also facilitates programmes funded by such agencies, such as its anti-corruption programme which is funded by Partnership (*Kemitraan*). As such, the issue of funding agencies cannot be seen solely in the context of foreign cultural penetration, or the capitalist/imperialist issue, but must be seen as a meeting between two entities that both have their own needs and interests. Of course it is not wrong to say that funding agencies have their own interests, but the NU youth active in various NGOs also have their own agendas and idealism. It makes sense that funding agencies want to influence the culture and world view of those they give money to. The greatness of a civilization in history is also a result of reciprocal influence.

I believe that in the context of the NU youth's intellectual movement, funding agencies only become a serious issue if they threaten the cultural identity of the NU tradition. As far as I have observed they pose no such threat. The majority of NU youth are also critical of modernization, capitalism, and neo-liberalism. This attitude is different from that of the Liberal Islamic Network, which openly supports neo-liberalism, as indicated for instance by the group's ad in *Harian Kompas* in support of the rise in the price of fuel oil in May 2003. It is only dangerous if the NU intellectual movement becomes dependent on funding agencies. As a result, the NU youth must think seriously so as to not continue to depend on funding agencies to meet their financial needs.

Finally, the NU youth must begin to think about finding peace within themselves, with their culture, and with international developments that are difficult to reject. Revitalization of tradition to undertake transformation is an important agenda to ensure that NU is not eroded by historical developments.

Notes

1. *Halaqah*, Study Together programmes, Bahst al-Masâil, and so on are the generic names the post-traditionalist community uses to describe the programmes they run to provide critical education.
2. *Halaqah* literally means "circle", or sitting in a circle to discuss an issue. The term is used in the traditional Islamic education system. See Mahdi Nakasteen, *History of Islamic Origins of Western Education (AD 800–1350)* (Colorado: University of Colorado Press, 1964), p. 45. In relation to the development of

NU intellectualism, this term was first used by the Jakarta chapter of P3M in an event on "Contextualisation of the *Kitab Kuning*" in 1987. P3M also produces a magazine with the title *Halaqah*. Prior to this, the term was fairly popular in the NU and *pesantren* circles, because the traditional study method where a teacher (*kiai*) sits and is surrounded by a semicircle of students (*santri*) was commonplace in *pesantren*. In time, the *halaqah* system developed amongst the NU youth community, naturally with modifications, or known by other names such as Study Together programmes, Bahst al-Masâil, and so on. It may well be that the term *halaqah* is also used as a way of becoming psychologically closer to the target audience of the programme.

3. Initially, LKiS was a group of activists with a traditional Islamic cultural background who cared about the development of transformative and tolerant Islamic thought. Individuals then followed the passion reflected in their ideas and formed the LKiS community. The primary activists of LKiS are *pesantren* alumni from a variety of areas, who continued their education at Sunan Kalijaga IAIN in Yogyakarta. Over time, their activities were honed and increased in order to respond to increasingly complex challenges, the demands of professionalism, and the desire to network more widely outside of their immediate group. As a result, they felt it was important to adopt a more systematic management arrangement by establishing a foundation.

    LKiS's vision is to (1) form a civil society that is committed to and recognizes the plurality and complexity of dynamic powers in all societies, like local wisdom on principles of leadership; (2) push for the establishment of an independent society and not deny the emergence of awareness of individual autonomy (both male and female), but value this as a dynamic factor that is important for the formation of social creativity and solidarity; (3) develop the natural, religious, and cultural environment of Islamic tradition and resources. This means studying, publishing, and appreciating other dynamic powers in society, such as local culture and religion, micro and macro socio-economic-political development, contemporary science, and cultural dynamics. Meanwhile, LKiS's mission is to increase the resistance of society and vulnerable groups within it against outside intervention that could isolate or persecute them. This kind of local resistance is considered important in leading society to independence and creativity, by enforcing values to ensure that it is (1) Egalitarian, or rejects systems that distinguish between gender, religion, social stratification, and economic class; (2) Transformative, or seeks changes that liberate humankind; and (3) Pluralist, or acknowledges, values, and is appreciative towards diversity, is non-violent, humanistic, principled, and concerned with the fate of fellow human beings. Read LKiS's profile at www.lkis.org.

4. Much research has already been undertaken on this group. Almost all studies of

the latest developments in NU intellectualism cite LKiS as an example. Studies that specifically discuss LKiS include Mochamad Sodiq's thesis, "Gerakan Kritis Komunitas LKiS: Suatu Kajian Sosiologis" (Yogyakarta: UGM, 1999) and the honours thesis by Muhammad Hormus, "Kritik Epistemologi LKiS terhadap Bangunan Keilmuan Islam dan Kemasyarakatan di Indonesia" (Yogyakarta: IAIN Sunan Kalijaga, 1998).
5. See *Tempo*, 10 June 2001.
6. Thanks to its pluralism-laden publications, LKiS won the Tasrif Award from the Alliance of Independent Journalists (AJI). According to the Secretary General of AJI, Solahuddin, LKiS was granted the award because of its ideas on pluralism. Not only that, he said that the institute campaigned for pluralism through a practical movement. One such example is its effort to neutralize the movement in Tasikmalaya concerning the implementation of Islamic *syariah*. In addition, LKiS promotes its ideas in the bulletin *al-Ikhtilaf*, which is handed out freely every Friday and has a circulation of 40,000. See *Tempo Interaktif*, 31 October 2002. In December 2002, LKiS also received an award from the Dutch Embassy in Jakarta for its efforts to develop democratic ideas and pluralism. See *Gatra*, no. 6/IX, 27 December 2002.
7. *Tempo*, 10 June 2001.
8. Abdurrahman Wahid, "Hassan Hanafi dan Eksperimentasinya", in *Kiri Islam, Antara Modernisme dan Postmodernisme, Telaah Kritis atas Pemikiran Hassan Hanafi*, by Kazuo Zhimogaki (Yogyakarta: LKiS, 1993), p. xiv.
9. Conversation with Farid Wajdi, P3M Jakarta Office, 8 January 2003. Farid Wajdi, an LKiS activist currently completing his PhD at Leiden University, told me an interesting story. In the lead-up to the 29th National Congress in Cipasung, NU youth who were involved with LKiS, Study Group 164, and so on held a series of meetings in Yogyakarta, Malang, and Cirebon to discuss a number of issues, both those related to national issues and those related to internal NU problems. The first and second meetings ran smoothly, but problems arose with the third, which was to be held in Dâr al-Tauhid Arjawinangun *pesantren* in Cirebon to discuss the "Reinterpretation of *Ahl al-Sunnah wa al-Jamâ'ah*". Initially leaders of the *pesantren* had no issue with the arrangement, but several days before the meeting, word spread that the NU youth who would run the event were left-wing, which meant they were communist. As a result, the event was eventually cancelled.
10. Akhmad Fikri AF, "Penerbit Alternatif tidak Sama dengan Pasar Alternatif", *Bianglala*, July–December 2004, p. 4. See also Jadul Maula, "Kiri Islam dan Kontekstualisasinya untuk Pencarian Islam Indonesia", *Bianglala*, July–December 2004.
11. Mochamad Sodik, "Gerakan Kritis Komunitas LKiS", p. 57.
12. Interview with M. Jadul Maula, director of the Yogyakarta chapter of LKiS, on 23 December 2002.

13. Interview with M. Imam Azis, founder of the Yogyakarta chapter of LKiS, on 24 December 2002. As a result of this incorrect method of Islamic education, religion, which should be portrayed as the saviour able to liberate humankind, has displayed a very different spirit. In other words, there are many paradoxes in religious practices or there is distance between the noble values of religion and religious practice.
14. Interview with M. Jadul Maula on 23 December 2002.
15. P3M's vision is to actualize an Indonesian Islamic community that highly respects values of justice (*al-'adalah*), freedom/independence (*al-hurriyah*), democracy (*al-syûra*), equality (*al-musâwah*), and brotherhood (*al-ukhuwwah*) amongst one another for the simple reason that we are humans, creatures of God, His servants and ambassadors. P3M's mission is to realize this social vision through cultural action on the level of religious discourse, empowerment of institutions, and advocacy. In order to achieve this vision and mission, P3M adopted a tiered strategy, from the development of religious discourse to undertaking social action oriented towards a resolution of humanity's problems, including social, economic, political, and cultural problems. The activities that P3M runs include: (1) Education and training to develop critical awareness and the ability to implement actions for change; (2) Studies and research to understand the social problems of humanity and strategies to change them; (3) Dissemination of information to develop wider public participation in actions of change; and (4) Advocacy to develop social synergy in the lower classes of society to help them resolve their own issues. See the profile of P3M at www.p3m.or.id.
16. For more see Djohan Effendi, "Progressive Traditionalists, the Emergence of a New Discourse in Indonesia's Nahdlatul Ulama during the Abdurrahman Wahid Era" (Dissertation, Deakin University, 2000), pp. 148–208. In this section, Djohan Effendi discusses P3M's implementation of *halaqah* from 1987 to 1998 and the topics they debated, including contextualization of the *kitab kuning* and discussion of concepts such as *dlarûriyyat al-khams* (the five key things to protect in religion, namely religion, the soul, the mind/intellect, lineage, and property), *fiqh al-nisâ'* (fiqh on women), and *fiqh al-siyâsah* (fiqh on governance).
17. For more information see F. Budi Hardiman, *Kritik Ideologi: Pertautan Pengetahuan dan Kepentingan* (Yogyakarta: Kanisius, 1990), pp. 35–46.
18. See Franz Magnis-Suseno's foreword in Sindhunata, *Dilema Usaha Manusia Rasional* (Jakarta: PT. Gramedia, 1983), pp. xix–xx.
19. See the article by Ahmad Sahal, "Kemudian, di Manakah Emansipasi? Tentang Teori Kritis, Geneologi, dan Dekonstruksi", *Kalam*, no. 1 (1994).
20. Emancipatory Islam education module, P3M Jakarta, 2002.
21. Profile of the Emancipatory Islamic Network, P3M Jakarta, 2002.
22. Ibid.
23. Ibid.

24. Ibid.
25. Emancipatory Islam education module (*Ma'had al-Islâm al-Taharrurî*), P3M Jakarta, 2002.
26. Emancipatory Islam education module, P3M Jakarta, 2002.
27. Booklet on *Emancipatory Madrasah: Religion, Gender and Culture*, Desantara Institute for Cultural Studies, 2002.
28. *Emancipatory Madrasah* booklet.
29. Ibid.
30. In the context of orientalism, Edward Said pioneered this kind of discourse analysis in his book, *Orientalism*, which was first published in 1978. In Said's view, the very critical orientalism towards the East (especially Islam) was the historical construction of Eastern culture and society as something foreign that had to be controlled. Over quite a long period of time, orientalist perspectives influenced the way people from the West viewed those from the East. Borrowing Michel Foucault's method, Said stated that orientalism was established through a discursive construction that had several theoretical implications: first, ideology operates not only through awareness or consciousness, but also through material objects; secondly, there is a complex and interwoven fabric between politics and knowledge/scholarship; and third, orientalism is self-generating. The important point is that scholarship from the West not only created knowledge, but also described the difference between what is perceived and what actually happens. See Luna Lazuardi, "Studi Kolonialisme", *Newsletter KUNCI*, no. 3 (November 1999).
31. M. Nur Khoiron et al., *Pendidikan Politik bagi Warga Negara (Tawaran Opreasional dan Kerangka Kerja)* (Yogyakarta: LKiS, 1999), pp. 33–35. This book was compiled by LKiS activists as a guide to political education that included religion as the instrument of political education. They argued that a critique of religious discourse is a part of political education.
32. Nasr Hamid Abu Zayd, *Naqd al-Khithâb al-Dînî* (Cairo: Sînâ li al-Nasyr, 1994), pp. 77–99. This book has recently been translated into Indonesian under the title *Kritik Wacana Agama* (Yogyakarta: LKiS, 2003).
33. Interview with M. Jadul Maula on 23 December 2002.
34. Moh. Yasir Alimi, *Jenis Kelamin Tuhan, Lintas Batas Tafsir Agama* (Yogyakarta: Klik, 2002), pp. 112–13.
35. The "binary opposition" concept was first theorized by the modernist linguist Ferdinand de Saussure (1857–1913) before eventually being further elaborated by Claude Levi-Strauss (born in Brussels, Belgium in 1908 before moving to France in 1914), which made Saussure very influential. Strauss was a structural anthropologist who used a lot of Saussure's theories of language as a structural system to analyse all cultural processes. For Strauss, binary opposition is "the essence of sense making", the structure that regulates our system of meaning

for the culture and world in which we live. Binary opposition is a system which divides the world into two related categories. In a perfect binary opposition, everything that exists can be placed in either category A or category B, and in using these categories we order our understanding of the world outside of us. Category A cannot exist alone without being structurally related to category B. Category A only makes sense because it is not category B. Without category B, there would be no relationship with category A, and thus no category A. In a binary system, there are two signs or words that only have meaning if each is positioned as the opposite of the other. Their existence is defined by the non-existence of the other. For instance, in the binary system of males and females, land and sea, or children and adults, a person can only be called a male because he is not a female, something can be called land because it is not the sea, and so on. Binary opposition is a product of "culture"; it is not "eternal/immortal". It is a product of the system of signs, and functions to structure our perceptions of nature and the social world through classification and meaning. Strauss also mentioned that part of the fundamental concept of binary opposition is the "second stage of the sense-making process", which is the use of categories for things that only exist in the natural world (concrete things) to explain categories for abstract cultural concepts. For a short explanation of binary opposition, see Nuaraini Juliastuti, "Oposisi Biner", *KUNCI Newsletter*, no. 4 (March 2000).
36. This issue is discussed at length in *Tashwirul Afkar*, no. 14 (2003) on the theme *"Islam Pribumi, Menolak Arabisme, Mencari Islam Indonesia/Pribumi* Islam, Reject Arabism, Find Indonesian Islam".
37. Eriyanto, *Analisis Wacana* (LKIS, Yogyakarta: 2001), p. 77.
38. www.lkis.org
39. Ibid.
40. Ibid.
41. From the editors, "Kris(t)is", *Gerbang* 2, no. 42 (1999).
42. The idea to formalize Islamic teachings in the state structure, especially those that concern law, is known as *taqnîn*. *Taqnîn* has a long history in Islam. After the rightly guided Caliphs (*Khulafâ al-Râsyidîn*), the idea was first put forward by Ibnu Muqaffa' (d. 142 H/759 CE) when he witnessed the burgeoning of different opinions, not only in issues of fiqh, but also in other scientific branches because of the climate of freedom of thought at the time. Seeing the phenomenon, Ibn Muqaffa' wrote a letter to Caliph Abu Ja'far al-Mansur (ruled 754–76 CE) that read:
"The *amîr al-mukminîn* (leader of the faithful) should consider gathering all religious legal opinions and decisions into a separate book that will be referred to by every person who argues with the Sunna or when making *qiyas* (analogies), then when the *amîr al-mukminîn* makes legal rulings or

political policies, and implements them in accordance with God's guidance, or when he forbids people from making their own decisions which violate said policies, and it is set forth in the authoritative book (*kitâb jâmi'*), then we hope God brings together these various opinions on what is right and what is wrong, and makes them into one law (policy) that is single and true (*hukman wâhidan shawâban*). We also hope that the meeting and gathering of opinions guides towards unity and centralisation of power (*ijmâ' al-amr*) in the hands of the *amîr al-mukminîn*. This also applies to subsequent rulers, until the end of time." See Dr 'Abd al-Rahman 'Abd al-Azis, *Al-Islâm wa Taqnîn al-Ahkâm* (Cairo, 1977), p. 240.

43. See Imam Baehaqi, "Membuka 'Ruang Pengap' Ideologi Aswaja, Mungkinkah?", in Editor's Introduction, *Kontroversi Aswaja, Aula Perdebatan dan Reinterpretasi* (Yogyakarta: LKiS, 2000).
44. See Said Aqiel Siradj, "Latar Kultural dan Politik Kelahiran Aswaja", in *Kontroversi Aswaja*, edited by Iman Baehaqi, p. 4.
45. Editor's research, "Memikirkan Kembali Ahlussunnah Waljama'ah NU", *Tashwirul Afkar*, no. 1 (1997): 4.
46. In *ushûl al-fiqh*, these five rights are called *dlarûriyat al-khams* (five key elements that must be present) and are the essence of Islamic law. For a discussion on this matter, see Abu Ishâq al-Syâthibî, *Al-Muwâfaqât fî Ushûl al-Syarî'ah* (Cairo: Dâr al-Fikri, n.d.). See also Abu Hâmid Muhammad al-Ghazalî, *Al-Mustashfâ min 'Ilmi al-Ushûl* (Beirut: Dâr al-'Ulûm al-Hadîtsah, n.d.), p. 234.
47. Editor's research, "Memikirkan Kembali", p. 8.
48. See Rumadi, "Teologi Kemanusiaan: Refleksi Kritis Teologi Aswaja", *Tashwirul Afkar*, no. 18 (2004). See also Agus Sudibyo, "Beberapa Tantangan Masa Kini: Upaya Transformasi Konsep Aswaja", *Tashwirul Afkar*, no. 16 (2004). See also Ahmad Baso, "Sejarah "Kebenaran" Ahlussunnah wal Jama'ah", *Tashwirul Afkar*, no. 17 (2004).
49. See Rumadi, "Agama Tanpa Tuhan", *Kompas*, 19 October 2001.
50. See the in-depth interview with Karen Armstrong in *Tempo*, no. 30 (December 2001).
51. Nuruddin Amin, "Pergumulan Teologi Kaum Sunni" (unpublished paper, 1994).
52. This reality has made a number of Islamic youth jealous of what occurred in Catholicism when the Vatican Council II (1962–65) reformed Catholic theology by adjusting understandings and internalization of the Christian faith to modernization. This had a two-sided effect. On the one hand, it adjusted religion so that it was able to guide changes that occurred in reality; but on the other hand, the authenticity of "religious teachings" interfered somewhat.
53. See *Statuten Perkoempoelan Nahdlatoel Oelama*, no. 9, 6 February 1930. See also KH Bisri Musthafa, *Risalah Ahl al-Sunnah wa al-Jama'ah* (Kudus: Menara Kudus, 1967).

54. Said Aqiel Siradj questioned this in his paper, "Ahlussunnah Wal Jama'ah di Awal Abad XXI". The paper was written in reply to criticism by a number of NU ulama of his paper, "Latar Kultural dan Politik Kelahiran ASWAJA". Details of the debate can be read in Imam Baehaqi, ed., *Kontroversi Aswaja, Aula Perdebatan dan Reinterpretasi* (Yogyakarta: LKiS, 2000).
55. For a short explanation of the debate between these two traditions of thought, see Ahmad Baso, "Posmodernisme sebagai Kritik Islam, Kontribusi Metodologis 'Kritik Nalar' Muhammed Abed al-Jabiri", in *Post-Tradisionalisme Islam*, by Muhammad Abed al-Jabiri (Yogyakarta: LKiS, 2000), pp. xiii–xvii.
56. Machasin, "Islam dan Revolusi", *Gerbang* 2, no. 2 (1999): 44–45.
57. Hassan Hanafi, *Min al-'Aqîdah ilâ al-Tsawrah* (Cairo: Maktabah Madbûli, n.d), p. 5.
58. For more information on al-Asy'âri's *kasb* theory, see *Maqâlât al-Islâmiyyîn* (Cairo: al-Nahdhah al-Misrriyah, 1950), p. 221.
59. See al-Syahrastânî, *al-Milal wa al-Nihal*, pp. 101–3.
60. This opinion is expressed by al-Bazdâwî in the book *Ushûl a-Dîn*, as cited by Harun Nasution in *Teologi Islam*, pp. 88–89.
61. See Said Aqiel Siradj, "Mengembalikan Aswaja sebagai Manhaj al-Fikr dalam Memahami Islam" (paper for the *Ahl al-Sunnah wa al-Jamâ'ah* workshop by PMII headquarters in Tulungagung, 20 October 1995).
62. Fazlur Rahman, *Islam*, translated by Afif Muhammad (Bandung: Pustaka Hidayah, 1984), p. 70.
63. Nurcholish Madjid, ed., *Khazanah Intelektual Islam* (Jakarta: Bulan Bintang, 1985), p. 14.
64. Al-Jabiri, *Post Tradisionalisme Islam*, p. 31.
65. The term secularization is often recklessly used, because it is still considered a threat to the majority of the Muslim community. This assumption is a result of the understanding that secularization is an attempt to divide religion from worldly life. I do not need to repeat the debate here. Nurcholish Madjid's explanation of the terms secularization and rationalization is more than sufficient. According to Nurcholish Madjid, secularization is rationalization, or making matters that are indeed already material, worldly. Secularization of theology, although not exactly the same as Nurcholish Madjid's secularization, focuses more on the effort to desacralize theology. Secularization of theology is often seen as the opposite of terms such as "theologization of fiqh" that I have used before in my work. The latter is used to express the tendency to make fiqh, which should be worldly, open, and flexible, into something "godly", closed, and rigid. As a result, fiqh, which should exist in the secular realm, becomes highly godly and theological.
66. For full details, see *Ulumul Qur'an* 6, no. 4 (1995).
67. Musta'in Syafi'i, "Islam dan Revolusi: Menggagas Teologi Antroposentrisme", *Gerbang*, no. 2 (1999).

68. Hairus Salim HS and Nuruddin Amin, "Ijtihad dalam Tindakan", in *Nuansa Fiqih Sosial*, by KH MA Sahal Mahfudh (Yogyakarta: LKIS, 1994), p. vii.
69. Hairus Salim HS and Nuruddin Amin, "Ijtihad dalam Tindakan", p. viii. Of these five characteristics, Abdurrahman Wahid firmly stated that adhering to the schools of thought in a methodological manner was the most fundamental and strategic paradigm, because doing so opened the door to making new breakthroughs in the setting of social, economic, and political transformation (*Editor*, 24 November 1990).
70. Badrun Alaena, *NU, Kritisisme dan Pergeseran Makna Aswaja* (Yogyakarta: Tiara Wacana, 2000), pp. 143–44.
71. Badrun Alaena, *NU, Kritisisme*, p. 147.
72. Final report, "Pendidikan Politik untuk Demokrasi dan Penguatan HAM bagi Pemimpin Pesantren dan Ormas Islam" (cooperation between P3M and the Asia Foundation, 1997–99).
73. Introduction to the report on Democracy Training, see www.lkis.org and the section on advocacy and network.
74. Ibid.
75. Interview with M. Imam Azis on 24 December 2002.
76. "Laporan Pelaksanaan Program Belajar-Bersama Islam Transformatif dan Toleran" (cooperation between LKiS and the Ford Foundation, 2001–2).
77. See Ahmad Baso, *Civil Society versus Masyarakat Madani, Arkeologi Pemikiran "Civil Society" dalam Islam Indonesia* (Bandung: Pustaka Hidayah, 1999), especially the conclusion, pp. 319–30.
78. Said Aqiel Siradj uses a different term to refer to civil society, namely *al-mujtamâ' al-mutamaddin*. The term *madaniyyah*, which was adopted in *masyarakat madani*, originates from the word *tamaddun*.
79. The Tsaqifah Bani Saidah incident refers to the power "struggle" after the death of the Prophet Muhammad (PBUH) between the Muhajirin and Ansor groups that seemed to be based on ethnicity. For more on this, see Philip K. Hitti, *History of the Arabs*, 10th ed. (London: Macmillan, 1974), pp. 139–40. This incident is an important historical event in Islam. Muslims were at the time faced with a difficult reality, that is, how they would arrange the life of the *ummah* (Muslim community), including how to select a leader.
80. For further information see my short article, "Paradigma Masyarakat Madani versus Civil Society", *PRANATA*, ISIS newsletter, no. 5, 1999.
81. Nurcholish Madjid, *Islam, Doktrin, dan Peradaban: Sebuah Telaah Kritis tentang Masalah Keimanan, Kemanusiaan, dan Kemodernan* (Jakarta: Paramadina, 1992), pp. 114–15.
82. Robin L. Bush, "Islam and Civil Society in Indonesia", p. 105.
83. For further information on the New Order's political accommodation of Islam, see Bahtiar Effendi, *Islam dan Negara, Transformasi Pemikiran dan Praktik Politik*

Islam di Indonesia (Jakarta: Paramadina, 1999), pp. 273–310. He argues that there is sufficient evidence, and classifies the types of accommodation into four groups. First, structural accommodation, which is marked by the recruiting of political Islamic activists and thinkers into the executive and legislative bureaucracy and the formation of ICMI under BJ Habibie's leadership. Secondly, legislative accommodation, such as the passing of Law No. 2/1989 on the Religious Court, and Presidential Instruction No. 1/1991 on the Islamic Law Compilation; changing the *jilbab* policy in 1991; issuing the ministers' joint declaration on the Zakat Collection Agency (Bazis) in 1991; and the abolition of the national lottery in 1993. Thirdly, cultural accommodation, or the excessive use of Islamic symbols, including the use of religious language and Islamic idioms in the repertory of political vocabulary and state ideology. Examples include the use of *assalâmu'alaikum* in national speeches and the implementation of the Istiqlal Festival. Fourthly, infrastructural accommodation, such as the construction of a mosque in the presidential palace, the charity Yayasan Amal Bakti Muslim Pancasila, the Indonesian Council of Ulama (MUI), and the Indonesian Muamalat Bank (BMI).

84. Ahmad Baso, "Neo-Modernisme Islam vs Post-Tradisionalisme Islam", *Tashwirul Afkar*, no. 10 (2001): 39–46.
85. Muh. Hanif Dhakiri and Zaini Rahman, *Post-Tradisionalisme Islam*, p. 48.
86. Ahmad Baso, "Neo-Modernisme Islam vs Post-Tradisionaklisme Islam", p. 42.
87. Interview with M. Jadul Maula on 23 December 2002.
88. Masdar F. Mas'udi, "Tanggung Jawab Publik Agama-Agama", *Kompas*, 7 February 2003.
89. Ibid.
90. In regard to this, there are at least three main currents in the movement for Islamic *shariah*. First, there is the group that wishes to formalize Islamic law. This group wants Islamic law formalized as the foundation to life in the nation and state. On the formal political level this movement is led by PPP, PK, and PBB, while at the level of social organizations it is led by KISDI, Hizbut Tahrir, and similar organizations. Secondly, there are those groups who want Islamic law not to be formalized (deformalized). These groups interpret Islamic law according to its substance, by allowing "private freedom" for individuals to implement Islamic law. Thirdly, there is the moderate current, which seeks to take a "middle path" and rejects both secularization and Islamization.
91. Jose Casanova, *Public Religions in the Modern World* (Chicago: University of Chicago Press, 1994), pp. 224–25.
92. Jose Casanova, *Public Religions*, pp. 228–29.
93. Interview with Hairus Salim HS on 20 December 2002 and M. Jadul Maula on 23 December 2002 in Yogyakarta.

94. Robin L. Bush, "Wacana Perempuan di Lingkungan NU, Sebuah Perdebatan Mencari Bentuk", *Tashwirul Afkar*, no. 5 (1999): 25.
95. Ahmad Baso, "Ke Arah Feminisme Post-Tradisional", *Srinthil*, no. 1 (May 2002): 37–38.
96. Ibid., p. 39.
97. Ibid., p. 51.
98. See Rumadi, "Agama dan Negara: Dilema Regulasi Kehidupan Beragama di Indonesia" (report on the joint research programme of the Indonesian Department of Religious Affairs and Leiden University, Holland, 2005).
99. "Laporan Pelaksanaan Program Belajar-Bersama Islam Transformatif dan Toleran" (cooperation between LKiS and the Ford Foundation, 2001–2).
100. M. Jadul Maula, in a recording of Study Transformative and Tolerant Islam Together, 1–10 April 2002.
101. Interview with Hairus Salim HS on 20 December 2002.
102. The discussion at Lakpesdam NU's headquarters on 4 February 2003 on *Pribumi* Islam talked about the difference between "*pribumi* (indigenous) Islam" and "*pribumisasi* (indigenization of) Islam". The latter assumes that Islam is a foreign object that needs to be grounded in a particular place. This understanding still assumes that there is an authentic Islam to be grounded. Meanwhile, *pribumi* Islam refers to Islam that has been allowed to grow without intervention. This difference is still questioned from several perspectives, such as exactly what is meant by the term "allowed". However, I do not wish to extend this difference because although there is a different emphasis, generally speaking the concern of the two is not too different; that is, they are both concerned with how locality can be in dialogue with and not oppressed by foreign objects in the name of religious authenticity and universality.
103. Posting on the mailing list emansipatoris@yahoogroups.com on 11 February 2003, under the subject "*Tentang Islam Pribumi: Dukungan buat Khamami*/On *Pribumi* Islam: Support for Khamami".
104. Posting on the mailing list emansipatoris@yahoo.com on 11 February 2003.
105. Ibid.
106. Khamami Zada, "Menggagas Islam Pribumi", *Media Indonesia*, 7 February 2003.
107. M. Jadul Maula, "Syari'at (Kebudayaan) Islam: Lokalitas dan Universalitas" (paper for the module on Study Transformative and Tolerant Islam Together, LKiS, 2002).
108. Ibid.
109. Ibid.
110. Interview with Hairus Salim HS on 20 December 2002.
111. For more on this matter, see Ali Haidar, *Nahdlatul Ulama dan Islam: Pendekatan Fikih dalam Politik* (Jakarta: Gramedia, 1998).

112. See for instance their work in the book *Fiqih Rakyat: Pertautan Fiqih dan Kekuasaan* (Yogyakarta: LKiS, 2002).
113. Abd. Moqsith Ghazali, "Wajah Fiqih Islam Klasik". I obtained this paper because I was involved in the same programme run by PPSDM of UIN Jakarta on "*Pendidikan Demokrasi untuk Guru Madrasah Aliyah di Lingkungan Pesantren*/Democracy Education for Islamic High School Teachers in the *Pesantren* Environment", held in 2003–4. This paper was also presented during the Emancipatory Islamic Education event, held by P3M, Jakarta and Ma'had 'Aly, Situbondo, from 5 to 7 April 2003, with the slightly altered title "Wajah Fikih Konvensional".
114. See Abu Ishaq Ibrâhîm al-Syîrâzî, *al-Muhadzdzab fî al-Fiqhi al-Imâm al-Syâfi'î*, vol. 2 (Semarang: Toha Putra, n.d.), pp. 254–55.
115. For further explanation on this, see Nasr Hâmid Abû Zayd, *al-Imâm al-Syâfi'î wa Ta'sîs al-Aidilojiyati al-Wasathiyah* (Cairo: Maktabah Madbûlî, 1996), p. 48.
116. Abd. Moqsith Ghazali, "Merancang (Kaidah) Ushul Fiqih Alternatif". This paper was presented on a number of different occasions. As for those I participated in, it was presented at a training series held at the PPSDM of Syarif Hidayatullah UIN, Jakarta, for the programme on Democracy Education for Islamic High School Teachers in the *Pesantren* Community (2003–4); and at a series of discussions on "Progressive *Ushul Fiqih*" held by the Wahid institute in November and December 2004. Recently, his work has been published in the book by Komarudin Hidayat and Ahmad Gaus AF, eds., *Islam, Negara, dan Civil Society: Gerakan dan Pemikiran Islam Kontemporer* (Jakarta: Paramadina, 2005), pp. 351–70.
117. For more information on the theory of well-being according to al-Thûfi, see Musthafa Zaid, *Al-Mashlahat fî al-Tasyrî' al-Islâmî wa Najm al-Dîn al-Thûfi* (Cairo: Dâr al-Fikr al-'Arabî, 1964), especially pp. 111–81.
118. Ibn Rusyd, *Fashl al-Maqâl fî Taqrîr Mâ Baina al-Syarî'at wa al-Hikmat min al-Ittishâl aw Wujûb al-Nadhar al-'Aqli wa Hudûd al-Ta'wîl* (Beirut: Markaz Dirâsat al-Wihdat al-'Arabiyah, 1999), p. 125.
119. 'Izz al-Dîn Ibn Abd. al-Salâm, *Qawâid al-Ahkâm fî Mashâlih al-Anâm*, vol. 2 (Beirut: Dâr al-Jil, n.d.), p. 72.
120. See Adonis, *al-Tsâbit wa al-Mutahawwil: Bahts fî al-Ibdâ` wa Itbâ' 'Inda al-'Arab*, vol. 2 (Beirut: Dâr al-Sâqî, 2001), p. 290.
121. Ahmad Gaus AF, "Kritik Nalar Dikhotomi Islam", *Panjimas*, 20 February–5 March 2003, p. 99. However, in his next piece he expressed more positive appreciation towards the intellectual rise of the NU youth. See Ahmad Gaus AF, "Kebangkitan Intelektual Kaum Muda NU", *Kompas*, 4 October 2003.
122. Personal notes from the seminar, "Mendialogkan Post-Tradisionalisme Islam dengan Islam Liberal dalam Gairah Baru Pemikiran Islam Indonesia", by BEM IAIN (UIN), Jakarta, in mid-November 2001.

123. For more information on *kiai*, see Zamakhsyari Dhofier, *Tradisi Pesantren*, pp. 55–60.
124. The term "Liberal Islam" is used here without any explanation whatsoever. This word has become rather a negative stereotype to refer to any kind of thoughts that endanger Islam, because they question parts of Islamic teachings that have always been considered well established. It is important to note that the majority of intellectual actors in the NU youth community are reluctant to be labelled as liberal Muslims. Hasyim Muzadi, the general chairman of NU's Central Executive Board, spoke at the *"Muktamar Pemikiran Islam di NU*/Congress of Islamic Thought in NU", held from 3 to 5 October 2003 at Pesantren Salafiyah Syafi'iyyah, Situbondo, and he touched on the issue of liberal Islam. Hasyim Muzadi specifically asked Ulil Abshar-Abdalla not to allow NU to be associated with the Liberal Islamic Network (JIL) and asked that he not refer to NU in his movement because it would have negative consequences for the very diverse NU community, which ranged from the conservative to the liberal.
125. *Panjimas* 1, no. 17 (October 2003): 29. See also *Tempo Interaktif*, 12 October 2002; and *Aula*, January 2003, p. 41. I also received the same information from Masdar F. Mas'udi, who was present when KH Masduqi Mahfudh spoke these words, because Masdar was to speak in one of the series of seminars. In fact, Masdar also revealed that Kiai Masduqi said that the thoughts of people like Masdar F. Mas'udi, Ulil Abshar, and Husein Muhammad could be listened to, but not followed.
126. Letter dated 4 February 2003, sent to NU headquarters after the Lasem chapter held a *halaqah* on 27 January 2003 to discuss the controversial ideas of Ulil Abshar-Abdalla and Masdar F. Mas'udi, which was then followed up with a plenary meeting at NU headquarters on 31 January 2003. Attached to the letter was a thirty-eight-page paper titled, "Bayân 'Aqâid al-Mu'minîn al-Akhyâr Dlidd Abâthîl al-Mâriq Ulîl Abshar" [Explanation of the Faith of the Chosen Believers in Opposing He who has Left his Religion, Ulil Abshar] written by Muhammad Najih bin Maimun Zuber, a *kiai* from Pesantren Sarang, Rembang, and also the son of Kiai Maimoen Zoeber. The paper was a word-by-word review of Ulil Abshar's article to prove that it contained many deviant elements. Najih Maimun had previously written a response to Said Aqiel Siradj's work, *Latar Kultural Kelahiran Aswaja* [The Cultural Background to the Birth of *Ahl al-Sunnah wa al-Jamâah*], which many people feel contains several mistakes. See Najih Maimun, *al-Ajwibah al-Sunniyyah ' an al-Masâil al-'Ashriyyah al-Nahdliyyah* (1996).
127. This is related to Masdar F. Mas'udi's position as director of P3M, Jakarta and the NGO's Emancipatory Islamic Network programme, which ran a number of *halaqah* in several regions that were always connected to the NU Central

Advisory Branch. I was also involved in this programme and am aware that branches of the NU Central Advisory Board are not their own "institutions" in the Advisory Board. Collaboration with the Advisory Board was purely for ease of implementation of the programme in NU pockets. Masdar F. Mas'udi stated in a meeting of the team heading the Emancipatory Islamic Network programme that it was done with the knowledge of the chairman of the NU Central Advisory Board, KH MA Sahal Mahfudh.

128. This data was obtained from the KMNU mailing list, a mailing list run by NU youth, particularly those studying at al-Azhar, Cairo, on 10 March 2004. Most media outlets did not report on this issue because they were more focused on political news and Gus Dur's candidacy to become president.

129. This event was held from 3 to 5 October 2005. It was actually intended to discuss the progressive thought developing within the NU youth community with all NU exponents — both NU management and the *kiai* from across a number of regions. Unfortunately the event did not reach its maximum potential, not only because very few *kiai* attended, but because of internal friction within the NU youth community. In fact, LKiS activists, who were known as one of the important driving forces behind the movement for the liberation of Islamic thought, did not participate in the event. Nevertheless, the idea of discussing the ideas and developments in Islamic thought within the NU community needs to be valued.

130. This statement was specifically directed at Ulil Abshar-Abdalla because he was coordinator of the Liberal Islamic Network (JIL) and his ideas had upset many people. However, I believe that this warning was not directed purely at Ulil, but also towards other communities in NU involved in similar movements but with different themes and perspectives.

131. *Tempo Interaktif*, 23 October 2004.

132. The weekly news magazine *Tempo*, no. 6, 12 December 2004.

133. Compare this with Hartono Ahmad Jaiz, *Aliran dan Paham Sesat di Indonesia* (Jakarta: Pustaka al-Kaustar, 2003).

134. These two books are KH MA Sahal Mahfudh, *Wajah Baru Fikih Pesantren* (Jakarta: Citra Pustaka, 2004); and Hilmy Muhammadiyah and Sulthan Fatoni, *NU: Identitas Islam Indonesia* (Jakarta: Elsas, 2004).

135. KH Husein Muhammad is known as the "gender *kiai*" because of his attention to women's issues. Recently, he had the courage to do something that is not typical of *kiai*, that is, to marry across religions — a Muslim man with a non-Muslim woman. See his reflection in "Wali Dua Imam", *Majalah Syir'ah*, February 2005.

136. For a response to this, see Novriantoni, "Mempersempit Ruang Tabu Pemikiran", *Indopos*, 12 December 2004.

137. Ahmad Baso, "Biarkan NU Membangun Citra atas Dirinya Sendiri", *Situs*

Resmi Nahdlatul Ulama, 12 January 2005 <http://nu.or.id>. Ahmad Baso's critique addressed Ulil Abshar-Abdalla's writing which commented on the 31st NU Congress, "Angin itu Berhembus ke Kanan", *Tempo*, no. 8–14, November 2004.

138. Ahmad Baso, "Biarkan NU Membangun Citra atas Dirinya Sendiri". Ahmad Baso is not the only individual to critique using this perspective. See, for instance, Umaruddin Masdar, *Agama Kolonial, Colonial Mindset dalam Pemikiran Islam Liberal* (Yogyakarta: Klik, 2003). See also M. Arif Hakin, "Watak Kolonial 'Islam Liberal' dan 'Kelas Terdidik' ", *ISTiQRO'* 2, no. 1 (2003), published by the Directorate of Islamic Higher Education of the Indonesian Department of Religious Affairs. This article is a review of Umaruddin Masdar's book, which is contrasted to those books that are described as manifestos of liberal Islam, such as Ulil Abshar-Abdalla et al., *Wajah Liberal Islam di Indonesia* (Jakarta: JIL, 2002).

139. See Azyumardi Azra, *Jaringan Ulama Timur Tengah dan Kepulauan Nusantara Abad XVII–XVIII: Melacak Akar-Akar Pembaruan Pemikiran Islam Indonesia* (Bandung: Mizan, 1995).

140. Khaled Aboe el-Fadl, *Atas Nama Tuhan, dari Fikih Otoriter ke Fikih Otoritatif*, translated by R. Cecep Lukman Yasin (Jakarta: Serambi, 2003), pp. 37–45.

141. <http://nu.or.id>. News analysis posted on 24 August 2005. The article was written by Abdul Mun'im DZ.

142. <http://nu.or.id>. News analysis posted on 24 August 2005.

5

CONCLUSION

This book was always intended to examine three key issues: first, the intellectual dynamics occurring in the NU community up to the development of the discourse of Islamic post-traditionalism; secondly, the factors that influenced the emergence of Islamic post-traditionalism; and thirdly, the forms and discourses that have developed in the NU community through the Islamic post-traditionalist paradigm.

Examination and analysis revealed that the emergence of a young NU generation with new and more progressive thoughts is indeed unique and interesting. It is unique and interesting because NU, which is seen to be traditional and is often stigmatized as backward, ignorant, and old-fashioned, actually has within it a group of youths who think and participate in movements in a way that is able to overcome this stigma. This cannot be separated from the NU Congress's decision to return to the Khittah of 1926 in 1984. The decision was to have extensive implications for NU, not just in political life, but also in terms of the orientation of its struggle. While prior to this decision, NU's success was always measured by how far NU was able to insert its cadres into strategic positions in the government and legislative branches, afterwards it was measured by how much NU contributed to alternative progressive thought and empowerment, especially for society.

This change in orientation was largely due to two highly influential figures, namely Kiai Achmad Siddiq and Kiai Abdurrahman Wahid. Both were important NU leaders who cared more about sociocultural development than socio-political development. Their existence gave the young NU generation an intellectual spirit. One of Kiai Achmad Siddiq's important contributions was his success in resolving the tension between religion and the state when the New Order launched Pancasila as the soul basis or ideology for social and political organizations. At the same time, KH Abdurrahman Wahid played a significant role as the social, political, and cultural umbrella for the younger NU generation to develop critical progressive thought within the tradition of NU intellectualism.

The tradition of progressive thought amongst the NU youth has recently been institutionalized in the NGOs they manage. This NGO tradition that develops programmes and is oriented towards social development, especially that of the *pesantren* community and all the intellectual wealth and traditions it possesses, has had a significant impact on the development of progressive thought in the *pesantren* community. Although the number of progressive activists is very small compared with the forty million or so NU members, their skill in publishing their ideas in books, short articles, journals, bulletins, and other forms of mass media has meant that their ideas have a considerable resonance, both within NU and outside the organization.

This small progressive group refers to itself as representing Islamic post-traditionalism, and consists of NU youth who use their tradition to revitalize tradition and undertake social transformation aimed at justice and well-being. This process of revitalization and transformation is undertaken through critiquing tradition — not only the traditions of others, but also their own traditions that they practise every day. Their contact with the wealth of social sciences, politics, and the humanities that they did not have access to in the *pesantren* has allowed them to use these new sciences to read their own Islamic wealth and traditions, especially those developing within the NU environment.

As a result of this criticism, their elders, who position themselves as the guardians of conservatism, are often suspicious of the NU youth. These youths' thoughts are often identified as "dangerous", and as such need to be watched. On one level, their thoughts and movements are not only considered dangerous to NU, but also a danger to Islam. As a result, critical NU youth such as M. Imam Azis and several LKiS activists have been called "infidels" by ulama or *pesantren* in Yogyakarta. In fact, LKiS was even said to be an acronym for *Lembaga Kok Isine Setan,* an expression of hatred and sarcasm equating LKiS with Satan.

Separately from this controversy, there are several factors that can be described as the social capital behind the emergence of the post-traditionalist community in NU and its progressive Islamic ideas. First, NU has an intellectual wealth and foundation that has been passed down from one generation to the next through its traditional education institute, the *pesantren* network. With all its advantages and disadvantages, the *pesantren* education system has been able to stand firm in a constantly changing world.

Secondly, after NU returned to the Khittah, the young NU generation found a new mobility which was marked by increasing numbers of NU youth entering higher education institutions after years of struggling with *pesantren* sciences. This made it possible for the wealth of *pesantren* sciences to intersect with new sciences that were richer in the methodologies used to view reality. A further implication of this was the intellectual diversification in the NU community, in terms of intellectual genealogy, religious understanding, and the type of sciences studied. This new mobility opened up a new horizon for intellectualism, not only related to the scientific traditions which developed in the West, but also the progressive contemporary thought developing in the Arab world.

Thirdly, on one level the NU intellectual tradition's display of enthusiasm in the second half of the 1980s can also be seen as compensation for the political disappointment as a result of NU's continual marginalization by the New Order government.

Fourthly, the demands of global development such as democracy, human rights, civil society, pluralism, and gender issues force not only NU but Muslims in general to rethink their religious traditions and doctrine, which have to date been accepted and believed in, almost without any alteration. The continually developing world demands that Islam and its adherents show a more progressive religious understanding, although within NU this can result in clashes with tradition, which sometimes can be quite sharp.

In truth, a wide spectrum of thoughts have been picked up and brought to the attention of the Islamic post-traditionalist community within the young NU generation. However, the themes that are most frequently discussed in journal articles, books, articles in the media, *halaqah* (Study Together programmes), seminars, and so on, can be categorized as follows.

The first category is the critique of religious discourse as a perspective for reading reality and religious discourse. This is important because all forms of religious discourse are formed through processes concerning power and interests, and not out of the blue. Critique of religious discourse is not only aimed at the great traditions, but also at NU traditions such as the *ahl al-sunnah wa al-jamâ'ah* ideology.

The second category deals with the politics of citizenship (civil society) and its political implications. In addition, the relationship between religion and state, along with its implications and associated issues such as formalization of Islamic *syari'ah*, is also a concern of the Islamic post-traditionalist community.

Thirdly, issues concerning feminism also receive attention and inspire varied and creative programmes.

Fourthly, the discourse of pluralism and interreligious dialogue, the discourse of Islam and local culture, and the renewal of fiqh and *ushûl al-fiqih* are adopted and approached using a framework for the critique of reason (*naqd al-'aql*) that breaks down the interests behind the dominant discourse. The implication of this approach is a "relativization" of religious exegesis. The process of religious interpretation is sometimes an unfair contest, and as such, a critique of reason seeks to cultivate an awareness that the marginalization and hegemony of one group over another is a product of this unfair contestation.

In this context, many people argue that the emergence of Islamic post-traditionalism is a new contest created by the NU youth to compete with the Liberal Islamic Network (JIL), which is viewed as a "modernist" product and pro–status quo. After examining the data, and meeting with Islamic post-traditionalist activists, I have discovered different motivations. There are some activists who are driven by anti-modernist views and attitudes. However, there are others who offer the Islamic post-traditionalist discourse as an alternative to the various Islamic understandings that are considered hegemonic and that do not clearly side with tradition and the marginalized, either socially, economically, politically, or culturally. They do so through revitalization of tradition, not by scorning or doing away with tradition.

On this basis, I believe that the Islamic post-traditionalist discourse that has developed in the young NU generation cannot purely be seen through a political lens as the continuation of the modernist versus traditionalist conflict, only dressed in "new clothes" and with more sophisticated theories.

Conclusion

Islamic post-traditionalism can be seen as an alternative and a model of Islamic thought which has been formed through a sufficiently lengthy dialectic process between the wealth of traditional Islamic science and other scholarship. This kind of alternative model of thought developed by the NU youth can emerge and grow in other communities, although with slightly different aspects.

However, because NU has a particular wealth of tradition, both intellectually and culturally, it is not surprising that intellectual transformation has occurred in the NU youth community, with its success in establishing dialogue between NU's tradition and progressive thoughts, both those developing in Islam and outside of Islam. The younger generation of NU is most fortunate in its wealth of tradition, because it allows the progressive thoughts that they develop to have stronger roots and thus to be less vulnerable.

Seen from this perspective, I believe that the Islamic post-traditionalist discourse is not merely a new contest intended to continue the traditionalist–modernist conflict, but is more a rational continuation of the overall development of NU intellectualism. There are indeed many factors involved in this phenomenon, from discreet intellectual competition with other groups, improved education levels, contact with other wealths of knowledge and the socio-political situation to the internal changes in NU itself. All of this creates a new psychological atmosphere amongst the NU youth which spurs them to revitalize tradition and find a new way of penetrating the rigidity of Islamic thought.

Figure 5.1 gives a general picture of the dynamics of the NU youth's intellectual movement, as explained at length throughout the book. It illustrates the dynamics within NU leading to the emergence of the Islamic post-traditionalist community. Starting with the traditional NU community with its unique characteristics, this community was influenced by several factors that allowed it to develop a movement marked by certain features that addressed a number of themes. This community continues to develop despite the extraordinary challenges it faces, both internally and externally. Internal challenges include the less than favourable response from NU ulama, while external challenges include global developments that increasingly tend to reveal an unjust world order.

The movement is a rational and conscious choice, not a coincidence. As a rational and conscious choice, the NU youth involved in this movement are very much aware of their position and the social risks they face.

FIGURE 5.1

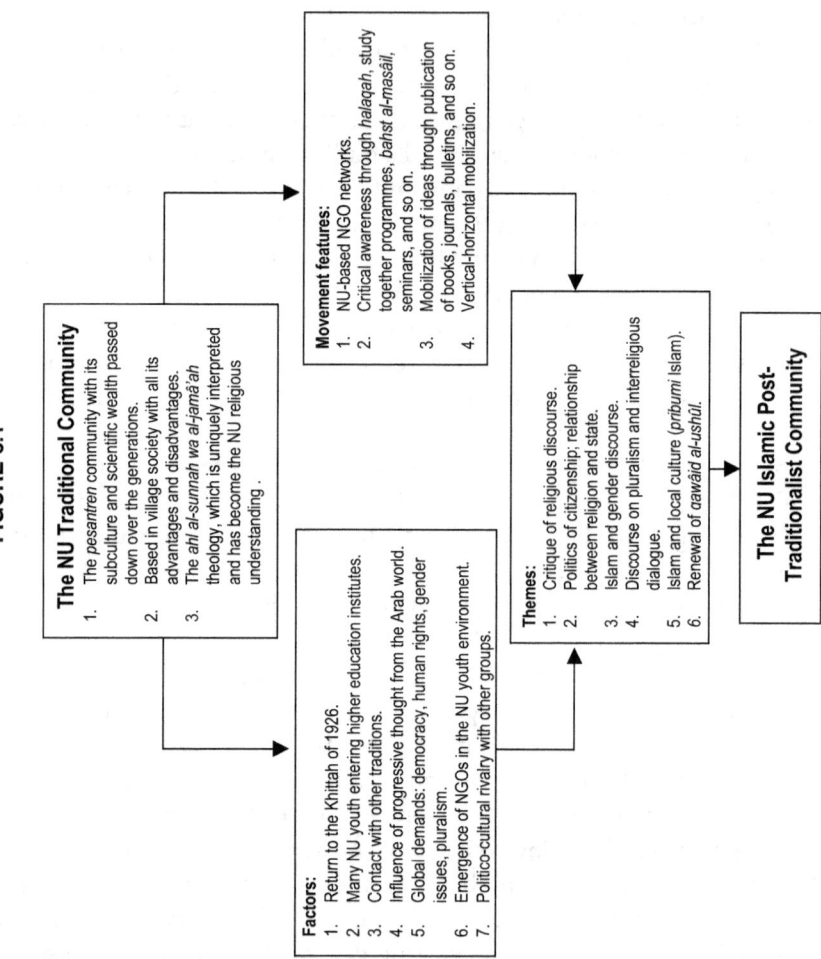

Conclusion

However, this rational choice is not merely based on economic calculations of profit as conceptualized in sociology theories, but takes into account the moral dimension. While rational thought in social theories places more emphasis on the will to follow the mainstream because doing so is profitable, the post-traditionalist movement uses rational choice as a way of opposing the mainstream.

Opposing the mainstream is not an easy choice, because it entails heavy consequences. If this group did not have sophisticated strategies, it would likely be rejected by the NU mainstream. However, history continues to unfold, and it will be history that tests the consistency and endurance of this movement in dealing and negotiating with the NU mainstream.

BIBLIOGRAPHY

Abdalla, Ulil Abshar et al. *Wajah Liberal Islam di Indonesia.* Jakarta: JIL, 2002.

Abdullah, Abdul Rahman Haji. *Pemikiran Umat Islam di Nusantara, Sejarah dan Perkembangannya hingga Abad ke-19.* Kuala Lumpur: Dewan Bahasa dan Pustaka, 1990.

Abdullah, Muhd. Saghir. *Perkembangan Ilmu Fiqh dan Tokoh-Tokohnya di Asia Tenggara,* vol. 1. Solo: Ramadhani, 1985.

Abdullah, Taufik, ed. *Sejarah dan Masyarakat, Lintasan Historis Islam di Indonesia.* Jakarta: YOI, 1987.

Abdullah, Taufik et al., eds. *Ensiklopedi Tematis Dunia Islam*, vol. 5. Jakarta: Ichtiar Baru van Hoeve, 2003.

Abdussami, Humaidy and Ridwan Fakla AS. *Biografi 5 Rais 'Am Nahdlatul Ulama.* Yogyakarta: Pustaka Pelajar, 1995.

Adonis. *Al-Tsâbit wa al-Mutahawwil: Bahts fî al-Ibdâ` wa Itbâ' 'Inda al-'Arab*, vol. 2. Beirut: Dâr al-Sâqî, 2001.

Alaena, Badrun. *NU, Kritisisme dan Pergeseran Makna Aswaja.* Yogyakarta: Tiara Wacana, 2000.

Al-Attas, S.M.N. *The Mysticism of Hamzah Fansuri.* Kuala Lumpur: University of Malaya, 1970.

Al-Azis, 'Abd al-Rahman 'Abd. *Al-Islâm wa Taqnîn al-Ahkâm.* Cairo, 1977.

Al-Bagdâdî, 'Abd al-Qâhir bin Țâhir bin Muhammad. *Al-Farqu Bayn al-Firâq.* Egypt: Maktabah Muhammad Sabih wa Auladuhu, n.d.

Al-Banjari, Syekh Arsyad. *Sabîl al-Muhtadîn li Tafaqquh Amr fî al-Dîn.* Cairo: Dâr al-Fikri, n.d.

Al-Ghazâlî, Al-Imâm Abi Hâmid Muhammad Ibn Muhammad. *Ihyâ 'Ulûm al-Dîn.* Egypt: Dâr al-Ihyâ al-Kutub al-'Arabiyah, n.d.

Al-Ghurâbi, Ali Musthafa. *Târîkh al-Farq al-Islâmiyah wa Nasy`'at 'ilm al-Kalâm 'inda al-Muslimîn.* Egypt: Maktabah wa Matba`ah Muhammad Ali Șabîh, 1959.

Ali, Fachry and Bahtiar Effendy. *Merambah Jalan Baru Islam, Rekonstruksi Pemikiran Islam Indonesia Masa Orde Baru.* Bandung: Mizan, 1990.

Alimi, Moh. Yasir. *Jenis Kelamin Tuhan, Lintas Batas Tafsir Agama.* Yogyakarta: Klik, 2002.

Al-Jabiri, Mohammed Abed. *Al-Turâts wa al-Hadâtsah: Dirâsah wa Munâqasah*. Beirut: Markaz al-Tsaqâfi al-Arâbi, 1991.

———. *Nahnu wa al-Turâts, Qirâ'ât Mu'âshirah fî Turâtsinâ al-Falsafî*. Casablanca: al-Markaz al-Tsaqafi al-Arabi, 1986.

———. *Post-Tradisionalisme Islam*. Translated by Ahmad Baso. Yogyakarta: LKiS, 2000.

———. *Al-Mas'alah al-Tsaqâfiyah*. Beirut: Markaz Dirâsah al-Wihdah al-Arabiyah, 1994.

———. *Takwîn al-'Aql al-'Arâbi*. Beirut: Markaz al-Dirâsah al-Wihdah al-'Arabiyah, 1991.

Al-Kasyani, 'Abd al-Razaq. *Ishtilâhât al-Shufiyyat*. Cairo: Dâr al-Ma'ârif, 1984.

Al-Qaththan, Mannâ.' *Târikh Tasyrî' al-Islâmî*. Egypt: Muassasah al-Risalah, 1992.

Al-Salâm, Izz al-Dîn Ibn Abd. *Qawâ'id al-Ahkâm fî Mashâlih al-Anâm*. Vol. 2. Beirut: Dâr al-Jil, n.d.

Al-Syahrastani, Muhammad Ibn 'Abd al-Karim. *Al-Milal wa al-Nihal*. Cairo: 1951.

Al-Syîrâzî, Abu Ishaq Ibrâhîm. *Al-Muhadzdzab fî al-Fiqhi al-Imâm al-Syâfî'î*. Vol. 2. Semarang: Toha Putra, n.d.

Amin, M. Masyhur and Ismail S. Ahmed, eds. *Dialog Pemikiran Islam dan Realitas Empirik*. Yogyakarta: Pustaka Pelajar, 1993.

Anam, Choirul. *Pertumbuhan dan Perkembangan Nahdlatul Ulama*. Sala: Jatayu, 1985.

Angeles, Peter A. *Dictionary of Philosophy*. New York: Barnes & Noble Books, 1981.

Anwar, M. Syafi'i. *Pemikiran dan Aksi Islam Indonesia, Sebuah Kajian tentang Cendikiawan Muslim Orde Baru*. Jakarta: Paramadina, 1995.

Arkoun, Mohammed. "Kritik Konsep Reformasi Islam". In *Dekonstruksi Syari'ah II, Kritik Konsep dan Penjelajahan Lain* [original title: *Islamic Law Reform and Human Right Challenges and Rejoinders*], edited by Abdullahi Ahmed an-Na'im et al., translated by Farid Wajidi. Yogyakarta: LKiS, 1996.

———. *Al-Fikr al-Islâm: Naqd wa al-Ijtihâd*. Translated by Hasyim Salih. London: Dâr al-Sâqi, 1990.

As'ad, Ali. *K.H.M. Munawir Pendiri Pondok Pesantren Krapyak Yogyakarta*. Yogyakarta, 1975.

Asy'ari, K.H. Hasyim. *Al-Qanûn al-Asâsi li Jam'iyyat al-Nahdlat al-Ulama*. Translated by K.H.A. Abdul Hamid. Kudus: Menara Kudus, 1971.

———. *Tsalâts Munjiyât: Muqaddimah wa Khuthbah wa Risâlah* [The Three Saviours: Fundamental Law-Speech-Important Advice]. Jombang: Pondok Pesantren Tebu Ireng, 1994.

Azra, Azyumardi. *Pergolakan Politik Islam, dari Fundamentalisme, Modernisme hingga Posmodernisme*. Jakarta: Paramadina, 1996.

———. "Islam di Asia Tenggara, Pengantar Pemikiran". In *Perspektif Islam Asia Tenggara*, edited by Azra. Jakarta: YOI, 1989.

———. *Jaringan Ulama Timur Tengah dan kepulauan Nusantara Abd XVII dan XVIII, Melacak Akar-Akar Pembaruan Pemikiran Islam Indonesia*. Bandung: Mizan, 1994.

———. *Renaisans Islam Asia Tenggara: Sejarah Wacana & Kekuasaan*. Bandung: Rosdakarya, 1999.

Azra, Azyumardi and Saiful Umam, eds. *Menteri-Menteri Agama RI, Biografi Sosial Politik*. Jakarta: INIS, 1998.

Baehaqi, Imam, ed. *Kontroversi Aswaja, Aula Perdebatan dan Reinterpretasi*. Yogyakarta: LKiS, 2000.

Barton, Greg. *Gagasan Islam Liberal di Indonesia, Pemikiran Neo-Modernisme Nurcholish Madjid, Djohan Effendi, Ahmad Wahib dan Abdurrahman Wahid*. Jakarta: Paramadina, 1999.

Baso, Ahmad. *Civil Society versus Masyarakat Madani, Arkeologi Pemikiran "Civil Society" dalam Islam Indonesia*. Bandung: Pustaka Hidayah, 1999.

———. *Plesetan Lokalitas, Politik Pribumisasi Islam*. Jakarta: Desantara and the Asia Foundation, 2002.

Benda, Harry J. *Bulan Sabit dan Matahari Terbit*. Jakarta: Pustaka Jaya, 1980.

Bush, Robin L. "Islam and Civil Society in Indonesia". Dissertation, University of Washington, 2002.

Casanova, Jose. *Public Religions in the Modern World*. Chicago: University of Chicago Press, 1994.

Chaidar. *Manaqib Mbah Maksum*. Kudus: Menara Kudus, 1972.

———. *Sejarah Pujangga Islam, Syaikh Nawawi al-Bantani Indonesia*. Jakarta: Sinar Harapan, 1978.

Daudy, Ahmad. *Allah dan Manusia dalam Konsepsi Syeikh Nuruddin al-Raniry*. Jakarta: Rajawali, 1983.

Dhakiri, Muhammad Hanif and Zaini Rahman. *Post-Tradisionalisme Islam, Menyingkap Corak Pemikiran dan Gerakan PMII*. Jakarta: Isisindo Mediatama, 2000.

Dharwis, Ellyasa KH, ed. *Gus Dur, NU dan Masyarakat Sipil*. Yogyakarta: LKiS, 1994.

Dhofier, Zamakhsyari. *Tradisi Pesantren: Studi tentang Pandangan Hidup Kyai*. Jakarta: LP3ES, 1982.

Effendi, Djohan. "Progressive Traditionalist: The Emergence of a New Discourse in Indonesia's Nahdlatul Ulama during the Abdurrahman Wahid Era". Dissertation, Deakin University, 2000.

Effendy, Bahtiar. *Islam dan Negara, Transformasi Pemikiran dan Praktik Politik Islam di Indonesia*. Jakarta: Paramadina, 1999.

Engineer, Ali Asghar. *Islam dan Teologi Pembebasan*. Yogyakarta: Pustaka Pelajar, 1999.

Eriyanto. *Analisis Wacana*. Yogyakarta: LKiS, 2001.

Esposito, John L. and John O'Voll. *Makers of Contemporary Islam*. Oxford: Oxford University Press, 2001.

Essack, Farid. *Qur'an, Liberation and Pluralism*. Oxford: Oneworld Oxford, 1997.

Fealy, Greg and Greg Barton. *Tradisionlaisme Radikal: Persinggungan Nahdlatul Ulama Negara*. Yogyakarta: LKiS, 1997.
Federspiel, Howard M. *Persatuan Islam, Pembaruan Islam Indonesia Abad XX*. Yogyakarta: Gadjah Mada University Press, 1996.
Feillard, Andree. *NU vis a vis Negara: Pencarian Bentuk, Isi dan Makna*. Yogyakarta: LKiS, 1999.
Foucault, Michel. *The Archaeology of Knowledge*. London: Tavistock, 1972.
Fyzee, A.A. "The Reinterpretation of Islam". In *Islam in Transition: Muslim Perspectives*, edited by John J. Donohue and John L. Esposito. New York: Oxford University Press, 1982.
Geertz, Clifford. *Abangan, Santri dan Priyayi dalam Masyarakat Jawa*. Jakarta: Pustaka Jaya, 1981.
Gibb, H.A.R. *Aliran-Aliran Modern dalam Islam* [original title: *Modern Trends in Islam*]. Jakarta: Rajawali, 1990.
Habermas, Jurgen. *Ilmu dan Teknologi sebagai Ideologi*. Translated by Hassan Basari. Jakarta: LP3ES, 1990.
Haidar, M. Ali. *Nahdlatul Ulama dan Islam di Indonesia, Pendekatan Fikih dalam Politik*. Jakarta: Gramendia, 1998.
Hanafi, Hassan. *Oksidentalisme, Sikap Kita Terhadap Tradisi Barat*, judul asli "*Muqaddimah fi 'Imi al-Istighrâb*". Translated by M. Najib Bukhori. Jakarta: Paramadina, 2000.
Hardiman, F. Budi. *Kritik Ideologi: Pertautan Pengetahuan dan Kepentingan*. Yogyakarta: Kanisius, 1990.
Haris, Syamsudin. *PPP dan Politik Orde Baru*. Jakarta: PT. Grasindo, 1991.
Harjono, Anwar. *Hukum Islam Keluasan dan Keadilannya*. Jakarta: Bulan Bintang, 1987.
Hasjmi, A. *59 Tahun Aceh Merdeka di Bawah Pemerintah Ratu*. Jakarta: Bulan Bintang, 1977.
———. *Sumbangan Kesusasteraan Aceh dalam Pembinaan Kesusasteraan Indonesia*. Jakarta: Bulan Bintang, 1977.
———. *Sejarah Kebudayaan Islam*. Jakarta: Bulan Bintang, 1975.
Hassan, Kamal. *Muslim Intellectual Response to New Order Modernization in Indonesia*. Kuala Lumpur: Dewan Bahasa, 1980.
Hidayat, Komarudin and Ahmad Gaus AF, eds. *Islam, Negara, dan Civil Society: Gerakan dan Pemikiran Islam Kontemporer*. Jakarta: Paramadina, 2005.
Hitti, Philip K. *History of the Arabs*. London: Macmillan, 1974.
Hormus, Muhammad. *Kritik Epistemologi LKiS terhadap Bangunan Keilmuan Islam dan Kemasyarakatan di Indonesia*. Yogyakarta: IAIN Sunan Kalijaga, 1998.
Hourani, Albert. *Arabic Thought in the Liberal Age, 1798–1939*. London: Oxford University Press, 1962.
Huda, Affan Ilman. *Biografi Mbah Siddiq*. Jember: Pon-pes al-Fatah, n.d.

Husein, Asaf, Robert Olson, and Jamil Qureshi, eds. *Orientalism, Islam and Islamist*. Brattleboro, VT: Amana Books, 1984.
Ida, Laode. "Gerakan Sosial Kelompok Nahdlatul Ulama (NU) Progresif". Dissertation, Universitas Indonesia, 2002.
Irsyam, Mahrus. *Ulama dan Politik: Upaya Mengatasi Krisis*. Jakarta: Yayasan Perkhidmatan, 1984.
Jaiz, Hartono Ahmad. *Aliran dan Paham Sesat di Indonesia*. Jakarta: Pustaka al-Kaustar, 2003.
Jay, Robert. *Santri and Abangan, Religious Schism in Rural Java*. Harvard: Harvard University, 1957.
Karim, A. Gaffar. *Metamorfosis: NU dan Politisasi Islam di Indonesia*. Yogyakarta: LKiS, 1995.
Keddie, Nikki R. *Indonesia Trade and Society*. Netherlands: Van Hoeve, 1967.
Khuluq, Lathiful. *Fajar Kebangunan Ulama, Biografi K.H. Hasyim Asy'ari*. Yogyakarta: LKiS, 2000.
Kuhn, Thomas S. *The Structure of Scientific Revolution*. Chicago: University of Chicago Press, 1970.
Kurzman, Charles. *Liberal Islam, A Sourcebook*. Oxford: Oxford University Press, 1998.
Lakatos, Imre. "Falsification and the Methodology of Scientific Research Programmes". In *Criticism and the Growth of Knowledge*, edited by Imre Lakatos and Alan Musgrave. Cambridge: Cambridge University Press, 1970.
Lee, Robert D. *Mencari Islam Autentik, Dari Nalar Puitis Iqbal hingga Nalar Kritis Arkoun*. Bandung: Mizan, 2000.
Littlejohn, Stephen. *Theories of Human Communication*. California: Wadsworth, 1989.
Madjid, Nurcholish. *Islam, Doktrin, Peradaban: Sebuah Telaah Kritis tentang Masalah Keimanan, Kemanusiaan, dan Kemodernan*. Jakarta: Paramadina, 1992.
———. *Tradisi Islam: Peran dan Fungsinya dalam Pembangunan di Indonesia*. Jakarta: Paramadina, 1997.
———. *Khazanah Intelektual Islam*. Jakarta: Bulan Bintang, 1985.
Mahfudh, KH MA Sahal. *Nuansa Fiqih Sosial*. Yogyakarta: LKiS, 1994.
———. *Wajah Baru Fikih Pesantren*. Jakarta: Citra Pustaka, 2004.
Malik, Dedy Djamaluddin and Idi Subandy Ibrahim. *Zaman Baru Islam Indonesia, Pemikiran & Aksi Politik*. Bandung: Zaman Wacana Mulia, 1998.
Mannheim, Karl. *Ideology and Utopia: An Introduction to the Sociology of Knowledge*. London: Routledge & Kegan Paul, 1966.
Marijan, Kacung. *Quo Vadis NU setelah Kembali ke Khittan 1926*. Surabaya, Erlangga, 1992.
Masdar, Umaruddin. *Agama Kolonial, Colonial Mindset dalam Pemikiran Islam Liberal*. Yogyakarta: Klik, 2003.

Masyhuri, Aziz. *Ahkam al-Fuqaha: Masalah-Masalah Keagamaan Hasil Muktamar dan Munas Ulama NU 1926–1994*. Surabaya: Dinamika Press, 1997.

Muhadjir, Noeng. *Metode Penelitian Kualitatif*. Yogyakarta: Rake Sarasin, 1991.

Muhammadiyah, Hilmy and Sulthan Fatoni. *NU: Identitas Islam Indonesia*. Jakarta: Elsas, 2004.

Musthafa, KH Bisri. *Risalah ahlus Sunnah wal Jama'ah*. Kudus: Menara Kudus, 1967.

Nakasteen, Mahdi. *History of Islamic Origins of Western Education (AD 800–1350)*. Colorado: University of Colorado Press, 1964.

Nakho'i, Imam, Abdul Jalil, et al. *Fiqih Rakyat: Pertautan Fiqih dan Kekuasaan*. Yogyakarta: LKiS, 2002.

Nasution, Harun. *Islam Ditinjau dari Berbagai Aspeknya II*. Jakarta: UI Press, 1986.

———. *Islam Rasional: Gagasan dan Pemikiran*. Bandung: Mizan, 1995.

———. *Pembaruan dalam Islam, Sejarah Pemikiran dan Gerakan*. Jakarta: Bulan Bintang, 1992.

———. *Teologi Islam, Aliran-Aliran, Sejarah Analisa Perbandingan*. Jakarta: UI Press, 1986.

———. "Antara Pembaharuan dan Pemurnian". *Pesantren* 5, no. 1 (1988).

Ngah, Mohd. Bin Nor. *Kitab Jawi: Islamic Thought of the Malay Muslim Scholars*. Singapore: Institute of Southeast Asian Studies, 1983.

Noer, Deliar. *Gerakan Modern Islam di Indonesia 1900–1942*. Jakarta: LP3ES, 1996.

Pijper, G.F. *Beberapa Studi tentang Sejarah Islam di Indonesia 1900–1950*. Translated by Tudjiman and Yessy Agusdin. Jakarta: UI Press, 1984.

Popper, Karl R. *The Logic of Scientific Discovery*. London: Unwin Hymann, 1987.

Qomar, Mujamil. *NU Liberal: dari Tradisionalisme ke Universalisme Islam*. Bandung: Mizan, 2002.

Rachman, Abd. "The Pesantren Architects and Their Socio Religious Teachings (1850–1950)". Dissertation, UCLA, 1997.

Rahman, Fazlur. *Islam and Modernity: Transformation of an Intellectual Tradition*. Chicago: University of Chicago Press, 1982.

———. *Islam*. Translated by Afif Muhammad. Bandung: Pustaka Hidayah, 1984.

———. *Neomodernisme Islam, Metode dan Alternatif*, edited by Taufik Adnan Amal. Bandung: Mizan, 1989.

Rahmat, M. Imdadun, ed. *Kritik Nalar Fiqih NU*. Jakarta: PP Lakpesdam NU, 2002.

Ricklefs, M.C. *Sejarah Islam di Indonesia*. Yogyakarta: Gadjah Mada University Press, 1994.

Rusyd, Ibnu. *Fashl al-Maqâl fî Taqrîr Mâ Baina al-Syarî'at wa al-Hikmat min al-Ittishâl aw Wujûb al-Nadhar al-'Aqli wa Hudûd al-Ta'wîl*. Beirut: Markaz Dirâsat al-Wihdat al-'Arabiyah, 1999.

Salim, Hairus HS and Muhammad Ridwan, eds. *Kultur Hibrida: Anak Muda di Jalur Kultural*. Yogyakarta: LKiS, 1999.

Siddieq, Ch. M. Mahfoezh. *Debat tentang Idjtihad dan Taqlied*. Soerabaia: H.B.N.O., n.d.
Siddiq, Achmad. *Khittah Nahdliyah*. Surabaya: Balai Buku, 1980.
Sindhunata. *Dilema Usaha Manusia Rasional*. Jakarta: PT. Gramedia, 1983.
Snouck Hurgronje, Christiaan. *Mekka in the Latter Part of the 19th Century*. Leiden: Brill, 1970.
Sodiq, Mochamad. "Gerakan Kritis Komunitas LKiS: Suatu Kajian Sosiologis". Thesis, UGM, 1999.
Steenbrink, Karel A. *Beberapa Aspek tentang Islam di Indonesia Abad ke-19*. Jakarta: Bulan Bintang, 1984.
———. *Kawan dalam Pertikaian: Kaum Kolonial Belanda dan Islam di Indonesia (1596–1942)*. Bandung: Mizan, 1995.
———. *Kitab Suci atau Kertas Toilet? Nuruddin al-Raniri dan Agama Kristen*. Yogyakarta: IAIN Sunan Kalijaga Press, 1988.
Suseno, Franz Magnis. In *Dilema Usaha Manusia Rasional*, by Sindhunata. Jakarta: PT. Gramedia, 1983.
Syarif, M.M., ed. *A History of Muslim Philosophy*. Weesbaden: Otto Harrasowits, 1963.
Thaha, 'Abd al-Baqi' Surur. *Alam Pikiran al-Ghazali*. Jakarta: Pustaka Mantiq, 1993.
Trimingham, J. Spencer. *The Sufi Orders in Islam*. London: Oxford University Press, 1973.
Van Bruinessen, Martin. *Kitab Kuning, Pesantren dan Tarekat*. Bandung: Mizan, 1994.
———. *NU: Tradisi Relasi-Relasi Kuasa dan Pencarian Wacana Baru*. Yogyakarta: LKiS, 1994.
———. *Tarekat Naqsabandiyah di Indonesia*. Bandung: Mizan, 1992.
Voll, John O. *Islam Continuity and Change in the Modern World* (Boulder, CO: Westview, 1982.
Waardenburg, Jacques. *Classical Approach to the Study of Religion*. London: The Hague, 1973.
Wahid, Abdurrahman. "Peranan Umat dalam Berbagai Pendekatan". In *Kontroversi Pemikiran Islam di Indonesia*. Bandung: Rosdakarya, 1990.
Wahid, Marzuki and Rumadi. *Fiqh Mazhab Negara, Kritik atas Politik Hukum Islam di Indonesia*. Yogyakarta: LKiS, 2001.
Wahid, Marzuki et al., eds. *Geger di "Republik" NU, Perebutan Wacana, Tafsir Sejarah, dan Perebutan Makna*. Jakarta: KOMPAS-Lakpesdam, 1999.
Watt, W.M. *Islamic Philosophy and Theology*. Edinburgh: Edinburgh University Press, 1979.
Wertheim, W.F. *Indonesian Society in Transition*. Bandung: Sumur, 1956.
Zaid, Musthafa. *Al-Mashlahat fî al-Tasyrî' al-Islâmî wa Najm al-Dîn al-Thûfi*. Cairo: Dâr al-Fikr al-'Arabî, 1964.
Zayd, Nasr Hamid Abu. *Mafhûm al-Nâsh, Dirâsah fî 'Ulûm al-Qur'ân*, 3rd ed. Beirut: Markaz al-Tsaqafi al-'Arabi, 1996.
———. *Naqd al-Khithâb al-Dînî*. Cairo: Sina li al-Nasyr, 1992.

Zhimogaki, Kazuo. *Kiri Islam, Antara Modernisme dan Postmodernisme, Telaah Kritis atas Pemikiran Hassan Hanafi*. Yogyakarta: LKiS, 1993.

Zuhri, Saifuddin. *Almaghfurlah K.H. Abdul Wahab Chasbullah, Bapak dan Pendiri Nahdlatul-'Ulama*. Jakarta: Yamunu, 1972.

Journals, Mass Media, and Papers

Abdalla, Ulil Abshar. "Angin itu Berhembus ke Kanan". *Tempo*, 8 November 2004.

Arkoun, Mohammed. "Topicality of the Problem of the Person in Islamic Thought". *International Social Science Journal*, August 1988.

Assyaukani, Luthfi. "Empat Agenda Islam yang Membebaskan". *Koran Tempo*, 13 July 2001.

Azizy, A. Qodri. "Mengibarkan Nalar *Ushûl al-Fiqih*". *Gerbang* 6, no. 3 (February–April 2000): 140.

Azra, Azyumardi. "Mengkaji Ulang Modernisme Muhammadiyah". *Kompas*, 9 November 1990.

———. "Ulama Indonesia di Haramain: Pasang Surut Sebuah Wacana Keagamaan". *Ulumul Quran* 3, no. 3 (1992).

Baso, Ahmad. "Biarkan NU Membangun Citra atas Dirinya Sendiri", 12 January 2005 <http://nu.or.id>.

———. "Islam Liberal sebagai Ideologi, Nurcholish Madjid *versus* Abdurrahman Wahid". *Gerbang* 6, no. 3 (February–April 2000).

———. "Ke Arah Feminisme Post-Tradisional". *Srinthil*, no. 1 (May 2002).

———. "Kritik atas 'Nalar melayu': Telaah atas Tradisi Intelektual Islam Indonesia dan Problem Rasionalitas". *Tashwirul Afkar*, no. 2 (1998).

———. "Neo-Modernisme Islam vs Post-Tradisionalisme Islam". *Tashwirul Afkar*, no. 10 (2001).

———. "Sejarah 'Kebenaran' *Ahlussunnah wal Jama'ah*", *Tashwirul Afkar*, no. 17 (2004).

Billah, M.M. "Intelektualisme Kaum Muda: Hasil dari Pergeseran Struktual di dalam *Jam'iyyah Nahdliyyin*". In *Wacana Postra*. Jakarta: ISIS, 2001.

Bisri, KH Mustofa. "Berpijak Tradisi, Mengkaji Hasanah Lain". *Tashwirul Afkar*, no. 9 (2000).

Booklet Madrasah Emansipatoris: Agama, Gender dan Kebudayaan. Desantara Institute for Cultural Studies, 2002.

Bruinessen, Martin van. "The Origin and Development of Sufi Order (Tarekat) in Southeast Asia". *Studia Islamika*, April–June 1994.

Bush, Robin L. "Wacana Perempuan di Lingkungan NU, Sebuah Perdebatan Mencari Bentuk". *Tashwirul Afkar*, no. 5 (1999).

Emancipatory Islam education module. P3M Jakarta, 2002.

Final Report. "Pendidikan Politik untuk Demokrasi dan Penguatan HAM bagi

Pemimpin Pesantren dan Ormas Islam". Cooperation between P3M and the Asia Foundation, 1997–99.
Gaus, Ahmad AF. "Kebangkitan Intelektual Kaum Muda NU". *Kompas*, 4 October 2003.
———. "Kritik Nalar Dikhotomi Islam". *Panjimas*, 20 February–5 March 2003.
Ghazali, Abd. Moqsith. "Merancang (Kaidah) Ushul Fiqih Alternatif". Unpublished manuscript, 2003.
———. "Wajah Fiqih Islam Klasik". Unpublished manuscript, 2003.
Hakim, M. Arif. *Watak Kolonial "Islam Liberal" dan "Kelas Terdidik, ISTiQRO'"*. *Indonesian Department of Religious Affairs* 2, no. 1 (2003).
Hanafi, Hassan. "Mengkaji Tradisi untuk Transformasi dan Revolusi". *Tashwirul Afkar*, no. 10 (2001).
Hasyim, Syafiq and Robin L. Bush. "NU and Discourses: Islam, Gender and Traditional Islamic Society". Paper presented at the Conference on Islam, Civil Society and Development in Southeast Asia, University of Melbourne, 11–12 July 1998.
Juliastuti, Nuaraini. "Oposisi Biner". *KUNCI Newsletter*, no. 4, March 2000.
Laporan Hasil Kegiatan Workshop dan Need Assessment Jaringan Islam Emansipatoris. In Ciloto 21–24 July 2002, in cooperation with P3M and the Ford Foundation.
Laporan Pelaksanaan Program Belajar-Bersama Islam Transformatif dan Toleran. Cooperation between LKiS and the Ford Foundation, 2001–2.
Lazuardi, Luna. "Studi Kolonialisme". *KUNCI Newsletter*, no. 3, November 1999.
Letter from the Lasem NU Chapter dated 4 February 2003, sent to NU headquarters.
Machasin. "Islam dan Revolusi". *Gerbang* 2, no. 2 (1999).
Mas'ud, Abdurrahman. "Mahfuz al-Tirmasi (d. 1338/1919): An Intellectual Biography". *Studia Islamika* 5, no. 2 (1998).
Mas'udi, Masdar F. "Tanggung Jawab Publik Agama-Agama". *Kompas*, 7 February 2003.
Misrawi, Zuhairi. "Dari Tradisionalisme Menuju Post-Tradisionalisme". *Tashwirul Afkar*, no. 10 (2001): 58–59.
Muhammad, KH Husein. "Wali Dua Imam", *Syir'ah*, February 2005.
Mukhtar, Naqiyah. "Hak dan Kewajiban Suami-Isteri dalam Pandangan Kitab Kuning: Studi terhadap Kitab Syarah *'Uqûd al-Lujain fi Bayân huqûq al-Zawjain* karya Muhammad Umar Nawawi al-Bantani". *Ulumul Qur'an* 7, no. 4 (1997).
Mun'im, Abdul DZ. "Gerakan Liberalisme dalam NU". Paper presented in a discussion at the Institute for Social Institutions Studies (ISIS), March 2000.
Najih, Muhammad bin Maimun Zuber. "Bayân 'Aqâid al-Mu'minîn al-Akhyâr Dhidd Abâthîl al-Mâriq Ulîl Abshar" [Explanation of the Faith of the Chosen Believers in Opposing He who has Left his Religion, Ulil Abshar]. Unpublished paper, 2003.
Novriantoni. "Mempersempit Ruang Tabu Pemikiran". *Indopos*, 12 December 2004.

PB NU. *Keputusan Munas Alim Ulama dan Konbes Nahdlatul Ulama di Bandar Lampung.* Jakarta: LTN PB NU, 1992.

Posting on the mailing list emansipatoris@yahoo.com on 11 February 2003, on the subject, "Tentang Islam Pribumi: Dukungan buat Khamami".

Profile of the Emancipatory Islamic Network, P3M Jakarta, 2002.

Rahman, Zaini. "Post-Tradisionalisme Islam: Epistemologi Peloncat Tangga". *Postra,* introductory edition, November 2001.

Rumadi. "Paradigma Masyarakat Madani versus Civil Society". *PRANATA,* ISIS newsletter, no. 5, 1999.

———. "Agama dan Negara: Dilema Regulasi Kehidupan Beragama di Indonesia". Report on the joint research programme of the Indonesian Department of Religious Affairs and Leiden University, Holland, 2005.

———. "Civil Society dan NU Pasca Gus Dur". *Kompas,* 5 November 1999.

———. "Islam Liberal 'Plus'=Post-Tradisionalisme Islam". *Kompas,* 23 November 2001.

———. "Wacana Intelektualisme NU: Sebuah Potret Pemikiran". *Tashwirul Afkar,* no. 6 (1999).

———. "Agama Tanpa Tuhan". *Kompas,* 19 October 2001.

———."Teologi Kemanusiaan: Refleksi Kritis Teologi Aswaja". *Tashwirul Afkar,* no. 18 (2004).

Sahal, Ahmad. "Kemudian, di Manakah Emansipasi? Tentang Teori Kritis, Genealogi, dan Dekonstruksi". *Kalam,* no. 1 (1994).

Siradj, Said Aqiel. *"Ahl al-Sunnah wa al-Jamâ'ah,* Asal-Usul, Perkembangan, Epistemologi, dan Doktrin-Doktrinnya". Paper presented in the *halaqah* on *Ahl al-Sunnah wa al-Jamâ'ah,* held by the Bahstul Masail forum and NU's Central Advisory board, 19–29 October 1996.

———. "Mengembalikan Aswaja sebagai *Manhaj al-Fikr* dalam Memahami Islam". Paper for the *Ahl al-Sunnah wa al-Jamâ'ah* workshop, PMII headquarters, Tulungagung, 20 October 1995.

Statuten Perkoempoelan Nahdlatoel Oelama, no. lx. Rechpersoon, 6 February 1930.

Studia Islamika 2, no. 1 (1995).

Sudibyo, Agus. "Beberapa Tantangan Masa Kini: Upaya Transformasi Konsep Aswaja". *Tashwirul Afkar,* no. 16 (2004).

Suharto, Rudhy. "Menimbang Pemikiran Islam Liberal". *Syi'ar,* July 2002.

Syafi'i, Musta'in. "Islam dan Revolusi: Menggagas Teologi Antroposentrisme". *Gerbang,* no. 2 (1999).

Tempo Interaktif, 12 October 2002.

Umam, Fawaizul. "Modal Sosial NU, Ekonomi Pemberdayaan Warga Nahdliyyin". *Gerbang* 5, no. 12 (2002).

Wahid, Marzuki. "Post-Tradisionalisme Islam: Gairah Baru Pemikiran Islam di Indonesia". *Tashwirul Afkar,* no. 10 (2001).

Zada, Khamami. "Menggagas Islam Pribumi". *Media Indonesia,* 7 February 2003.

Index

A

A. Gaffar Karim, 6, 13n2, 92n182
A. Qodri Azizy, 85n104
A.R. Ibnu Ubaidillah Syathori, 257
'Abd al-'Azîs Ibn Sa'ûd, 26
Abd al-Karim al-Banjari, 30
Abd al-Karim al-Bantani, 30
'Abd al-Mâlik al-Juwaini, 36
'Abd al-Qâdir Audah, 60
Abd al-Rahman al-Sagaf, 54
Abd al-Rauf al-Sinkili, 18, 29, 48, 65, 86n116
'Abd al-Raziq, Ali, 137
Abd al-Samad Ibn Muhammad Sâlih, 44
Abd al-Shamad al-Palimbani, 21
'Abd al-Wahab Bugis, 50
Abd Moqsith Ghazali, 233, 245, 247–50
Abd Rauf Singkle, 41
Abdel Wahab el-Affendi, 104
Abdul Djamil, 85n98
Abdul Mun'im DZ, 98, 241
Abdul Rahman Haji Abdullah, 16, 20, 38, 40, 85n106
Abdul Wahab Hasbullah, 25, 78n41
Abdullah Abbas, 257
Abdullah bin Umar al-Hadharami, 54
Abdullah Faqih, 257
Abdullah Laroui, 137
Abdullahi Ahmed al-Na'im, 104, 138
Abdullahi an-Na'im, 137
Abdurrahman Mas'ud, 139
Abdurrahman Wahid, 4–5, 67, 70–71, 96, 102, 121, 171–72, 215, 256–57, 284
Abed al-Jabiri, Muhammad, 8, 98–100, 107, 114, 125, 141, 151
Abshar-Abdalla, Ulil, 117–18, 241–42, 251, 257–59, 262
Abu Abdullah Muhammad bin Yusuf al-Sanusi, 42
Abu al-A'la al-Maududi, 119
Abu Bakar al-Baqillani, 35
Abû al-Hasan Ali ibn Isma'îl al-Asy'ari, 83n74
Abu Hamid al-Ghazâlî, 41, 63, 208
Abu Hamid Muhammad al-Ghazâli, 29
Abu Hanifah, 28, 246
Abu Hasan al-Asy'ari, 23, 29, 69, 202–3, 208, 210
Abu Hâsyim, 36
Abu Mansur al-Maturidi, 23, 69, 202–3, 208
Abu Musa al-Asy'ari, 33–34
Abu Qâsim al-Junaid al-Bagdâdi, 23, 29
Abu Qâsim al-Rafi'i, 61
Abu Syuja', 246

Index

Aceh, 16, 20–21, 40–42, 46–49
Achmad Siddiq, 4, 25–26, 28, 71–72, 81n58
Ackermann, Robert John, 145
Adi Sasono, 172
Adian Husaini, 229
Adorno, Theodor W., 178
al-Afgânî, Jamâl al-Dîn, 132, 134
al-Afkâr, Tashwir, 78n41
Africa, 11, 39, 49, 119, 206
ahl al-sunnah wa al-jamâ'ah, 31–32, 43, 45
   doctrine, 1, 23, 25, 102, 111, 139, 201, 204, 208, 219, 256
   Fiqh, 45–56
   ideology, 263, 286
   Tasawuf/Tarekat, 62–66
   theology, 32–45
   tradition, 27
Ahmad Baso, 80n55, 98, 105, 110, 121–22, 126, 136–38, 142, 164n90, 223, 234, 251, 260–62
Ahmad Rifa'i Kalisalak, 30, 42–43, 53
Ahmad Surkati, 25
Ahmad Wahib, 120, 121
Aisyah, 34
Akhmad Fikri AF, 171
al-Fatihah, 43, 246
al-Irsyad, 21–22, 25–26
Ala'i Najib, 234
Alexandria, 120
Ali bin Abi Talib, 34
Ali Haidar, 6, 23
Ali Harb, 112
Ali Ma'shum, 72
Ali Masykur Musa, 97
Ambon, 53
Amin Abdullah, 153
'Amr ibn al-'Âs, 33
al-Anshari, Zakariya, 48, 50, 61
al-Ardabili, 48

Armstrong, Karen, 207
Asaf Ali Asghar Fyzee, 123, 161n63
Attaturk, Musthafa Kemal, 26
al-Attas, Husein, 38
al-Attas, Najib, 38
al-Attas, Naquib, 16
al-Audarusiyah, 47
Averroism, 227
Azra, Azyumardi, 21, 29, 38, 48, 133–34

B

Bahtiar Effendy, 23, 114
al-Bakr bin Muhammad Syatha' al-Dimyâti, 53
al-Baghdâdî, Junaid, 63, 208
Bahts al-Masâil, 57, 59, 60
al-Banjari, Arsyad, 49, 51
al-Bantani, Ahmad Damanhuri, 30
al-Bantani, Nawawi, 30, 54
al-Baqillâni, Abu Bakar, 35
Barton, Greg, 114, 120–21
Baso, Ahmad, 80n55, 98, 110, 121–22, 126, 136–38, 223, 234, 260–62, 281n137, 282n138
Benda, Harry J., 18, 37, 84n82
Bidâyat al-Hidâyah, 42
Binder, Leonard, 123
Bisri Musthafa, 29, 70, 78n46
al-Bisyri, Thariq, 137
Boneparte, Napoleon, 120
al-Bujayrimî, 61
Bush, Robin L., 7, 13n4, 115, 117–18, 159n48, 234, 251–52

C

Casanova, José, 231–32
civil rights, 224
civil society, 221–23
Crawfurd, 16
critical analysis, 192

Index

D
Dâr al-Arqâm, 172
Dawam Rahardjo, 172
deconstruction analysis, 109, 167n119, 213
democracy, 204
Desantara, 105, 188, 233–34
dialectical theology, 209
discourse analysis, 187, 198
Djohan Effendi, 6–7, 121, 271n16
dlarûriyat al-khams concept, 204–5, 274n46
Drewes, G.W.J., 17

E
emancipatory Islam, 127, 129, 179, 181–82, 185, 188–89
Esposito, John L., 121
eurocentrism, 152, 167n118

F
Fachry Ali, 23, 114
Fahmina Institute in Cirebon, 233
al-Falimbani, Sayyed Muhsin, 30, 42
Fanon, Franz, 234
Faqih Hasjim, 77n36
Farid Essack, 206
Farid Wajdi, 270n9
al-Fatani, Zain al-'Abidîn Muhammad, 44
Fatima Mernissi, 136
Fazlur Rahman, 76n22, 117–20, 122, 148–50
Fealy, Gregg, 6
Federspiel, Howard M., 114
Feillard, Andree, 156n6
feminism, 173–74, 286
Fiqh al-Wâdlih, 54
Forum Umat Islam Indonesia (FUII), 257

Foucault, Michel, 196–98
Friedman, R.B., 265

G
al-Garuti, Hasan Musthafa, 30
General Election Commission (KPU), 257
Giddens, Anthony, 9
Gujarat, 17
al-Gurabi, Ali Mustafa, 83n74

H
H.A. Mukti Ali, 92n183
Habermas, Jurgen, 178–79
Hadith, 146
Hairus Salim, 244
halaqah, 221, 268n1, 268n2
HAMKA, 16, 77n36, 86n116
Hamzah Fansuri, 19–21
Hanbali, 23, 27, 57, 69, 155, 202, 248
Handramaut, 16
Haramain, 263
Harun Nasution, 10, 73, 120
Hasbi ash-Shiddieqi, 55–56
Hasyim Asy'ari, 2–3, 28–31, 57, 61, 64–65, 68–69, 72, 90n169, 91n177, 140
Hassan Hanafi, 93n186, 98, 100, 104, 107–8, 112, 125, 136, 138–39, 141, 152, 167n118, 170–71, 209, 215, 251
Hijaz, 26–27, 78n44
Hilmy Muhammadiyah, 260
Hinduism, 20, 37, 42
Hisyâm bin Mâlik, 213
HMI, 99, 160n49, 251
Horkheimer, Max, 178
Hululiyyah, 20
Hurgronje, Snouck, 17, 22, 30
Husain Ibn Mansur al-Hallaj, 64–65, 76n14, 89n167, 216

Husain Makhlûf, 60
Husein Muhammad, 233, 260, 280n125, 281n135

I

Ibn 'Abd al-Wahhâb, Muhammad, 24
Ibnu Rusyd, 140
Ibnu Hajar, 48, 61
Ibnu Hajar al-Haitami, 50, 246
Ibnu Muqaffa', 249, 273n42
Ibnu Qâsim al-Ghazi, 54
Ibnu Sa'ûd di Hijaz, 27
Ibnu Sina, 140, 150
Ida, Laode, 7, 100–101
INCReS, 4, 97
India, 16–17, 21–22, 38, 46, 75n7, 84n81, 119
Indonesian Communist Party (PKI), 105–6
Indonesian Democratic Party (PDI), 92n182
Institute for Social and Institution Studies (ISIS), 98, 155n1, 157n8, 165n98, 251
IPNU, 219
IPPNU, 219
ISIS, 98, 155n1, 157n8, 165n98, 251
Islamic Legal Compilation (KHI), 56
Islamic Students' Association (HMI), 99, 160n49, 251
Ismail al-Khalidi al-Minangkabawi, 30
Izz al-Dîn Ibn Abd al-Salâm, 249

J

Jabarite theology, 34, 40, 210–13, 215
Jabir Ushfur, 112
Jadul Maula, 132, 170, 270n12, 271n14, 272n33, 277n87, 277n93, 278n100
Jahmiyyah, 20

Jalâl al-Dîn al-Tursani, 51, 52
Jamâ'ah Tablig, 172
Jamâ'ati Islâmi in Pakistan, 119
Jamâl al-Dîn al-Afgânî, 24, 82, 132, 134
Jamiat Khair, 22
jam'iyyah (organization), 263
jam'iyyah diniyah (religious organization), 4, 23
Jam'iyyah Ahl al-Tarîqah al-Mu'tabarah al-Nahdliyyah, 65, 90n169, 91n173
Jaringan Islam Liberal (JIL, Liberal Islamic Network), 118, 251, 257, 259–61, 280n124, 281n130, 286
Jay, Robert, 18, 37
JIL. *See* Jaringan Islam Liberal (JIL)
Jombang, 31
Johns, A.H., 17–18, 49
al-Juhani, Ma'bad, 213
al-Jurjâni, 60
al-Juwaini, 'Abd al-Mâlik, 36

K

Kacung Marijan, 6
Kamal Hassan, 114
Kant, Emmanuel, 101
Keddie, Nikki R., 38
Ketib Anom Kudus, 42
Khaled Aboe el-Fadl, 264–65
Khalil Bangkalan, 30, 91
Khamami Zada, 242
khilâfah, 26
Khittah, 71, 96, 99, 103, 283, 285
khurafat (superstition), 19
KISDI, 229, 277n90
KPU (General Election Commission), 257
Kuhn, Thomas S., 150
Kurzman, Charles, 120, 123, 132–34, 162n68, 163n80, 163n86

L

Lailatul Ijtima' Nahdlatul Oelama (LINO) bulletin, 56
Lakatos, Imre, 150, 167n116
Lakpesdam NU, 105, 118, 172
LAPAR, 4
al-Laqani, Ibrahim, 44
Lembaga Kajian Islam dan Sosial (LKiS) community, 17–71, 233, 268n3, 284–85
Leob, Edwin E., 38
Liberal Islamic Network (JIL), 118, 251, 261, 280n124, 286
LKPSM, 105–6, 219
LP3ES, 98, 172
Luthfi Assyaukani, 130

M

M. Imam Azis, 106, 271n13, 284
ma'âni (part of the essence of God)
mabâdi' khaira ummah, 67
Madjid, Nurcholish, 80n54, 115, 117, 120–26
Mah'ad Aly, 245
Mahfudz Abdullah, 54
Mahmud Mohammad Thoha, 105
Mahmud Yunus, 54
Mahrus Irsyam, 6
al-Malibari, Zain al-Dîn, 54
Maliki, 23, 27, 57, 69, 202
ma'nawiyah (not essential aspects of God's being), 41
al-Maqassari, Muhammad Yusuf, 18, 21, 29
Marcuse, Herbert, 178
Maria Ulfah Anshor, 233
Marxian paradigm, 98
Marxism, 170–71
Marxism–Leninism, 171
Marx, Karl, 101, 178
Mas Subadar, 259

Masduqi Mahfudh, 256
Ma'shum, 31, 72
Marzuki Wahid, 157n20, 233
Masdar F. Mas'udi, 102, 125–27, 182, 228, 256–57, 259, 266
Masduqi Mahfudh, 256, 280n125
Masruri Mughni, 259
Masykuri Abdillah, 139
al-Maturidî, Abu Mansur, 35, 203, 211
Mathla'ul Anwar, 22
Maulana Abu Ishak al-Shirazi, 40
Michel Aflaq, 137
Miftâh al-Jannah, 44
al-Minangkabawi, Ahmad Khatib, 30–31
Minhaj al-'Âbidîn, 44
Mir'at al-Thullâb, 48–49
Mohammed Arkoun, 98, 136, 141, 147, 149
Mu'awiyah bin Abu Sufyan, 33–34, 82n71
Muchith Muzadi, 255
Muh. Hanif Dakhiri, 98
Muhaiminan Gunardo, 257, 259
Muhaimin Iskandar, 97
Muhammad Abduh, 119, 132–34
Muhammad Arsyad, 51
Muhammad bin Abd al-Wahhab, 134
Muhammad Ilyas, 3
Muhammad Khafullah, 137
Muhammad Shahrur, 125
Muhammad Syahrur, 100
Muhammad Taib ibn Mas'ûd al-Banjari, 44
Muhammad Yasin al-Padani, 30
Muhammad Zain Faqih Jalâl al-Dîn al-'Asyi, 42
Muhtaram, 31
Muhyi al-Dîn Abu Zakariyya Yahyâ bin Syârif al-Nawâwi, 61
Munawir Sjadzali, 92n183

Mu'tazilites, 35
Muzadi, Hasyim, 258–59, 267

N
Nadham Tasfiya, 43
Nahdlatul Ulama (NU), 1, 23, 97, 100–101, 134, 170, 172, 192, 203, 207, 211–12, 233–34, 240, 245
Nahdlatul Ulama Students' Association (KMNU), 93n186
Nakamura, Mitsuo, 69, 91n179
Napoleon I, 120
Naqsyabandiyah, 21, 66
Nasaruddin Umar, 266
Nasr Hamid Abu Zayd, 98–100, 125–26, 136, 148, 182, 192, 194
Nawal Saadawi, 137
neo-modernism, 10–11, 115, 118, 137
neo-revivalist movement, 11, 119
neo-sufism, 63
Niemann, 16
Nur Khoiron, 137
Nur Kholik Ridwan, 251
Nuruddin Amin, 170

P
P3M, 172, 177–78, 184
Paku Buwono, 42
Parmusi, 71
Pekalongan, 53
pesantren community, 22, 27, 68–69, 177–78, 253, 256, 284
Pijnappel, 17
Pijper, G.F., 25
PKB (National Awakening Party), 96–97, 99, 137, 156n6
PMII (Indonesian Islamic Students' Movement), 102, 104, 160n49, 219
PPP (United Development Party), 71, 97
Popper, Karl R., 150

PPWK (Education for Development of Ulama Awareness), 105, 172
PTAI (private Islamic tertiary institution), 3, 72
PTAIN (Perguruan Tinggi Agama Islam Negeri), 3

Q
Qadariyah, 20
Qadiriyah wa Naqsyabandiyah, 66
qadli (magistrate), 51
al-Qalyûbi, 61
Qanûn Asâsi, 28, 69
qawâid al-fiqhiyah, 58
qawâ'id al-ushûl, 244–50
Qodir Azizy, 139
al-Qusyairi, 22, 63, 86n111
Qutb, Sayyid, 104

R
Raden Ngabehi Yasadipura I, 42
Raja Ali ibn Raja Ahmad, 44
al-Ramli, Syams al-Dîn, 48, 50, 61
al-Raniri, Nûr al-Dîn, 19, 41, 47
Rasyid Rida, 134
Rifa'iyah, 47

S
Safiat al-Din, 20, 21
Safînat al-Hukkâm, 51
Saghir Abdullah, 86n116
Said Agil Siradj, 139–40, 201, 203, 275n54
Said, Edward, 272n30
Sahal Mahfudz, M.A., 255
Salim bin Abdullah bin Samir, 54
Samaniyyah, 20
al-Sambasi, Ahmad Khati, 30, 91n174
Samudra Pasai, 85
santri (Islamic students studying at pesantren), 3, 31, 73, 269

Sayyed Hossein Nasr, 8
Sayyid Ahmad Khan, 119, 132–33
Sayyid Sâbiq, 60
Sayyid Usman bin Yahya al-Betawi, 43
Serat Cebolek, 42
Sheen, Fulton J., 207
Shimogaki, Kazuo, 170–71
Shirâth al-Mustaqîm, 47–48
Siffîn, Battle of, 33
al-Sinkili, 48
Siti Musdah Mulia, 233
Srinthil, 105, 234
State Islamic College (STAIN), 3, 13n3
State Islamic Institute (IAIN), 55, 72, 93n183, 93n189, 139, 160n49, 269n3
Steenbrink, Karel, 49
Sultan 'Alâ' al-Dîn Mahmud Syah, 42
Sultan Alaiddin Johan Syah, 51
Sultan Iskandar Muda Mahkota Alam Syah, 46
Sultan Mahmud Syah, 39
Sultan Malik al-Dhahir, 39
Sultan Malik al-Shalih, 39
Sultan Mansur Syah, 40
Sulthan Fathoni, 260
al-Sumatrani, Syams al-Dîn, 80
Sunan Amangkurat IV, 42
Syafi'i Anwar, 114
Syafi'i, 53, 246
Syafi'i Ma'arif, 115
Syafiq Hasyim, 13n4, 233, 260
Syaikh Abd al-Malik bin Abdullah Trengganu, 51
Syaikh Abd al-Muthalib Aceh, 52
Syaikh Abdurrahman, 42
Syaikh Abu Ubaidah, 42
Syaikh Abdul Aziz, 42
Syaikh Abdul Hamid, 31
Syaikh Abdul Malik, 42

Syaikh Ahmad Nahrawi al-Banyumasi, 30
Syaikh al-Azhar, 26
Syaikh Dawud ibn Abdullah al-Fatani, 44
Syaikh Ibnu Atha'ullah, 51
Syaikh Ibrahim al-Kurani, 51
Syaikh Muhammad Zain bin Faqih Jalâl al-Dîn, 52
Syaikh Usman, 42
Syarh al-Aqâid al-Nasafiyah, 41
al-Syarbînî, 61
Syarif Husein, 26
Syekh Ahmad al-Mutamakkin, 42
Syekh Yusuf al-Maqassari, 49
Syir'ah, 105

T
al-Taftazani, 41
tahlilan (prayers for the dead), 24
Tahmidullah bin Sultan Tamjidullah, 50
Taimiyah, Ibnu, 122, 134
taqlid (imitation), 61
tasawuf (mysticism), 62
Thayeb Tizinî, 112
Thoha, Mahmud Mohammad, 105, 138
al-Thûfi, Najm al-Dîn, 248, 279n117
al-Tirmasi, Muhammad Mahfudz, 30
al-Tursani, Jalaluddin, 51

U
Ulil Abshar-Abdalla, 117–18, 160n49, 241–42, 251, 258–59, 261–62, 280n124, 280n126, 281n129, 282n137
Umar ibn Muhammad al-Nasafi, 41
Umdat al-Muhtajîn, 41
Umm al-Barâhin, 42, 44
Uqûd al-Lujain, 54

V

Van Bruinessen, Martin, 44, 61, 65, 103, 137
Van Leur, 38
Voll, John O., 121

W

Waardenburg, Jacques, 143
Wahab Chasbullah, 28
Wahab Hasbullah, 72, 81n58, 91n177
Wahid Hasyim, 3, 31, 81n58
Waliyullah, Syah, 132, 134
Walisongo (Nine Saints), 37
wasîlah (meditation), 25
Wertheim, W.F., 18, 37

wihdat al-wujûd, 64
wujûdiyah, 19, 21, 47

Y

Yûsûf Mûsâ, 60

Z

Zaenal Abidin I, 51
Zain al-Dîn ibn Muhammad Badawi al-Sambawi, 44
Zaini Rahman, 98, 121
Zainul Milal Bizawie, 85n95
Ziaul Haque, 104
Zamakhsyari Dhofier, 29–30

ABOUT THE AUTHOR

Rumadi was born in Jepara (Central Java) on 18 September 1970. After completing Primary School (1983) and graduating from a State Islamic Junior High School (1986) in Jepara, Rumadi went on to study at the State Religious Teacher Vocational School in Kudus. In 1989 he studied at the Faculty of Syariah at the Walisongo State Islamic Institute (IAIN) in Semarang, graduating in 1994. From 1995 to 1997 Rumadi completed his Masters at the Imam Bonjol IAIN in Padang, and later, in 2006, he obtained his PhD from Syarif Hidayatullah State Islamic University (UIN) in Jakarta.

Rumadi taught at the Bengkulu State Islamic College (STAIN) from 1997 to 2004 before moving to the Faculty of Islamic Syariah and Law at Syarif Hidayatullah UIN in Jakarta. While teaching, Rumadi was also senior researcher at the Wahid Institute (2005–present) and editor of the *Taswirul Afkar* journal published by NU's Institute for Human Resource Studies and Development (Lakpesdam NU) (2000–present).

Rumadi has published several books, including *Masyarakat Post-Teologi/Post-Theology Society* (Jakarta: Gugus, 2002), *Fiqh Mazhab Negara, Kritik atas Politik Hukum Islam di Indonesia/Fiqh and the State: A Critique of the Politics of Islamic Law in Indonesia,* co-authored with Marzuki Wahid (Yogyakarta: LKIS, 2001), *Renungan Santri: Dari Jihad Hingga Kritik Wacana Agama/Santri Reflections: From Jihad to a Critique of Religious Discourse* (Jakarta: Erlangga, 2007), *Post Tradisionalisme Islam, Wacana Intelektualisme dalam Komunitas NU/Islamic Post-Traditionalism, Intellectual Discourse in the NU Community* (Cirebon: Fahmina, 2007). In addition Rumadi has also contributed to and been the editor of a number of books. Besides being well published in several academic journals, his articles are frequently published in a variety of newspapers such as *Kompas, Suara Pembaruan, Koran Tempo, Media Indonesia,* and *Suara Karya,* amongst others.